Roots & Branches Series

The Art of the Serial Poem

Richard Blevins

*For all construction is made of debris,
and nothing is new in this world but forms.
But you must destroy the forms*
—Marcel Schwob.

Spuyten Duyvil
New York City

The author wishes to acknowledge the following editors & their work on my behalf: the late John Moritz for *Court of the Half-King* (Tansy, 1980) & *Taz Alago* (Zelot/Tansy, 1984); Bill Shields for *Letters from Kansas* (Zelot, 1986); Richard Aaron for *Clarel's Motel* (Am Here, 1987); Peter Kidd for *Three Sleeps: A Historomance* (Igeneus, 1992); Beth Shabel for *The Morrison Poem* (privately printed, 1992); Steve Ellis for "Voyageur," *:that:* 8, 1993; Pat Smith for "Slight Return," *Notus* 12, 1993; Edward Mycue for *Longplaying* (Norton Coker, 1994); Steve Ellis for *High Season: A Sonnet Cycle* (Oasii, 1995); Ed Foster for *The Collected Later Poems of Philip Marlowe* (Jensen/Daniels, 1998); David Baratier for *Fogbow Bridge: Selected Poems, 1972-1999* (Pavement Saw, 2000); Vardo Rumessen for *The Eduard Tubin Society Yearbook for 2004* (Tallinn, Estonia, 2004); Peter Temes & Jed Hickson for *Castle Tubin* (Press One, 2006); Tod Thilleman for *Captivity Narratives* (MEB/Spuyten Duyvil, 2008), *Breathing Bolaño* (Spuyten Duyvil, 2009), *Medieval Ohio: A poem for d.a. levy* (Spuyten Duyvil, 2011), *The Opening Day* (Spuyten Duyvil, 2012), *Naked Noah* (Spuyten Duyvil, 2014), *Gadsden* (Spuyten Duyvil, 2014), & this book. Special thanks to Cara Gilgenbach, curator of the Special Collections and Archives Library, Kent State University, for her aid in gathering images from the Richard Blevins papers. Thanks to Henry Denander for permission to reproduce his watercolor portrait of Tom Kryss (p. 419); to Heriberto Rodriguez for his photograph of Mexican prostitutes (p. 589); to Tom Kryss for his snapshot from Hart Crane's boyhood house, Garretsville, Ohio (p. 94); to Anne R. Bertholf for Bob's snapshot (p. 679); and to Mathilda Blevins for her portrait of Doris Blevins (colophon).

©2017 Richard Blevins
ISBN 978-1-944682-25-5

Library of Congress Cataloging-in-Publication Data

Names: Blevins, Richard, author.
Title: The art of the serial poem / Richard Blevins.
Description: New York City : Spuyten Fuyvil, [2016]
Identifiers: LCCN 2016027364 | ISBN 9781944682255
Classification: LCC PS3503.L635 A6 2016 | DDC 811/.54--dc23
LC record available at https://lccn.loc.gov/2016027364

To Dick Martin
To Peter Kidd
In Memory Of Tessa Lowell
In Memory Of Ken Irby
In Memory Of Kenneth Warren
In Memory Of Bob Bertholf
In Memory Of Love

Castle Tubin

(2006)

For M., & in memory of Jim & James

The drama of our time is the coming of all men into one fate
—*Robert Duncan.*

"Bitter Eclogue"
To Eleanor Falcon

> *In Love's deep woods*
> —George Meredith, *Modern Love.*

The day I left my wife
I told her
keep the house
to live in.
I was thinking

she would need gardens
to work,
cats for evenings,
and familiar rooms
of furniture.

(I planned my speech
for weeks,
driving the car,
sleepless on the couch,
and especially

while reading—
first a biography of Keats
and then, surviving
his death, a book on
Dickinson's passion.)

Things went badly,
as things do. The speech
was a speech.
She never flinched.
(At least I had taken
the precaution of packing
the Robert Duncan
self-portrait, "a drawing

of somebody else appearing
in avoiding
my face in the mirror,"
into the 10-year-old Spirit.)

I drove off the hill
to my new address.

She worked quickly.
Sold first my books,

a car, the house, and then
the tree in the back yard.

Next the cats:
declawed

before she sentenced them
to the pound.

For months,
When I wasn't poor Heine
writing in bed (working
on my speech),

I was imagining
her suicidal reaction
to the news.
Wood to wooden;
Would to would then....

No need
to worry.

Any woman who'd sell
A Cowper oak for lumber
will live
to buy another house

and fill it
on credit
with new furniture
made from the trees
she's killed.

      *

"You don't read
Catullus, but
he would say:
Hating me
you despised he tree.

"A big tree like that
must be declined
top to bottom,
but its roots
are impossible.

"They remain,
a rock in their fist.
Too late
my branches had lately
flowered again—

"a laughing baby daughter!

"The tree did not betray you,
it grew
in rings
into circles of outward
on the water's surface
where my children will walk
hand in hand
and carelessly toss
the rock in."

ROMAN ZERO
For Martha Koehler

> *Im Traume war ich wieder jung und munter*
> —Heinrich Heine, *Romanzero* (1851).

"Lazarus"
1.
Desire is the town
You drive thru
When you leave
On long week-

Ends upstate.
I've never been
Beyond Desire
Like you have.

II. *Mathilde's letter to Harry*
"I thot I was home
Sick, now I am too
Homesick. Coming back
Home is god (I mean good),

But I miss Paris.
I miss you, shopping
The boulevards. Don't miss
The housework, too!"

III.
The woman is a paragon.
I've been reading her
Dissertation. She understands
How love letters work:

If Clarissa gets on top,
We have a whole new ethos.
She reads XVIII-century novels
The way others have sex.

When we're apart, I wonder
Which character she thinks of me.

It excites her
When I'm behind
And she can't read
What I'm doing.

When she quits me
I'll cease to be—
Really—I'd return
To the pages of

Evelina's masculine:
Only alive when
She writes,
Reads me.

IV. *Harry's to Mathilde*
"I've been dead for some time, so
If my responses seem slow to you
It's because they come from so far away.
Try to be patient for a while longer, young one.

Your hair falls in dark
Brontë curls across
One eye I take two
Fingers move it back

Into place so many
Times our first day
Together, you ask
If I don't like it;

I'm looking for any excuse
To touch you.

This happened so long ago,
Being in love with you I would have died
From old age years ago anyhow.
Nickels seem the size of dimes.

I liked to watch you undress in what
Light we get from stars. Not nearly enuf light
To read by: a column of blood hardly counts
As a tower: dimes the sighs of nipples.

Lift your skirt for me
Like a bad school girl (no panties);
You saw my eyes cloud over
Sealing up a last image at death (white panties).

Your fierce eyes posted sentries
Either side of their paradise;
Your mouth gave away nothing.
Your chestnut hair always falling

Across your face my lap.
If I slip I was in love with the curve (I admit)
Of your ass, you won't like it (you'll contend).
This many years and you'll give me an argument.

Maybe on a night in someone's future,
My observation will come home. It will be early
Spring for them. They are readying themselves
For bed and because he once told her

How much he enjoyed watching her move,
She thinks tonight to open
Their one window and let in
A camisole of light from a dead star.

When they x-rayed the master's painting,
They found the stars were always there—
Behind the cobalt sky—a noontime for lovers
Navigating by other lovers' suns their way back."

V.
The only German that Mathilde knew:
"Ich bin eine Wilde Katze!"

VI.
Nobody
Ever
Owned a cat.
Anywhere.

When they shaved her belly
The long-hair discovered her nipples
The motherless one, childless one,
She comforts herself

"Sits a throne of her own
Leaping
Eyes," as in the phosphine hieroglyph
For pumpkin.

(Zukofsky's Cats,

His translation from Catullus,
Brings love in
Off ancient streets
But keeps it feral.)

Oblivious, the woman on the couch
Above the dreaming cat tries
First one breast then another
In the incipient poet's wine glass.

VII. *Dreaming "Le rêve"*
"I never dream of you,"
She told him
After they had been lovers
Seven months.

Rousseau was wondering
Whether his easel could
Fit thru the blue
Door to her atelier nursery.

(So much furniture

It's hard to
Move around.

My violin
Goes where?)

He realized she was
Still addressing him,
In tones usually
Reserved for his own
Unsent love letters:

"...I dream about animals."

This was the week
Before he died. One of

His last letters,
April First, 1910,
Explains to a critic
Why he had painted

A red divan

In the middle of his jungle.
A woman sleeping
On the couch, dreaming
The jungle around her.

VIII. *The Theriophile*
Thru the long late-January week of days, the animals wait only for them.
The zoo is open all winter

To lovers with no place of their own, and children inside inherited snow suits
Who must wait for their own first day of school,

And to those native birds who choose to hang their nests
On the very fences meant to keep other birds in.
There are also the boulders some sit on anticipating an hour's blood-warm sun.
Otherwise, there is no witness

To the elephant's dance,
Back and forth on alternating front legs, each weighing what,
While swaying her head, ears tight to her head, exact to the rhythm
She alone hears.

The keeper I asked, who was not in love and no kid anymore, explained
Elephants do not dance. This female felt anxious,
Displaced on loan from Toledo, Ohio. Brot here to breed. Her picture
Comes at our end from the renaissance engravers

Who attempted their elephant
On the basis of travelers' descriptions. Otherwise, there is no witness
To the kodiac's circus catch, no hands, of the lofted apple eaten whole
(A whole new ball game if Lofton swallows the ball he runs down)

To the leopard's cry that's a cough
To the old lion, more like an actor or Bert Lahr burlesque, whose skinny ass is draped
In boxer shorts, mounting and remounting the bored lioness (porn flick)
To the graffiti giraffe who would hide somewhere if he could

To the gorilla, you said has the face of a worn catcher's mitt
To the antelope's wishbone
And the sorrow of the one-armed monkey climbing away
And the gibbon, watching the watchers, who's seen all this rise and fall before.

In this zoo, the animals are housed open
According to the natural habitats
Of groups of words

In a living syntax:
From those who need no punctuation (gazelles)

To those who are all-vowels (leopard)

To those who parody the swift (zebra)

And including those who regularly rhyme (peacocks).

Here is spoken the language of the animals,
The wake beyond the bestiary,
An unlocking of the verse cage we always thot held thot.
When Ulysses tests all the animals

In Gelli's Circe,
It's the elephant
Proves worthy
Of philosophy,

Returns
To human
Form,
The philosopher.

Ganesha proclaims:
   "Shit
Or get off
      The Rock,
Man!"

IX.
Your cats watch us
When we make love.
One positions her head
Beneath the tv: wide-

Eyed, belly-up:
A plaster cast of eruptions
The town the mountain buried.
Her catamountain brother steals

Past, not moving
His big head on his
Neck: cruising pussy
In a '57 Chevy.

You say they
Miss me
When I can't
Be there—

I'm a disruption
In their routines.
They despise change.
I envy them

Their eyes see
So much
Of you
In the half light.

X.
In the end, when we read Heine,
Mathilda, the girl he imagines,
Becomes a reference
To Crescentia, the one we live with.

XI. *Roman [fold] zero*
Being in love means
There is no poetry
Of reference. No literature
Of romance or, if there is,

You'll read it later.
There is no metaphor—
All likenesses are unlike
Her, no image that is not her.

XII.
No more reference to the external, then,
Than Beethoven's first movement.
You make me want to write
Simple love cries emitting no

Reference outside the bed, faithfully
Keeping between themselves hushed secrets
Of faithlessness. I try to learn to use
The many words for happiness you do

But I'm frustrated thru the day
When milk and sugar in my coffee becomes
A point of reference if I don't
Drink it black, as you do. You are present

Like trying to separate the music of the next moment
And the mind of Beethoven, L.
After the fourth movement I lose count
Somewhere between last thots of you

Before sleep and first thots of you waking.
It's over. Previn is spirited away in a white
Stretch limo, even before the audience
Makes a crowd in the street. Someone is humming

A crazy snippet from the music,
Teasing his date with it, as if holding
A bright object at the end of his long arm
Away from her frustrated reach.

XIII. *Fourth and Pennsylvania*
Poems are only forms that Poetry takes;
Hardly the only form. The parking ticket explains:
If he pays his fine today (before midnight),
It costs him 3 dollars;

After that, it's a 6-dollar ticket; if left unpaid
Within 10 days, the whole thing's turned over
To the commonwealth and we all know
We know what that means.

Of course, he had no money in his pocket
To pay the meter or the fine, that's precisely
Why. Or he would have made the meter
Eat quarters until we all know what.

The red parked car
Keeps following around
The illicit lover
All thru the next day. And the next.

Zum Lazarus

I. *For Blue Dress*
Richardson entreated his daughter,
Refrain from marrying until
You and the boy have enjoined
In a lengthy correspondence.

I edit letters never meant
For books or more than carbon
Copies. One thousand letters
Passed between two poets

Between two continents, to us.
Once met, their letters stop:
Daily saw their differences,
Fell famously out of love.

Sharing her bathroom
Mirror, careful, not to,
After making love
For hours, bump.

II. *La Mouche*
What happens if I ask
In a letter I am writing,
Do you still care? When
You are sitting down to

Write I love you, to me?
My letter carrier is Madame
Bovary, who leaps across fields
To deliver your epistle. Flowers.

At your end, it's Saturday;
The mail has been slow in coming,
When our letters cross
Like simultaneous orgasms.

III. *La Mouche*
In the time it takes to read
The thousand pages it takes
Clarissa to ready herself
For dying, you and I could have

Fucked thru the night for a month:
Propping your exquisite white
Bottom at the requisite angle
Atop the abridged version.

Clarel reads best in two volumes;
One to place your nose in
While you wait on hands and knees
For the other to spank you hard.

IV. *81 Bleecker Street*
The fact that the Patchens
Let this loft half a century
After the Melvilles spells
More a disruption than

Lettered community. Poor
Novalis sees his Sophie
Everywhere: her face
Is the blue flower's calyx;

Since what was left
Of Nerval proved
Insufficient weight
For snapping his neck,

Aurelia obliged
By assuming the form
Of a convenient
Lamp post.

V. *Katharina*
What must the first have thot
To feel their souls fly out—
Then rush back again—into
New orgasmic bodies?

When they had evidence
The corpse is not the body.
Sense, being jarred
From dreams of being in a world,

Of the ancient earth's heat.
That the book is not the poem.
Keats eats from paper plates
We keep.

VI. *Phatic Head*

>   *...deep, Sir, deep!*
>   —George Eliot, "German Wit: Heinrich Heine."

My phatic head
My phatic head is in your slender lap
My phatic head is in your slender lap and you are reading
My phatic head is in your slender lap and you are reading aloud

a passage
a passage from somewhere
a passage from somewhere I have never been
a passage from somewhere I have never been in *Middlemarch*
on how

how tiny
how tiny is
how tiny is the human
how tiny is the human soul, unborn child, in the wide world.

In my good ear,
you do George
Eliot's voice
like yours;

in my other,
the ear in your lap,
I hear deep
inside you.

I may be just
a big fathead,
but I think
the small noise
your body
makes
narrates the new
book of

Mary Ann Evans.
The one
who is buried
in Eliot's grave.

VII. *Angelique*
      If love be
Seasonal,
It is
All fall.

Fall lasts forever
Longer
Than we ever
Remember it:

A whole childhood
To the child.

LAMENTATIONS

I. *Something Duncan said, makes me*
Think of "Tapiola."
Art is when we are
Entertained
By the artist's pain.

Breathing space,
For one nostril
At a time, beneath
The ice sheet.

II. *Snow Pack*
"When I finish this,
I won't be," I heard her say.
She was packing to leave.
Learning to breathe,

Out beyond my depth
Into your open mouth,
Panicked me.
Waking together, our

Kisses were like dawn
Scattering
The dark birds of insomnia
From the sleepy lawn.

Neighboring plots
Like consecutive days together.
Everything ending at the street.
"I feel I'm disappearing," she was saying.

There can be beauty
In pain. Only there
    Is so much of it.
Utterly without plan.

"I'm careful to leave

No trace of me
For wifie's eyes:
I pack the things

I'd thoughtfully brot
To make me
Beautiful
In his sight.

Pluck my own eye
Pencil from her
Sink, toss it
Into the overnight—

I am blind.

Recovered is the tube
Of red lipstick he favors—
Silences me.
These stains are deep

Into the pale sheet
A childish me had appropriated
To make a spooky ghost
Of love's unmade bed.

My comb, a grin of mirthless
Laughter, into the maw of the bag, too.
Two rolled stockings
Shapeless smoke.

His gift bracelet
May yet come to light,
The cigarette lighter found
In the split-open gut of a marlin.

I'll go along
With the assassination attempt
He thinks love is. The idea
Had been to stay

Under the covers
Thru a winter
No bird in the open
Can survive.

Some unnoticed kid at our door
Has made boot prints in the new
Snow leading away
From here and now."

III.
Why should sadness take the form of lamentations
Beginning "You don't read women writers, do you?"

Poor bastard, strip
Teased to an ugly public
Execution from the inside
Out.

The way the northern painters liked to skin their saints
Alive for us. Ignorant of anatomy, especially female.

IV. *Caller ID*
[Phone rings.]
[He answers.]
[A woman's voice,
Without prelude:] How will you comfort me / in my hour of need?

[He does not speak.
Is she quoting
A song he wrote?]
[She has her answer. Hangs up.]

This occurs,
In Heine's mind, sometime
Before the invention
Of the telephone.

V. *The Great Figure, 4 or 6*
I had to slow up
Or we would have met
No matter how hard
You tried to run ahead

Inside that tight blue dress
I had written the poem
In praise of
We would have crossed paths

There would have been
More cross words
To prick myself with
When I am almost

Most alone
On the city street
After the firetruck
Is swallowed

By the commotion of
Anthologized
Bad poems
Your high heels pounding

Long blunt spikes
Thru the complaining
Boards of the pedestrian
Bridge, killing the ugly

Troll of my desire to see
You, even under these
Circumstances, show me
What's up

The sheath of that
Tight blue dress
As you walked
All over me

Even as it happened,
As you gained the steps
Before me,
I wished aloud I hadn't

Seen
Left me
Nothing
To say

VI.
By the time they scored his lines,
Heine had said them to himself
Like a faucet dripping
On dishes in the next room

In Helen Adam's apartment
After her sister died. He'd memorized

The poems for mantras
Thru the first hours
Of his day, their night;
Then dictated them whole

To whoever finally noticed
The sun's back for more.
Such poems live nocturnal
Lives, bean-dark and bitter

As his morning's coffee
Without bread or sugar.

VII.
"Besides dear Insomnia, you are
My most faithful visitor,
You quatrains who come to me
When we have the place to ourselves.

You come in one door
And leave by another:
Eros before I die, or thanatos?
Where do you send me?

Can I come back from there?
Don't tease me like this.
(Both, indeed!) Please,
It's still dark out. Tell me another."

VIII. *"I'll Take the Sublime"*
"Poem, show your calves
To a dying man. I promise
I cannot touch you. One
Last look, what do you say?

And when I open my eyes
Again—well, let's just say
I'll have no one to tell.
Not to mention a little peek

At those thighs. We won't meet again.
Where I'm going there's no need
For poems: past loneliness,
Beyond the threat of death."

IX. *[Inclosed in the preceding Letter:]*
"I'm warning you—Don't come round here
Humming national anthems
Unless you want to play the game.

Why learn anthems anyway?
The worst sort of singer
Imagines we've bot tickets
For the game to hear her!

The sport must be greater
Than a singer's voice,
Or we could not
Presume to print our love poems."

X. *[Inclosed in the preceding Inclosure.]*
"The opera glasses I once used
To spy on the audience below
Worked too much like poems
To take me out of my hard seat.

The strangeness of self-exile
Is another history
Including the everyday,
The faraway nearby:

Close enuf to overhear—
Dirty words in a lover's ear—
What the jazzman sings to himself,
Urging himself on, as he plays for them."

Histories

Ah! We truly need the gentle, indestructible, melodic history of humanity to comfort our souls amid the discordant noise of world history
  —Heine's "French Painters."

"Hello To All That"
When you finally get around to it,
To printing the anthologies of war poets,
And the poets who refused to go to war:
Picture Heine before Delarouche's picture

"Cromwell Opening The Coffin of Charles I."

He stands for hours overhearing
The opinions of the day from those
Who come to see History for themselves

At lunch hour. The painting spoke
To him. The decision to open a coffin
Is always risky; to reconsider—

"Diaspora"
After Joel Oppenheimer

the door
of your
refrigerator's
enamel white

is not quite
like mine,

where magnets have attracted things
to die there of neglect,

bugs to neon
summer,
nor Williams' door

with its handle
on our speech.
Fact is,

inside
and out, there isn't much
too go on,
see, or eat.

you appear to live on nothing,
type up your notes
from the faculty meeting
instead of early lunch;

reconstructing what the dean said,
as if he were a character
in Richardson critiques Richardson.

clean
white enamel.

after we fuck, I stand
naked before it, swallow
cold tap water
direct from the mouth

of its bottle. I recollect
the dean had wanted to fuck you
read *Clarissa* like an expert
and wrote the anonymous valentine.

    I see again
the postcard
you must have bot
for yourself,

its photograph
of the Seattle campus
you must have walked up and down
in your first years

of teaching years before we met.
there isn't a lot
to go on,
no date

no address
no lover's name
(thankfully)
no cancelled stamp

in inky lines
like an international sign
for river
once waded thru

no writing on the back
(I've looked twice
to make sure)
"wishing you were

here,"
not in your handwriting,
your handwriting hasn't changed
over years, the "you" for "I."

LETTER 1
Crescence Mirat Heine to Heinrich Heine

Normandy, March 5th

Dear Henri,
      I thot I was homesick, now I am homesick. Coming back home is good. But I miss the city. Normandy days and Paris nights would be dreamy in one week. I miss you, shopping on the boulevards. How are you—better? (Don't miss the housework too!) Your Mathilde.

"Intermezzo"
Because it comes for me below
The one window we own,
Like my window blowing dust off
Her side of our headstone,

Proud, her housework is a blank
Space by which I measure
Weeks endings, weak poems
Ending. Maybe like reading,

Not living thru it.
The Second Coming that was
Louis-Napoleon, all those souls
Only a little dirt blown away.

Why I can never picture myself
A corpse,
Or a baby,
Just dust.

Scrubbing the floor is not kneeling.
"Understand me, dead is nothing;
Whereas here we want each other…,"
She wrote to his son by another woman.

LETTER 2
Madame Amandine Lucile Aurore Dudevant to Heinrich Heine
                                        Nohant, March 10th

Dear Henry:

The wasps have made my writing paper
So I can tell you this secret.
In the painting pretty
Girls are picking apples from unseen boughs,

[*tear in
manuscript here*] horizon;
Limbs
Beyond our ken,

Not drawn yet drawing us
[*tear here*]
Their promise
Of roundness.

Love,
George Sand.

LETTER 3
Heinrich Heine to George Sand
Paris, March 29th

Dear Geo. Sand,

    This is my dream
Of the garden below
My window, dreamed
From my mattress-tomb:

Sit still long enuf—
Cold shadow of a leafless
Tree inches across this page
I am writing on—and Nature

Returns to its place,
Place. Small animals ignore
My intrusion, sounds come up
To feed from my hand

(Water on a nearby rock
I hear now), the noise knows
Flowers from the Catholic cemetery.
Look, they've gone home

And left the tombstones
Out in the rain. The mourning family.
A young man they call Mondrian
Comes every Sunday

To paint the trees."

"'She sat like patience on a monument, / Smiling at grief'"
(to me by way of her Richardson from Shakespeare)

The good model
Holds her pose
For the artist
Until she becomes
The painting.

(What more is a cycle of love
Poems, after the inevitable
Breakup, if not lies then beautiful
Snapshots of her in love with you?)

His picture conveys emotion
Along with the possibility
It may all have been a pose
Demanded by the artist.
How she looks

When no one is looking,
When she is quite alone,
The artist has no picture.

LETTER 4
Rahel Varnhagen von Ense to Heinrich Heine
Holborn, April 28th

Heinrich:

[*Indecipherable text.*]
As if deciding one season
Or a single memory
The more real and present;
And summer only false winter.

Immer, Rahel.

LETTER 5
Heinrich Heine to Rahel Varnhagen

Paris, May 13th

My dear Rahel:

    A burial is when we can look nowhere
But up, wearied by the obscurity
Of our own chosen work, before continuing.
Continuing in the obscurity of our words' worth.

    This came to me
When you were sleeping:

        Brief   letter:
          Lied   lied.

I call it "Broke Quatrain."
        All my Undying Love to you, H.H.

LETTER 6 (unsent)
Heinrich Heine to unknown

May 26th

All the letters
All for you,
In all ways;
Always yours.

How can you be
Lonely
When all I do
Is think of you?

"There Is No Desire To End It"

       Caught you unawares
Of Williams' great line,
"There is no end
To desire,"

But you were the one
Found the title
I'd forgotten. Now
We both know better

Than the poet himself
When he wrote it.
We know the future
Of his marriage,

How he died eventually
How he wrote—
Never in fashion
And not about

His wife except
In apology
After opening the
Bathroom door

Exposing her
By describing
Ways a man sees
Girls walk past him,

And away.

What Flossie thot about
His love poems to other
Women is unrecorded.

In the end, she spoke
For him, after his
Series of strokes
Left him too tired.

(But this is years
Into the future.
Finish the next
In your head.)

A poetry of
Desire mounting
The stairs to his
Attic study

Skipping the one he knows
Will give him away
Wake the sleeping house
To his squeak of desire.

This is not the night
Past midnight,
But the summer day
It storms suddenly;

Just another recurrence
There is no end to.
But always a surprise.
Is the way of his poem's

Coming, after I thot
The cycle was done.

It came like a letter
Undelivered
All these fifty years,
Now the letter in hand.
I sit down at once

As if it needed
Answering. Have to
Turn on my desk
Lamp at noon. Sequitur.

"Sequitur"
For Mathilda Clare Blevins

Your mother's hometown comes at the end
Of *Tender Is The Night*, of all places.
She showed me the passage proudly
After we'd made love for hours.

Ours. (Each time I wrote a new poem,
I sent it to her and kept no copy myself.
I'd never worked that way
Before her. Not the usual chaos. Trust.

The series came email
From her, thru me, then I
Would make the drive to her place
To visit both of them at home.)

Medina County, country I'm from,
Is the source for Wine
Creek when it rains in *Winesburg*—
She pointed out during a break from lovemaking.

I hadn't known that either.
She also told me your name
Would be Mathilda, after she read these poems
You may never be the right age or mind to read.

I continue to dislike Fitzgerald's prose.
You were born with your mother's long fingers.

"For My Daughter"
"You'd be better in another *life*,"
I thot I overheard her say to him.
Walking away, I knew it was "*light*."
She'd already cut the guy dead.
She's one tall coffee; he's a mug For Here.
Seems I've joined the regular
Barns & Noblige group
meeting weekdays noon
in order
to avoid
cross-town traffic
two of four times
driving my daughter to Montessori.
That's me!
That's my car
In your parking lot!
I'm so glad there's always
Room for one more!
We think Frida Kahlo's eye-
brows fashionable.
We understand the background
sounds of beepers
grinding beans
and laptops
of cell phones leaving
a message, like Gerrit Lansing
knows the backyard
birds of Cape Ann.
We grow Frida Kahlo's eye
in the fore of our grey heads.
Find Poetry right beside
Antiques & Collectables.
We are not amazed to see,
on public shelves the height of school-
girls' tiptoes,
along the lengths of spines on books
on Dickinson and Wallace Stevens:
the word "desire," like "life," in their titles.

A student from somebody else's workshop
who thinks she's Weldon Kees' daughter
is busy revising
her new poem on her
laptop atop
a table meant for four
in the middle
of the busy room
oblivious
while demonstrating the dramatic monologue
("like overhearing like
one side of a phone conversation")
over her cell to the guy
on the receiving end
who cannot know she is
retyping then omitting without printing
the word "desire"
as she speaks and sips coffee.
On second thot, I too dislike
Kees' poem for his daughter
because of his use of the word.
He will never know
the workshop poets he's sired.
I suddenly worry
the sounds kids make in a reading circle
make a raft in water
way over their heads.
Local Interest.
New Arrivals.
Inspirational Journals.
Large Print.
History
At Bargain Prices.
Former Best Sellers.
I walk among tombstones,
Never encountering my own.

"Revolt of the Flower-Sellers"
For Peter Kidd

Daniel Defoe, from Newgate Prison,
knowing he would be standing in the pillory
before mobs that were known to throw eggs
and brickbats, being himself a magistrate, wrote
"Hymn to the Pillory," a lampoon on his judges.
The illustration from George Lee's biography
shows the local flower-sellers
so moved by the poem
being hawked in their streets
they threw flowers at Defoe
three July days in the pillory.
A long-time instructor of French, a Jew
who lived from town to town in Vichy
France, always a bicycle ride ahead of the Nazis,
came to my office yesterday. Her problem is
always a new crisis of identity.
A black male student on her roster
quit coming to class after failing the midterm,
his seat to be filled by a succession of
other black male students, signing his name
on her attendance sheets. Her problem is,
she's forgotten what the real student looks like.
And who will sit tomorrow's final exam
on the ambiguities of French verse?
My sister in law, on the eve
of her flight to interviews at MLA.
has a nightmare about her grandfather Mal.
Sometimes the wrong student
will get the right answer.
I have it now. Peter Temes resembles
Apollinaire in some photographs. While I'm
aging into Dante Rossetti's round little body.
Rossetti's paintings and poems,
and the poems about the paintings,
are windows we'd throw open to—do we
"breathe"?—a symbol world. Only to find them
sealed shut by paint. Or at least as hard to pry open

as Lizzie Siddal's casket of poems.
Weighing the body, before and after death,
I read a biography of Roethke, a poet I dislike,
to learn the secret of his celebrity in the classroom.
To know the volume of the flown soul.
I swear this happened. After suffering
the horrors of the flu, all night long, it is
given to Martha to hear, round 8 a.m.,
the first bird song of this coming Spring.
A redbird outside her window!
We sleep in separate bedrooms
so the song came to me as a description.
Should I worry about the sleeping arrangements?
I have one story of a bird in the house.
Helen Adam told me
she'd known her sister would die, when
a bird came in a window, flew around
the rooms, and nested for a moment
on Pat's pillow. Helen explained to me
the bird was Death's fetch. This happened.
You had to know Helen.
I'd visited the apartment. I knew
the windows were decades painted shut.
Unbidden, Helen and Pat's walkup, a stroll
from the steps of the Met, comes vividly to mind
today. The faucet drips there still.
I have had bats come down my chimney. Also
carpenter bees in the eaves, field mice
in the family room, a raccoon in the garage.
No one would ever mistake a bat for a bird.
Batness is retained verbatim
in our most permanent mind.
Along with every spider and snake we've seen,
we see them move toward us
as only each can move.
Never mistake a pillow for a pillory
when one is offered to you,
the wag's pillow of a wig.
Always knowing a pillow can be a pillory, dear.
All love lyrics were first written by Attis.

Attis on board the ship!
Attis forever in the woods!
Doctor Snowman says I must take the pill
three dollars every day the rest of my life.
My urologist's name really is Snowman.
My necessary angel.
Possible side effects from the pill, size and shape
of a finger nail's crescent, but purple, include:
enlarged breasts; reduced sex drive. As I recall,
Tiresias's prostate finally had to be
surgically removed by his female self. He had
put herself thru med school only to be divorced.
I'm mistaking Tiresias for Orlando again, aren't I?
I've frequently admired weeds for flowers.
Those little wild flowers are my favorites,
the impolite varieties
that my ex-wife weeds
from lawns, gardens, her life. (We weeds thank her kindly!)
I'm willfully mistaking signs of an early Spring
the third week of February. But, hell, Carl
Rakosi is 100 years old! More ancient
than San Francisco. I'm telling the truth.
And my friend, who teaches Spanish,
has just made triple-bypass surgery.
Martha bot him a card to send—
so I thumb
thru Lorca—to find a quotation, something
to make the card more personal,
but all I read is death
and the bleeding heart.
Instead, Bolo gives me
a quotation from his hospital bed!
He insists: "Mala hierba nunca muere."
And it's true, Weeds never die!

Bed of Glass
To Mathilda

Rapt
as stained glass,
carried away
in place,

light
long withheld
within the church
next door,

vaults—
its alleyway passage
washes my high

walls
its opaque
of hours

into
our first
night

together:
resurrection
—to joy.

"Prefatory"
Tho they could never have
predicted us, they have framed
this moment for us, those

dear anonymous glaziers
of the high plank work,
the unseen os, sisthcundmen,

who built the wall, brick
by brick, (rock upon which,
etc., a holy ghost building)

art above no net of platitudes' attitudinalizing
art from no shaky allegorical Scaffolding
their blue collar windows suit me fine

they leave no reading
that is not ours tonight
their stained glass is

blank but for color
unfinished
as Melville's head-

stone ("stain" from *stone*).
I live above
what was to them, 1906,

the city block-long factory
manufacturing
marble headstones.

I will lean
out my open window
and extend my hand

and write my own legends
in the accumulated dust
of the ten church windows.

I.
Peace of being
is a window
place I wish
to be tonight's

untoward rapture;

patch of sun
on a blue rug opposite
the first window
where I wrote this morning

where our sleek cats

sleep, or what we have of

temenos:
a short path downtown
where the earth is
as it has been

small wild animals
at home in
eyescape's
landscape.

So love *is* a stain

upon this world
after all.
Cozens, preparing to paint
his world a skyscape

that makes good sense
to us,
first stared
at the stains on his walls:

"carried away."

II. Emily's homily
Threatens me
With Heaven—
All homely
And choir-lofty—

Til all Eternity—
Sounds—quiet.

"Marry me in Heaven"?
Where do we go, dear,
When it's past Time
For Divorce?

is the next window closing.

III.
That congregation's got it wrong
Don't you see, your light *bathes my walls*
Come on over to my side, Baptists
I'll host

the choir in my shower
(better to be cast out than lukewarm)
the preacher in her closet
I'll request "I'm Working on a Building"

and someone could maybe explain
why the Holy Ghost
makes noise upstairs when I'm sleeping
but doesn't seem to be at home

the early mornings of my insomnia
I'll propose
the immediate secularization of all church property
including parking spaces of light

to result
in a retroactive tax
going all the way back
to Adams' blue Chartres—

"where LaFarge not only felt
at home, but felt a sort of ownership—
a member of the Church
[who] worked in glass"—

delivered to us express
by fat-assed Brooklyn workmen
after dropping off
Duchamp's Large Glass

by dropping it.
This is the stained glass window
that I shatter,
for the quality of found art is profound.

To find your way in a city
is fine
much luckier to lose
your way somehow;

the legend of the 55
times Baudelaire moved
to the next new
atelier in Paris, or

one Sunday,
at his breakfast on the edifice,
a red squirrel
is our gargoyle!

IV. *Stuart Z. Perkoff*
After I move in with the church
windows,
I spend the hours when she's asleep
frequenting the hangouts

in Voices
of the Lady
so many hours in the company of your poems
that I come to dream I met you

when you were
writing these poems
in the untranslatable light
of the morning suns

you've always been up all night;
only dawn
is more inevitable
than your insomnia and obscurity.

In my dreams you are always wearing
sunglasses,
it could be
inside or out of doors

but your shades are
tiny twin panels
of stained glass
across them play ecstatic

figures of suffering Crashaw never felt—
the darts that killed you,
darts of pure light—
your eyes must be, I cannot see them,

madly dilated
you live on a planet
with two black suns
in the yellow sky.

For this
window, the poet who
used himself up,
instead of a saint.

V.
Pigeons on the glass
Pigeons on the glass
alas, my ass
must be three dozen pigeons Come

here, honey,
to the next window
and count them
with me!

The allegory of the windows
is alive in her movements
Martha opening the windows
to air things out.

The wind, o, which is what
she feels warm on her skin,
of unity
coming thru.

VI.
I thot I had a story but I missed
it, it didn't seem to me to be
rain but what there is
accumulates on the church roof

like the million words
in Martha's beloved
Clarissa, a flood plain
drains off.

The flood that washes
Over me
Waters the one coleus
That is washed

Out its bed:
Untended flame
Lights the alleyway's
Concrete neglect.

(I trace the image
of seed and
leaf
for this window.)

VII.
Round about mid
some knight
I never see
practices violin

within the chapel
hollow. Another
alleyway free
concert.

VIII.
A
 found
of riddles,
it begins

reading for comfort
in the apartment we
rent waiting for
devorce, baby, the

morning it begins again.

How many families
have lived in these rooms
what strategies did they employ
against the high unreachable ceilings?

It does not begin again
because it never ceased
we only start it
a next time

it is unchanged
we come to it
transformed
a car under a foot of snow.

IX.
The cat that makes me sit
The cat on my lap that makes me sit
still enuf to look

see the ways
the stained glass looks
in the vertical light
at noon,

Pumpkin is my design for the next window.

X.
    Some light,
      light,
      or none:

an alleyway
for a clock.

When you wake up nights / a whole window
for our nightlight.

	Each	New
day's		
	Brick	first
rays		
	Distinct	strike
this		
	It's	
window		
	Noon:	looks
white,		
stained		
		glass
panerian		
		bow
trans formed		
		to

true fog bow,
                              our
car touche,
                      for an
hour.
Some word,
A space
Erased   —a prosody a day.

XI.
Last night, I dreamed I was writing a section of a poem called "Glass Bed," about the four-window main piece of a wall of stained glass, one window each, for George Butterick, joel oppenheimer, Robert Duncan, and Sherman Paul.

Then one day word came that Ed Dorn had died.
The news is in forever.

One would sooner
doubt the wilderness,
mock the frontier…

That one won't last for long
what I drew on this window cannot endure
the next
ten minutes.

Throw open the windows
The wind that blows thru the stained glass city

needs in
Open windows for tornados in spite of your impulse

and save yourself, hurry
leave behind your treasured editions and journals,

the collections
of incisors of every French pope and the lock of Milton's hair

take the time
for one last look around

leave nothing to the attorneys who will live on after you
and their sons, after them

Save yourself, Laius

before the pressure of being inside

explodes your astonished face

into shards of the one true Glass!

XII.
I yearn for a world
whose philosophers
do better
than write about themselves,

for a world
whose poets sing
philosophy
with their mother's milk.

Only when a hand,
unbidden from this side,
flicks on
the lights inside the chapel

that is opposite
my window,
be they 10 percent
tither or cynic janitor,

only then do I make out
The Four Angels on Four Clouds
(one well drawn,
the face

of a girl)
painted on
that side
of the glass.

For her nursery,
I paint yellow walls and
doors of robin's egg blue.
Baby's window frames

the four-glass section
its four angel
babies on their four
pillow clouds.

*When it happened
there was water everywhere
So much water
on the face of the earth*

her cloud mother rained;

*then, after days of rain,
as if a light turned on,
Mathilda Clare
is born, January 6, 2000.*

*It is the date of
Fanny Burney's death and Carl
Sandburg's birth.
Something from both parents,*

*of prose and poem genders.
The rain turned to ice.
Icicle writes roofwater
on the church beyond*

her window, her sight just now.

She looks into the light
when she is calmest, rapt,
already wanting
to figure it out. Making

the zoo animals on her walls
across her floor, an ark of
animals, jealous
of her blue-eyed gaze there.

I realize what I took to be
concrete for my doorstop
is a block of marble
with a faun in it finally I see her.

But it is Martha, nursing Mathilda
Clare, who reads aloud from
Tom Meyer's new book
finding the poem "January

Sixth" open on her lap
so that
it will always make perfect sense
as the baby's day

and no one else's,
and language's poem to her alone:
"This morning has that clarity, a sureness
in the eye, as clear-cut as animal tracks."

"West Urn"
(on the death of Edward Dorn)

The news is in forever.
The On is turned to Off.
All the many-mouthed
agents for the singular moment
essay one tongue,
a fungible one they appropriate
from the poet's estate, usufruct,
in the days when the history of futures,
reading ever like letters from home,
is fallen out of print;
when even occasion is borrowed—
their obit Gist
Ain't quick enuf
to catch the poet at home—
a morning's brisk exchange
of nummular pictures from the ekphratic
deathbed mask.
Their notorious corpse
rests on edge,
leaned on display
in main street
in a pine box
unfinished but for
a window for his face's
face. Here no building's
second story is not false.
The silver barrels of pistols
are all plugged.
The spokes on speeding coach wheels bend
optical illusions, that history might
spin itself backwards
to a time in the country less convivial
to satire; when gunslingers were just
down the street
breaking into jail.
  Now vox-mail
  Answers itself—

    Carpe noctem,
    Turner's o'erturned—
the frontier forfeits closure,
at least as early as the Donners,
believing its well-trampled grave
safe from disclosure beneath
the trail heading out.

But enclosure forgets closure;
attention, fence-denied,
will simply detour,
deeper down.
If only the dust seems real
to us and more conspicuous
than the brilliant ribbon of civilization
that ties up the traffic to the far
fair coast,
where even the jeans they wear
endear them to the Erth
a gain again;
if only the dust is less
conformal than the mind of the east
requiring a legend on a map;
then only the dust, the red
dust is a purer calling,
tho we choke on it,
than the one the vast super-
market the midwest declares
above the otherwise mollifying
hubbub of the New World
it replaces endlessly
by inventing a mouth for food,
not words,
an appetite for appetite.
Only the plainsman could
call the high haulm
home. Hear him
in his death He calls
us to ourselves—
Rochester Haniel Sauer

Souse da Vaca Ungar—
in one voice.
One would sooner
doubt the wilderness,
mock the frontier.

"Night Paving"
With Bill Pamerleau

> *In hours when I am full of images,*
> *then young people should be all around me*
> —Rilke, *The Worpswede Diary.*

> *I was unbelievably alone…*
> *It was about two hours past midnight*
> —Rilke, *Schmargendorf Diary.*

What are the chances of

whichever green apple you pick,
for whatever reasons of taste,
from what seems (now) a desirable tree
in this sector of the well-strolled orchard,
that is, it is everywhere
morning outside Ware,
New Hampshire, tasting familiar?

              How did you come, to know
this apple among countless apples you might eat
is the one word in a poem
grown inside the mountain
state of language, the right word
for the woman you miss?

In the trip report you'll be sure to remember
("Extract the juice which is itself
a Light," says di Prima's Paracelsus.)
how, after biting into not one but two

nails, picked by our rental's flat tires
both coming and going, served continental
(what are the chances of that?), the tires tasted.
High time to retire the house dice, Sucker;
they've been Mallarmade. His contemporary,
Charles Sanders Peirce, writes: "Chance is
First, Law is Second, the tendency to take habits
is Third" ("The Architecture of Theories").
He did not mean to write a poetics.
He did not know he was writing your poetics.

Looking for two hours for the house described in Brent, a bit like
understanding William Wilson's mind from his account of the
architecture of his architectonic schoolhouse.
Arisbe!
         Which afforded its philosopher-builder a view of the Delaware
turns out he could not particularly afford, stands these days cut off—by
a busy 209N then dense trees and condos—from a distant river. Our
first tries were to find the house along the river. Stop at downtown
Milford real estate office open Sunday, where the female version of
the German bookstore owner in *Vertigo* ("He true her avay!") gives us
directions. The house C.S. Peirce built is rented for office space by the
U.S. Parks Service, which operates its four air conditioners.
Peirce's biographer claims Arisbe was "intended, like its ancient
namesake on the banks of the river Selleis…to be a colony of
Miletus…." In our century, H.D. "traveled to Miletus / to get wisdom,"
meaning to London for Freud's couch. A transverse.
Katheline Hayles has come to live, among the SUVs with government
plates, at Arisbe, and Prigogine beneath the second roof that Peirce
built. Some local poet picks up his mail here, not c/o of the local bar.
Tubin's castle.
         *

You can't write your poem deliberately
Without literary reference
Unless you can stand traveling
Without a road map or a radio…

from the Delaware
up the Hudson to
the Connecticut…

poesy and philosophy—and *jazz* on the cd—carried us
past our exit at Carlisle
til Mason-Dixon signs wake us and we clowned.

It is only natural to talk about Stanley Coveleski
when driving past Shamokin.
Never to forget his forgotten brother.
We carried the Brent on the trip
with the maps. Ives' town, proving
You can never nose
your auto

into the same traffic
jam twice.
In Keene, Ms. Falcon's directions to campus
make precisely what
Pound demanded of a poem:
lead us to an office on the campus
tho the college's street sign be
as modest.

(My mother would be a falconress
made Duncan the falcon he arrived at!)

only the insomniac is free
to imagine his biographies of friends and lovers
will never reach their living subjects, hurt.
Here goes.
Tomorrow I will ride with Jed, to Brattleboro,
in his green convertible
bot for maybe three years, he says,
til the Parkinsons
takes his reflexes:
his strong hands shaking on the wheel—
but his driving was precise and joyful—
someone among us
to witness and adjust.
Failed to recognize the old man
in the snapshots Jed layed out

from G's birthday party.
I still wished to deny him
for a stranger, some poor relative
of Jed's I'd never met. No matter
how many times I make myself look
at Ehrbar's photo of Bruckner on his deathbed,
I can only see my father's mouth
the entrance to a cave on the river Sandy
in the moment
after death.
An oil of the taxpayer stood wake
from one wall of our parlor for the night. Luckily,
I didn't have to meet him,
or the painter.
Jed on the couch, the others arguing Just War,
(I'm happy to be quiet after my reading), his hands
always whittling a walking stick handle. It was late
in the history of night, early
in the morning
of the apple-picking.

    *

Put aside Rilke's journals. 4 am. Descend instead
Someone else's pine stairs, this old farm house,
Step, in the dark, everyone is sleeping I pass
Their closed doors of innocent sounds, bump
Black looming shape no shape til dawn. At length,
I step outside
To be under the roof
I know well
To call you and talk about the starry night
That covers us.

"I have always had a horror of listening to music
with my eyes shut." That's Stravinsky.
As far as seeing makes a poet,
Prèvert is a great poet, I'm
thinking for some reason.
  Apparently, the theme
Of the reading was my insomnia.
I hadn't planned it.

What is it
we do
control?
Not even the invitation to poetry was my own doing.
Peter Temes' invitation to come read poems in New England
made the theme. The invitation
(is always)
to the journey.
Insomnia has extended my attention, like H.D.'s
"jelly-fish" vision, past that last exit
and beyond my natural endurance
to a place where dawn is a flicking tongue
in and out of sleep's slack mouth.
I decide to say nothing of this to my audience,
pick the frost heaves poem to start the reading,
writ for George on the trip to joel in Hibbing,
knowing I'd written it for this audience
George Eliot would say "choir" for audience
that still
includes them.
This trip, another road sign
swims into my ken, threatening
NIGHT PAVING.
Trip reports must still go out, I realize now,
to Sherman and Dorn, forever.
What then has changed?
This trip, get to meet Peter's daughter,
12-year-old! who was born the night of the first
time I read for Temes, at The West End,
thinking of the poet ghosts
crowded onto that dias.
Experience of reading aloud an old poem,
abandoned a dozen years back,
as if for the first time. Whittling.
Much as the body is the source for all wise mysticism,
so is insomnia the only poet of everydayedness.
For insomnia is not a longing to join the sleepers and succumb,
But rather the drive to stay impossibly alert forever,
—or else swoon, as the poet said. Please know,
a man standing in front of his insomnia's sun

only appears to be
black as a hole
punched into daytime.
Only the insomniac is at leisure
to recall his day. Earlier,
my philosopher host had proposed a game:
we were to name
who our wives
most resembled.
Easy, I said at once, The young Virginia Woolf,
thinking Steve Ellis had remarked she's Edith
Sitwell, a poet only Duncan loved.
  Martha, left behind, works at home
Beauty among her faultless monsters.
I dial our number, long distance,
4:30 in the morning
just to hear her voice
on the answering machine.
   *

"Your voice: the only antidote to this vile despair," I read in the Mason
Rimbaud I've just bot second-hand in Brattleboro. Green pine hill along
the eastern spine of the town, back turned to the buildings in the posture
of the reclining nude posing. Face-to-face
the church steeples below me on Main,
one white wooden warden
and one of red brick.
Only the white church chimes
5 o'clock. What are
the chances of Pope spending
the middle one-third of his career
translating Homer? And of
Robert learning to read the Greek
only after writing "The Dunciad"?
What are the chances of H.D.
having read Ann Finch's
Pindaric Poem on the Hurricane
("the planted mast," Finch writes
when no trees remained in England
to make ships' masts from; thus,
the Weymouth pine) before she

wrote "Hermes of the Ways"?
What are the chances of identifying Nietzsche
as the composer of "Nachklang einer
Syvesternacht" for two pianos?
What are the chances of Fred
Astaire being present, the early
morning of January 8, 1925,
at a party in New York when Igor
Stravinsky and George Gershwin
improvised a duet on piano?
What are the chances that anyone built
remotely like Anton Bruckner could
block from his mind the chance-encounter
panties of the young and unrequited
long enough
to write the divine Seventh
Symphony?
What are the chances that Artaud
knew something?
What are the chances of Weldon Kees being
turned down for a Guggenheim in 1942,
having been recommended by Tate,
Cowley, Sandoz, Ransom, Farrell,
and Horace Gregory? What chance is there
of ever writing a memoir so perfect
as Elizabeth Hardwick's pages on Billie Holiday
in *Sleepless Nights*?
For jazz is night music, the imperative
of those who are up all night.
It is the sound of night paving
in the hills that pillow one ear.
For Amy Mann has named it
Driving Sideways.
What in hell might be the chances of Peirce writing
"Love, recognizing germs of loveliness in the hateful,
gradually warms it into life,
and makes it lovely," of evolution ever being
thot lovely? Of him writing from deep hell like H.D.?
What are my given chances
of finding somebody around here

who will give me some answers
to Whitman's "The Sleepers"?
Fat chance that you and I are talking
about the same thing when she said
"Ipso facto" like that. So what
do you think are the chances of ugly Addie
Joss pitching so beautifully?
What are the chances of the sincerity
of The Pisan Cantos?
What the chances of a boy growing up in Ohio
finding Jim Lowell and books?
For "tychism" is the word I've been looking for,
Peirce's term, meaning absolute chance
(not probability)
is spontaneity, a world
out of nothing.
It's there, in "The Law of Mind."
What are my chances of ever thanking Bill Pamerleau,
for sharing the spontaneous drive
and the world of the trip,
by writing this? For

finally we arrive
at a place only
because our travel
toward it must
eliminate arriving
at any other place.
That is, we drive in a tradition of arrivals.
For the river must ever forget its source.
For the river will change its course.
Drove all day back across Pennsylvania,
day unto night in Enterprise's car, knowing
the nail was There in their Tire,
too tired to figure our chances.
The philosopher and the poet
shared the driving, therein
happy a man
cannot know
the day of his exit.

Preludes & Fugues

A tap with your finger on the drum releases all sounds and begins the new harmony—Rimbaud's *Illuminations*.

Music resembles Poetry...that Licence is a Rule
—Pope's "An Essay on Criticism."

"S, no. 1"
This prelude is Shostakovich
This prelude is Shostakovich writing
Writing his 24 Preludes & Fugues.
He is thinking of Bach

Of Bach's 48 Preludes & Fugues
He is thinking of Bach on the anniversary of Bach's death.
This is Bach playing thru Shostakovich playing thru his work on two successive nights,
Myopic before fidgeting censors.

This fugue is Rimbaud writing the prose poems of his *Illuminations*, in London in 1872, the year Walt Whitman received John Addington Symonds' letter asking after Calamus and before Verlaine shot a bullet into the teen's left wrist. Writ being beauteous, the ancient circus lives make us, not yet 20 years old, into mystic vagabonds on the morning of our drunkenness or metropolitan barbarians brot to our knees before an historic evening. You say you've read all this somewhere before? Sharp. Swift or Smart. And cagey, too, John. To accuse me, the composer, of simply realigning the lexicon. Use the notes.[1] Note how Zukofsky notes Henry Adams' *Education* for A. The letter is likewise a note. So it sounds. Like his. Voice. "Araby" is a fugue writing James Joyce in three voices: blindness, pneuma, lumen. Like that. If brass wakes up tomorrow morning a trumpet, it's not its fault.

"C, no. 2"
Please consider
H.D.'s Claribel
In terms of
Ruth's Clarel.

For the trope of the ekphrasis,
The formality of writing it
Down, eyes open:
Picture Oppen.

In Doody's usage, the ekphrasis is a pictorial representation (in a novel). Mathilda, who is one, just fell asleep on my lap as I was typing this fugue. wait a sec. she shifts so I cant use the shift keys. but the thot continues, now one finger at a time. of necessity. that's mararet anne doody says she wrote this book, the true story of the novel, necessarily out of her interest in the history of the novel during the writing of her third novel. she writes about ekphratic figures of eros and place, which to my mind evoke duncan and dorn. on proust: "'form,' which is also 'history,' is deformed by time and the viewer, is reformed, and then launched in flux again." take that as the informed epigraph for *free for m*. I see the young poet's phosphene hieroglyphics were crude pictures of the poem in progress that was his to be. Not "Clarel's Motel," but a Clarel Motet. Not the travelog in *Three Sleeps*, the map revisited, but a nap. The baby is lately awake from.

"O, no. 3"
The Oppen's left
For Mexico, 1950,
In the year Shostakovich
Began his Wordsworths & Fugues.

Write Ralph Maud asking
If his book has humanized Olson
After Clark's suggestion, now in paperback,
It wz Frances B begat O?[2]

In this poem, I learn...

A view of farm requires eyes open.

The young poet's phosphorous h.zeoshperes were snapshots of architects of future eve in pose

Not the traveling in 3 sleeps revisited, how a nap.

"C"

Please consider
H.D.'s Claribel
in terms of
Ruth's Clarel.

For

On the trope of
the ekphrasis,
(a pictorial representation in, *The p.2 mt. spins.* move to footnote
in Doody's useage, a novel), *she spins*
picture Oppen. Mathilda, who is one, just fell asleep on my lap as I was typing this. wait a sec.
she shifts so I cant use the shift keys. but the thot continues, now one finger at a time. of
necessity. margaret anne doody says she wrote this book, the true story of the novel, necessarily
out of her interest in the history of the novel during the writing of her third novel. she writes
about ekphratic figures of Eros and place, which to my mind evoke Duncan and Dorn. On
Proust: "'Form,' which is also 'history,' is deformed by time and the viewer, is reformed, and
then launched in flux again." Take that as the epigraph for *For M*. The baby is awake.

The fugue is an old email from June from David Zauhar, who, as it turns out, occupies an office at U Illinois Chicago a few doors down from Chris Glomski's, who I know as Sherman Paul's grad student. Seems my line, "Gerrit Lansing and Hart Crane are not read here," has "been a running joke upon walking into any redneck bar for the past few years" with them, "So your work has passed into the living discourse…," like Blackburn's poem "The Continuity" and the liquor store robbery. The new harmony.

"P, no. 4"
In Geo O's practice,
The writer's perception
Of form, in winter
Objects, groupings,

A landscape of their
Relationships become poetic form.
It is the poet's sincere hope
Into ethos

that the clearer the perception, the truer the experience. The subsequent record of perception is thus divorced from inherited literary form, ahistorical. A sheet of music / The record of some song. Tho his poems do exhibit a Marxist's distrust of the mythopoetic impulse to make histories of our lives or to live by their culturally imposed guidance. Came home last night with the Mravinsky Shostakovich Eighth, after reading M's the man who most closely knew what S wanted the music to sound like (later on, M became afraid of his association with S and betrayed him to the Party). The recording, the 1960 UK premiere, is compromised by English coughing spells from the audience; but the Eighth Symphony, with the Fifth and his String Quartet No. 8, is obviously my Shostakovich alright. George Oppen / Melville's fiddler. I can't concentrate. That coughing from the front rows! John Lennon's proletarean wisecrack about them rattling their bourgeois jewelry, in the Queen's time, for applause.

"Q, no. 5"
Kind of rattling around,
Like driving to Malabar
Farm, taking down the
Occasional note in a jeep;

Queequeg was all morning's tour
Of the farmhouse. Watching
Tilly, it begins to rain out. She notices
Otherness past the screen door.[3]

"Questions (Maybe) on Her Mind": Why is there this music when it rains? The wind comes in what flavors? What sense does the cat's blur make? Why read to me poetry when all books fit the tooth-sore mouth? Why learn to become a poet when words play so nicely by themselves? Why wish more than laughing to make Momma laugh? Of Oppen, her mother likes best (or only) the poem in which the boys in their boys' rooms are Shelley and Keats. Douglas as a toddler laughed pointing at the blue book Daddy called "A." Today the name of the rock band Douglas plays in is Imminent Groove. If there can be said to be a Mozart Effect on pre-schoolers, then how about playing Duke Ellington's "Tone Parallel to Harlem" over the nursery intercom with mother's quote milk? Open Oppen poem nope. Eh what? X amply follows:

"X, no. 6"
"Land,
A place to die!"
Opens
Echevarria's *Cabeza de Vaca*

Esteban silent
As Queequeg.
"I have a world
Even tho I am lost!"

Prophet on a rock calling to bird; exile in a tent sustained by ant. *Virgin Spring* closest to what I know of this beauty, the ritualistic pace. Figures painted in mud and excrement, smokey procession to the girl's pyramid tomb, burial in wicker casket. De Vaca is crazy to intercede—she's dead, ex—believing he can raise her (not a surgery this time). What would it be to emerge, naked, from your new tomb? "We'd better stop talking about magic if we're going back to civilization. We're going to have to lie." Unfinished cathedral image from start of film. "What day is today?" Reject Captain's order excathedra to help build the extravagant cathedral on the backs of natives. The city of Cibola, its women with three breasts, the soldier lies. Truth and lies. Final image of slaves hauling, to drummer, across desert waste, what looks like an x-aircraft that won't fly for another 400 years.

"H, no. 7"
Carpe noctem
Epyllia
Carmen epicum
Poeta doctus:

From Michael Schmidt:
My first Dad's Day
Gift from Martha and Tilly:
Eclogues in Don's backyard:

Letting Bill Miller talk, which does not constitute talking *with* him, yesterday in Hornell, something interesting from his recent reading for his book on courage—that started out a book on cowardice—about Ulysses S. Grant's prose. Can its influence on modernist prose style be measured? No Hemingway or Stein or Anderson would admit it, certainly. Who won that war anyhow? The loss, downtown Hornell, NY, of Union Park to 1960s highways. Davy Jones tobacco card, 1901, for sale downtown window.[4] Lines for a poem mixing Don Koehler's and Basil King's bowers, beginning "The backyards of Brooklyn and Hornell are a temenos" and unfinished. A second try, before leaving Hornell, gives me: "In order / to take the river to the hills, / you must first / drown yourself / in the monotony of the trees' green // The astonishment / there is too much / green in one day / Then the relief / of reaching the lava fields / and new meadows / they've made for us." So now the poem, before it's abandoned, includes the day I drove Duncan from Eugene to McKenzie Pass and Three Sisters.

"B, no. 8"
<u>Reading Donner's Beddoes</u>
Lovell B. (for Lowell Blevins)
Fyttes (unpubd Oregon mss, "Enoch")
Eros-Thanatos (Marlowe poems)

A study of being a poet,
Or just short of, nerve,
Cannot publish *DJB* so writing more
Poems becomes untenable.

Structure of a sustained improvisation.[5] The body of Beddoes lies buried beneath the contempt of two centuries' readers. Beddoes' thinking is *the* example of the Romantic return to The Ideal. Mother Death. He dissected to find the spirit in the body. An autopsy on the Go-Getters will reveal the same energy that drove the American engines, in Ed Dorn's era, to a new poetry.[6] I finish my poem on Dorn's death, beginning "The news is in forever." The newly fallen poet. West Urn. Looking for Visesimus Knox at the Hillman library, I use the dictionary for "dorn" and learn:
1) Never put a dornik in your hand unless you mean to throw it; and 2) never throw it unless you're sure to hit.

"N, no. 9"
No Fogbow in print
No part-time instructor to fill the last two
Comp sections
No way to see Douglas

No license plate from the Commonwealth
No no-fault divorce really
No word about Doug's U Mich loan
No Ken Irby at our doorstep

Could Dr. Williams have had in mind Montaigne's definition of man, as "ondoyant et divers," when he wrote the "undulant" in his later poems that caught the young Creeley's eye? Apprentice poet Allen Ginsberg formed a personal relationship with Williams, but not Pound, who refused to read his poems forwarded by Williams (anti-sem?). I have long thot of my own poems as inevitably what they are. My god, what if

I'd spoken to Ginsberg at Kent in 1971—I'd wandered lonely in a crowd up to the stage to talk to *him*, not to Duncan, who was on that stage too—had given him my poems and, like Williams to him, he'd responded...Or if I'd followed up with Kenneth Koch, in 1970, and attended Columbia after his letter inviting me...AG assembles his first book of poems out of journal entries that WCW passes on. On not no.

"M, no. 10"
Unlike me to fall asleep listening
To music, but a few nights back,
When I'd bot head phones in order
To listen to Mahler's Tenth

While mother and child sleep,
I'm jolted awake—at the noisy end
Of movement one—by the apparition
Of Martha entering my room,

a room filled with noise! (The ghost of Hannah, Frederick Goddard Tuckerman's wife!) I'd pulled out the plug and treated everyone in the apartment house (Melville's inmates) to a dose of late Mahler after midnight. I've admired M's unfinished symphony since 1973, when I played it during the time of Marie's cancer treatments. That lp was the George Szell Cleveland and, as I remember, only the completed Adagio plus a fragment M set before dying? The sound was the sound of death: M's, his pre-war Europe, if not yet Mom's. Finally, I've bot the Slatkin St. Louis cd—the version edited by Remo Mazetti. Thinking of the versions by Cooke (two), Wheeler (four), and Carpenter (six)—reminded of Boar's and Butterick's reconstruction of last Max. Know not noh.

"T, no. 11"
Confirmation of
Creeley's definition
Of art being the
Artist's "attention":

Shostakovich clinking
Vodka glasses
With a bumb on the street—
And hearing a triad.

Worried when the film *Tom and Viv* opened with its dedication to her memory, is a funny thing, thanks to her brother, o brother! Opening voiceover tells us more than it can know: TSE's falling in love with V was his desire to become "more English than the English." Bert Russell on a picnic! How *is* Tom the only one not to note V's craziness? Effective scene: Eliot outside and Viv inside door on their honeymoon…Also, Eliot, next, staring out into ocean—turns out, he's standing *in* it…Then there's Eliot walking to work at Lloyd's. Great scene, in which T and V do the voices, cops and all, a dramatic reading of what we are to understand is the first draft "Waste Land" for her family; awkward as must be. Filmmaker has the poet "explain" to a listening audience (behind door closed to us as V leaves the house) that "poetry is an escape from emotion," in context of V's hysteria; strong mix of essay and speech, audience for audience. The visits by the vicar culminate in the one when he and TSE find V collapsed: a clear visual journey to Tom's entering the church at the height of his poetic powers; i.e., he was alone there. Did she really insist that, because the poems come from their life together, she wanted co-credit? Scene during WWII, V long hospitalized: Russell and Eliot descending lift to their own personal hells. Tippett agonistes.

"W, no. 12"
Martha tells me,
All of Richardson's
Male protagonists
Are 26 years old.

I was still a grad student
Ignorant of my father.
Grigori Kozintsev's *Hamlet*,
Music by Shostakovich.

Martha has finally done it. I do believe Mozart's *Requiem* is immortal sound, after thinking I dislike WAM for being frivolous or merely mathematical these years. Listen to his *Requiem* on headphones before bed…Middle of the night, I dream boyhood best buddy Ed Meserko is sitting with me in the Western Reserve—I swing at his jaw—and my fist meets nothing—I realize, in a shock, my fist is noncorporeal—that I'm dead!—then sensation of blacking out—to nothingness. I wake up remembering Ed's favorite player was Willie Tasby...Next night, I dreamed I was West, talking about "The Winter Log" with a smiling and relaxed Ed Dorn. Both Ed's live near Denver. Each one of Hilda Morely's poems is a requiem dream of Stefan Wolpe.

"F, no. 13"
A work of no beginnings
And no end; all
Middle,
And yet no development,

No periods of
Writing therein.
Engagement, fresh
Each time.

Perchick is our Satie. He has compulsively written thousands of one-page poems, each one delicate and subjective; each one the same poem; each without external meaning. How does the next poem, perfectly articulated, come, after 51 years of writing without a topic? I read, in Serres' *The Parasite*—"'Free of parasites, free, free, free of itself, absolutely purged of ego. The more I [Rousseau] write, the less I am myself. Finally free of this noise'"—what Perchick is not. He is placeless. Ahistorical. No stands for number.

"J, no. 14"
Texts for Mahler's
"Song of the Earth"
Mostly Li Po's
In German (sic.);

Pound, in a couple more years,
Would have straightened things
Out. Funny to find M and P
Working a field.

A 4 a.m. vivid dream: Martha and I are in New England, in the paneled lobby of an inn, when we come upon Donald Justice (I've no idea what he looks like, etc.), who sits plaintively on a high stool in the middle of the great room…We approach; Martha, anxious, turns her back…The little old man in the dream warns us that, as the poet ages, his poems become "limiting," more and more so, until they go away. At breakfast: Martha says my dream came of our discussion of the concept of Justice, after sociologists' assigning of gender. O, I get it: the jouste.

"I, no. 15"
The feel, gradual,
Of the need to
Write is prelude
To the poem.

Not a good feeling,
One of necessity;
Not anxiety, but an emptiness
Soon to be filled.

Prep a lecture, How to Read Joyce, for common-text project history class I'll guest. Start with Icarus. This working in the apartment beside M and M, thru play and sleep, together with rereading Joyce, a first love, and locating poems in *Fogbow Bridge* for upcoming reading—but especially just now, it's 5 p.m., returning to the table from the screened back door, having the smell in my nose of rain drying on the tar roof—I feel I'd like to write a *new* poem for the reading. Of course, Duncan said it's *a pouring out*, having been filled up, of language and experience. But I try not to write when the only thing in my head is writing. It's Shostakovich's birthday, 25 September 2000—Keep your eye on the ball, Ishmaelite!—Chico Salmon is dead.[7]

"L, no. 16"
In *The Golden Book of Springfield*,
The year is 2018:
That's when my daughter will
Graduate high school, Vachel?

Stan Musial, Griffey Junior, and…Frank L.
Amprim, J. Edgar's agent in Rome,
Who tracked down Pound:
All born in Donora, PA?

Ladro, the DTC night cat[8]…then Macaulay reminds, not 30 minutes later, Johnson's cat was named Hodge. An odd moment yesterday: I've had a postcard version of Dante Rossetti's self-portrait thumb-tacked below my light switch in the office for several years now (since, I guess, I finished the "High Season" sonnets that start from Rossetti's sonnets). Well, yesterday Judy Zimmerman—before I was to lecture on How to Read Joyce in her history class—remarked, as if I'd known, that dearly departed old friend on campus Guy Rossetti was a direct descendant? At lunch, news from the Vatican that Oscar Wilde has been recently absolved, on the basis of his deathbed conversion. <Is nothing sacred?> After midnight, playing new cd of Bruckner's Ninth (Carragan fourth movement), I realize, just now, on the 104th anniversary of the composer's quiet death. Eric Dolphy's last sound on lp, *Last Date*, was spoken work: "…you can never capture it again."

"G, no. 17"
When Puskin looked in his mirror,
A slave looked back.
When a woman……………
In the poem……………..

One of those
Hopelessly scattered
Periods, when
It needs focusing.

Today, at a used book store, I buy Feinstein's *Pushkin* for no reason, Schuyler's *Diary* for old reasons, a Fulcrum *Briggflatts* to rescue the poem from the store; tonight, a full-price for H.D.'s *Collected* to replace the books I've lost. Life is never / In the middle. Why is there such pleasure always in reading Schuyler's prose? The relaxation of reading writing. In the hands of a sure observer, for once not a guide to culture. The oddness of reading about his insomnia, after the event of his death. And references, as in Pisan Cantos, only when and as they come to a gossipy mind. Diary's description, 21 December 1968, of baby Leon Porter—"It's like having a foreign friend, to whom one can say only, 'Milk,' 'Bot-tle,' 'Bowl,' 'Light,' 'Spo-o-on.' The friendship is almost non-verbal and understood…He walks around like a little drunk…," etc.—are terrific. Do I like these, too, because JS is not always in NYC? But do not like his hot-house life, kept by friends; tho I dig, when Barbara Guest was visiting the Porters' he didn't go downstairs! JS Diary=second reference, in a few days, to Dr. Johnson's dog. Martha says Pushkin would make a great name for a cat. I say (our female cat is Pumpkin or Pumpy), "Pumpkin and Pushkin." She: "You can't call a cat Pushy."[9] Martha is gracile, graceful and slender as the letter "I" should be but seldom is.

"A, no. 18"
Schuyler, I too suffer
"Aesthetic hangovers," unable
To simply enjoy a walk—
We must remember fit, look on

It as a poet would look. Relax!
(Maybe baby Tilly
Saves me, I simply
Delight in watching?)

Keeps playing thru my brain that Pushkin is so much a part of Russia that gradeschool children who leave the door open are still chided: "Who'll close the door—Pushkin?" At end of Jim Lowell's Asphodel Book Shop catalog no. 203 find the sad note that Tessa's original drawing of the asphodelus albus, on the cover I guess of 202 catalogs, is lost when Jim's printer "went under." When Schuyler, in June 1987, resumes his diary, he "has religion." Save me from that fate, as I near death. Feinstein reports that, bleeding to death in his study after the fatal duel, Pushkin, when asked if he wished to say farewell to his friends, addressed his books, "Goodbye, friends." Later, he hallucinated that he'd climbed his bookcases and was dizzy. "I find myself rushing thru," as they say, Feinstein for biographical bases for reading Sinyavsky's *Strolls With Pushkin*, which scans as if it is written with a poet's sense. Eugeny, Oregon.

"R, no. 19"
The Russian proverb
For tonight, 1:00 a.m.:
"Sleep! Morning is
Wiser than evening."

Little Mathilda, born on
The feast of the epiphany,
To lunch with Sam Slote,
A Joycean from Buffalo.

The monotonous motif of the opening movement of Shostakovich's Seventh is obviously meant to damn the mindless bureaucracy to it own hell, and take the censors with them—*never* to glorify the siege of Leningrad. Pushkin, meaning to kill the man, rushed him. This action made d'Anthes shoot first, and badly. It was January in Tzarist Russia. The knee-deep snow had had to be removed by the seconds attending. Tertz sez "Pushkin was the first civilian to attract attention to himself in Russian literature…The biographies of poets before Pushkin were almost unknown and held no interest outside of affairs of state." Sez P stopped short of identifying with self-made hero Napoleon because he saw Byron's mistake (in "The Corsair"). P. instead, in "The Bronze Horseman" and "Poltava," links himself with Peter the Great, by creative character and black Hannibal. Second night of bedtime reading in Carr's *Mahler*: "Mahler did have a very odd, jerky walk which no one who saw him could fail to notice…[His daughter Anna] said Mahler simply changed his rhythm every few steps."

"V, no. 20"
I listen to Bruckner's last
As if, in a dream, content to
Wander a night thru a Victorian mansion.
The ghost of Tilden

Wakes me twice from troubled sleep,
For radio election results and on
Cable tv, with Martha, also restless.
We voted for Nader.

Green Thoreau's idea of a selenitic journal, after the stone (Selenites) in Pliny, white, "which increases and decreases with the moon," for a title for a poem cycle? Martha's comment, about citizens in West Palm Beach streets arguing for Bush or Gore, is smartest I've heard: she likens it to Frederick Douglass' accounts of slaves arguing over whose master owned the most slaves. Overheard from a next room in the house, the sound of a hammer (driving a nail into our common wall?) seems a rash thing, all overconfidence—a noise that mars—when somebody else does it. "Violinists," confided the musicologist who was a pianist, "have the biggest egos because they play notes no one else has."   The score is too numerous to enumerate the every day and every night sounds of life, ever increasing and decreasing, in an apartment house with George Aperghis's six musicians above and below us.

"D, no. 21"
Firemen returning up the street
They'd marched magnificently down,
Looking too human now, only
Frozen like us.

Cold turns us away
From Tilly's first parade,
Thanxgiving gave out
Downtown Greensburg.

Schoenberg was right to predict a world in which milkmen would someday whistle his music. Now it is the winter of Scriabin's insect sonata. The bottles of milk might freeze on our porch even in this brilliant morning sun. Another way to distinguish between two eras: Mahler's First was ill received by his contemporaries—they had no dragoman for the music—but his Third, that dinosaur body with the brain, philosopher's, that's the size of a man's, made his reputation as a composer! How did M know he was great? How did he compose every summer? How did…The cd player breaks, just finished ape in the cemetery of "Song of the Earth" to the counterpoint upstairs woman sobbing in our midnight hallway about the depravity of love.

"Z, no. 22"
I poured two glasses
Of wine. We argue.
Now it's approaching
Midnight and the new

Year. Alone in the room,
I drink both glasses
Carefully. Fireworks
Somewhere northwest

in town scare the cats from my bed in the floor. Vexed, certainly, but not so far as Satie's 409th, I, zelot, still have big things planned for tonight: the first hour of 2001 will be Bruckner, thru headphones til I sleep the zzzzzzs of his dead knights. Unheard parties are sweetest, neighbors. Straight enuf to straighten a picture in our apartment: an ancient b/w Pound at the end, cap and cane, visiting Joyce's grave. His face betrays no indication that he hears the animal noises from the Zurich zoo nearby; it is the silent Pound staring at a whimsical statue of his long-dead friend. (Could death look like that, like a joke like that, after all?) And humor in writing came between Olson and Dorn, old and new years, after mid-century. Fanfare for the American century: Bill Monroe's high lonesome mandolin. When Bill came to town, he challenged all comers to box; he played first base against your best all-stars team; then, when the park grass was full of summer dew and the sun was finally down, he sang "Heavy Traffic Ahead" before hitting the road in that bus and writing a new song, maybe it would turn out to be "Jerusalem Ridge," before your town woke up in the morning. Monroe's fugue required simply stepping up to the mike for a solo, a step back for accompaniment.[11]

"Y, no. 23"
Great beauty too needs
Reassuring.
Her hat must do
More than

Fit.
I've lived with you 18 months;
Every time
You walk in, I'm astonished.

What different decades make of Charles Ives is about as interesting as his music and usually more interesting than his thundering bidness life.[12] Apparently, his experiments grew out of Yale College fun with a game of varying *one* musical factoring a piece he was playing. Reading dossiers for search in music, I learn that music is most alive in America in the local church, where, o, Bruckner, o Ives, o blind Vierne, ah Messiaen, these Ph.D.s play the organ, lead the choir, sleep at the Y. One interview is expert in the music of George Crumb, of Charleston, West Virginia, y who has set poems by Lorca. Start Russell Banks' narration of Owen Brown, *Cloudsplitter*, its fictive narrator/ son of John Brown immediately takes me to sites I know in western Pennsylvania and northeastern Ohio. Decide, after weeks of wondering if I'm up to the text, to buy translation of Constantin Floros' *Mahler: The Symphonies*. Seems serious business when nobody's looking but me. Plan is to work my way thru the 10-plus-"Lied von der Erde," listening and reading in order, nights, when the girls have gone to bed. John Lennon died 20 years ago this day, Doug's email reminds me. Yclept away.

"E, no. 24"
Poor Nerval's life long hanged from
That corset string: Cameron's
Herschel (1867) is Ed Dorn's face: never realized that
Bonnard took pictures, too:

Open to Alice Boughton's 1905 portraits
Of Ryder I do not see
The mystic they all talk about: he evades her, camera.
No visionary eyes staring us down, infidels.

Watching pictures of the erratum in Palm Beach Co—Martha quips that the canvassing board, sitting at table in front of cable tv cameras, reminds her of the composition of bodies in a painting of raft-and-shark-in-water…Watson? or I guess, it's "The Raft of the *Medussa*"? Altho I admire Mahler's First Symphony, and parts of Second thru Fourth, it is only with the Fifth—last night's listening as I track it thru Floros—that I find the structure I've wanted to know for poems.[13] Nachtmusik. Reading *Cloudsplitter* and, in turn, listening to M, about as disparate as the Eighth's Latin hymn/*Faust II*. Still nothing as agreeable as the opening movements of the Ninth and Tenth. Open Gass' *Reading Rilke* (why does he insist on the spelling Duchamps?) on our last day in Hornell, on what turns out to be the anniversary, as they say, of Rilke's death. The idea of Rilke's poems of "Self-Portrait." Autobiographical writing has a way of involving fugue voices, layers in songs of myself. Rimbaud's "I is another"; the self-portrait Duncan presented me, Fall of 1972, swapped for a drawing of my own—he has inscribed it "a drawing of somebody else appearing in avoiding my face in the mirror." A recount. As a boy in Seville, I witnessed the linotype form letters of hot lead. The lack of information to go by, when you need tv weather to plan a winter's drive of five hours. What exactly is it we watch? The etaoin shrdlu.

"'The true, lost face of music,' no. 25"
After Rodez,
Artaud could believe
In no part of the
Anatomy

Excepting
The human face. He
Wrote: "...the human face
Has not yet found its face...."

The image purported to be Emily D. found on eBay, in 2000, supersedes, for me, that photo of the poet at an awkward sixteen.

I greatly admire Artaud's sketches of the face not like I admire Schoenberg's paintings or the b/w photograph of Tubin from the cover of the cd of Symphonies Four and Nine.

Schoenberg reports that he saw only *gazes*, not faces, when he looked into people's eyes. These Blicke, along with his self-portraits, comprise much of his best painting.

A family snapshot of Schoenberg playing tennis with the Marx Brothers.

Benny Kauff looks into the Greely wire service camera lens of the last pitch of 1915, and swings.

All photographs of Pessoa.

We have the expression, Face the music. Messian wrote, waiting for his Catalogue to be performed: "In my hours of gloom, when I am suddenly aware of my own futility, when every musical idiom—Classical, Oriental, ancient, modern and ultra-modern—appears to me as no more than admirable painstaking experimentation which cannot ultimately be justified, what is left for me but to seek out the true, lost face of music somewhere off in the forest, in the fields, in the mountains or on the seashore, among the birds."

The composer Eduard Tubin is not so much looking out into the vista of his retirement at Ruda Lake as he is caught in the moment just after the act of his peering for a long time down the bank and into the water that mostly submerges a rowboat. He looks, well, composed. His is the air of having already and thoroughly considered. He has decided for himself but not yet moved from the spot to tell anyone. The boat is swamped. The water in the boat makes a little lake too. At once, I see it as the cover art for the book that would contain this poem and the image of the very human composer. When I write to his son, Eino Tubin, in Turkey, he apologizes for not locating a print or the negative. He does tell me that his mother is the photographer and suggests that Vardo Rumessen, in Estonia, might have the print. As I write this sentence, I haven't an answer to my search for the picture or for Artaud's search thru the darkness of being conscious. If David Baratier has published the photo, you have it, dear reader, in your hands now. Look at the face.

"U, no. 26"
Front-yard elect-me signs in season
Looks like the neighborhood's being
Sold off
By two real estate agents.

On Man Ray's tomb,
In English, so we might read it straight:
"Unconcerned
But not indifferent."

Martha sez it's Beethoven's birthday, as I'm off fishing listening to Delius in Florida.[14] Last 3 a.m., finish the John Brown novel and start Stephen Minta's Byron in Greece, which turns out to be told by a reluctant 'istorin. Sample: "When traveling, it is always better to listen than to talk." In Ann Arbor, to pick up Doug on Xmas break, the university town is next to immobilized, or snowmobilized, by 15 inches of new snow atop old. On drive back, gratified to hear my son's appreciation of the Firelands' scraped-out landscape. One of JoAnn's smarter observations about me, in response to my expressed interest in traveling to Ohio, "You don't miss the people. You just want to see the landscape again." Ubiety. Return to Greensburg to card and gift from David Baratier, of Tom Bridwell's *Notes from the Cistern*—a model, as it turns out, for the prosepoem fugues here. Dear Martha has given me the most appropriate of Xmas gifts, a remarkable print, passes for watercolor, of a Robert Delaunay 1909 interior of St. Severin.[15] Its design and color I've admired since undergraduate days at Kent, when I kept a cheap calendar reproduction of one of his Eiffel Tower etudes in a little red frame. Minta is right. Hobhouse was disappointed by the ruins at Delphi, but Byron "could claim a new legitimacy. His excitement still depended on all that had gone before…But his relationship with the landscape was new, personal, and direct. The Muses, he knew, had long since departed. Something, however, remained in the air. A sensation more physical than literary, deeply connected with the past, yet not confined by it."

"G major, no. 27"
Last September, I prepared by falling
Asleep in the early mornings listening
To Ashkenazy's fingering the 24
Crazy to figure a way

To use the form in poems at last
Falling asleep after two often
Dreaming of three in G major.
Martha sd Graham Nash for Ogden.

So this is the 27th Prelude & Fugue. I'd hoped for 26, a kind of alphabetical complement to Shostakovich's 24 (and his to Bach's 48); letters for notes. So do you think I need a system of sharps and flats to justify my continuing? So the structure challenges the form to the collapse of one, or both? Isn't writing like a madman from October to February, as Shostakovich did in 1950-51 and I aim to do, enuf to unify this cycle? Who the hell are you, Kabalevsky, in my face? Didn't you hear me play my 24 before you and the rest of the Composers' Union censors, on this very keyboard? Didn't you listen to me explain afterward that, after the first few, my Preludes & Fugues were no longer interesting to me as technical exercises for keeping fit at the bench? (Ms. Livanova was the worst of the lot from the Union. But dear Yudina, the pianist, I shall never forget her.) Well, there are more. Perhaps many more, I don't know yet. Exile me for a formalist. You have my leave, so go fuck yourself to your own satisfaction. Gass: "The *Elegies* tell us to listen as hitherto only holy men have listened…The *Duino Elegies* were not written; they were awaited." Difficult to contemplate the opening of that first Elegy, in the family context of John believing himself to be an angel among jackals. Martha shows me, reads aloud, George Eliot's poem "O May I Join the Choir Invisible," from the 1900 Little, Brown edition we brot back from storage in Hornell. Poem defines GE's kind of tradition; Martha's, too, I believe. My tradition is to have written, in the months of the 50th anniversary of Shostakovich's composing his cycle, these Ps & Fs. The dizzy dance of being at work on a long poem keeps me up til past 4:06:32. Monk's awkward dance / beside himself / beside his piano / and back. The form Thelonius Monk took is not replicated in nature: splayed fingers thinking to strike beside Haeckel's table at the Blue Note.

"K, no. 28"
First teaching day of Winter Term,
The anniversary of Byron's return
To Mesolongi.
Yesterday, at parents' request, graded,

Wrinkled and soiled from the car crash,
The term paper on *Vertigo*
My student died trying to deliver. And Byron died
There, on 19 April, last teaching day of this term.

Offer John K_____ a ride, it's 9 degrees and snowing, to his local bar where I surprise him by accepting his shy offer, car door in his hand, to come inside for a beer. We are kith and extended family kin. The bar is Lucy's and it stands, or rather leans, beside a bar with a male name, both directly across the street from the long-deserted train depot, a great last century seat of the Erie Railroad that Webster traveled to Hornel on his own flatcar for. Sit with him in his public loneliness of bad cases bumming smokes and buying a bag in awful restroom and the girls just or never out of local high school old already. Enter his bedroom, at home, to be reminded how at Kent I was entertained by the proximities of poetry and insanity. John fancies himself a writer: i.e., he writes on everything—dresser, walls, ash tray, statue of saint—tho I can't concentrate, he explains, to read a book. His notebook actually has dust on the cover he doesn't seem to notice when he shows it to me. (Martha's gift, years ago, of Art Pepper's autobiography is the only book I think of him reading.) Fugue is also a term in psychology for the mind fleeing. Loneliness. Obsession. Cryptic witty talk—great synaptic leaps, often very funny when I can connect one—reconnecting unifying lines from somewhere beyond my vanishing point, before gathering for next leap, exhausting, sometimes into a darkness beyond me, sitting with him. And poets, too, do they not, talk on and on this way, believing their auditors follow? "K is for Mozart," he might well have said. "I haven't had sex in two years," he does say. He used, in conversation, the word "Republican' as a verb. He says he's an angel. His power is the terrible burden of knowing what's going to happen, like one of Homer's gods helpless before Fate.[16] This is not so much sad, but basic human condition exposed. John complains he's lost the things he's written. Investing the attention of symbolism to the smallest particle of debris, picked up, now, between fingers and stored in shirt pocket. Dating, as I do, poems or books I buy. He's Ezra Pound looking for the gloss to the Text. Do the words "poem" or "book" redeem the madness of our own methods? I question my ethics in making this most personal record, like Charlie Parker's breakdown on "Lover Man." A single night in the tragedy of having a long life before him. A drunk in the bar approached our booth and called out like a knife presently unconcealed: "I envy you!" he was talking to me and I thot of a dozen things I'd be proud to be envied for that he couldn't possibly, of course, know, a stranger in his town, bar. It was my head of hair, his bald spot.

"C major, no. 29"
Will the poem admit
The unwanted voices of schizophrenia
To the voices of the ongoing fugue?
The work in fits and starts, as usual:

Transfigured
Or disfigured in the transfer
Nonetheless
Figured.

Since Oregon, the poem has always come to me in fytts. A unit in prosody. It comes again. Overcoming me with the way things suddenly seem obviously to fit in the universe of things. Blake and van Gogh and H.D. and Rilke and Ryder and Hartley[17] and Scriabin are the great late artists of fytts. Radio in Orphee's car in Cocteau's film by Jack Spicer. Admit it. Most poets only wish to be schizophrenic, for one sitting at a time, which is the very least of what Rimbaud must have meant by derangement. When H.D. wrote "In resurrection, there is confusion," of course, she was not thinking of the simplicity of Mahler's Fourth Symphony. Gustav Mahler's second voice, not the Viennese director's orders to musicians but the one speaking to us from the invention of the modern language, dates from 7 February 1960 and that day's Young People's Concert broadcast. Schizophrenic Mahler? Alma's Mahler?[18] Lazarus Mahler (as in that Fourth)? Both eras have their ears full, Walter's and Lenny's. Time signatures. So this is the afterlife (played in major) some artists would die for countless times.

"A minor, no. 30"
A minor consolation
For living
In a Woodrow-and-Edith-era apartment is:
Our steam heat, cock full

Open, makes all the plants—
Orchid, Xmas cactus,
Hoya—in the dining
Room bloom.

Gass cites Edmond Jaloux on meeting Rilke: "When I began talking with Rilke it seemed to me that it was the first time that I talked with a poet…all the other poets I have known, however great they were, were poets only in their minds; outside their work they lived in the same world as I, with the same creatures…." A good way to describe what crosseyed Duncan means to me. Gass' way of translating seems pretty close to how poems are written in the first place, tho on first draft the rush of inspiration may obscure the many directions taken by the poet being in his colloquy.

"E minor, no. 31"
All change is crooked, camb,
If brass awakes to find itself trumpet;
Extreme xenophilia begets handfasting
And ithyphallic soldierish is straight talk

By Rimb and by Monk, bang on Large Glass.
Thelonius always too big for the raincoat he's in
Dumb hat. You can still paint after Duchamp
But there are no more walls to hang it on, hat.

Dance like he broke a leg, circle back to the stable stool suspended above
fumes his middle name[19] to play thru.

"D major, no. 32"
"Bill,
The apples!" The telephone
Pole in Sommer's water-
Color means to

Look like
The Chinese
Character for "sun
Rising in the east."

Call Lowell to buy the William Sommer watercolor he advertises in the
latest Asphodel. Sommer was a northeast Ohio artist who eschewed fame,
even galleries, and, at 54, taught Hart Crane about the art and music of
the modern era. To me, an ideal artist not dissimilar to Gerrit Lansing or
Ken Irby or Carl Ruggles. Buy it on Tilly's first birthday. In four days, the
apple crate arrives (I'd been thinking about Jim muttering "Don't know
how I'll mail it" into the phone), wrapped as only a package from Ashpodel
can be. The last, strips of masking tape across the glass, like unwrapping
the face of a mummy. Mathilda watched, interested in every layer and my
expression, from her highchair. When I call Jim to accept delivery, I hear in
the background (kitchen) Tess say she misses the picture. Strangely, the best
view of the watercolor is now, in the dining room lit by a chandelier—not
during the day, when light glints off the 1930 glass—when it looks glowing

golden from within. The artist's bold, broad strokes for snow and hill and telephone pole, in contrast to the lithographer-precise ink dictation of the house. The foreground makes me feel what I feel in the northeast Ohio landscape with ground covered by snowfall. (The last was my first impression, this afternoon.) From a distance of 10 feet, from my table, the impression is one of depth—foreground and up, across hill. A picture to live with, then.

"B minor, no. 33"
Inman's Garrison Hall
Sounds like college basketball,
A character's name in a novel,
Or a military threat.

Ann Arbor is not to be
Confused
With Garrison Hall, with life
In Garrison Hall.

Gregory Corso is dead. At midnight, from my pallet in the dining room floor, I can see what looks to be a Minataur's head hanging in the walk-in closet, back-lit from all-night hall light, whose door opens in, maze-like, to my room's door, frame intersecting frame. In what childhood's childish movie did I see such a cow's head speak the voice of a goddess—was it to Jason or Telemachus? I misremember. I wish it to open its big cow eyes and speak to me now, tonight. To dictate a new old poem thru me, or a way. (Find a new version of Hart Crane's "C 33" in the core of a snowball in the freezer since 1916.) And when the world awakes in the morning, I would go to sleep at last with my secret Dedalus wings hanging from wire coat hooks…Lost my way in the dark, in the college town snow, in the neighborhoods of the unshoveled, coming down from my son's dorm on Hill, or really years before aware that I hadn't somehow dressed for the cold first breath goes to the quarter that goes into the frozen public phone to call for a ride to the host's home to drink and wait for frozen dawn.[20] Corso, you are my true Elpenor.

"A major, no. 34"
My son Douglas suffers
Ignorance
Of Rimbaud's example
How to subvert education

And save the artist's soul.
His father lives on
No poet
Survives his own adolescence.

Imagine Hart Crane listening. Because Hart Crane never looks the same in any two photographs, he never seems to be listening. To Bill Sommers, or to Ivor Winters, or Miss Monroe or to Marsden Hartley who was in Mexico with him. Only, at the end, to the sea. Sound of Sibelius and sleeping in a cabin by the lip of the sea. But, near the beginning, when he was young he drank and played Sibelius on the piano with Bill Sommers at the old converted schoolhouse in Brandywine. Teaching *Gulliver's Travels*, Book III, Martha mentions the Academy of Projectors; does everybody but me see that *Slinger*'s Projector is here? Steve Ellis sends me his *Full Tilt Flywheel*, one of 20 copies. Prose-line sonnets. Comes in at just the right moment to inform my writing of more fugues. Only bad part, some of his poems read like ones I must write, stop me nearly in my tracks, like "Hymn" ("You can think in the 90s about listening in the 80s to the Stones / in the 70s…") or "Call" or "Torch Song." Gulliver would have Pound bring, instead of an Objectivist poem, a bag containing the tree and the sun. A list in listen.

"F sharp minor, no. 35"
It was the Zutiste Cabaner who
Taught Rimbaud piano
According to the method duly recorded
A vox set. Colorful language.

William James visited Helen
Keller and brot the girl a gift of
A vowel she never forgot:
A peacock feather.[21]

The radical empiricist. Bogg notes: "Anyone who left home as often as Rimbaud inevitably spent a great deal of time there." Is there a term, there must be, for the sub-musical utterances that come from the musicians as they play a piece? Name it and it is the title for every poem I've written, recording my non-singing while the poetry plays. Imagine the 18-year-old Rimbaud in the Reading Room of the British Museum with Swinburne and Marx, without meeting Swinburne and Marx. Continue to be put off by Coltrane's table talk about spirit, but know now that the *Ascension* session, 28 June 1965, happened during divorce/new baby time in his life similar to my year. Maybe he gives me, at 50, permission to sometime use the word "soul" in a poem? Rimbaud's "Spiritual Hunt," evidently a prose poem mss., was destroyed by Mathilde Verlaine. When his first solo emerges, a miracle birth, from the chaos of creation all around—prelude—you can hear he's a finer player than Ornette, whom he's followed here…Second lead is a point of unity? Freddie Hubbard, who was trumpet on Ornette's *Free Jazz*; or is it Dewey Johnson, a more mysterious empiricist, who, in another kind of sense-making in this fugue of players, disappears from jazz after this session?

"E major, no. 36"
Inspired
Breathing the fire
That leaves
No air

Wayne Andrews
On evaporating piano
The single realistic detail of Lazarus
Arisen but stinking of the tomb.

Our writer of the sonnet "The New Colossus," Emma Lazarus, remembered at least *at* the Statue of Liberty, did the translation of Heine (1881) that still stands up. Note Ms. Lazarus and the Laz of *Roman Zero*, dear. Note her sonnet's "air-bridged" and not between the strong legs of a hero. Note her false line, first of the sestet, is dropped from the plaque; her poem was used to raise funds for the masonry base America had to build to foot the gift. "The dead in a photograph reveal a forward look like a face among cloud and wind such as a rock grows to express" (LZ's *Arise, arise*). Liberty's green face around the corner from Baz's studio, a sweatshop next door where Asians made shirts for what Passeo calls the clothed animals. Brad Mahldau's *Elegiac Cycle* playing…What does it mean that Kate Chopin should choose the music of Chopin for the awakening that kills?…playing in my head.

"C sharp minor, no. 37"
The only time I saw Sherman Paul
He let me pick
One b/w picture
Of Duncan Dorn him

Around a table in Iowa City.
I have no idea where
That enlargement of
My three teachers got to.

Picture three voices for me. Voice-over by me pretending to be the writer, narrator, and reader of the *Illuminations*: "Life to me seemed a popular film narrated by my ex-sister-in-law, the once and always homecoming queen of Kent now in her 50s and matronly twice over, who had the bad habit of telling you every minute detail of every minute of the plot, and only the plot ma'am, of the last film she'd seen before I'd had a chance or even the impulse to see it myself.[22] That is to say, I did not feel, in my unhappy first marriage, as if I were living in a movie; I distinctly felt I had been previewed by the yuppies and found to be as banal as conversation in Cincinnati, not to say Columbus, Ohio. That all changed. One day (or maybe evening, as I recall the lights were up), you, dearest, bot a ticket and sat down in the seat next to my usual at the Norka in Akron. I'd heard all about the film that was on the screen, as usual, but something was funny—the continuity a bit off?—Fred Astaire referred to things we should not know while Edward Everett Horton was doing a double-take like only he can in front of something we already missed. In one particular scene, b/w, Woody Allen is Ingmar Bergman's father, and so on. In another, Gide is the Widow Rimbaud bitching about her son.[23] In short, it was love, Martha, in all its extra-marital confusion. "The Gay Divorcee" was not its original title. Turns out, the projectionist had switched Reel IV for Reel III. In the end, we'd already made love the night before we met ever after."

"B major, no. 38"
Damfino, Keaton's homemade
Boat is prelude
To the family soon to be lost
In the stage dark. Some Sybil

Asks like a wife, "Where are we?"
And Buster mouths
(For this is a chaste and silent film),
"Damfino!" He is beside himself.

That's *The Boat*. But *The Playhouse*, the film he made before *The Boat*, is Keaton's silent-film fugue: he played all the parts in that film, like a poet fabricating the impression that a cast of voices, not just his own, the lyrical one, plays in the poem. From September to February 1921 to 1922, Keaton the not Keats made *The Playhouse, The Boat, The Paleface, Cops*, and "The Poem beginning 'The.'" Shostakovich, age 17, plays the piano to illustrate silent films at Bright Reel Theatre, Leningrad.

"G sharp minor, no. 39"
Try
Playing Bruckner's Ninth
And not
Disturbing the neighbors,

All bold now hushed
Really the most serious kind
Of party
It ends after 3 or maybe 4.

In her self-portrait, hard-hearted Penelope parodies something he once said to her without first thinking. The paintbrush squirms in her free hand. Dried, among gold apples, the tabled brush is the formula for obdurate dawn, when it is still moon in Odysseus' head. Must be the ghost of Sherman Paul in Iowa City sends me a review copy of Hollenberg's *H.D. and Poets After*, with Robert Kelly's call therein for, after Dunc's H.D. Book, "the sensuous [I'd first typed "serious"] discipline of reading and of following the text wherever it leads."

Also with an essay by Sharon Doubiago, whose place, in our generation, is with H.D., in hers. Meaning she is our H.D. of the long poem, but plays to nobody's DHL or EP or WCW or Freud. Reading a few lines of Kelly's "A Joining" sets me off on pages of couplets for a poem on dis-joining, divorce, beginning "The day I left my wife / I told her // keep the house / to live in…." Kelly's useful distinction: H.D. wrote "Long Songs," not narrative poems. Are we to play the songs loud or circumspect, in afternoons or late into the night?

"F sharp major, no. 40"
The commission
Went to Britten.
A propeller starts—
Rimbaud to Africa

Antheil to Hollywood
And tv, crossing
At McKonkey's Ferry—
A pianola loop.

Learn that Benjamin Britten set the *Illuminations*. I've got to consider that combo for my poem. Antheil might have made a better choice, early (Bad Boy) George, of course: sounds of industrial London, images from the Chrystal Palace in the boy's head when Rimbaud visited it, cry of a shrinking stomach.

"E flat minor, no. 41"
I'm thinking in quatrains.
I thot I needed to
Hear *Ballet Mechanique*
Then, abruptly,

His Symphony 6.
Tilly smiles and dances
In her highchair. Served up
A child's dish.

She smiled and stepped toward the sound, knowing it for a dance. Modern music for a postmodern girl, born in 2000. I don't actually mind grandmother's Guardian Angel on your shelf as long as it doesn't fuck with the tin wind-up parrot brot home from the Warhol. You never realize just how many times you *do* step into the same river, more than twice, until baby spills her water on the rug: your sock foot is wet all day. There is the old thotfulness father newly acquires, babe in arms, to telephone or open a bill. For dads there is no bio*logical* niche in the hip—I lift with one arm stronger than I remembered, a place in the heart.

"D flat major, no. 42"
Wolf Kahn calendar
For February:
An old barn sags
Inward, upon itself

The tree beside it
Branches up and out.
Arms would not hands
Could not reach him.

I had always wanted to be an artist, thot of myself as an artist, looked at the world with an adolescent's artist-in-training eye. I turned out on request charcoal portraits of friends of the family, drawn from photographs. Norman Rockwell wrote back to my 5th grade teacher: "Thank you for the drawings by your student…If Richard applies himself and works hard…." By 16, I realized my limits. I could not mix paints, I was impatient at building up an area in a picture, thinking that way, and, as with my lackadaisical attempt at playing the trumpet, I was frustrated then bored to inactivity by the thot of daily practice. When I first read poetry, about then, I mean the poems they did not mention in school or seem to have read—some pages of Pound, then the Donald Allen anthology that starts with Olson and Duncan—I hoped I could learn to work in language. In the abstract. I could draw a competent likeness or toot a simple tune, but I could never *think* in line or music. I was, in short, landlocked in Ohio. George Butterick once told me it was the Allen anthology for him, too, early. I was still drawing when I met Duncan. Traded him drawings. Publishing cartoons. And I'd by then seen Apollinaire and Joe Brainard, read something of Williams. All that remains is my interest in placing words on the page. Hold the typed page backwards, to the light, it's a picture.

"B flat minor, no. 43"
What is it makes Max Jacob
Fade so, or Picasso,
A plump 37, embolden?
Including perhaps the only photo

Of Modigliani smiling.
The buildings of Paris
Unchanged behind these men
Unsmiling, unposed, unmoved by them.

Stravinsky once said, "The voice is perfect on the telephone." The book *A Day with Picasso* is snapshots by Cocteau and not all of the pictures, or the best, feature Picasso. I like seeing Satie, posing with Valentine Gross (what a name! what a hat!) when he was working with Cocteau on *Parade*. In the photos the sun is out—Kluver uses the shadows of 12 August 1916 to date each frame—and the war is something only I am aware of. The climate is summer-, not war-time. Our grandparents look drunk in midday and too at home and happy with themselves to be battling Modernity. The monologist in Poulenc's opera eventually strangles herself with the phone cord.

"A flat major, no. 44"
Gift to the New World
From Rimbaud's order
The Statue of
Liberty then in Madison

Square tourists
Pay to climb
The disembodied
Limb

The hard lesson of the amputated limbs of Cendrars and Rimbaud should be a warning, what's enuf is enuf, as the captain of the "Samuel Enderby" told Ahab. The mistake of *The Rake* still makes the fugue progress apace; Stravinsky's error of infecting Auden's inflection, as if there is no music in the words. Craft sez it's pitch valued over rhythm, plus Stravinsky mistook some parts of speech. Hard to mistake Baba, the bearded lady or Mother Goose's brothel for anything else. Helen Adam wrote the best songs for whores. The best whores have Scotts accents. George Grosz drew a better Orgy than Hogarth's. Let's include their voices then. Let Felicity Lott, who sings on a cd of Britten's *Illuminations*, sing the final voyage of the "Aphinar." Aboard the death ship "Aphinar" leaving the port of Aphinar (AR's last words return to themselves). A is the only vowel remaining.

"F minor, no. 45"
May*be*
We *can*
*R*eread
John Wieners'

707 Scott St. journal
And leave out
All the bad
Days?

One aftereffect of reading Fowlie's Rimbaud translations each night: I forget to read the verso pages of books all day, only recto. So Frank O'Hara's poem to Helen Frankenthaler, "Blue Territory," is gone and what was once facing, his poem to Franz Kline, "Poem," now ends with the couplet "I thought it was outside disappearing / but it is disappearing in my heart," effectively rewriting the history of art in America. In Hollywood in November, Auden stays with Stravinsky to work on *The Rake*. The composer called the poet "Ow-den." (Stravinsky writes Act III while Shostakovich writes P & F. (A year before his death, Stravinsky was reading Troyat's biography of Pushkin.)) Auden left the Stravinskys' house only once, to see a doctor when he went suddenly deaf. It turned out to be earwax. Stravinsky, at 70, had never written an opera or a composition on love.

"E flat major, no. 46"
Abyssinia
And the River
Awash,
Rift Valley,

And further out
The Ark,
The Garden
Where elephants go to die.

This fugue will end with no buttons. In Dornac's photograph, Verlaine's bald head floats above his drink. His head has no body but rather a sinister shadow for a black suit blending, like a urine stain into buttoned trouser fabric, into café booth. Verlaine's bald head like a light bulb, which means an idea in cartoons, is only empty. The incandescent light bulb has not been invented yet. The head cannot comprehend Africa. The head has just published Rimbaud's poems without Rimbaud's permission. Verlaine's mustaches, wide as the head-splitting grin not forthcoming in this life, point downward to his neglected glass of absinthe, milky white on the table and glowing from within, a reference to an era and a consciousness. Slits for eyes. Dim wit lyricist. He of the head is alone at his table. Perfect harmony on "Get Back" by John and Paul, perfect opposites in life and in death. Karel Syzmanowski's Song of the Night playing in the next room. Meanwhile, on another continent, Rimbaud makes plans for a photo album of Abyssinia. "His caravans set off for the coast like long, repetitive poems in four-legged stanzas...." (Whole caravans of preludes!) Abdo Rinbo is noted locally for never wearing a hat. Sun-baked skull hatching plans. Seldom in control of his hands, when talking. Threw a rock and killed a man.[24] Visited the kings of East Africa and survived.[25] Made a fortune he never spent. His tall, thin, coffee-skinned Mariam survives in a photo from the period. Snapshots of Rimbaud in Africa are entirely lacking in contrast, as if he's elected to become part of the background amidst the sand and sun and air. Fade out. His hair was turning prematurely white when he died. He was busy leaving the inaccuracies of old age for his critics when he died. He was busy leaving and taking leave when he died. Makes his own clothes. No buttons.

"C minor, no. 47"
Don't say rivulette
When we both know
You mean banjo.
All day the wind

Corrupts the winter.
Cui bono?
Igitur's month
To be endured.

The shortest death over many agonizing passages. The shortest month of the year. The obese Roman governor raises a wristless arm that sends the 28 runners for ice for his drink from the glacier. Meanwhile, February elects to fall on a dull spear.

"March March, no. 48"
A fragmentary music clears the room—Ted Berrigan.

"Sadly, the piano
Is become an, oh, a
Historical instrument. You have to pay
To have them taken away."

The reed organ predates the piano,
And now the keyboard, in American
Homes. "Hayden sat at the table
With the other servants."

Her Claudio Monteverdi and my William Carlos Williams. How basso continuo and word painting, 1610, argue Williams' beats, the line breaks that stress in him a word. Monteverdi writes in defense of a music no longer restricted to mathematics.[26] Schubert's "through-composed" lieder, each stanza its own discrete musical drama; opposed to the old practice of "strophic setting" and maybe the preface to why stanzas in our poems can and should vary? Ives' characteristic gesture: spitting into the fireplace. Anywho, the fugue part is that I've plagiarized these voices, two women and a man, scholars all, we're interviewing for the tenure-track music position. Trying to find Schubert's Seventh. According to plan, things went. The man informed me that William Thomas McKinley is still living; indeed, he'd been born in the county we were sitting in. I suddenly knew nothing about WTMcK, or my Olson, both too "impatient" was his word to write masterpieces always going for the impromptu. I hadn't planned on the patience of masterpieces. Shostakovich, "divorced from himself," left playing out his lonesome hand. According to plan, I would end with Hayden's *Farewell Symphony*, only transcribed for piano so there's no one from an orchestra to leave the pianist, already alone on the stage. According to plan, I would write my Preludes & Fugues during the months that Shostakovich wrote his, ending in February. Now it's March and the series is unfinished and unabandoned.

"Double Preface with Double Fugue, no. 49"

    Coltrane's in   Tubin then
my daughter's childhood house.   Syzmanowski
The a/c off &   sustain me
one night's air, this   before sleep

night's, breathing in   a weekend in Ohio.
& out the house.   Could have used them
The lift of   Pursuance,   when I was an o boy
the Psalm   after Ives'.   weakened in Ohio.

A prelude is a test of will that only rhymes with "skill," a sketch the man makes of himself then grows into it. But a fugue tells itself in many voices, past and present, in an order that comes only after the poet swallows language whole as pride.

It's worth the drive to the Flint Hills to confirm the sunset. When I enthuse about Syzmanowski to Ken Irby, he tells me the quote in *Catalpa*. So, I've known and not known the composer's name for 25 years. Wallace Stevens' comment that music is feeling, not sound, goes for Syzmanowski's music. Two years writing his unrecoverable novel. Thinking about writing about Robert Duncan, I only tonight realize he used Rousseau's "The Dream" in the Venice Poem, so my poem at the end of *Fogbow Bridge seems* to read ironically. Ken has already been where, many times in poems, I'm going.

"Quodlibet, no. 50"
This sestet is Shostakovich
This sestet is Shostakovich playing with one hand
Only the Intermezzo to his Piano Quintet:

> All sonnet chance,
However handsome or sound,
Once counted on, now counted out.[27]

I wrote the three couplets, then managed to lose the slip of paper. What's next is not the only end. In Gorky, on 23 February 1964, Shostakovich, his right arm by now useless, played the Intermezzo to his Quintet in G Minor for Piano and Strings, opus 57, written 24 years earlier. It was to be his last performance. On my cd, the movement lasts six minutes and 32 seconds. This end is only what's not next.

This is not, defiantly not, Zichy's sinisteria.

This is the lefthandedness of Jimi Hendrix.

And Hendrix was the next Art Tatum. What kind of fugue would be the last in the series beginning with Shostakovich at the time of my birth? Beginning with Pessoa is a fugue for three voices, sometimes called Symphony of a Restless Night, whose fragments endlessly reorder themselves like ancestors of the hours of insomnia. What's next?[28]

The word "face" occurs sixteen times in this poem. Now it's seventeen.

This is not the.

Notes

¹ "*Can*
   The design
   Of the fugue
   Be transferred
   To poetry?"
   —Zukofsky's *A-6*.

² The name of the woman Charles Ives married was Harmony. The title of Mary Oppen's book, her auto/biography of a marriage, is *Meaning A Life*.

³ Samuel Coleridge- / Taylor had it / right, not backwards.

⁴ A member of baseball's first platoon, 1911, in an outfield with Sam Crawford and Cobb. Author of a baseball memoir.

⁵ See William Thomas McKinley's music.

⁶ Charles Ives' Mutual Life

   Wallace Stevens' Hartford
   Walt's "commerce" with
Pound's dollar signs throughout Alberti's church, and the pun on a British pound echoes in the chapels. Decades of tomb dust make the carved drapes there seem all the more real. DO NOT ERASE on blackboard when I enter the classroom. His not he / lied.

⁷ Cleveland Indians' infielder-outfielder from 1964 to 1968. When he smiled, for after-the-game tv interviews, kids saw the gold heart between his two front teeth. In August of '64, he smiled quite often.

⁸ Frank O'Hara writes, in "Chez Jane," that Saint-Saens' music makes a sound like steam from cat piss.

⁹ See Pushkin's "Mozart and Salier" in *Little Tragedies*.

¹¹ The technique is known as "ganging the mike."

¹² The parents of Eliott Carter bought life insurance from Ives. A mutual life.

¹³ Schoenberg's homage to Mahler is nine bars for piano. Also see his painting of Mahler's burial.

¹⁴ It's always Irby's / Delius I hear. East / of Texas.

¹⁵ O, the / Ogives / Satie gives us.

[16] Max Jacob's Christian poetry often sounds like John speaking:
"He has named me secretary.
So during the night I decipher
A paper he covered with figures
Which he writes with his own hand
And placed in my mind."
(Wallace Fowlie trans.)

[17] Until reading about Marsden Hartley recently, I hadn't thot about Richard Rolle or fyttes since graduate school. Ryder is his master. And Hartley's cubism begins with his painting the Bach Preludes, "Musical Theme #1," 1912.

[18] Alma mater / Alma matter / Alma Mahler's memory.

[19] Why did you bother to look here, if you knew it was Sphere?

[20] Ruskin once asked Lewis Carroll to write a novel that was not a dream. Cobb once asked Addie Joss to kiss his ass.

[21] "Heidegger never thinks 'about' something; he thinks something," Arendt.

[22] Poe writes in *Eureka*, his Big Bang book, that the universe is a plot of God's. God could not be contacted for her response.

[23] Minta recalls Gide claiming that happiness resides not in freedom but in the acceptance of duty. That's precisely what Rimbaud's mother preaches.

[24] Rimbaud killing a man // Rimbaud teaching the Koran.

[25] "The strangeness of palaces for a cowboy," Frank O'Hara.

[26] Webern's rows for a time returned music to math. Vic Davalillo's uniform number with Cleveland in 1963 was 25. His dissertation subject was a composer of the 15th Century; note his use of medieval canon structure.

[27] Forty-nine octaves are left dissonant and open without this. ("A dissonance is any musical sound that must be resolved, i.e., followed by a consonance; a consonance is a musical sound that needs no resolution, that can act as the final note, that rounds off a cadence," Charles Rosen, *Schoenberg*.) Cp. Field composition, as dissonant.

[28] An answer to note 1 above: Paul Zukofsky played Glass' Einstein, his voice of a violin.

Page 1. From: Vardo Rumessen <rumessen@uninet.ee> on 7/29/2002 10:29 AM +0300

Dear Mr. Richard Blevins.
As far I was away, I got Your message in this morning.
What do You think, if I'll send this Tubin's photo to You by email?
Could You use it as scanned version?
If You will prefer to send it by mail, i'll need Your mail Address.
Best wishes Vardo Rumessen

-----Original Message-----
From: martha koehler [mailto:mjk7+@pitt.edu]
Sent: Sunday, July 21, 2002 8:19 PM
To: rumessen@uninet.ee
Subject: Eduard Tubin

Dear Mr. Rumessen:
  I have been in touch with Eino Tubin, who has given me permission to print Mrs. Erika Tubin's photograph of the composer at Ruda Lake (the photo
appears on the cover of the BIS cd of Symphonies 4 and 9, as you will know), for me to use on the cover of a book of my poems. It turns out, however, that he could not find a print or the negative of the picture, and
Eino suggested I contact you. Do you have a print that you could sent to
me? Please let me pay for any costs, including postage, of course.

Best,
Richard Blevins

What I Hear in the Music of Eduard Tubin

"First Essay: Castle Tubin"
For Vardo Rumessen

<u>English, "castle."</u>
<u>Estonian, "loss."</u>

I mistook the mourning
dove of our late winter
mornings for an owl.
In my country, Vardo,
they don't like McDowell
because he isn't Ives;
and they've never
liked the likes of Ives.

II. *The Legendary*
My Martha knew his song
like she would call to mind
yet another of her
Bing's or Big Band tunes,
as if she had been thinking
of it all along and not just
out of the blue. We saw him once
close up, only the glass of the
unseen window made a
breathing in between us,
I swear his feathers looked
the color of the fat gold
crayon I wrote it down with,
not trusting to recollection.
Such is the clarity
of her memory.

III. *The Heroic*
Now in early Spring
when the dove sings,
and our daughter dances

a circle the room squares,
she in the certainty
that he sings for her,
I bury the memory
of my confusing
the dove for the owl.

IV. *Siinfonia lirica*
As Pound learned:

Odysseus begets Elpenor,
the young poet's

long ignorant midlife.

Losing them again,
grandfather would fume:

"If I ever

find those keys,

I'll keep them

in the ignition!"

Please place this

note inside the drawer

under Dimitri's

Four. Bring it

to light in

some next age.

See Rossetti unearthing
his early poetry,

but published *with*

wormholes. Unscored music
Tubin left behind,

a telescope collapsed

on his table

another man sits.

V.
This sovereign state
insomnia
is an ache
might last all night;
which, too,
too far north,
could mean
days. In the shadow
of Juhan Liiv, where

everything lyrical
turns nocturnal,
here without the sun to pace,
the music becomes eternal—
time's signature.
Even his beloved landscape,
"place the eye takes in,"
needs be the
landscape recalled;
or what you *can*
take with you.

VI.
Unexpectedly a moon no man has ever touched
rises directly behind a child's head.

If there is a cathedral, it is modest. Contemporary.
Happily mistaken for a shelter for small animals.

(His music secrets me
across moonlit borders—

Estonia to Sweden—
places I'd have never been.

Rapid changes in point of view,
in tempo.

Breathe again.

VII.
(Diminse
Lt. Chas. Wilkes explored,
while Pym, silently mouthing
the words, wrote letters
to his southern editor.))

VIII.
There is no Dante to speak for
thee, twice-exiled.

                    And Elpenor
is your martyr.

IX. *Sinfonia semplice (the passing note)*
        Sibelius gives us:
One happy nostril at a time
into the inches of pure air
beneath the ignorant flow
of ice and the black water
that numbs the body so
only the calming mind is
left to its enclosing each
smaller box inside a larger.
               While Tubin swears:
Even this glacier that has changed everything
will melt. In another world, children will drink it and mothers now
unborn will know its cleansing properties. And when this glacier recedes
from our feet and up the u-shaped valley, it will leave a stone behind on
the grave of Kalevide. Give us the patience to witness great change.

X. *for Christine Quintasket*
On the first true warm day
In May,
The mourning dove sang
All day.

XI. *The Unfinished*
The ducks have come back to campus
to nest in Slate Run, before finals.

Call it "Notes Toward
the Foregone Beginning."

"Second Essay: Incidental Music"
For Eino Tubin

1.
Americans find the gerund *tubin'*
If they search the net,

Meaning to ride an inner tube
(The augmented fifth

Tire) down a wild river a
Few hours' retire from home.

This spot is
Considered by many
A purely recreational
Sport.

2.
The mourning dove is one of two Pennsylvania birds
Who drink without, each time, tipping back its head,

As dancers might
In one of Cendrars' ballets…

3.
A government without paper!
Rumessen's email reminds me
Estonia is exclusively e.
The next logical step:

E-liminate all government.

4.
The composer tried applying

To Sweden's office of taxation
For the status of "work-at-home seamstress."
His was a writing of the dining room table,

Overlooking the overlooked backyard.
Piecing together daily
All the brilliant bits of sound.

5.
...The identity of the second Pennsylvania bird
Remains a mystery at flight time.

6.
By the time
I read in *Newsweek*

Estonia is one of
The if not the hot

Destinations
For this year's tourist

After the fall
Of the Soviet Union,

And thinking how much
I'd like to fly

To the Tubin Festival
This is June and
I'm already
Too late to see it. Anyhow:

7.
Tubin's Second, the first
Five minutes, how happy

It must be
To wake up
In Old Tallinn.

8.
I send an e-mail half a world away
To Tubin's son, Eino,

A working journalist in Turkey,
Satisfied

That I'm in touch with the living at 1:00
AM, whatever hour it is with him.

9.
Martha has, since college,
The perfect title for *someone's*

Autobiography. She calls it,
I'll Take the Sublime.

This is the unshakable impression
I have listening to Symphony Seven.

10.
It turns out, Tubin has provided
A staff for these notes of mine.

I had worried
That the title "Castle Tubin" was not right.
Perhaps too close to Wilson's Russia.
Or simply pretentious.
(When I'd addressed letters to the Princess
c/o Brunnenburg Castle,
the postman laughed twice.)

Today Eino Tubin sends me his "Tubin
In Sweden," and I read about the man who loved:

"...History, old castles, art, architecture, engineering, politics, aviation, small Arms...
football...audio recording techniques...mushrooms...wild birds...
[Father] loved to...talk to animals...He built a large carton model of a French
Castle and several houses to my model railway."

11.
We say they *play* music,
The revenant truths in us.

"Third Essay: At Alatskivi Castle"
For Nancy Birk
   I can remember much forgetfulness—Hart Crane.

Bus thru a landscape of good wood furniture
Not the kind pounded together for Rudge,
but room upon room's stunted growth midwinter.

Frozen back of the maker's hand, a veiny leaf.

What memory was like, leaf-like I mean,
before the torture of remembering.
Sometimes a blizzard come,
but more usually flurries,

accumulate
never quite scraped away.
(High temperatures below freezing here
too the first three weeks of the year.)

Their bus driver wears shades.
The glare off the snowpack, abedo,
makes the world black.

 Vardo Rumessen, in his memo to The Tubin Society, writes that *"When we arrived [earlier this month] at Alatskivi castle, we were greeted by a rather sad sight. It was terribly cold in the castle. The renovation works had stopped because of lack of funds and the castle is falling apart. Tubin's Challen, grand piano of red wood, which was donated to Estonia by Tubin's heirs, has been brought to the great hall of the castle, where the[re] are not adequate means of preserving it. There was also Tubin's Schroder, grand piano from Tartu.... On those pianos Tubin composed nearly all his musical works."*

The snowy desert only preserves
(huts of explorers still out for a walk, leather thighs
of fallen climbers) if
temperatures stay freezing

or below. Great thaws in
the political climate
(see the Balkan states)

tend to obliterate
the record. Fresh snow
makes good hunting.

No less than (Darwin
thot him "glacier-mad)
Agassiz" needed an Ice Age
destroying everything before
it, hunted it down, to Brazil
to make sense of its racist
science that paid his bills
in Cambridge, *during*
the Civil War. A world
lost many times over.
  Henceforth:
all scriptures
should be
ice sculpture!

*"The castle also contains Tubin's photo exhibition, which was formerly
in the Liiv Museum. It had been transferred because of lack of space.
Tubin's nature photos were also in the castle…. Although…asked…to play
something…on Tubin's piano, I afterwards regretted it, since it was not
possible to play anything with fingers so stiff from cold.…"*

So the piano is a tree again:
spiked by white light, noon,
drugged to stupor in a northernmost forest,
as innocent of song as snow on the grave;

leafless again, revenant,
all body, like furniture in a landscape
but wholly without irony,
all body, before making

leaf, piano, song…

Emily's herbarium,
a book of pressed flowers
Zukofsky's pick of 88
or grey Enno, whose grey songs
the young Tubin loved.
(And what's this funny balalaika
I find stuck in a snow bank,
like a Russian hockey stick
or a new design for a bad
shovel, doing in my concerto
anyway?) Jack London is the poet of snow
where winter is Addie Joss, writing in the off
-season, in Toledo, in Ohio
in the days like months
splayed before its dream
of leaf,
spiked now, by white moon,
the north star lost overhead.
                              Ahead
must be the lonely lamp of the lucubrator,
reading and sometimes writing this
far north of midnight?

Horror Vaci
To Peter Temes

And let flatness light up in volume—Artaud.

In the same way as our visual field is without boundary, our life is endless—The Tractatus.

Angel Heurtebise, in robes of water—Cocteau.

The Allegheny is first and last to speak.

"All wars are immoral.

All wars are one war.

All wars immemorial.

All wars are this one again."

There was always the one guy on campus who'd run ahead the otherwise sagging line of demonstrators, snatch up the sizzling canister, and throw it oh so deftly back to the flak-jacket who'd shot it. Here's to him. To the never-ending next one of them.

SCENE, at the altar within St. Nicholas Croatian Roman Catholic Church, Millvale, Pennsylvania. At the time of the U.S. invasion of Iraq (but easily mistaken for 1916 or 1941 or 1991 or now). As each player speaks in turn, he or she lights a candle or extinguishes a candle or lights a stick of incense, according to his or her notion.

The rituals of war and the rituals of art in arches above my head.

This is not a stage drama, not even a one-act or a closet play, but a succession of choruses. The sound is not to be contained by the ceiling and walls of murals.

Dramatis Personae {would have included}:
Pilgrim
Ghost
The Allegheny River
Maxo Vanka
A Belgian Red Cross ambulance driver
Mother Mary
Vanka's aristocratic genetic mother
Vanka's peasant adoptive mother
Lady in Blue
Jesus
Father Zagar
Louis Adamic
Margaret Stetten
Douglas Chandler
Labor
Johnstown
Eduard Tubin
Haniel Long
Josh Gibson
Malcolm Cowley

"You will not find him on his back on the scaffolding this time. He leans out, into space and away from his body, as a river can do. His arm is fully extended to touch the ceiling with just the red-hot tip of the flaming tongue of his brush—a pistol shot, already drying. Around him, the neighborhood in slips, all saggy-assed porches off stretch-mark alleyways that shortcut vanishing pointers down the hillside, slide along, spider veins to reach the highway, train tracks, me; the mill and the vale are foreshortened here, as surely as the slender immigrant bride becomes the lace parlor face of her peasant mother—recorded in smiles, but at war with her eyes.

"I see them, without looking,
Instead of dreams. (For a river never sleeps.)
They are the naturalized workers at dusk

Climbing their hill to supper.
Dawn come, they descend again
To mills of greater darkness and light.

"I am called the Allegheny,

Tho I am never the same water

Within the same banks. I am

The strong right arm

Of Pittsburgh's fist."

Capt. James Sample settled on this land in 1789, and built a grist mill.
(*Grist for the Mill* will be a title of a book of poems by Haniel Long.)
An early resident, H.B. Lyons, named the town for its mills in the vale.
Adamic: This is not Croatia
Old dog, white muzzle
Slobbering weak eyes
Covering the same old
Ground for lost bones.
We have come to Millvale, Pennsylvania, the New World!
(Hitchcock's vertigo
is an immigrant's too.)
The angle of repose needs an angel of repose,
Or it will roll out of town.
Its church is a yellow bird asleep her perch.
But the whole stands up somehow:
Now on one leg, then the other.
From the road below, behold a miracle
  To sleep that way!

Black spider crossing the painted battlefield, its path undeterred by
the violence, crawls across, without disturbing, the painted smile on a
corpse's face.

In the choir loft, a nun is seen cutting with small, precise scissors the preRaphaelite virgin's halo!

Driver: We never witness the votive candles replaced. We light them, for other hands To minister. Lines of lit candles, a line of nuns around the coffin in the foreground, to the background of neat lines of soldiers' white markers. Beneath, every corpse facing the sun rising. So young to sleep that way. The sentences of the Tractatus are lines from the trenches. One nun, on her knees beside the open casket beside the open fields of rows of new graves, holds a lighted candle that resembles a bone finger. The joint is the white flame. A line of saints in phosphene gowns and making the same faces of the tenured faculty, eyeless at commencement.

Bunting chose prison. Rilke went to war too quickly. Celine. No one escaped it.

This is not a poem you can keep in your head all day, taking notes, taking time. I find I can start it up again for two-hour writing sessions by reading Celan. Other times, Neruda instead. When I save the poem to file, this is what the program makes the title: "Not a painting to hang on someone." From the couplet at the start of the first draft page that read: "Not a painting to hang on someone's wall finally / But the public act of painting on wall and ceiling."

Hard on the eyes, my 'istorin. The murals of Vanka's second commission are. Stan Brakhage will come to Pittsburgh thirty years later to film a trilogy ending at the Allegheny County Morgue and call it "The Act of Seeing with one's own eyes." Films of three days of autopsies I had to walk out on, in front of Brakhage, thirty years ago now.

In February 1952, Celan writes to Ludwig von Ficker: "Sometimes it's as if I were the prisoner of these poems…and sometimes their jailer."

On vacation in Luxembourg, I learned you can still find the detritus of the Great War—tank parts, bunkers, wheels, cogs—it is still lined up in the plowed fields facing the fast freeways to Belgium. (I imagine, closer in, shells, buttons, pocket watches, teeth.) A cason rusting like a shopping cart nobody bothers to return.

In time, we must leave even what is left on a battlefield. The point
in coming to a place many hold sacred.

Note the weapon of choice on this modern battlefield.
It is the bayonet.
No light bulb goes off over Guernica. The bayonet is
Strictly low tech.
Born in Bayonne, France
And perfected how long
Before the Romantic revolutions?
To kill with the bayonet is personal.
It requires the fortunate recruit to feel
The loser's death.
(Weight at the end of his brush.)
The navigator's view of the pinpointed city
Is unavailable to the bayoneter, who must suffer
The whole weight of his person forward,
Then into, the resistance that was not a wall at all.

Bayonets lace open
The bodies of saints
And folks
Choir loft gallows
Soup kettle helmets
I, Infidel, look
At the Croatian lace at Mary's neck
And think it holy

A student returned from Rome put on my desk today her
photograph of a statue of a saint, its metal wings more like an
opening rib cage. Hand to hand, feet to feet, man to man, the eyes!
What sound this makes remains un-recorded in the walls.

Driver: The whole point
Of a bayonet
Is the edge.

Priests use it
To lace the wafer
That clogs
The throat making speech
Impossible.
The very whiteness of the wafer is convincing.
Blindness can be black or white. Even blue.

"I was walking in a field in Belgium on a beautiful day in May, and I saw a soldier lying down, looking up at the sky. I stopped and said to him, 'Good morning. So you too are a lover of clouds!' He neither answered nor moved, and I saw that he was dead." Maxo Vanka, recalling his experience as a Red Cross ambulance driver, age 26.

My father once built me a kite, from two sticks and a newspaper. In the manner of the kites over Harold, Kentucky, Appalachia, in 1937. Maybe the bad news (the death of Kennedy) made it too heavy to fly?

The view of the murals is short of iconographic, more personal, freshly discovered, a wound in your side (not his).

Try to find a Lady in Blue. Run into the nun with gas mask and sword, who blocks my way across the wall. Her scales are tipped, heavy gold coins in favor of bread. Dread.

Where in the murals is love? My notes of the visit don't say
There was a bell ringing
But I want one in the poem. Where is
The pearling ocean that has left, after unthinkable violence, these smooth
Stones on the Croatian beach?

Maxo Vanka's early portrait, "Lady in Blue," might be by Balthus, whose madness proclaimed the purity of prepubescent girls is not erotic. The observer feels guilty for having looked! At Millvale, female is woman and woman is a peasant Mary thirty-six feet high. In both cases, the viewer must consider himself.

I taught myself to read Pound standing before the ruined walls
of the Schifanoia, no cameras allowed, thanks. (Vanka's link to
Pound would be thru his in-laws' pursuit of Douglas Chandler.)
Thanks to you, I know where I go when I look. It's the place in the
mind where Shelley saw the Witch of Atlas and the same horror
Melville knew in the whiteness of the whale. It is annihilation of
the self into the blank page.

Horror vaci, the muralist's dread of unfilled spaces.

I am not here.
I come from undistinguished Welsh stock, coal miners there and
here, who were among those easily assimilated, married early and
often, into the Cherokee nation and soon displaced, again, with
them. Those who stayed hid out in Blue Ridge caves, crouching
so near the soldiers' horses they could smell them. Hard scrabble
farmers, or operating below the notice of the professions. Lots of
James and Richards according to the online search, but otherwise
and always
I am not here predicted.
I have come as a native stranger
Against my will and better judgment
This is not my fight
Landlocked, inbred, ignorant
No memory of leaving
Or arriving
Lost in America
An immigration so thorough it has left no track back.

"I haven't gone back," a student blurts, meaning no revisions on
the poem he is just about, mouth open,
to read to us. Could Vanka revise his mural? How does egg
tempera on plaster dry?

I return to my Leopold to be certain Vanka returned in order to paint the blank spaces he'd left—to silence the ghost of the mural's white spaces. His second commission. My first visit to the church, house painters were painting the white wall between the murals a less startling blue grey. The smell of paint filled the dome of the chapel like an apt simile.

Maximilian Vanka was born a "fachook," second-rate, an illegitimate child, perhaps the son of nobility. He was raised by a peasant wet nurse, Dora Jugova, his artistic ideal woman. He met his genetic mother, perhaps, once. Could never return to her.

I'm afraid to eat with them. Their bread is probably His body missing in action. I'm afraid it will become real in my stomach. The word made flesh would kill me. (Ghostly Jesus hovers behind the Croatian family.)

Vanko's bosom friend Adamic once said: "My grandfather always said that living is like licking honey off a thorn."

The blood is unseen, unspoken,
Underground among the underclothes of priests and nuns.
Do not spill this wine
This is Christ.
Unwashable blot.
Silvia Pinal
Climbs down
From the cross,
Her wounded crotch,
Into your jittery lap.

"Battlefield," under the choir loft, depicts the moment after
the mustard gas incense has been inhaled.
The odour of death that fills and never leaves their nostrils

Drives them mad,
Jesus and Mary.
Only a mother could stand to
Touch the green skin
Of these slaughtered boys.
The water she secretly bathes them in,
The water no cloud will reclaim,
Constantly rains.

Lachrymose, to borrow Hart Crane's word.

On first entering the church, the grand scope of the murals
took adjusting to, after studying photographs for a month. The
adjustment of holding up one hand to shield your eyes from the
obliterating sun from the windows was easy.

Surprised to find angel's green wings in flames after Blake (or Blake's
source, Michelangelo)!
The constant little surprises of the painterly details of the tears of the
mourning nuns, the tiny white wild flowers on barbed wire, the tiny
white stars on the lapels of the fallen son.

There don't seem to be entrance wounds in the victims he painted.
I search for corpses resembling my father after the machine stopped
breathing and he sat upright, blind and suddenly comprehending.
O is the hole,
my father's mouth,
he left thru.
Only an exit wound.
The dead are those among us
Who know
There can be no resurrection.

The painter's aubade escalade.

In the murals
The bullet travels faster
Than sound
Not bang you're dead
Just dead.

All the murals were painted, he recalled, in three levels, each requiring the interruption of the moving of the scaffolding. He would leave an incomplete image still drying on the ceiling, going on to the next—never seeing the whole with his eyes, but keeping—what? —in his head those months of work? Joe Reed writes in a poem he read to a café during the writing of this section of my own poem: "a picture of three things at once, like Christ."

Bill Shields always wanted me to tell him what sense The Holy Ghost makes.

Curious to be reading Fisher's Hart Crane these early mornings in bed in order to calm down from working on the poem. It took visitations from Vanka's ghost, Adamic tells us, to drive him from the scaffolding each morning. Once, Vanka climbed up the scaffolding, having adopted newspapers for blinders and cotton balls for earplugs. The newspaper is ironic; the murals are news of the bloody war. The detail of the earplugs seems to me the most important. Did his visitor give him instructions, like Hamlet's father, when the natural order of things had run out?

When I was a boy, a friend of my father gave me all his campaign ribbons and medals. I was heavily decorated. In those days, ten years after the peace, I was making a little Eisenhower jacket for war games in the backyards of Seville, Ohio. I remember especially the feel and smell of the infantry badge. Its blue enamel. Rifle like a stroke of lightning against blue sky. In the car driving home, Dad explained quietly in his low voice that his friend did not like to remember the war. Our worst arguments would be over Viet Nam, my refusal to wear the uniform. That Dad had earned a Bronze Star in the Pacific I was to learn forty years later, at his funeral.
Mary is larger than life, the scope of Doris
Day's star ass, set in motion
Across the screen of the dusky drive-ins
Unto dust. Dante employs the word "stars"

As the final word in all three sections
Of the Comedy. Blue Sky Drive-In:
Metal box speakers hang from
Rolled-up again window glass, their
Umbilical chords link each parked car,
All face one way—Miss Day
In the darkening sky without stars.
Still another source of the vertigo in the church on the hill: The Byzantine Mary, the Theotokos (whose foot established in the clouds has been painted over!), plus various supporting stiff saints…But the swirl of the battle being won and lost by expressionists!

In his final state, Artaud believed himself capable of self-combustion.

Who lights the capitalist pig's cigarette, while he sits without appetite
At the end of his long table attended by his black servant?
His top hat begs
To be pulled down, with the statues of Milosevic in the plaza.
Why, naturally,
It is the bones of some missing skeleton's extended right hand—
It comes right out of the corner of one wall—
         For his
          match.
In my reading, the quality most frequently associated with egg tempera painting is "luminosity."

What is the light source
On the livid battlefield?
It would be perpetual midnight
Save for the sudden piercings of flesh trunks, a farmer
Unearths a shard of Roman sun in a far field.
Odysseus was a farmer first.

Artaud at Rodez was preoccupied with pokers and knives. He threatened the visiting Prevel with a knife slammed into the table between them. On walks, he hacked at the trunks of trees.

Irby reminds me that Robert Duncan "long ago pointed out…our victory in WWII was not really to get rid of Nazism but [to] inherit it," when I complained about George W.

The modern invention of Christ's barbed-wire crown.

With the brothers van Eyck, the invention of oil painting supercedes egg tempera, tho a Victorian translation of Cennini into English realized a little revival of the technique, and another following the Second War. The egg yolk is the agent binding the artist's mix of dry pigments. This dries fast.

So the revision is another layer envisioned.
It's the blind spot, the optic disk, where the nerve connects, eyeball to brain, makes vision possible. We do not see the horror vaci but because of it.
In Duncan's seminar, we read *Scientific America* on how we see and made connections with the visions of Kit Smart and Blake.

(A revision, after asking: Not egg—they don't know the binder Vanka used—"something cheap.")

This late revision to the poem: "Between *the upstream* (Pastor Russell's pyramid, the grass uncut, since the end of the world, around it; but his black stare from the photograph fused to the headstone, unforgettable), and *what's downstream* (Gertrude Stein's birthplace, still a residence, in a modest brick house on a last-century street that somehow got spared if not for her sake), find Walt's *instream*." And later add: "Burchfield is a tributary. Below's a stream of pissing loss from Kiskiminetas: a kiss then kismet met. Ida Tarbell, Nellie Bly, Rachel Carson contributing to the flood."

A river chorus: A river like me
Is geography; an ocean is the moon.
Hart Crane's train crossing and
Recrossing, thoughtlessly.

A short history of tributaries: Did the waste, the acid and the human piss, from John Brown's business reach the Allegheny? Or did the tannery poison the grave of his wife and the wells of his neighbors? Michelangelo, Vanka's self-portrait as Christ, John Brown—the self-martyreds' wounds will not heal.

Vanka completed his first commission for Z in the summer before 7 November 1937, Artaud's day for the end of the world. He completed his second commission weeks before 7 December 1941. Time runs only one way between the two dates, like the unnavigatable northern stretch of the Allegheny. Above the locks at Brady's Bend.

Brady was an apostle for the Northwest Territory, a map of a man. I lived directly across the river from Brady's Leap in Kent. Bend and leap are verbs describing the figure.

Apostle among the throng on the ceiling that is The Last Judgment, Bartholomew sits, holding his own skin in one hand, the one not thumbing a ride (a skinning knife for a thumb!) on Christ's cloud. The leathery face on that skin is the painter's. Robin's egg blue sky all around the figures. Michelangelo's second commission opens the Romantic era.

"In resurrection, there is confusion," H.D. writes in "The Flowering of the Rod," and for weeks I've been trying to keep it out of my poem. She imagines, in that section, what it would be to participate in the annunciation of the faithful. I can't see the chance of it on these walls.

Lean against one wall, hoping to overhear what has never been near to me. What would be the effect, on people my age, parishioners over fifty, who have grown up and lived with the murals? Who have seen, every Sunday, the murals, and been photographed standing stiffly in front of them and underneath them at their weddings and confirmations, or bent for funerals? Zagar smiles from a frame, smile like Dr. Delmas', between two cousins. Kids climbing the walls, dads hit the ceiling headlong. What will it be like, this Easter mass, when they are dismissed by the young priest to return to their homes on the hill with Christ dead? Death is by no means dead; she's fucking us into oblivion. Even here, she exposes that dark cunt of hers that drains the chapel, making the dark more appealing to some poor sucker putting himself into a crack in the corner. Her children are born of this seed, the kind released by trees only when they are up in flames. Her progeny are wars. Born of lightning between the legs of redwoods tourists drive cars thru.

I ask my guide, Diane Novosel, who has come to the church every day since first grade. Growing up, "I had dreams," she confides.

Find a wooden bench in the spring sun at the front of St. Nicholas, beneath its twin bell towers. Yellow brick building. Façade spoiled by the additions of glass doors and foyer over the decades. View of Rt. 28, stone's-throw close, 'spoiled' by billboard for Chevrolets to be read from cars passing. Train goes by, much louder than the constant car traffic in and out of Pittsburgh three miles downstream. Rail tracks on an artificial hill, other side of the highway, mean you'd have to climb the bell tower for a view of the river. All buildings surrounding the church are yellow (a paler brick, later on), a European color. Two other churches up the vale, the same yellow. Street is the same-color brick. Undistinguished stained glass windows. Mostly old ladies but exclusively women emerge from the church basement with covered dishes to wash from afternoon bingo. An old man drives up next; he waits in the shade, at one end of a small dog's leash. We both face the church. The dog looks unfriendly. His owner had arrived with such sense of purpose that I took him for groundskeeper, but the silly, over-indulged pet gave him away. He is wearing a blue dress shirt, like me, but we don't talk. For a time, women continuing to emerge from under the church call to the dog. Their claps echo in the breathing space between the yellow buildings. When their cars leave from the asphalt all around the church, the building looks smaller, hollowed out.

Vanka lived with the priests, during his months of painting the Millvale murals, in the brick residence on the east side. He had a walk of only a few feet from his room to the church each morning and night.

"Whatever I gather, I pass down. Among the locutions of location which you name place, I float you—a secret—to shore. Promise to take it up the hill next you go. The secret is: The ghost is me, Allegheny! My own secret is how to be ancient and always new. Current.

"But a river is a visitation, no kind of guide. Poor Vanka could not hear me from his church on the hill above, so I came to him on those mornings of his greatest disillusionment.

"I'd surfaced in Ruskin's chapter, Cumae under earth and running over it.

"I told them both, no one is more weary than a river. No one.

"You cannot hear the river from the church, no matter how hard you listen."

[Finished on May 4, 2003]

"False Unicorn"

> *…the Bee that comes Home sober is the Butt of the Clover.*

> *Not greatest, thou—not first, nor last,—but near*
> —Hart Crane to Whitman.

> *There is a woman who resembles the sentence*
> —Robert Duncan.

> *Dressed all in white or all in black, she seemed to float over my canvases for a long time, guiding my art*—Chagall.

> *At 57 I have two people ED and LZ, after a lifetime, almost, of reading…*
> —Lorine Niedecker to Louis Zukofsky.

    In this my fifty-fifth year, I come calling.
"I had been hungry, all the Years." Route 9
into Amherst, not horse and hearse
but a slow road still.
For I, too, am a sensualist,
arriving after Lyman,
whom all good men must
denounce even while following
him, to you. You who
teased that "All men say 'What' to me…."
Whose flirtatious words were your "fictitious lips."
Who did not so much inquire: "Dare you see a soul at the 'White Heat'?"
Who, in hot weather, would have in all hours heard from open windows
the train report to Amherst Station.
Poetrix of "Wild nights and the Road," who childless
remained. My wife,
Martha, is thirteen weeks
with our second girl child. I've crossed the Connecticut—
I've come alone—To Pelham Hills, by gaslight.

Concerning the difficulty
of our age difference
(120 years, tho we are both fifty-five),

my probationary period

extends up the street like a line of parking meters

to Pleasant and the commons Olmsted designed.

You'd promised me afar

a garden for my sun-dial, if not

a writing table for my hour-glass, meaning

to replace the pocket-watch brother Austin broke inadvertently while climbing

the conspicuously located bell tower stairs

in pursuit of the pocket of happiness which took him

regularly to the other side of town

(the whole town was in on it,

before the intervention of reality

tv) and, late in his married life,

from his office and back to his own bedroom

in the Evergreen manse downstairs,

a room adjacent the yellowing parlor's

walls of pallid Hudson River landscapes

like portraits of New England aristocrats

in heavy collars of crafted frames.

Your legs were never photographed.

No guest put his hand on a knee.

(She declined a

walk next door

to meet

Emerson.)

Too many

underthings in the way

of biography.

In Alice Fulton's poem, "Maidenhead," the white dress is beheaded but otherwise "so alive." The head is on display in Carnegie libraries across the nation; its brain powers a whole intellectual industry. But what has become of her body? Every time we look at the dress in the case, a little more of it disappears—until her body of work, the female form, is that brain again. (I heard no one exclaiming a missing head when I stood before Cy Young's Boston uniform in southern Ohio.) No, Emily Dickinson's stolen body is one of the dark crimes in our fascist time.

I touch

opon

the poet's

pun, her
maiden's head

To touch the dead, even in dreams,
strikes
a nerve

        in me
to touch the virgin
is abhorrent
(I lose
    my nerve),

tho we say we are all
touched
      by her. Or make her
the old maid aunt
who's good with others'
kids.

Into this small-town world
I was borne, bearing relics
for future curious.
                You were born to it,
and were fifteen before you could tell
time by the hall clock. Inside out
his cancelled envelope;
pencil in your new love poem.
Turn the table over
to start fresh.

Enter a spirit clad in white, figure so draped as to be misty, face moist, translucent alabaster, forehead firmer as of statuary marble.

You appear as a small, white object in the dark, either big as a star or compact as a flashlight, advancing or receding from us at the velocity of her grave across the buttercup fields (now houses and lawns) in West. You're not at home in your own (father's) house, along with the locket of your red hair (at Amherst College) and your writing desk (to Harvard): our guide, a recent graduate, announces at the start of the tour that the poet was not isolated; then she spends eighty minutes relating anecdotes of your increasingly eccentric and isolating behavior. Are you aware that the locals called you the Myth of Amherst when you were alive? (My world, which embraces its several inventions of her, has printed a postage stamp with a likeness, but the image of The Master's Daisy masturbating in that short bed in the corner room on the second floor, as she must have, will earn this poem the royalties of censure in what is still a moralistic age.) In Alice Fulton's poem, your white wrapper could be alive but for the missing head. She wants to see you like what remains of a Greek statue of a female form, but I want to watch your lips move while we ravage an hour. Know for myself MacLeish's "being spoken to."

(((I thot you'd be upstairs.

There's the stairway! I see it.) "Stop,"
our guide calls me back,
"at the white
dress" (only a copy). Then

a sudden white like Indian Pipe
discovered
at the top of the forest
stairwell.
(Rarest
fogbow dress
she wore
a uniform.))

Your bed is the only original
furniture
in the room.

Not exactly your Wild nights—nor
death throes, nor fucking to climax—yet
a midnight ride alright
beyond the radios of puzzled security
on a borrowed golf cart
Peter drives, no headlights, out
across the Amherst campus.
Twice passing Frost
Library, he asks if I thot you had made a "happy" life.
"Frost is…a powerful brigand
in Dickinson's peculiar cosmos."
He'd been reading anew Frost thru Dickinson. (It pleased
me secretly
to misread Farr
in this bad light.) In my boyhood memory, the field
still closed, hard frost on a tennis court,
from the year
of the day JFK came to town
to dedicate the library.

                I'll model myself privately
a Robert Walser tourist,
the kind of man for whom
the act of being shown a room
[to let] was close to composition.
It should be
an attic room,
with a view of the [German] landscape.
So he could get inside
the dwelling, and look
where people had
lived, without the risk
of relationship (perhaps
allowing himself
the stray
fantasy about the landlady).

"While Rapture changed its Dress
And stood arrayed before the change
In ravaged Holiness."

Joseph B. Lyman was a boarder.

"…He has in mind features he does not mention. The face is particular and vivid to him as he goes. But the reader sees in his reading a particular and vivid face of a person in the poem or he misses a face in the poem." *Caesar's Gate,* 1972 edition.

I frequently wonder how much Helen
Adam resembled you in life.

Beautiful kangaroo.

PROSPECTUS FOR "STUDIES IN IDEAS OF THE POETIC IMAGINATION"

The texts in the course:

1) Pound's PISAN CANTOS
2) Williams's PATERSON
3) Christopher Smart's JUBILATE AGNO
4) Blake's JERUSALEM II, from his p. 42 to end of II; and JERUSALEM IV, "To The Christians"

are to be common ground of reference for those participating in which they may research and from which they may draw illustrations. It will not be a course of study _of_ these poems but a course from these poems toward a picture of our current idea of the Imagination and a mutual understanding of our individual experiences of the Imagination.

What I mean by "our" idea of the Imagination is first, the one we have in the general understanding and prescription of our education--this will, I take it, consist of the conglomerate of permitted and prohibited ideas of what the Imagination is that we can find in our own thought; and one of the projects of the seminar will be to compile a lexicon of such ideas and a series of diagrams showing schemes in which they may be placed as say "above" or "below", "left" or "right", "central" or "outside" and conglomerates of related ideas of Imagination may be traced.

Second, I want to keep in mind all references to the pictures that have been raised in the Sciences concerning the nature of our physiological and psychological experience of sight. Previous to the course, read on the Morphology of the Eye in any thorough medical text; read some textbook on general physiology relating to the senses (I have at hand, for instance, Karl von Frisch, MAN AND THE LIVING WORLD, Chaps. 8, 9, 10, 11 & 12, Part II), read articles on Seeing and Vision from the Scientific American and/or from Science over the last ten years. What I want is for all of us to have some idea of the range of ideas of organs and functions current in the "scientific" world. There is one work here that is, for me, of the order of the four above as a text:

5) Sir Charles Sherrington, MAN ON HIS NATURE.

In our projected lexicon of ideas of the Imagination, we will be concerned with whether we consider the ideas to be phantastic, scientific, known, eccentric, psychotic, etc. What we can hope to "learn" in the course of study is some more informed and extensive idea of what is involved in the question of Imagination, and, in turn, of how ideas of Imagination in poetry relate to the fields of religion and the psychological and physiological sciences.

In conjunction with the poems of Pound and Williams taken as common references, each student is to take a text of his own choosing from a twentieth century poet for reference; and in relation to the texts of Blake and Smart likewise, to take a poetic text from the Romantic movement of the 19th century.

ROBERT DUNCAN
San Francisco 1972

...Eyes once bright hazel now melted & fused so as to be two dreamy, wondering wells of expression, eyes that see no forms but glance swiftly to the core of all things—

The iris is a rainbow
stemming from a bulb.
With anterior ureitis,
the iris is inflamed.
The patient will avoid
Sun off the snowbank.
No books
for eight months.

        Duncan's required reading for the Imagination seminar:
               Jerusalem, *Paterson*, *The Cantos*,
                 and articles on rods
                    and cones
                 in *Scientific Monthly*.

(Sensitive to light, but she wrote in a letter
her eyes were "like the Sherry in the Glass, that the Guest leaves."

       My favorite eunoia.)

You garden at midnight to save your eyes.
I type this letter to you when one day ends and another starts. A new poem
starts up.
An eclipse of every morning's sun,
the Christian God to you.
An error in Calhoun's new life of Longfellow, "Father
Marble" for Mapple, is one you'd savor.

It's the diction, in your conservatory letters and poems, that
forces the bulbs to startle in every season we may read. You do not think to save
our eyes.
One oak remains

in the yard you saw out
your conservatory.

Aunt to those of us who must believe good poetry will somehow survive,
published like perennials we bot in December with the house.
You never saw your father's grave, and were buried beside him.
Unable to read *Leaves of Grass* with your own cultivating eyes,

you were told Whitman
was disgraceful.
I find myself trying to think what you would write, in gnomic letterpoems,
following such observations. Try out:

"No need for Directions to her father's House,"
"This is the Law of all biography."

On your stay in Boston
we see you absentmindedly
walking off with a magazine
from the doctor's office.

When you were under treatment for your eyes you frequently wrote about water.
DeKooning liked to compare Mimi Kilgore to water, his highest compliment.
You get the sunrise
120 years and an hour before we do. Tonight, I go

online to download
the Gura image,
then
enlarge it:
you
fill my screen.
The sensation of
               seeing you / looking back.

...hands small, firm, deft but utterly emancipated from all claspings of perishable things, very firm strong little hands absolutely under control of the brain, types of quite rugged health

To say she gardened at night
is not to employ
a metaphor. Same
fingers quick to
recover
paper and pencil
record a line
safely returned
to pocket. Once,
you brot a dying tiger
water in the cup
of those hands.

The biographers disagree on the specifics: Therefore, her contemporary Rimbaud wrote with the right or the left hand.
                                                 My mother's dad was a Tennessee farmer.
                                                      It was not dirt in his hands.
                                                  I saw him taste the red soil
                                                           for information.
                                      The first poem I wrote was for him.
                                         I have inherited, alas, his temper
                     and nothing of all he knew about the land
                               the weather and how things grow.
                          Dad's was a Kentucky miner, a divorcee
                       with a new family in Florida I never met,
                                      and a magical story-teller.
                                    I have his eyes and his hair
                                        and a second family.
When I use the Rimbaud book, my therefore bookmarker, I lose sight of it, out of hand, inside the Dickinson volume; need to rediscover its other context.

                                               Rauschenberg's Perpetual Inventory.
When our local postgrad docent does point out the especially designed pocket, right-hand side, in Dickinson's True Dress, one designed for quick notes for poems, I get self-conscious about writing down these notes on scraps and

shoving them into my own pockets, among the detritus of small change, rental car keys, Jed's and Temes' phone number, and receipts, as we walk thru your father's house.

> You nicknamed the ball clubs in Troy and Worcester
> for local flowers birds insects long
> before Marianne Moore wrote
> her letters to Ford. Last
> year, the ivory-billed woodpecker was seen again.

Not at home at home
        with Mahler in Manhattan
        with Pound in Wabash
        with Sherwood Anderson in Ohio
        with John Brown in Akron
        with Maxo Vanka in Pittsburgh
        with Haniel Long at Carnegie Tech
        with Warhol at Carnegie Tech
        with Vachel Lindsay in Kansas
        with Zukofsky at Brooklyn Poly Tech
        with Schoenberg in Hollywood
        with John Adams in Paris
        with Rimbaud in London
        with Degas in New Orleans
        with Pessoa outside Lisbon
        with Jack Spicer in Minnesota
        with Dirk Peters in Illinois
        with Hart Crane in Mexico
        with Eisenstein in Mexico
        with Hopkins in Ireland
        with Trakl at Grodeck
        with Montgomery Clift in a western
        with Poe at West Point
        with Grant in the White House
        with Charlie Parker recording "Lover Boy"
        with Laura Riding in Wabasso, Florida and Duncan at the front door
        with Duke Snyder in Southern California, Willie Mays in a Mets uniform, and Mantle playing first
        with Melville coming home from The Battery
        with Bergman on Faro

    with Strindberg watching The Growing Castle from his window
    with Benjamin Paul Blood in Amsterdam, New York
    with Vincent on earth.

In our news: Thieves stole *copies* of Mŭnch paintings in an Olso hotel: today.

                                      The white dress was stolen once
                                            John Wieners wore
                                                          it
                              to a ball behind the State House
                                      The dress danced all night
                                                    til
                          his date went home with a taper
                               and Longfellow's
                                             wife
                   the following morning found the dress
                            abandoned on a dirt road
                        From that night on, the poet of
                                             Joy
                                            Street
                became more and more like the dress material
                                        izing at
                                    poetry readings
                                    from Beacon Hill

When I was small
I always wished
for a little sister.
The closest I got
was my ex-wife
in the final years
of that two-sided
triangle.

Inheritor of none
Mother of nobody
Never bitter sister
Aunt never old
You didn't want
to be doing

anything you
weren't doing.

Duncan's vow in 1968 not to publish poetry until 1984 released him too from the antics of the poetry attorneys. His drawing of the Ideal Reader depicts a middle-aged woman, in a garden, bent to her reading.

Did you ever wear a sun-
hat like that?

You replace my head
your hands back into your lap
I quit
realize the white dress empties out into a lawnscape with untitled graves.
Not every parent
names its child;
not every child
is a parent.
All those bodies
holding their breath
to hear the revelation
we are living down.
Therefore.

You are the Economist of Therefore.

...mouth made for nothing & used for nothing but uttering choice speech, rare thoughts, glittering, starry misty figures, winged words.

I hear your lips
once tasted
rum. Open them.
(Her spelling leaves
"opon" for *upon*.

She must have
said it thus:

"A spoonful
of ashes
opon Jim R. Lowell's

flower bed
in Ohio."
Wish she would
say it
for me.)

What was held to be
upon
is really
open.
A bolt

of cloth, heat
lightning
in a drawer suddenly opened.
The whiteness of her dress has been addressed by Clarel, the Riding Chair
Professor in Time at the University of Colour, and found to be the annihilation of
the self.

Here I am myself
curiously
reminded of
the accident of
my Midwestern
accent, sometimes flat
like Ohio in places,
like talking to Creeley
at his kitchen tables; of
my poorly front tooth,
killed by a soldier's punch
in the street of My civil
war and, a week before this
trip, broken in half,
to my ear slurring my speech
so someone's description of
meeting me

would be
partial, like the North portrait's
teenager out of her sick-bed.
Dear Friend,
I'll bring you up to speed
      fast:
Amerika is still a lousy place
for poets
      who are immortal, and
Robert Lowell
is its poet.

Critic Higginson writes to his wife, from Amherst, on August 16, 1870: "E.D. dreamed all night of *you* (not me)!"
      So my Martha is circumference, too, even of
          this
remote.
Even when I think
I am talking
to Emily, I am
connected with
the other
brown-eyed woman
who too
wears size 6 or 8
and takes
George Eliot
to her heart.

In the weeks when we tried to conceive,
following the winter miscarriage,
Martha took a daily dosage of False Unicorn.
I find no mention of the herb
in the Farr and Carter index. I had thot seriously
then of forever renouncing the writing
of poetry.
So False Unicorn belongs
to my own herbarium,
properly

consisting of the single
item.

Researchers have extracted
the newest fertility drug
from the urine
of old nuns.

My poem is becoming a rude
portrait, perhaps
too much

resembling Bullard's
Emily, at ten,
the open book prop propped
and a rose opon
for her bookmark
—but her head stuck
opon a formula body,
at odds preserved
—a cubist Stein. Even
Martha's bedtime reading to
Mathilda suggests another index:
Cicely Mary Barker's
flower fairy watercolors!
Only now in the poem do I remember
Tilly's delight
in repeating,
like learning a step in her weekly ballet,
the line Mommy read to her:
"I cannot dance on my toes."

Only now in the poem do I remember
I was reading *Dickinson's Passion,*
getting off the couch only
to let the assassin cats in and out all night,
when I left my first wife
who was a day gardener.
At our new house, the trees suit themselves.
I even hire the lawn cut.

You didn't walk
to church—
made stanzas—dance
—to hymns. And now
Mathilda has me read
to her Heine's story of Giselle, the whitest dancer, a
Wili, the ghost of a girl
dead before marriage.
She threatens to dance to death
the boy on the boards of her grave.
                              Opon
the dance cyard for the Wili of Amherst
(unpublished in her lifetime and hung
like a dress in a closet maintained by the historical society), we can still read the names
Pym,
Ishmael,
and black Wili Otey,
thru the ash from the Java volcano Wilis where, offshore, the long, white arms
of Carlotta Grisi meet to a wave of applause in a vortex above her head and ours.

                    But
she did not think in series. She is the only economist of
therefore.

She is the only truly great Amerikan poet who did not attempt a long poem dedicated to Thomas Cole. The white dress every morning like dawn is not thinking in series.

The white
dress is a
technology
(Heidegger)
its space in
the culture
of loneliness
produces time
for poems.

She fears
the ball
in her lap
is chaos
raveled up
tight again.
At least letters
come back to one.
Copeland, Carter, lately Michael Tilson set songs to her poems not choral
symphonies.
She stays on the page
in her room on her father's fourteen acres. Yet

you teach me
we must feed
off the light
but never, never
deceive ourselves
It makes us
see better.

Martha tells me she sits each day for an hour
waiting
for the baby to move inside her.
I concentrate on Gura's portrait on my desktop
til I can only feel my blood in my back.

Again,
the poem becomes the father's field, opening for a month now, process of what
goes in (e.g., Mee) and what does not fit (or *The Mouse of Amherst* comes in the
mail, for Tilly).
It should
read
like "random scatter,"
tho the art itself selects.
Margaret Mee watches with you for—
in the dark yard the Amazon rushes by like blood
circulating to the provincial in a body
of text—

the Moonflower blooms
for a single night.

───────────────

Dash is geography.
<u>Untitled, history.</u>

Let's both take the path between most resistance, this is a poem, my
conservatory to
the open field across the street, or
Homestead
to Evergreen

                    to niece Martha's old typewriter,

                    adulterous love you condoned, the inward curve of all
velocity

                    to the family's last child.

I walk undisturbed in her abandoned garden. Visit her grave, where I try to call Martha on the cell phone. No—Seeing Gib's unrestored nursery, site of the poet's collapse, was too horrible. "Open the door, the boys are waiting for me!"—answer.

O, send down your basket opon us
We've played all day starving
Gypsies lost in a country
We were never in

O, send down your basket opon us
Lift us up with gingerbread cakes
It's too late for anodyne
If your window sinks.

"And yet I was a living Child
With Food's necessity

Opon me."

  I realize, four weeks now into writing the poem, that my Emily Dickinson is the eternal amateur, the subterranean zealot, the anti-professional career poet. And the energy that is dictating the poem about Emily Dickinson is the revulsion I feel, like the taste of blood in the mouth, I feel toward the professional breed, of magazine writers and endowed chair-holders, retreaters and prize contestants, who follow in a line from Simonides of Keos, the first who went pro (try to imagine ED interviewed by a magazine). "Poetry hath ravaged me" is the only line I wrote all that season. I realize only now that I've never recovered from winter's crises; an ancient oak snapped in the wind as we slept, and its limb brot down the electrical wires to the house; the shock of Martha's miscarriage, on the day of Tilly's school pageant in an audience packed with children, there is no grounding from. My mood, by extension from wintertime, had been toward renouncing the writing of poetry in my life. I'd been writing from the age of sixteen, landlocked in Ohio. Laura Riding's early prolix prose made vital sense to me for the first time. So I drove myself to Amherst to court Poetry—only to be returned to children's play in language. "Self is poetic self. Nature, mathematical life, is the become, the eternally grown-up; History, logical life, is the becoming, the eternally childish." Riding says in "Jocasta."

      I could
pull it myself, right now
my tooth's so loose in front
I could plant it
among your bulbs; I could
toss it from your window;
draw on it
for scrimshaw some next visitor might
take it for ivory
midst the pebbles and buttons
people leave on
your headstone
to weather.

      When 1882 was a season,
Tim Keefe and Buck Ewing were battery mates
inventing the changeup in Troy, the year
you wrote box scores like "The Bible is
an antique Volume" and "My
Wars are laid away in Books."

A scorekeeper is another economist of therefore.

Bill Shields, in 1982, gave me a photocopy (now at Kent) of what he claimed to be a page, kept in the family, written in Dickinson's hand. It may be that I have played among

        child zealots we
whistle thru missing teeth
below her closed tight
Main Street window,
sun bouncing off
like a ball into shadow.
Her chat with children,
the voice of *chora*
Kristeva describes.
I entered
a suitor—
to exit
a child—still—
playing.

[July 10-September 5, 2005]

Court of the Half-King

(1980)

For Ken Irby

Their hopes again
Come unexpectedly to men—Haniel Long.

1

Our farmer knows
 his chore,
the coughing tractor-
starts
to Spring's.

His discs,
 keen to hill geometry,
turn up gardens lost in blossom,
scented still
with wind-grey flint,

cut the ridge as it has been cut.

Unspecific redbird—
② shaver in Jeanette ① before morning's foggy mirror
③ deliberately slits his throat—

with a cry, a flight.

Unspecific redbird—
another before steel's filmy mirror,
shaver in Jeanette
deliberately
slits his throat — a cry, a flight.

The furrows are not Homer's,
 are this time spiritless
and they do not speak to why we've come,
looking
for Bushy Run.

1
Our farmer knows
    his chore;
compare the coughing tractor-
starts
—to Spring's.

His discs,
    keen to hill geometry;
turn up gardens lost in blossom—
scented still,
the rows of bone and wind-blown flint—

cut the ridge as it has been cut.

The furrows below not Homer's
    are this time spiritless.
They do not speak to why we've come,
looking
for Bushy Run.

2
        There is no song,
        sings Guyasuta

        no voices recall
        an Ice Bridge.

        There is only you,
        your word my
        heir may remember
        it for the story.

Ruins of kiva factories smolder at sky's bottom…

        Young braves learn
        no dance

              for our singing The Steps
              Leaving Us,

        behind the migration,
        dead to Anasazi.

...by 1840, Sharpsburg had its Guyasuta Iron Works.

3
Is the Savior of Pittsburgh
                            the day's H. Bouquet
smoking dope in stereo vans?

          Is it that E. ALLEGHENY's
a whole bus load
        only *sounds* Mingoes rushing?

Picnics are set all around, like nothing they could have predicted.

Small boy finds sleep in sun
                            his ear to the grass
Who will wake instead?

4
Colonel Washington, that fine flaming
        ponytail
a burning bush beneath his tri-cornered hat,
        gaining
the advantage of elevation long before
        celebrity,
overlooks the swampy triangle a darker,
        bushier
Maiden of the Run controls, sees France,
        Aliquippa,
and the river's progeny....

5
There is nothing here to see

but those who come to see.

        Anniversaries,
                a variation
                      supplies the Flour Bag Fort,
    young highway patrolmen
                blockade backroad to Jeanette

    that labor decked in redcoat
            We Stand Behind Our Bread
    might chase management,
            native-clad,

    into the besieged night
            of picnic sounds
  softball
                      in the seventh.

Indian, "where we bury
the dead." A transition,
no one speaking French here,
no more to be visited than the Great Vowel Shift.

Lemieux's the only poem they know in French.

6
There is nothing here to see
but those who come to see it.

  Perhaps the girl—a music never heard,
        unselect
  of the softball draft, lone blue
        fare
  on the parked orange bus—
        whose lips
  are moving, move me, as they

        mouth
her reading a passage in Long, in
        Notes
For A New Mythology—

Is she the unpicked bouquet?

Her own bush is crushed—
  a sachet of strong herbs
  is pressed to the nose—
beneath the jeans fabric

barriers to exploration

That delay the fingers
already frantic from delay
must smooth roads, separate
the matted frontier,
"an Ocean of Trees,"

        before

           again

       before

7
A sense of wholeness surely haunts

this amputated limb of the city

A carved box of Army Surgeon's tools

spills in the rushhour noonlight

Our sense of what this was, empty

Here and now twists a tourniquet

Ties with the only sash we have

The bouquet of today
Ere the days spill away, too

P.S.

Thanks so much for your praise of the scholarship in Sun Stands.

Not many understand the "art" involved in that area, and nothing of writing praise is more rewarding than to encounter those who do understand it.

You have made my day.

—Will

Taz Alago

(1983)

For Will Henry

*Lost…as in a forest, I do believe the average American
to be an Indian, but an Indian robbed of his world—
unless we call machines a forest in themselves…*—William Carlos Williams.

*…alone. Not so much from choice as from necessity—
I generally prefer to go into places where no one else
wants to go*—Edward Abbey.

*The American West is the place men of our local
civilization travel to in wide arcs to reconstruct
the present version, of the Greek experience*—Ed Dorn.

"Asks Me Too In"
For Bob Gale

"What
do you people
want?

asked
Boyd, his whitebird
flag,

of
Perry, Ad Chapman
Trumpeter

Jones.
Asks me too in
pursuit

one hundred
six years late I chase I
chase:

Appaloosas—
spooks with spots the hands can
feel!

—race
before my days, *thunder
cluds*

set
wind   shield   north
toward…

too
short, the lines too short
to last;

skirting
the Sweetgrass
Arch,

toward...
The Invisible
forty-nine,

Queen's
Land, medicine line and above it,
beyond war.

I surrender
stripped of weaponry, not to
Monteith

Never.
But to the spirits who
guide.

Travel
alone to this
lonely

spot
in my heart,
Wallowa.

To
meet you, my Wy-ya-kin,
pledge

on
your father
's

grave.
This page, my white
flag,

that
I have dreamed these dreams
without sleep.

"In the Dream a Pony"
You make my typewriter go all night,
my idea of you

strengthens. A pony gains its legs
may run away with me yet.

Would it take me to you
if I went?

>	I fear you, Appaloosa
>	hear you in the darkness
>
>	closing circles
>	curious
>
>	to eat from my hand.
>
>	In the dream when I touch you
>	soft, the moon makes the tepee breathe
>
>	you spit and turn to fight.

Waking—my fingers frozen to the keys, morning
your breath coming

hot
on the backs of my hands.

"Four Chiefs of the Nez Perce"
1	 Step
	back from the brink of a
	detail—
		Hell's Canyon;

                    See

            the crease at the edge of
            his dying
                        smile: "Never sell

            the bones of your father...."

    2   Angry in the blood,
            I too have "seen red."
                    Old
            Joseph tearing up
            the bible.

    3   In Sohon's sketch
                    29 May 55
            the old chief resembles

            later photographs
            of Ollikut,
            his second

            born.
            "He who led the young men."

    4   So,
            bloody ground grows screaming
            plastic carnations. They

            overspill
            the rim of the melancholy rifle pit
            where Ollikut
            bled to death

            His precious head
            -waters, unstoppable
            outbound

When the snow left the coulees,
two thousand miles
from Eagle Creek to the Milk to

the Missouri gone to wandering,
crazy with blood—Sand Hills Flint Hills
Badlands Black Hills

outbound

5   C.E.S. Wood tried
to dip a page in the young chief's blood,

as a warrior in battle might
fashion a mad headband; a banner;

tried to
the rest of his life.

6   A tall drink from this slowe creek
might just kill a man

(Would it take me to you...?)

7   Tuekaka's body——-
                  eventually——-

returned
    to Wallowa.

8   Being the last
to die in battle,
the death of Looking Glass,
not necessarily
the most unfair

I'm asking

            A fourth to die at Leavenworth.
            More at Ponca. At Colville.

    Worse?

        Nespelem.
    Thunder's grave
    Its marble palisade
    Casts its
    Smaller shadow
    Below
    The church spire's.

    I'm asking.

9   "Incarnation, as One Sustained"
    red and white
    the sun turns them
    red to white

    Someone sewed the cutbank
    in carnations
    a pale plastic.

    To see the spirits you must climb
    the mountains south of here.
    Up the anticline toward

    one sustained
    view.

"A Traveler's Check"
    Excepting the exceptional Al
    Schulmeyer's Wisdom,
you do not claim the Nez Perce
Oregon Idaho Washington—do.
    Montana, you remain
    vacation buffalo grounds
for warriors without buffalo.

                              Their camps were not strategic.

All the stops remember
    (a) fool who would be Prez, or
    (two) tools
               of a sitting exec.

I hear of Xenophon, the Tartars, of Napoleon
(from Howard, OO, on
                of "retreat" and "massacre"

                              Their camps are unmarked.

White history
white noise
rapids
below dam,
with all the vapid authenticity/ISBN/
of Bede's.

Montana, you are a tourist in your own state.

"Lapwai"

Poverty is like the moon but with air.

"[I am standing here where they]"
I am standing here where they
      told McWhorter, repeatedly, that
      it was here that Five Wounds sang
      the death song Rainbow so carefully
      taught him, then sang his own; where
      the pregnant squaw shot the pony soldier
      (Logan?) who had shot Wahlitits, the hot head,

    before the soldier shot her head. Because
    only the land moves slow enough, it becomes
    an exacting frame for war.
Though the tourists drive back to Missoula disappointed,
    Big Hole's "bullet-ridden trees"
    all rotted away
    as if flesh left by Bannock scouts,
      the picket-pin squirrels still go off on time, salute
      you all along the footpath by the creek—
      IZH KUM ZIZ LA KIK, the Flathead named this camp—
      the camas still blues in the bogs above the willows.
I do not know how much the creek has altered course
    since Five Fogs fell in,
    already dead.

"[Time was]"
Time was—-
before the apparatus of history landed on this mare
before the glacier came and, leaving, left kames
(efficient gravel dams—
the whilom Missouri was a straight and northrunning river,
all the way
to the arctic.
You can see Big Sandy Creek
in the bottoms.
The Upper Missouri winds like my line, nearly finds
itself, thinks better, shakes hands with itself
as if in the telling of Yellow Wolf or the man by the stove
in the store at Loma, spinning yarns.
Four times
it cuts the engineers' highway
between Craig
& Cascade.

"The Death of Looking Glass"
After Looking Glass

"Looking Glass the Asotin will not
    dig camas
when he can kill meat.

"Wives, it is high time
    to go
to the buffalo;

"Expect me when you
    see me,
descending the Lolo."

"The Death of Looking Glass"
After Will Henry

      accuracy is not to be confused
with any one pursuit
of truths.
Will Henry's. Yellow Wolf's. Noyes'. Beal's. Brown's. Shields'.
Sutherland's. Schulmeyer's. Brumble's. Haines'.
Tho we might agree to argue that—-
standing over the frozen body of this chief
who, shot once thru the forehead, was
last to die in battle
and who, more than Lean Elk or Chief Joseph,
made the tragic mistake
of thinking like an Indian
even as the white world telegraphed ahead—-
that he is truly *dead*,
"accurate"
merely describes the aim.
Our astonishment at the unseen aim
of one who dropped the smoking rifle,
to join the ranks of those absent we now consider.
A long shot.

"The Death of Looking Glass"
After Robert Penn Warren

If scholars and penmen from Guthrie, Ky.
visit this spot
tenaciously, then
will we live to see the coulee of his final couch
carried off
in their pockets.
One lunch bucket at a time
over 35 years,
and the factory worker has smuggled out his own

home Bear Paws.

"I've Never Been That Cold (October 1, 1877)"
Cold?   why, simply

run down your own private bison,
drink the blood hot from

its beating heart
for your nightcap, munch

the delicate raw
liver, and

crawl inside
the bull's carcass still steaming

snug as a
bug in a

cornhusk
bag.

"Common Knowledge"
The Milk's in the backyard. An' I don't know what to do about it.

Thru the yellow duststormdistortion
3 Indiancowboys in our common "Spanish" motel "courtyard,"
on a barBQ drunk

All mixed-up like
w/ Ollikut's blood, the cowboys being
Injuns,

the Alberta dirt
blown down here to pepper the burgers they are inhaling, and
oblivious to

"Fine red dashed lines indicate selected fence lines"
—legend, USGS map

            Cope's dinosaur diggings
     at the Bear Paws, only
a year before

    looking for the 3-toed horse, fossil hooves pointing from the cut bank
    a way to get back to,
    at Marsh

    found upon arriving Ft. Benson,
    Custer lost, Sitting Bull driving—-this way.

Onto the stranded shores of these brown mountains, rolled the end

                        of the "thunder horses,"
                        of the buffalo, north herd,
                        of the free Nez Perces,
                        of Looking Glass,
                        of Ollikut,

              of the great Appaloosa herd,
              of the good chase,
              of the open rangeland, U.S.A.

Last camp
Trip logged
This account
Clo-sed.

"Taz Alago"
       I prefer
the pale-green flower.
    Blue only tortures the mind.

The mirage of wind-tricked ponds;
of the gathered lily-eaters' cries:

            —-Taz alago. *Good-bye.*
            —-Taz, taz. *Good, good.*
            —-Taz taz. *It is good.*

dissolve
   at out remark.

[Havre, Montana
June 25, 1983]

"Bear Paws Wo-man"
For Sharon Doubiago

Other
side this gibbous moonrise, re
sides

ray
less night wrapped in its own black sack.
Over

Id-
a-Ho tonight, men spin to keep
hid

den
their far half. I write to you from
home,

across what seems   centuries.

Over
and over on my wallpaper, I notice for the first
time,

some
hand has traced, unwitnessed,
petroglyphs:

each
depicts a man——hunter——moving inside the moon
-white

skin
of his feminine
prey.

"Nothing So Lovely
Escapes Our Mouths"
After J.L.

Reading Laughlin's Nothing
That's Lovely Can My Love

Escape only confirms it
has taken a written his

story of war to scratch
East and West on a ball

In the misnomer *Indians*
we declare the original

error in our thinking that
long usage has fenced off

Krishna's milky cowgirls fr
om Wister's prancing cowboy

"Hers How"
For the ancient volunteer in Charlie's house, I
shooed the big black horse
fly out the screened front door. Blam, ma'am.
We stood alone then, facing his house, our silences I gather
from her echo chamber
of commerce history,
clearly *the wife's* frame house, piano, wallpaper
        from the start
the painter's studio came later on,
        and detatched.
Rarely had my hostess reason to leave Great Falls.
She was older than his death, in the picture her
class excused to line his funeral streets even then,
<u>the skull was his signature.</u>

"Hers how" (sic.) is a Charlie Russellism on display at the CMR Museum, Great Falls, in an illustrated letter to the Hon. Sen. Paris Gibson. The letter is dated Feb. 2, 1902. That day, the author of *Roughing It* would celebrate his 32nd wedding anniversary and, on the opposite shore, an unknown James Joyce, his 20th birthday; that year, *The Virginian*, dedicated to Pres. Roosevelt, would first appear in print.

So, "Here's how, Charlie!" Two rider, their lines intersecting by chance the vanishing point of the otherwise impersonal tableland, demonstrating:

The methodology of sharing / a bottle / before / Riding On.

Rarely had my hostess reason to leave Great Falls.
Like the fly, dive-bombing the porch now, I was
days old and loose
                larger than death for my moment
in Montana summertime
breathing in
         that endless sky

"Dance Mud Wrestling"
Malta ahead of schedule
anticipating July's coming
attraction billboard
by the pole barn fire station:

****DANCE MUD WRESTLING****

Depart Malta on time, 1:40,
not ahead.
I will have it
for my tribal name, bear
the power of
Dance-Mud-Wrestling
every day of my living,
name my sons for it
from the flashing window of this train car.
I will have it
as the Dakota farmer has his,
testing his soil in his mouth.
I will have it rolled in dirt

(Bathing, the common crow is buff-colored,
his feathers are lance-shaped).
Everything seems east
of here, now
even Thomas McGrath

The Test
supposedly making it big in Zurich London Paris.

But who can get off this train, two bags
first, as if throwing the canteens
into the canyon—-Decision made,

and make themselves *fat*?   Who among us
can accommodate the dance
and mud?

"Home, Pennsylvania"
For Paul and Edward Abbey, who hunt among stones

"I am off to Cuba,
a week
Saturday," to carry

the gift of his gifted son's
Brave
Cowboy to Fidel.

After eighty-two summers,
burning
to see the Isle of Youth!

A lifelong lapidary habit's
rocks—
he has lugged here, treasure

from years of trips West

from Home,
Pennsylvania

Only to overrun his hand
-hewn
shop, spill down

broad slab steps and back
to habitat,
the emigre rocks scattered

like grown sons one
famous
away from home

might mail a card to say
I AM OK, BUT
DON'T KNOW ABOUT THE WEST.

When I supply the V.
between
Debs, Eugene

says he, "Let me
shake
yer hand!" When he

heard the speech that sent Debs
not to PA Ave
but to prison, Paul Revere

Abbey was pushing
seventeen
Sends me home

with a Soviet Life,
an egg
carton filled with rocks

for my son, and "The Claw [or was it
Call?]
Of the Caribbean" sounding in my brain;

a narrative poem in many parts
arranged
like boxcars in lines that belie contents,

pulling slowly out of Salt Lake
first heard
at twenty and memorized as the hobo repeated

in the darkness of their boxcar and, as he tells it,
"improved
with sons on each knee."

As Abbey recounted the
legend
of the name "Apache

tears," I knew he
too
would leap to death,

preferring it
to life
in captivity.

Letters from Kansas

(1986)

To Sherman Paul

It is nowhere flat,
What the tourists drive thru all night, to escape,

but regular
The features of western Kansas

are regular.

Like the expression on the faces of american presidents
after Lincoln, only the rows of haircuts vary much
over 50 years; seasons of chief executive facial hair
from side whiskers and full beard—-to trim mustaches—-then
vanishing buffalo grass or "the flower-fed buffaloes of
the spring" Vachel Lindsay never saw.

For it is nowhere flat

grain elevator or,
gaining combine-status, your seat:
You do not peer over,

$\Bigg\{$ from the village

into Colorado.

You see the next village,
its elevator, back.

Trained
eyes and hands

unable
over a lifetime of trying to draw the human face, why, what

annihilating flatness of character did Lindsay see there
in the open   faces of those who took him in? When
the young student of Alexander Campbell knocked at the screen,
The Plain People of the midamerican plains, he tells us,
Stopped their singing the plainsong long enough to let him in.
This is what the Mennonite farmwife, east of Emporia, said:

"Nothing had been prepared for you coming

You were quite unexplained

I did not mean to admit you

My husband would soon be returning

You simply appeared at the door as I labored

I recall it was nigh 5 o'clock

My husband was working the far field, stacking behind six horses

I looked up and you were asking

'I shall pay with an entertainment this evening
or half a day's work in the morning'

For supper, lodging, and breakfast

I recall

The grasshoppers have taken heart-shaped bites, I was thinking,
from the tract that you hand me, beaming."

Certainly, I would never have **called** *for Vachel Lindsay in the poem I was writing. I did not know his poems, except for the loud anthology pieces we'd beaten to death, I guess, in grade school; I had not read his life, warned away by his zeal for Anti-Saloon lectures. That day in Springfield, coming down from Lincoln's tomb after the rain, when we called at 603 South Fifth the Lindsay House was closed. Regular hours. Twice-a-week tours that would frustrate most pilgrims drifting thru the city. So we took each other's photograph— balancing on the high steep front porch—and drove off. Quickly ("Let not our town be large," 50,000 dream population compares to the Emerald City's exact 57,318), we were south and west of Springfield on 36 and among the first waves of the corn prairie that moved ahead of us, tonight toward Hannibal. Only later, back in Pennsylvania, did I read about your walk that way, starting out May 27, the eighty-first anniversary of Jedediah Strong Smith's murder in Kansas.*

Recombinant————
is the smell from the porch of your house, remembering

Lincoln's tomb
after rain. Makes a powerful memory that waits for me

among July-
        high weeds in Illinois————

That pulses with a power invisible to me, another farmer's grandson,
on the day I pissed on the wire cow fence I did not see————Its shock
leaving for life the metal taste; smell of porch and tomb (how
it would have tasted, to kiss the bronze sarcophagus holding
Lincoln's dust?)————Smell of porch and tomb————Its current in me,
is currently running thru a rainy field to the Westfield farmhouse,
as old as this house, to Grandma, screaming for her, Veachel....
Vachel, I am the quick unwilling ground   for your power.

Ford County, Aug. 11, '86

Dear Lindsay,

Denver must be cinders by now.

I am sitting by my darkening tent, the wind too high to light a fire to see by, watching, the last of the sun in Kansas. Denver's sun has rolled downhill some 2,000 feet in 300 miles. The plains sky above me is black already as the remaining light comes in beneath the even blacker leaves of the trees I am leaning against. My wife and son are asleep inside the nylon tent. Out in the new night, I believe that the Cimarron runs somewhere below its dry bed—marking the depth of my belief in anything I cannot see. A steady 20 mph, this wind from Liberal will let up only to draw a deep hot breath at dawn, and blow again for a day. Even at night, the sun and its wind rule Kansas as they have long ruled.

While we were staying at Irby's I read that your mother suffered sun-stroke as a girl; that you angered the foreman, that Balaam, in Great Bend when you got too much sun one afternoon and quit on him.

I like best your ink drawings of the sun in the Montana book. I wrote a Montana book, too. But shouldn't the American Hieroglyph for Kansas be a sunflower (and not the "wheat field where I, once, was a guest")?

Later,
Clarel

Coming back from Asphodel
I drove to Hiram Hill today,

looking around for your ghost
or something still here

you might have seen
or wanted or despised.

(Last week at Wabash, I found the library
and fingered the card catalog for Pound.)

The campus was deserted
All the wood recently painted

but dry.
Garfield had been a janitor here;

Gerrit Lansing and Hart Crane
are not read here.

Only a family getting into their 'wagon
in front of daughter's dorm moved.

I didn't park the car, squeezed
the wine bottle tighter between my legs.

Driving the three hours home I felt
not even the ghost of a poem.

 I've been putting together the Kansas poem, now a Vachel Lindsay poem too, from dozens of pages of notes and stray lines and only some whole pages and sections, set down in Kansas and Ohio and Pennsylvania over the last two weeks —and the poem's epitaph arrives (epigraph, tho I place it here in its place of event in the composition) with its semantic rhyme (Springfield, Lindsay's "Pilgrim City"/Clarel et al.) and its articulation of the meaning of travel and poetry. Deborah C. Andrews and Thomas Fahy write:

"*The full title of Melville's poem…reads* <u>Clarel: A Poem and a Pilgrimage</u>. *If*

we take the title seriously…the poem itself is the pilgrimage, the artifact of the

poem is the journey." Melville Society <u>Extracts</u>, 66 (1986), 3.

Bed-less or –bugged———
sometimes you would stand up all night writing letters

to Penelope
————ghost spooking a Kansas P.O. lobby, your Spencerean

penman
-ship, round inky letters as regular as the sunless fields outside,

unchanged
since childhood————warping flat from fatigue by first light————

Writing the letters———
till————"The harvester is indeed harvested."

[August 9-30, 1986]

"Remembering the Future"

The cats have eaten all the dogs tonight
Hush pretty baby
The bad dogs buried all the food in the world
And forgot where tonight,
But the cats are wise, pretty baby
The cats have dentists' clocks for eyes
Tic, they lick their paws and wait their turn
Like acid heads knowing just where to lick
Where and which period
Is the microdot at the end of what sentence, too.
Tic, their black and yellow tails are full of novocaine
Toc, they strike like pendulums when lightning kills

from Three Sleeps: A Historomance

(1992)

Richard Blevins

~~REMEMBERING THE FUTURE~~ (inverted, crossed out)
REMEMBERING THE FUTURE ~~A BOOK OF FURTHER STUDIES.~~ (crossed out)
~~A CONFLUENCE OF MAPS~~

THE ZELOT: NO. 1

ONE DOLLAR

"'The Prairies' Dreaming Sod'"
—*Hart Crane*

Seated according to Milton's reading list,
the seventeenth century occupies my seat.
Opposite, you nap
approximately the birth of Suckling

The experience of america is to look
up from Donne, into
MISSOURI, MISSOURI

Ahead, three sleeps out:
forwandred, sad as rubbed wood:
riding his hard bench as it is
at the hands of the bus station clock
whittled down to nothing:

    The Village Atheist waits
inside an empty hour all must fearfully occupy
who slit
the throat
of sleep.
[Eugene, Oregon, Dec. 1975]

"Clarel's Motel"
For Jerry Cooper

THE CATS HAVE EATEN ALL THE DOGS TONIGHT
Hush pretty baby
The bad dogs buried all the food in the world
And forgot where tonight.
But the cats are wise, pretty baby
The cats have dentists' clocks for eyes
Tic, they lick their paws and wait their turn
Like acid heads they know just where to lick
Where and which period
Hides the microdot at the end of what sentence.
Toc, their black and yellow tails are full of novocaine

Tic, they strike like pendulums when lightning kills the lights,
Like the sound of the birth of a rose.
Now the cats have eaten the last of the dogs tonight
The sound of that,
Scratching to get in.
Sleep tight pretty baby don't let the bedbugs bite
Lies are the world in tune. Tic-toc tic-toc tic-toc tic

TONIGHT I BED AGAIN IN KENT
Or stay awake eschewing drugs
High lonesome
In the land of the western reserve-dness
Outside my attic ledge
There is not the treeless track of the Old Zest
Tho I half expect it
The west has moved on from Ohio
Diah Smith from Ashland Crane to Mexico forever
Beneath a tree in Idaho
We can dream we know the stars by heart as they crystallize
"Both hemispheres?"
Both.

Because the west has moved on from Ohio
And because his dream was a hard object in De Vaca's boot,
The asking needs the inverted question marks of Spanish sentences
Somewhere a recorder underscores the moment
"Dalé, si le das"
Stream between the teeth between the lips of two times
As I read this only the tape there is an overlay of your infant cries, recorder on recorder
Listening, I am drawn
Into the passing of the lonely recorder's time
As a man from Iowa might
Stand before a waterfall.
All night I strike bugs from my paper
As I write from the recording, drawn to another light:
Dirk Bouts in Oregon
"Deer Bull" in Paterson
Duchamp meaning "of the ground"
Fly cast from left and right banks beneath the falls of the
Mississippi—

Gulf, where precious stones wash up!
College of the confidence-man.
Field at the end of the fogbow.

ONE MINUTE I WANT TO DRIVE OFF SLEEP
Or stay awake eschewing drugs
Or chew peyote buttons
Off the tight red blouse of insomnia
(The ash on my cigar a good two inches
I'm working on it
Approximates the thickness of the collected poems of Stephen Crane)
I see Bertholf's old house on Mantua, the visiting poets before and after their readings
The Master talking in one room beneath the signed and numbered Master on the white wall
The denim poet with the talking horse having walked all the way from the massacre snorts
Another line in the room adjoining
Torn, even in the remembering,
Between talking myself into exhaustion
And cookin all nite long
I try to find my voice to tell *them* that.
One minute I want to drive off sleep
Til my personality is unrecognizable to close friends of the family
Except for the single memory of sleep we have in common
An unplugged radio plays "White Room" beneath my head
When the song ends
It starts again
No one remarks on it.
After the acid the I reassembles
According to cut flowers beside a vase the wallpaper or the song playing then

But I have not returned to Kent to turn on
As I have not returned to Kent to turn in

For I am aware
That the ash will never be the thickness of *Clarel*
That the finish of the world is in the hands of those who cannot read *Clarel*
For I am aware of what even Dos Passos became
That hypocrisy is immune to dying in its ovoid sleep
For I have come to turn in my Self

Copyright Richard Blevins, July 1981.

"For D.L.B."
I mean to write a poem for you
and everything else comes thru
Melville in Jerusalem
never left home
When I picture you reading this
twenty Mays pass away
It happens like this
First,
the poet must carry his poem in his head
he must live with a poem as man and wife
And only then the writing
After the living
it is the sensation of remembering the future
of translating Rilke
or planning a baby
Above everything else,
I have created a world I must let go.

The Zelot Press
Greensburg, Pennsylvania

REMEMBERING THE FUTURE: A CONFLUENCE OF MAY

The cats have eaten all the dogs tonight
Hush pretty baby
The bad dogs buried all the food in the world
And forgot where tonight.
But the cats are wise, pretty baby
The cats have dentists' clocks for eyes
Tic, they lick their paws and wait their turn
Like acid heads they know just where to lick
Where and which period hides
The microdot at the end of what sentence.
Tic, their black and yellow tails are full of novoca
Toc, they strike like pendulums when lightning kills
    the lights,
Like the voice of Yeats in a close room driving Poun
    crazy, tic
Like the sound of a piano melting
Like the sound of the birth of a rose.
Now the cats have eaten the last of the dogs tonigh
The sound of that,
Scratching to get in.
Sleep tight pretty baby don't let the bedbugs bite
Lies are the world in tune. Tic-toc tic-toc tic-to

Tonight I bed again in Kent
Or stay awake eschewing drugs
High lonesome
In the land of the western reserve
Outside my attic ledge
There is not the treeless track of the Old Zest
Tho I half expect it
The west has moved on from Ohio
Diah Smith from Ashland H. H. Crane to Mexico
Beneath a tree in Idaho
We can dream we know the stars by heart as they cry
Both hemispheres?
Both.
Because the west has moved on from Ohio
And because his dream was a hard object in De Vaca'
The asking needs the inverted question marks of Spa
    sentences
Somewhere a recorder under-scores the moment
"Dale, si le das"
Stream between the teeth between the lips of two ti
As I read this onto the tape there is an overlay of
    infant cries, recorder on recorder
Listening, I am drawn
Into the passing of the lonely recorder's time
As a man from Iowa might
Stand before a waterfall.

To write down the poem of the ash falling bodily
As Melville turns from prose to poetry
And Cendrars from poetry to prose
As in the romance when the broadsword neatly falls
And the rider splits into alliterative halves
Falling to either flank of his charger
As the right arm above the elbow falls away, a stanza
By the etherized French poet predicted in *Clarel*
"The testimony of the hand Gnawed in the dream…"
As love letters pump the stump each heart's throb
…Til he bleeds to death.
…Til cauterized by a lie.
(Writers as a rule take sides.)
Lo, the stone over my eye is rolled away and Christ my Christ is vanished!
We all grow up.
Clarel haunts the one true tomb of Melville's eye.
Lies are the world in tune.

Cendrars' arm surfaced the other day
Item 24 in Lowell's catalog
One of two copies
Very good to good
Unsigned.

A Cendrars who had never written prose
Menaces his brand new stump at the cameras
The dirty bandages threaten
To unravel
Painfully like a narrative by Cossery.
Tho fame has not come to the poetry, alas,
Cendrars remains himself
I come to the poetry
Precisely because.
He has taught me
To live with the feeling
You've left something essential behind;

To pack my suitcases with my unpublished books
Wear five pairs of winter socks and four golf shirts if you have to
Your books
Are the valise of a burden not shared
But carried yourself up the stairs
They open
Like a butterfly from Blake on the hotel bed, like a memory of the future.

If there were no afterlife no promise of the afterlife
Could we send our sons to war?
There is no afterlife.

Tho I am aware
That Vaughan's star in a tomb was a glint in his eye,
I cannot
Clear my own dust from my eyes
I fear in the night for the demise of my consciousness
I am strapped
Even as a patient with a tumor as he is wheeled into the O.R., I am strapped
I have come to turn in my Self
But I cannot
It is not within my power
Practicing Dadaists have amputated my religion
So that I am afraid to sleep or go too long without sleep
I cannot close my eyes now that their cruel images have sliced away both lids
This poem fits me like a prosthetic arm I'd love to leave behind in a newspaper train station with a busted clock
It is always noon or midnight there
The hour needs inverted question marks as in Spanish sentences
The arm scares all the children, their faces cloud up like ruined picnics
It scares all the vacationing women, sends them tottering like septuagenarians on spiked heels
It scares me
Like nothing else
I fear for my consciousness
It is all I have
As tho thot were a way thru unhappiness
As though thought were a way thru
It is *not much to go on*

Come morning we might sit in the kitchen
Without eating breakfast
Plenty of coffee
Sugar
Milk
The open back door hungry for fresh air
Our feeling for food slow returning
And I might read to you from across the tablecloth
The feast of the Prose of the Trans-Siberian
The fast of the Prose of the Trans-Siberian
Just when the sun most resembles the orange you peel with your thumbnails
I could easily touch you.
I will put off reading you this
The fruit and the sunshine spraying the walls and our eyeglasses: light, orange.

Timing, for the poet, is everything.

Lefty,
Your poems move toward what is,
Even now,
Past.
Ancient history.

The cleaner stars burn the skin of men in the fields of Ohio
It is a genuine mystery
On Luyten 789-6 radio-astronomers jump to hear the rifles' report at Kent State
Remind me again exactly
How many years must light travel from your brown eyes
To reach me
That I might forget
¿It is a journey thru oblivion much like bringing a poet into the world, no?
Look, I've already poured your second drink.

Few poets can read their own poems
With anything like enjoyment
It should be as when we first asked"

"Do I remember that, Dad,
Or did you tell it to me once?"

Cendrars, I have a complaint
Our poets make much out of what seems worse than nothing
Christ!
Our prophets of the faraway nearby are simply suffering the final stages of echolalia
Christ!
Our slogans have deteriorated into private enthusiasms for the unlikely
CHRIST!
The streets of Kent are as empty
As heaven

Tho the time I know is ripe to change the world from the bottom up,
I write to kill time. Tho my love insists I have thirty days to change or she walks,
I write to be alone for part of each day.
Tho the police are on to me,
I must forge this last check in the name of Poetry.
Will you accept it?
I've acquired a slew of new identities
Assuming the Social Security numbers of American poets who died writing long poems
They remain the safest bet
(Jerry tells me an Akron musician goes by the stage name of Willie Tasby!)
When Picasso's signature, and maybe a quick owl, became more prized than the sum on his bill,
The artist
Traveled free.
We are that far gone, tremulous flower of Lorca's flown soul
A dry mouth propped open for the high-speed drill
A rotten window exhales into the furnace of the night
Night folk prowl Water Street in the light of the heat of their own bodies like embers
The Cuyahoga on fire in its banks
Silhouette
Someone with the voice of Blake is reading aloud from *Tristram Shandy*
From the two black pages
A little following gathers self-consciously like false dawn at the foot of the campus
The sleeping suck the night into their lungs

All night I strike bugs from my paper
As I write from the recording, drawn to another light:
Dirk Bouts in Oregon
"Deer Bull" in Paterson
Fly cast from left and right banks beneath the falls
       of the Mississippi--
Gulf where precious stones wash up!

One minute I want to drive off sleep
Or stay awake eschewing drugs
Or chew peyote buttons
Off the tight red blouse of insomnia
The ash on my cigar a good two inches
I'm working on it
Approximates the thickness of the collected poems of
       Stephen Crane
I see Bertholf's old house on Mantua, the visiting
       poets before and after readings
The Master talking in one room beneath the signed and
       numbered Master on the white wall
The denim poet with the talking horse snorts another
       line in the room adjoining
Torn even in this remembering
Between talking myself into exhaustion
And cooking all night long
I try to find my voice to tell them that.
One minute I want to drive off sleep
Till my personality is unrecognizable to close friends
       of the family
Except for the single memory of sleep we have in common
An unplugged radio plays "White Room" beneath my head
When the song ends
It starts again
No one remarks on it.
After the acid the I reassembles
According to cut flowers beside a vase the wallpaper or
       the song playing then

But I have not returned to Kent to turn on
As I have not returned to Kent to turn in

For I am aware
That the ash will never be the thickness of <u>Clarel</u>
That the finish of the world is in the hands of the
       reactionaries
That hypocrisy is immune to dying in its ovoid sleep
For I have come to turn in my Self
To write down the poem of the ash falling bodily

As Melville turns from prose to poetry
As in the romance when the broadsword neatly fal[ls]
And the rider splits into alliterative halves
Falling to either flank of his charger
As the right arm above the elbow falls away, a s[ ]
From the etherized French poet predicted in <u>Clar</u>[el]
As poems pump the stump each heart's throbbing
. . . Till he bleeds to death.
. . . Till cauterized by a lie.
(Writers as a rule take sides)
Lo, the stone over my eye is rolled away and Chr[ist]
        Christ is vanished!
We all grow up.
Clarel haunts the one true tomb of Melville's ey[e]
Lies are the world in tune.

Cendrars' arm surfaced the other week
Item 24 in Lowell's catalog
One of two copies
Very good to good
Unsigned.

A Cendrars who had never written prose
Menaces his brand new stump at the cameras
The dirty bandages threaten
To unravel
Painfully like a narrative by Cossery.
Tho fame has not come to the poetry, alas,
Cendrars remains his own man,
I come to the poetry
Precisely because Cendrars remains his own man.
He has taught me
To live with the feeling
You've left something essential behind
To pack my suitcases with my unpublished manuscr[ipts]
Wear five pairs of winter socks and four golf sh[irts]
        if you have to
Your books
Are the valise of a burden not shared
But carried yourself up the stairs
They open
Like a butterfly on the hotel bed, like a memory [of]
        the future.

If there were no afterlife no promise of the aft[erlife]
Could we send our sons to war?
There is no afterlife.

The opiated lump of morning bubbles under match
Dawn is the glow returning to the habitual user's face, fixed
I think I can sleep now.

"Gregg Is A Babe Williams Delivers"
For Bob Bertholf

like babe in the cradle, or Saul among baggage

Charlie Russell drawing wages

Melville dry in Illinois

wood & canvas, wood & canvas

the frontier interviews its author prone
his skinner's wagon struck—for Santa Fe!

1
"Faced inland to originality," Gregg is
another babe Williams delivers: "a sense of
stripped, being clothed, nevertheless."
Among doctors, a doctor between patients
sits, a poet
between cultures, ages,
who cures us of this laryngitis.
Who speaks to us in our own accents.

"Is Saul also among the prophets?" in the
"Olympus of Prairie mythology?" Doctor
and Major?
Gregg declines the titles. Acts.
Tho his cutting Smith's trail at the Cimarron would
station Gregg among the fathers, Strong
is not his middle name.

"O you must try to stich up some way or other"
an ear
for prose & poetry, epic & idiom. Act II.

The bullwhacker to this start is Parkman, following,
who found among all doctors
one
who prescribed "Far Zest."
Josiah means "Jehovah heals,"
tho the healer of Saltillo credited
instead
the prairies "for their sanative effects."

2

                Eternal commerce:

                    res and place

3
They say, *wood & canvas*, Monet wished to be blind
temporarily!
You have two wishes coming….

The dream of the child in the bed going West
is, yes, a land wedge, in the shape of
what small shade he makes, going into.
It is sundown, the shadow parts
the tall grasses all around.
His world moves the infant to exclaim
the names of a terrain, yet
his language is another world's….

4
The rain here

falls all one
shade: New
York, N.Y.

5
"my book piled up,
my days
in Santa Fe."

The objective presses: "jot down assures

life a note(book)." "Others

send you poems," Tobias notes, "I give you bibliographical cards."

Gregg the great note-taker, "his habit
from early youth...a mere book of reference

to strengthen
his own memory."

King Josiah discovers the lost book of the law
Gregg failed at reading the law, and *Commerce* lost among Bigelow's review.

Taking notes against loss, between patients, on the desk calendar,
the thrust
is not
to make books
to lyricize life
(*The night was not a poem.*),
but an objectified daylight
and its champion,
Paterson.
Tasistro is of the east and dis-ease
(*Our feelings make poor verbs.*);
at tables couples around us
saw us.

6
1844, they've named this inn:
nine rooms, nine fireplaces.
You were east of this
farmhouse that year.
I wonder aloud at the crossada,
writing and printing the Commerce
even William Cullen Bryant in my poem
                              tonight!

My wife smiles
up from her pregnancy
interest in the antique
white cradle smell of
dried flowers
I do not like the
white spray job
She declines a strong drink,
No, as you would—
My lone dispute with you,
yet less, surely, than with those "throne of Grace" letters home.
(Happy the Mad is not the Virgin.) "De biggest boy in all de town
loving the belle of the city…
'That's some,' you'll say…."
(But there will be no more.)
We leave too easily satisfied
with the meal and our weekend
"discovery."

7 *Gregg, for himself*
You do not know me
1844 is no more alien to you,

as you look I become another
mile in your marches across Kansas.

When you recall this crossing think of me,
it will make a poem like the news of gold.

Only then does speech make sense
of the trail of notes.

Like a child realizing his fist,
I am newly a part of Kansas.

[Read at William Carlos Williams Special Session,
1983 MLA Conference, New York]

"The Whiteness Of His Tomb: A Trip Report for Ed Dorn"

We two have come to him, late
as the day is
attenuated.
whole districts
of city empty too as eternity is at death the blood

pools
in Baltimore's
extremities, presumably
as far as
Richmond.

                                For it is (only) proper

with Lawrence & Williams, Baudelaire bearing elegant prose wreathes,
chrestomathies
And Whitman, for once the lone beard as advertised,
          attending the November dedication
          of his by then *Victorian* cenotaph

          tho late, not emptied yet of meaning
          but its sense making

          mean echoes within that new tomb,
          the gothic moment having variously

passed on
(1849-75).

                      Admitting That
If there be a coin of ad
mission, then
it is gambled away
frivolously in this air.
That we have carried it individually
between us all along
but casually, as loose change
down backseats of cars, is not so
noteworthy.
But this is no place of commerce.
Mr. Poe reclines
in the narrowest of
contexts, a brick alleyway
to prop his marble pillow
white as the proudflesh ghetto
that constitutes the terms
of The Recovery,
as the late empire
reckons it.

In Hollywood,
Poe grows
luminous—
tho in more specific terms,
he rots,
emitting a strictly low-level energy like tv.
Lo, the whiteness of his tomb
a tenement gutted nearby
like a tomb enrapt!

To understand his death
in the word intensely felt
was premature,
a faint
feint sham of
what is
the great unread on-deck history
PYM
"A scene of the most horrible butchery..."
we are already
deep inside of

Finally, to visit I must

Finally to ingress this egress I must
     squeeze into the unlit hold of his Grampus,
     a stowaway
     inventing in the darkness methods to read in the darkness
     in the sudden inrushing claustrophobia
     transforming our familiar
     study:
     a buddy's note unexpected
     arrives, ensanguine
     while, unknown to me,
     the latest mutiny storms across and across the sick blood-slick
     deck above my head.

                         To discover only that
Pym lies here, beside Virginia, the accumulation of his many
premature burials fashioning the irony
The white veiled figure which breaks off without saying why
the vision of the narrative, goodbye color of enaw
of the One Bright Star in Eureka, a
boxed set in the whiteness of his unused tomb.

And in the end,
in this Baltimore
corner, restless for
summer nightlife,
the absolute quality
of his whiteness
is no more mysterious
than blackness.
                    (Why, instinctively,
                      I hold my breath passing

                      sprung iron gates, eyesockets
                      in neighbor tombs; tho

                      I know
                      nothing's there but

me.

"At Melville's Tomb"
He who walked in love with truth,
enamored of its fragrance; a mortal
plucked by ambitious living—

Repulsed, the glove that cut the pool

She who opened to his eyes
now cold contemplates the closing
flower, the polished stone—

I've acquired a slew of new identities
Assuming the Social Security numbers of American poets
          who died writing long poems
They remain the safest bet
(Cooper tells me an Akron drummer goes by the stage
       name of Willie Tasby!)
When Picasso's signature, and maybe a quick owl,
          became more prized than the sum on his bill,
The artist
Traveled free.

We are that far gone, tremulous flower of Lorca's
          flown soul
A dry mouth propped open for the high-speed drill
A rotten window exhales into the furnace of the night
Night folk prowl Water Street in the light of the heat
       of their bodies like embers
The Cuyahoga on fire in its banks
Silhouette
Someone with the voice of Blake is reading aloud from
       <u>Tristram Shanty</u>
From the two black pages
A little following gathers like false dawn at the foot
          of the campus
The sleeping suck the night into their lungs
The opiated lump of morning bubbles under match
Dawn is the glow returning to the habitual user's face,
          fixed

I think I can sleep now.

            "The Dream including Gypsophila"

Char was a dead man in 'sixty-eight
In twenty-four months May returned
And the dogs,
"Each grape to his cluster clung."
I was not twenty
Still reading women Shelley
Honestly believing <u>may</u> should be <u>can</u>
A room above an epic
Kent State
When the maying gave birth to death
An age stillborn
And died herself, exhausted.
Same old story.
We are that far gone, flower of Lorca's soul
When eleven Mays give way, I will be your father.

    O, battle the pieces, draft the fragments!

covers the hand that leaves no clue.

"Clarel Meets Vine"
We laughed to break their backs, slightly rusty hinges
Cracked between my touch-type vise: "Today,
We put our ears back!" Practiced sucking
Strip-tease strings off the unlit floors of
Baltimore, up
The broken straws of their own missing legs.
   A scale wood hammer
    Opened majuscular Claws.
Soon, for us, it was money for old rope.
Noetic behind a line of swipes,
Saw Sol exhale tar & carbon
Then douse the day-old fuse in skim milk bay.
   A perfect pearl sank
   In each beer bottle
Of a sunset.
The bouquet of boiling cayenne & sea
Salt stuck to my cut fingers
For days.

"Monody, from the Pack Mules"
Tho their mules could not smell water ahead,

Two zealots found
A pool of shade
Floating the rock
Of Geo's Butte.

Cans cannot rust in this desert.

Above their noise,
Graben bathtub
Rings marked the done
Demersal days.

The feral sand resmoothed her skirts.

Felling themselves,
They lapped the sand:
Like tumid fountain
Pens, her ink.

Two mules stood by, illusionless.

"American Larch"
Our lone tamarack lacks the faith
Of evergreens. Its needles fall
To cynic winter.

Barren, the shadeless larch
Most anticipates the ship's mast
It will never be.

Astride, instead, a sandstone crest
Its roots sound ground waters deep
Beneath the upheaved floor
Of the once and future inland sea.
Its stoic fruit, a cone.
Its needles fall. Still,

Your change distinctly speaks to me
Of what eternity must be.

Each spring you seem "astounded
Into heaven…." A bit later, each year,
For your own resurrection.

"Interview with an Archivist"
"I can no longer believe in vampires.
Oh, I've known a few live ones
left them moaning 'Marry me!' in my warm bed
easy as I'd left that factory job in Rittman
the printing presses still running onto the floor of my father

and bot an unlisted number, formerly a funeral home's,
when they started calling the house after midnight.
I don't worry anymore. I figure
since there is no god, vampires are unemployable.
The are no better in this economy than ghosts
and everybody's already got his own ghosts.
The sharpened stake would begin to look inviting.
They would stay awake all day in their coffins watching
equestrian events and volleyball on ESPN.
They would cease criticizing Lon Chaney Junior's acting.
They would look into a mirror one night and find a visible grey hair.
They would gradually forget about their war with the dead Melville
and teach the bible as lit once a week evenings.
They would come up for tenure after seven centuries
and make a flurry of phone calls to Kent State
asking for letters of recommendation from deceased faculty.
The suicide rate among the undead would soon prohibit the issuance of insurance
policies. The sharpened stake, etc.
Noting how life mirrors b-movies,
they would look like Bela Lugosi between takes shooting
up beneath his redlined cape. Not even Dracula
could be monster enuf to watch
everybody else in his world
age, sicken, and die.
Poe couldn't.
They could not go on.
No one could possibly say 'Good-bye' that many times."

"Life Along the Connecticut"
*...the drive to explore and dominate
the landscape turned inward*—Paul Metcalf.

I.

Am somewhere between Amherst and Greenfield,
   Emily's dash—
Driven east out of Arrowhead, west from Gloucester—
   And Tuckerman's accretion:
North between storms, February in remission.
   It should be snowing
Another thermal dermis to be scraped—
Their snowplow blade looms, not his bowsprit;
   Their fields reconvey, creak
Shut behind our entrance. Our car on display
   Sinks as it makes the grade.

II.

You drive. I cannot ask why the whiteness
Of old snow does not annihilate us—
Why mid-life's midwife to mizzen winters—
In we breathe. Hold the unspoken word. Air
(Forgotten heater, stilly zealot)
   Burns in our bodies.
I ask instead about the roadsigns, new to me,
   Warning FROST HEAVES:
   "Is it a *verb*? A poet's disease?"
(It is a sign Tuckerman would have hoarded
Never understanding its description
   Of his own cycles.)
Past the Greenfield exit before I think this.
   I "witness and adjust"
   You handle the heavy, white car.

III.

Next turn—a frozen lake:
A few pure products have sunk
Holes thru to the black eye of water.

They sit unseen and staring,
Into that unblinking eyeball
In the floor of their shacks
Atop Lake Franklin Pierce.

IV.

"You're Midwestern!"

                                                                          you tell me

"My head's in Idaho!"

                                                                              I duck.

We both know that

I am here and here

Tonight is Henniker

And the Henniker, NH Zip Code opens

With the precise number of blue

Degrees

Outside,

0.

V.

Your cancer is in remission. Along your jaw I note
Three faint blue dots: Rilkean quarter notes? Tattoos
  For lining up
  Their white machines?
Our mission today, this Valentine's Day, is to carry
Seventy newly printed books
To their author,
To the poet of Henniker,

Who is living too with cancer and smoking cigarettes
   Between his drug therapy
   For his one lung.
You are the great Gloucester poet's editor and a poet
So rare that you seem never
To have read the great poet;
Our host is a poet so memorable
It is impossible for him
To have been a student of the great poet's
Or to have attended any mountain's college,
Beyond the brilliant course he skiis
   In his talking.
   The new poem
In each of the seventy books tells the same story
Of the poet's cancer, the irony
Of the simple government
Directions for eating his medicine—
Every line break
   A seminar
   In prosody.

We can see the ski slope on Pats Peak
From his upstairs apartment. Two wood beams
Brought here and set at five feet ten inches
Divide the main room like a worry
Both poets either think to stoop their six-foot frames,
Or headslam
Every time
One gets up to pee or hunt a book
I sit, inexperienced, between them
Comparing the brutalities of life-saving;
Eye admire
The framed snapshot
Of some old geezer in a plaid wool shirt:
   Open
   Fishin'!
Zukofsky's black eyebrows land on another frame
   And twitch.
I clear the ceiling nicely; duck anyway.

VI.

But when we drive the three hours back
Over the same frost
Heaves now the desire to hurry
Driven out of us. Now in darkness
The bumps in the spiraling road feel
   Comforting
   As Braille.
We drive back past the same ice-fishers' huts
Their small fires squat on the unmalting lake,
Windham Lewis self-condemned
Inside his ice cave west of here,
   You tire
   Testing recovery—
And I know I have been lost all day in New England,
This easement, a hole in the dark ice
Thru which to pull
Up the bloodless fish
Into the freezing
Air of our warm
Suffocations.
In some milltown we stop, idling beside an iron bridge
You turn to me from somewhere for directions
   To your own house
   In Willimantic.
I can only sit up straighter
Pretend to read the road map, this time more carefully
But I know already
The car's interior is glowing from the tiny dome bulb
As the first flakes come alive
Multiply on the windshield
Inches from our eyes

In Memoriam, George Butterick and joel oppenheimer.

"You Mend Our Punched-Out Smiles"
The Olson Manual sits on your bookcase

like a beaten fighter in his corner.

Your office has two doors, no windows,

his library. When you leave the room I

cradle Olson's copy of *Moby-Dick* and it

opens. His annotations like the arches of

broken and swallowed teeth. You return

and tell me That typewriter's missing a

character or two I immediately forget

which you say thinking as you talk

that you are here to fill in all the

awful blank spaces he left us.

hiram college
HIRAM, OHIO 44234
(216) 569-3211
ENGLISH DEPARTMENT

November 8, 1983

Dear poets,

Here, finally, is our list of all of you who will be participating in the Special Event celebrating William Carlos Williams at the MLA. Robert Bertholf and I will preside at the event, but we will ask each of you to introduce the poet who follows you on the list. Robert will introduce James Laughlin, who, after his reading, will introduce Paul Mariani, and so forth.

In order to save time for the readings, we request that you take no more than 30 seconds introducing the poet who follows you. Each of you will have five minutes for your reading. In the interest of fairness, we will keep strict time, so please plan your reading within that limit.

We will all be able to continue the celebration and tribute to Williams at the centennial dinner at the Harvard Club, 27 West 44th St. (cash bar at 6:00; dinner at 7:00) Several of you have already sent checks to cover the cost of guests for the dinner. Please send me their names, so I can make a check list of those attending. If any others of you want to bring guests, please send me a check for $30.00 made out to the William Carlos Williams Society for each guest.

We are looking forward to this special event. Feel free to write Bob Bertholf or me if you have any questions.

Yours,   list in order of reading:

1. James Laughlin
2. Paul Mariani
3. Charles Tomlinson
4. Allen Ginsberg
5. ~~Richard Eberhart~~
6. Daniel Hoffman
7. Joel Oppenheimer
8. Sam Abrams
9. Neil Baldwin
10. Richard Blevins
11. Charles Bernstein
12. Theodore Weiss
13. Milton Kessler
14. M.L. Rosenthal
15. Louis Simpson
16. Mary Ellen Solt
17. ~~Nathaniel Tarn~~

"A First View
of Gloucester,
You, Too"
For Gerrit Lansing

Where the land begins, we meet

At land's end we climb, individually,
to meet the common present: a path you seem to know,

through Dogtown Square.

*"Unfruitful, with parched, thorny shrubs, monochromatic, ochreous,
the wilderness…stretches out, so weird and creepy that nothing that looms up
in the way of beasts and monsters or preposterous edifices can possibly
astonish us,"* Max Friedlander on landscape art.

Travel is the methodology.
The present slides
along a continuum
of unremarkable tendencies:
hillocks, like rows of graves, blocking the ocean;
a girl, who slipper slips,
dives beneath a pile of leaves: emerges
from the ocean foam, triumphant, laughing—
a girl again (Tragabigzanda?);
I bring the incubus home, as I must do,
and place it on the table, as you once did,
where my family, like yours, gathers around
where the incubus sits, stalled
in the middle of the room on the table
like a platter of meat
that has been prepared beautifully for us
meat we cannot eat of;
snagged my pants on your deathbed, brought my ear
across the room, to your last words,

a bowl for
the flowers that
float, shallow
on their pastel backs
at your side
as I leave;
fell on my nose amid the fluffy petticoats norns wear
you used for pillow cases;
sensation of floating, little feel for the raft underneath,
the morphine falls audible always below our voices, asking:
"Where does all this water
come from?";
only guilt is not instructive—
we live in spite of it—
guilt's assassin has not been born;
"And where does it all
go?";
when she said, "Go there in your mind"
I thought she meant it;
you cannot get there mathematically
always 1/2…1/4…1/8…1/16…1/32…1/64…of the way there—
but when the poem stops,
everybody gets off;
poems come of necessity,
but the local is a principle;
Your leaves blow in my yard,
My leaves blow into yours—
Like the soil, then souls, leaving Oklahoma;
There is no end
To the new old leaves;
yesterday, after the eulogist read
joel o's new poem, wherein the poet wants
the bird (of poetry) to please visit
the feeder he has built and stocked with seed
(his neighbors' feeders are full of
beautiful songbirds!), a bat woke up
and circled, six times,
inside the Congregational Church at Henniker; today
the sky is preparing to snow, the boulders
to receive it.

Where it is
we say we
stand upon.

Travel is the methodology.
In America where nobody hitchhikes, I pull over
let out
my only son.
The distortion was heavy for early morning. I saw
an old face
in city traffic
trying to remember
different.

We can say accurately that we have finally reached Dogtown,
but no
                        yapping guardians of the culture are alive to
greet us too, only
berry brambles snap at our heels, dry turds of the fossilized village.
Other barks, past our hearing, wake ghosts, our ghosts.
And only
the carving in the boulder
still announces it:
We have entered the region of
        BEON
          TIME
arrived on time and exhibiting the effects of
the last of many elaborate stages
of travel. Is why
I've never practiced writing poems, writing short poems
The journal I keep could be Scobie's when he kept honest
It doesn't work, the work is not there to work with
any more than our laundromat trip
every few days (our well's run dry)
can be a dry run for say a train ride to Kansas
(each time I turn on the tap and nothing happens,
is a big superannuated surprise).

The wind here is colder than water
A few birds swim in the air

or sit on the folding chair
of breakers, equally.
All my life I've heard about many, too,
of the few men who
make a difference.
They grew up beside the ocean.
Landlocked, in Ohio, I memorized their books
never seeing their ocean.
We pass a few stragglers who quickly realize themselves
mistaking headland for heart-
and return to their rooms in town,
as people might put on a coat
for warmth.
The city, at the Fort, is a window to the sea beyond me,
at my back the continent
shoves me
so far east, it becomes west again.
It remains for the shore
to explicate the ocean floor,
toss at our feet
what we cannot possibly
reach for ourselves

[Storrs—Henniker—Gloucester]

"Going to the Source"
To Steve Clay; at Sherman Paul's

When you are there, everything else is there, Suzuki

Hears, here where the line is undiminished in its utility as the rule of the horizon
                                                sustain
                                                ing sustain
                                                ed Olson's
                                                "vertical list
                                                ening," even
                                                ing's ear to
                                                the ground.

Not on top of the world, but high up
    on her one hip
        so close
            her unfocused face
   fills my eyes.
I feel wrapped in the earthen smell of her movements with the wind
dampness of her long hair drying, milky   glacier lakes.

                            Only 1,500 feet, and level
                                but effect
                        of being brot up close to night
                            sky, never
                      leaves me during visit.

                      "The boreal forest," my host turns to me,
                      "begins here. Goes all the way north."
                      Sensation of having for once both ears
                      to the vertical ground.

Basil King is right.
"I was here, I trod across"
is what the WASPy poets write.
I envy the well-driller

asleep on his rig,
        a sunny platform in Iowa:
with every blow
he gains an inch below.
I can only drive the
miles ahead.

Mary Butts tells of her childhood desire to taste the mud.

                                                                                                       (Tradition.
                                                                                     or when we Read,
                                                                                        we pick up

                                                                                         things

Hard not to

                track in
                a certain amount
                of black
                sandy
                loam

onto your clean kitchen
floor,
Jim, I have simply

        "come in."

There is a kind of memory
I know it
beyond experience
you'd never heard of Wade
Boggs didn't believe me
his average is a throw
-back to Hamilton & Burkett
This is a kind of memory
what decays in bogs we wade

brims again with life clings
like death to our boots
like to swamp us taste of
Scotch whisky over time the bog
is solid enuf to support
the weight of a drunk man.

                                  He spoke, by the burial mounds:
                                  "I like to think man's first words were
                                  uttered in imitation
                                  of the soughing of the wind
                                  in big trees like these."

II
After two days of driving the need to drive had left me
by the river, north of St. Louis, I am
wholly inside I hear
me traveling thru the world I talk to myself when I stop in truck stops
uncharacteristically ask for receipts

The body,
      after ten hours in a car seat,
becomes mindful:
                it has covered a lot of ground
                            without once touching
down. Home pulls
like love's gravity   even while the road leads
                                suddenly, up Emerson's tree!
                                One-car crash
                                picture of useless spinning
                                tires horn stuck coming to
                broken consciousness broken

No room in
Heidegger's "houses
                of fiction" Whitman walked out on
                their perfumed rooms disinfected
                for your convenience a century ago
the amerika I am driving at, across.
My car envelopes me
is Clarel's Motel.

Outside my white room
there is no trace of Clemens
in Hannibal, billboards mark only Twain
And he leaves off navigating in St. Paul
so I turn inland
This is the Heartland
idle beside a field to watch Jake Beckley
play a slick first base and double off
the wire fence then into Iowa and wind
steady all day at forty miles per hour
starts to worry me staggers 'em,
nearly knocks me down at the self-serve
pumps learn to hold the tank cap,
suddenly lightweight, in free hand
        and concentrate
till a farmer bangs diner door
claps his dozer cap to his head,
        bends sharply
into the wind and yelps "Whoooo-eeee!"
to the tune of Anderson's midamerikan chant
One of those who never read it nevertheless
"who read their own lives there"
        in the Iowa sky
always changing left to right
as if across a vast unwritten
            page

The wind to young Pound is magical in those poems
is, at Pisa, "part of the process."
OED, suffing, as Jim pronounced it for me.

                        That the lexicon erodes, land to wind,
                                  until only the poem
is left.

                        Journey to the End of the West
                        West in a random universe
                        The Last First People

>   Finding the Way
>   High Lonesome
>   One-man posse
>   Periplus
>   A flock of landscapes
>   Drive, he sd
>   Common knowledge
>   Zelot's Logbook
>   Overland
>   Outland
>   Outis
>   The Confluence
>   The shapes of western states
>   How far can it be (if you can think it)?

Driving north, thru Minnesota, I jot down titles for a book, for company, my notebook beside me on the seat like a passenger. I remember the first time, San Francisco, I read Dorn's *Gran Apacheria*, mistaking the table of contents for the first poem. *Read* it, that way, for a poem.

[Notice to be Posted on Motel Doors in This State]

(1) Get a good, early start, and lunch in a diner down the road that serves breakfast twenty-four hours.
(2) Start late, and lunch in a diner down the road that serves breakfast twenty-four hours.
(3) Try to keep the trip episodic. Skip breakfast. Forget the mathematics of the miles; dig what Don Gordon calls "the secrets in the landscape."
(4) Call home before you dream in your motel bed that you called home.
(5) Never eat Chinese in states beginning with the letter "I."
(6) In your room, watch only local news, never network. Watch only network news in the lounge.
(7) The correct response to the challenge "You're not from here, are you" is "Please ask that as a question."
(8) The best street directions assume it is nighttime.
(9) For the kingdom of insomnia is greater than money.
(10) At 3 in the morning, it is not loneliness or fatigue but the realization of the annihilation of the individual one feels shaking apart the bed.
(11) Remember, some fuckers will never know what 3 in the morning feels like.

As if he could, by driving north, reverse the overconfident trend, the man in the cream-coloured Honda, etc.
Play car radio all
   day
Against isolation of taped
   music
Want to laugh at the local
   DJs,
hear what it is they're listening to
in the farmhouses and tractor cabs I pass all day.

phosphine hieroglyphic roadsigns lead to Clarel's Motel

The slow road to Bemidji
fills my windshield,
like Thoreau's day; each mile
reveals herself for me alone
reading the whole anthology
and not once peeking
at a poet's name or Bio.
I brake, full stop, beside
convex bubble shore
of unknown to me lake
somewhere in country
I will never find again
but in memory or smell
of sun on small flowers.

Veblen in MN……………………..stuck behind
traffic……………………………………………..
                                            ……………...fat-assed RV   from TN….
Dorn at Kent State in 1972 turning finally to each of us seated around the seminar table to ask (we've been reading on our own about Josiah Gregg and Geronimo, Diah Smith and John Wesley Powell): "On this map, point to, The Prairie." Simple.

Nobody knew. He sent us off to the stacks to read the sources, USGS documents, to see for ourselves. Never with the sense of somehow coming back to class and "justifying" one's data in an academic defense, never "controlling" sources—but to extend one's own measure into that real and measurable world, too, of the primary experience of men. What he saw in The Max. About then I ran across a library copy of *A Bibliography on America*.

The river undulates I ride beside   going to the source
out of the heartland   up to the headwaters   your door is near
Agassiz,
        extinct lake
        drained off. Source.
        of the river

        Zeb Pike explored
        as far as Cass L.,
        1805-06.

'Istorin is amateur and hence pure.
Without the language and Pound for guide, we found each site—
        in Rimini, Ferrara, Siena, Rapallo, Venice, Arles, Paris—
           and were comfortable
Our method was to drive into the center of town and get a room.
'Istorin is rank   amateur to the professional—
        Pound's Chinese,
                Olson's archaeology.

And Nietzsche wrote in his lifetime,
        three footnotes.

III
Nature is that in which no thing can be lost
does not mean we come here, to Itasca, to find
things or those who are gone or especially ourselves;
for the transformations of Nature are inhuman.
Even in the canoe, time pulled against us downstream.
But having climbed this far above the river, I had hopes
my poem would open up to democratic vistas;

whereas I found at the top I could not bring myself
to drink the cold beer, drinking in the scale,
you had to port the bottle down the bluff.
The first mile runs north
upside down, facing Hudson Bay, ignorant of downriver reputation
below it the long backwards fall to Hannibal and below
at this stage loved by immediate family only
its life is not much longer than our own lives.
Antipodal Alberti was unaware,
upside down as he was in Mississippi history,
of mound-building culture.
Pelegrin, Dante's word for "pilgrim."
What bird was it our canoe started from the wild rice?
But also *peregrine* the falcon.
"Have you noticed," she sd, "only men
   know the names of the stars?"
She who knows every bird, mushroom,
   the sources of flint by name.

   ITASCA
From *veritas* and *caput*, "the true source"
               of the Mississippi
               Schoolcraft's name for what amounts to
               his claim, Morrison before him
               (no government man, he)
               did not stop to
file.

               CAPUT
               source of the river
               root of plant
               top of tree
                  my dictionary tells me,
               main point
               chapter
               capital.

To my ear, Itasca makes vaguely Chippewa sounds
   or Ojibway, Marx brothers Italian.

The Chippewa girl who sold me gas
    made no sound at all. Unspoken hope
of the tribal Bingo Palace, beside

    The Great River Road:
trying to raise a family on roadkill.

"Anywhere," cried the poet inside Europe,
"out of this world!" But at the end of all
that travel, travail,
one must stand somewhere. Anywhere,
clearly will not do.
Except for men who confuse
weather for climate.
Travel only in-
tensifies the local,
multiplies it times itself
to the point of universality.
The business of
Melville's Cosmopolitan
is to know the native
taboos the business
of whitened amerika is the Calvin
in Coolidge, is what made him
leave evergreen Vermont.
And no river can run from that lowland puddle
Washington built on a slimy pool
Head not a source
but a dead and fetid end.
Ignis fatuus, the light
on Pound's grave?
Johann Bachofen drained the swamps
where the farmers till,
I work the flooded ground below.

IV

        Scent of slab wood
        heat from my stove
        the sleepy taste
        layers of comforters

                pillows for my head
                on the bed you have
                made for me makes
                a female appeal
                to drive into and thru
                still I am up driven
the idea of the poem is a source of irritation, a life beneath the host skin
                    insomniac with a flashlight
                    reading outhouse walls rush
                    light prose. Too nervous to
                    read biographies I've brot.
                    A tick on the prick.

Out   is   also
outis.

                                "Time Zone"
                  You Are Leaving the State of Solitude
                          Entering Loneliness
                        Be sure to set you watch
                              accordingly

After Husserl, Nature is a bracketed word.
And all nature-writers, philosophers.

                        "Turner's Minnesota Returned"
              FRONTIER, define as
those regions in the country
where books have to be carried in.
("Carry them out again, please
when you leave our park leave it
as you found it.")
                MEASURE the megalopolis
not by the circulation of newspapers
or the length of tv cables
or the written census of the illiterate poor

    but by mapping the reach of inter
        library loan

"This is the land of libraries and schools. St. Paul has three public libraries, and they contain, in the aggregate, some forty thousand books." (Life on the Mississippi)

The names of the winds,
                threnody
I have forgotten the names of the winds,
                            blow thru me
      Owl sounds
changes of direction inside the unfixed darkness
                        Duncan writing to Helen

Adam names birds.
Grown, in the dominion of old age, to look like birds.

V

                                      Home
last three days of writing the poem
brings back the mind's habitat, solo drive in the car, lines like roads on a map
                              periplus

Using the Cantos
        to prop open, at typewriter,
    The Sea of Tranquility, from which I copy out
                                          a poem in a letter
to Bemidji

Just when we ask Itasca, "Where can all this water come from?"
      there is more.
         At forty, I have thot of myself a poet
for twenty five years
and some days, I cannot
imagine writing a poem.

These words scanned randomly out of Williams' *Collected Poems*, Volume I:

                                                                twigtip   heartbreak
                                                             _____
                                                             lakewater horseplay

"I've carried around the intent [to write the letter] for many months; carried it with me to all the places" (a letter in today from Sharon Doubiago).

When letters go unanswered
When you begin to fear for the work,
The silence out there big as the shape of
     the unexplored Midwestern states
Is as nothing
Thinking of the immigrant wife's unwritten
               agoraphobia unto death.
She is lost in the world
It is a lost world
Poets cannot say they are neglected
It is beauty that is neglected.
It will not be as before
It will not be like saying good-bye
This time will not be a renunciation
Of having made a life in poetry.

              "How Far Can It Be If You Can Think It?"
                   The miles between us
                      never disappear.
            But they no longer separate
                     what we have
                  between us, pooling
                    our resources.

[May 12-June 12, 1990]

THE ZELOT PRESS

"I examined the Zelot all over for every small
snag and tiniest blemish, I repaired them with
patches, oversewing, inlets, pleats, it depended
what kind of tear . . . . in the end I got quite
caught up in the job." Celine, Death on the
Installment Plan (tr. John H. P. Marks).

Distributed by The Asphodel Book Shop, 17192 Rav
    Road, Route 44, Burton, Ohio 44021.

Chapters from

The Morrison Poem

(1992)

> Carpenter: Do you still read a lot?
> Morrison: No, not as much as I used to. I'm not as prolific a writer either. Like when, a while ago, I was living in this abandoned office building sleeping on the roof…I threw away all my notebooks…and these songs just kept coming to me. Something about the moon….(LA Free Press)

Chapter I
I don't like people
So
if my office resembles
the walkup dumper
Ch&ler built for Marlowe
you should know
not to be the first-
term coed who comes
to my closed Door for
IV answers & stays
surprised I have
nothing to offer
not even a remake
of The End the lizard's at
being the end of his
hypnotic chain swings
him teaching in PA
this time around.
The individual never does die
we are all lords who suffer
to know our own fate.

That was the first mistake.
From which all follows.

I've spent as if one night
what adds up to
twice my life
professing to teach i.e.
dancing with my pants down
film & poetry poetry &
film at eleven state schools
two generations of all wet
yet unwashed masses
out of which I myself
emerged. Flopped on the first shore
coughed water out of my lungs
& grew legs. Maybe four

percent would correctly
identify Raymond Ch&ler
on a multiple choice quiz
& maybe half would spell
"Philip" with one "l"
after three weeks of lecture.
The demigod "Rimbaud" a phonetic freak
punchdrunk & jogging forever in Philly.
So I've earned my dislike
& learned to stop giving
pop quizzes.

I'm Jim Morrison, alive all these years,
teaching at a private girls' school.
You should also know
I prefer Private Eye
to private dick or
any other form
of **Private Dozent**.

Hemingwaytao somewhere wrote
in one of his visionary modes
when he forgot to tell us
he'd grown a beard
on his boxing glove,
you should never let 'em
see you working. I liked to
keep the place littered
with cardboard boxes
styrofoam coffee cups
old bluebooks looking as if
no one ever worked there
or as if I hadn't quite
decided to take the job.
A bower as warm as human nature
or the indirect lighting above me.
Since the good men & 10 women
in the state legislature
saw fit to put up the funds
that were frittered away

Aber
sein Torso gluht.
(Rilke)

until only this white-
walled cubicle a window
overlooking one brick wall
of the library could be
built for my office hours
(a waste of space at that
I occupy it
fewer than four hours
a week 30 weeks a year)
I don't have the luxury
of collecting dustballs
in an outer office
Marlowe-style.
The dust stays with me
& the grey-brown metal
officefurniture gravemarker
desk I inherited
from a dead instructor
of English the joke goes
How can you tell? where I am
writing this tonight
a filing cabinet
I didn't ask for
issued because
I have an office
its horizontal files
never got unpacked
I use the shipping box
for my doorstop
a bookshelf with books
I don't need at home
where I work when eye works
the uncomfortable
institution-style chair
nobody is sitting in
comfortably or not
The two objects of value in the room
are my paper weight a marble chunk I stole
from the cemetery isl& the other Venice
near Pound's grave & a letter from Jean

Béliveau my childhood eyedoll thanking me
in broken dictated English for a poem
I'd written and sent him.

There are no papers
under that weight
I had the letter
properly matted
in Habs' team colors
& framed
then nailed it
to the thin wall
my shoe for a hammer.

No visitor has ever asked
about the paper weight or the letter.
Nothing was meant to impress
my visitors these days
mostly fellow instructors
the radical tenured as they say
bored between a day's forced
march of lectures or
the very occasional
student who thought she saw through
her instructor's well-cultivated cynicism
& into what was supposed to be
my intricately defensed love
for love read passion
passion for the printed word.
I liked to watch their long nervous legs
still growing out of the open
bottoms of their short skirts
as they took the chair beside my desk
& recited the speeches
that were just entering
their excited minds speeches
I'd heard and categorized
you see more is really one
to me since 7/03/71
Speeches not yet song.

The red marks
on the insides
of their knees

left from crossing
their legs for the
length of their
campaign
speeches

matched
the blush
on their cheek
bones
when they'd
finished
& walked
out.

The ones who were miserably failing
had stopped coming to the office
years before when I was no longer young
& tragically flawed. I missed them
& their calculated bullshit
"I need a good grade in your class
because I'm a pre-Med major"
more than I like the bright kids
"Isn't it true that the creator
of the character Billy Budd
was, himself, a repressed
homosexual?" who wanted to
adopt me as father & then
murder me.
But I was given
along with my tenure
which wears like religion in eternity
an office & a name
plate screwed to the door.
These benefits I treated

like the story of heaven
of retirement in a Miami courtroom
on social security
or the continental breakfasts
you sleep through
in the cheap motels of Iowa.
But I kept four hours
of office hours
about every week
during the two academic
terms in the year &
Philip Marlowe paid the rent
on his office
the first of every month. Doing the scales
for the 23,750th time like
the only prisoner in New Haven
that ordinary nite
who was not enrolled at Yale
or decoding Stevens by nitelite.
It was Fall Term last year when she came
through the door of my memorial to myself
like the angel appearing in 1922
after years of a dry spell & not writing
in Rilke's elegy.

There is a sense that no one is going to leave the room, ever.
(Joan Didion, THE WHITE ALBUM)

    How can eye describe her? Let's say
it would be easier for a UNLV basketball player
to graduate. For once it seemed
10 million years of evolution on earth
had paid off in the creation
of something more than AIDS
& a discrete system
of major credit cards
& 900 numbers
for phone sex
to subvert it.
Her lips were an argument
in favor of Darwin.
Milton would have written love poems
upon hearing her voice.

Strindberg would have made
a fool of himself
on the phone with her. Artaud
would have found her just right. She was
the one sweet-
est flashback. The only
woman on the atoll of von Sternberg's last vision
the only woman & all those soldiers
Not the blonde Ololon & not the soldiers at all
of a different army & TV.
Later her name would be to me
like an epithet for Athena & I
repeated it over & over
like one of the rhapsodes
singing Homer's epics.
Her breasts launched
a thous& dreaming
mountain men toward Wyoming.
Her dress & fashionable heels
were of dark blue the color
of blood returning to the chest
her stockings lighter blue.
Her hair was red
blood rich with oxygen.
Black eyes like dried
spills of your own blood.
Her eyes were set too wide apart
beneath eyebrows that were too fine
almost colorless so that
the overall effect of her face
was like the chivalrous concept
of Beauty we put in museums.
Those lovely, dreamy maidens—
500 years in the grave.
A man knew she was beautiful
the way he knows THE CANTOS
is great poetry though he cannot
read it all. She spoke first.
> "You're a hard man—
> to track—to earth,"

        She must have been using
telepathy I hadn't seen
her lips
move
as she
said this as she
looked at me
with her "I"s.
     "Not really," I tried to recover & the professional added: "My office hours—"
     "Look. You're never
in this office
Tuesday *or* Thursday
from noon to two o'clock.
You've got a secretary
paid minimum wage
with no benefits
who is either incredibly
loyal to you
or a neoNazi
& refuses to give out
your unlisted home phone
even when I claim to be
Robert Creeley
& on the fourth ring
your answering machine asks me
in a Parisian working class accent
announcing the next stop
is Pere-Lachaise
to leave a message
you never return."
     "Guilty. Okay, you've got me now. Please, sit. What can I do for you, eh, Ms.—?"
     "I have in my possession
as safely locked away as the thread in a plot by our boy
a certain notebook
Raymond Ch&ler kept
while they filmed
THE BIG SLEEP & murdered
his book."
     "Nice. Of course, I'd be very interested in reading anything—"

"You don't underst& Doctor.
The blue notebook is mine.
No special collections curator
in the country
including one who could
identify the bookstore
which published the memoir
A Shithead in Paris
is aware
of its existence."

"Then you should be advised to get it appraised & arrange to sell it, it's priceless, at an auction say—"

"Please. Don't interrupt
& don't treat me
like one of your lit majors.
I am fluent in 10 languages
& four systems of phosphine
hieroglyphics
I remember where I was
the day Douglas Woolf died
Beckett told me why
he married before he died
I know the Latin names
of south American birds
I've learned the legal birthdates of
anarchists poets & Louis Tiant
on 1/30/73 I see
I underlined in my copy
"In A. Huxley's phrase,
as Doors in the
Wall," so I knew early
never read *Perception*
without *Heaven & Hell*.
I was a film
star with Brakhage
& James Broughton
wrote my dissertation on Zukofsly's *A*
taught myself the music to
Helen Adam's ballads
& one night as San Francisco burned

I am on record
I outtalked Robert Duncan.
You have no time. Unless
we move right now tonight—"

      "Wait. Now, whoever you are & whatever you're selling, I'm afraid I have to butt in here. What do you mean by 'we' doing whatever 'tonight'?"

      "—The notebook proves
that the man we call Ch&ler
was not the man of Hollywood
& the biographies. It proves
conclusively
that Raymond Ch&ler was
not a man at all but a fictive
character created by the four
-fold mind of
Philip Marlowe."

      She claimed the notebook
      was at her house
      an easy four-hour's drive
      from campus.

Chapter II

      The house turned out to be in Ohio, the part they used to call The Western Reserve. At the close of the Twentieth Century, the lots of first-growth forests that had been reserved for Connecticut veterans of the Revolutionary War were all sub-developed into mowed lawns & developed into a strong of malls & drive-thru stores that lined the old highway like the skin of a snake that needed shedding. As we drove in her car west on the Pennsylvania & then the Ohio turnpike & the hills flattened into corn fields, the sun seemed to take an unnaturally long time burying itself into the brown horizon. The l&scape could not escape itself on this flattening plain between bands on the car radio. (Her one joke the whole drive was, dialing the radio, "Write it down if a poem comes, eh?") She did the driving & did not speak or invite small talk, so I concentrated on devising ways to keep the sun out of my eyes as I caught glimpses of her good legs expertly working the floor pedals.

      What is it, poets, about travel that makes us
      hungry for everything?

When we left the turnpike somewhere in Ohio, we drove for about the time it takes to proofread two chapters, in what I expect were a series of loops through the burned-over countryside, until she stopped the car in what seemed to be an arbitrary if not nonsensical place on Gambetta Avenue & announced, "We're here, Doc."

There was no need to drug me or blindfold me; the monotony of the l&scape worked just as well so that I could never get back here, or away from here, on my own.

Pam, her name was Pam, had spilled the map backwards across her folded lap.

Chapter III
    Philip Marlowe was doing more smoking than typing. Four typed pages had been turned through the wringer of his typewriter; beside them, enough cigarette butts to form the broken fingers of two corpses. He needed the money he knew a new novel would bring in &, increasingly since the unexpected success of his first attempt at writing a mystery, he needed to hear the applause one more time. Williams said we write out of need, but he didn't mean this kind of necessity. When he'd finished his smoke & the words still would not be still for the paper, he took up his ink pen & the blue notebook that was always at his right h& & made another entry:

There was no need to drug me or blindfold me; the monotony....

from

The Collected Later Poems of Philip Marlowe

(1998)

"Pick-Up On Noon Street"
A detail
not a
fragment:
the finger

prints
to study
like brush
strokes,

plays of
light
or word, guns—
an I.

"Why It's Only 'It's Only a Scratch'"
1
Because my blood tastes sweet to me,
I lick it off my finger.
2
A hero's blood tastes good
to everybody.
3
You scratch me; I'll be you.

"Farewell, My Lovely"
Some fatman's jeans
hanged by the cuffs until dry
without the unpainted house:

the little general's
private flag.

"The Little Sister"
…gist ain't quick enuf, Amigo.

"Death of a Hired Man"
He expired with the ease that work gets done
when you watch
somebody else
do it.

"The Flash"
For David Abel

might be gunpowder from a snubnose,
some photographer's bulb in your salad,
a badge in a wallet,
a white leg,
a phosphine hieroglyphic,
a climax, a conclusion, spittle,
Melville's Truth, a pearl-handled letter opener in the lumbar,
or Jacob Boehme selling something.
Better
answer it.

"And the Dodgers Were Bums in Brooklyn"
I consider myself
a small businessman,
got me an ad in the phone book the monthly light bill
& a key to the wash room
one floor down—
but, honey, what you're selling
requires a whole new kind
of buying.

"File"
He sold bold
songs to bored troubadours
of
unrequited vice
—just to watch.

She was the answer to the question
Why is it LA women seem to have
read
Sir Thos. Browne
too early?

Their affair makes the headlines:
Another foreign war
I never voted for;
another place in the world
where we send youth
to die.

"The Finger Man"
Luck does not accrue
It only makes you feel

lucky.

"The High Window"
A child who died a child
haunts this gap in the mountains.
Though the tooth is lost,
the tongue returns to it.

"The Wounded Partner"
The clearer outline,
as in Blake's drawings,
this time drunken laughter

READINGS ETC. AT THE BRIDGE BOOKSHOP

APRIL

21 THURS 8PM JANE BRAKHAGE The Autobiography of Stan Brakhage, chapters 5 & 6, can be found in the latest issue of "Motion Picture" magazine.

24 SUN 6PM GAVIN SELERIE British poet, author of Azimuth and Strip Signals — this is his first reading in the USA.

MAY

1 SUN 4PM DAVID ABEL Mayday! and the store's ½-anniversary.

5 THURS 8PM PIERRE JORIS An all-too infrequent appearance of the Luxembourgish poet & translator. Brescia, his selected poems, recently out.

8 SUN 6PM NICK PIOMBINO's long-awaited Poems is out from Sun & Moon Press, & this will be a publication party — no admission.

12 THURS 8PM RICH BLEVINS & BILL SHIELDS Rich is the editor and publisher of Zelot Press. Bill's Sparks from Hell is available at the Bridge.

19 THURS 8PM PETER WORTSMAN Eridanos Press has just published his translation of Posthumous Papers of a Living Author by Robert Musil. He'll read from that and from his own work as well — no admission.

26 THURS 8PM BILL KUSHNER & GEORGE FERENCI Check out Bill's book Head, published by United Artists. George will read stories and translations of contemporary Hungarian poets.

ADMISSION TO ALL EVENTS $3.00 UNLESS OTHERWISE INDICATED.
TIMES & DAYS VARY — PLEASE NOTE CAREFULLY.
SEATING IS LIMITED, SO DON'T BE TOO LATE.

THE BRIDGE BOOKSHOP — 117 EAST 7TH STREET
212 533 3459 (BETWEEN FIRST AVE. & AVE A)

HOURS: TUES–THURS 4PM–MIDNIGHT; FRI 4PM–2AM; SAT NOON–2AM; SUN NOON–8PM. CLOSED MONDAYS.

against a hospital block.
To enter here, we must
do the essential things
alone. Back on the street,
the stars above your room
open catalog of what
we cannot buy.

[Boston cancer ward]

"Scotch"
For George

Your jaw brushes her, her beautiful indifferent hem.
Years ago, cut your private eye
teeth elsewhere on her; these were the wisdom.

What were you doing down there, partner, did you think you were doing?
Silken slip soaking in hem
lock nightly nightie.

You've scraped your jaw against the wall supposed to be
keeping out infinity.
No—-infinity is not, in any century, white;
it is the blonde of our desire.

Our ghosts are tyrants—-
They cannot die.
Because we do,
We know too much.

Singing to herself, she hears you. She must have been waiting for a very long time keeping an ear out for you for a very long time yet apparently intent upon her polishing job. She answers in rehearsal as if you had buffed both brown shoes on the nervous backs of trousered legs, adjusted your dick side-right, and then knocked on her parents' front door, secretly knowing that they were already settled into their motel in Pasadena for the whole weekend.

Your touch reverberates inside her.

When nobody answers, the girl resumes her task, polishing next a pair of red pumps with a bow. It does not seem an ambiguous statement to her. She keeps on singing, keeps on beaming, almost at home in her body.

"Lowered to his Office like a Soldier"
She came to Hollywood Boulevard to hire me
at twenty-five dollars a day
two-hundred minimum
plus expenses;
I gave her the view from my office.
She seemed unimpressed when I told her
we're one-hundred and fifty-six feet
beneath the tallest buildings
city hall allows.

"More Free Advice to his Client"
Yes, a hero is always in love
with two women at once,
his muse & his
death.
No,
your husband cannot be
considered a missing person
if he does not try to be
found.

"Poem Noir"
For Bonnie

Low in the seat in my car in your street,
I doze below the snapbrim horizon

the dream of not having to
make love with our shoes on.

The biggest dream,
of having time:

You see the moon once
in a bucket of water,
& think you'll find it
there when you get back.

"Room Service"
Moonrise

My part of the day. Awake now,
with the moon above my head like a fresh bottle of blood
the lovely, cold nurse has just brot just for me I see
by its dripping
light, into the corners of my room,
all next day.

"Red Wind"
In his running to & fro without headlights
unmarked nevada roads
ventilating cool desert night
past asbestos towers
beyond the burning city—
Marlowe,
the wounded healer,
passes himself driving the other
way before doubling back
on the same
tarot roadkill skull.
Other/wise,
how to describe the sensation of being
hard inside an even
harder woman?

"Hum"
In LA, where the
cars they do not
rust, we must
crush them.

"The Paranoid Crematorium"
This place needs dusting
for fingerprints:
Someone who came thru here
must have been guilty
of Something.

"Exhibits"
She stabbed him to death with a knife of ice
then cooled her gimlet
with the evidence.

Ax murder in a tiled bathroom;
making love in a tomb.

Neat, professional jobs.

"A Portrait of Madison"
For Bill Shields

The insane one, chicken-
fucker neighbor, always trims his dead lawn
in tightening concentric circles, so that
his clippings will not need raking, will
necessarily as a result of his meticulous weekly process
fall all in a pile
(for his good wife, my lover, to tote to the curb).

Life, Ptolemy, is never so neatly carried off.
Instead we find, after years on the same block
living in the land where daddies always die first
sucking up the calm dinner hour of welcome home daddy,
next door lives insanity divorce murder ruin disgrace impotence
ambsace AIDS incestuous stupidity infirmity fugue poets in drag
or anything this time but
the other fucker

"Clue to Emily"
After Camille Paglia

She dealt her pretty words like blades—Dickinson.

A finger—-a middle finger—-rolls in—-
Dropped thru the mail slot—-in my outer office—-
Under the door of my—-locked—-private one—-
And across both dusty floors—-to me—-in medias phone.
I finish my call, roll a cigarette—-I pick up the visitor—-
Ruin a good hanky—-marvel at its momentum, its aim—-
Its instantly dominant pronoun reference—-Thinking
To use it, in some—-other—-epic.

"The Long Goodbye"
Wally's poem

Somebody's always writing incorrectly
a poem about a flower,
when it is the flower
with a poem in it.
We write in the presence of death
mostly lies, suicide notes
about "the death we wade thru" to get to the typewriter,
misrepresenting the cautionary one
about the posy.
The lady of the lake, it turns out,

is the lady *in* the lake.
The tragedy of mid
-life is not, finally, its proximity to Death
but the growing need to fabricate
more lies
before dying.
When Her promise should
clarify our thinking.
The black rose unfolds: it is
the end, with the poem inside it,
we sniff at, eventually pluck,
and take inside

"Black Mask"
[At 40]
Letters from my death make me crazy,
but I live—-for the next one.

[At 20]
Poems from the muse drive me mad,
but I'd die—-for another one.

"Colorized Version of Basic Black"
The way other people start to believe in God at 80,
the drivers of the politic cars formed a black convoy,
doing 80 on the freeway, back from Forest Lawn.
Serra's sun
made venetian blinds from a stand of palms,
for maybe 10 seconds, in passing—-
adding a lyric head
to the epic ache.
"Your dress is very becoming," I offer to the black widow.
"You're late," she shoots back.
"It's always
already there."

"'There is a moment after death when the face is beautiful...'"

Quick, before the muse comes down, I go thru her desk...

The top drawer is a box of neon light,
everything objective in the room
falls in & doesn't
come out again.

Next drawer is a draw-er
in the court of the Queen of the Angels,
falling in & out of favor,
he makes sketch upon sketch for her portrait.
It's hard work to draw her out
of the sheets, white upon white.
She won't sit still for it.

Quick, while steps are returning, I rifle the contents of her desk:

Find
a mouthful of blood,
a drawer of her perfume,
a bottle of Kennedy Scotch,
pearls for a necklace fired as slugs
from a chrome .38, a stone from the bottom
of La Brea, a glossy of me, age 6, laughing in a cowboy suit,
train tickets for two, rain checks for one,
a cigarette radio lipstick davenport
on which Jackson MacLow sits reading a newspaper,
a gothic arch with a false bottom,
a French kiss (English text facing),
her bound leather appointment book
with the time, day, & place of my death kissed on a page in red lipstick.

I just manage to close
the drawer containing a phone call coming in the middle of sleep, when
she enters the long room & I am
for some unexplained reason
sitting in her chair

behind her desk
drinking her Scotch
watching her
face, as she comes on.

[Read at the Granary, May 1, 1991]

"'The drunkenness of great fear...'"
The girl in the next room is why I write,
but she cannot know I'm here. Always
listening at the membrane for her
acoustical return—-door slam, air space, spigot.
I imagine a design on my eardrum
to match the design of the wallpaper.
The sound of her turning on
the bedside lamp, like crickets
lost inside a dark trim lawn.
Once when I suddenly felt sure she was
bending there at her end table writing a poem
about me, I panicked for a minute
before reason returned alone to its
own rented room.
If I go outside to eat,
they'll lock me out
and sell my clothes.
Some days the drink I am drinking seems too weak,
but it means I can stay like this virtually forever.
She never
answers the phone. I never call.
I can make love in this position virtually forever.
Sometimes
about suppertime I play a tape to make it sound
like a family on this side reuniting
after its members' various days.
When I know she's in, I try to use the water
about as much as an LA family of 2.8 would.
But because she grew up in Portland
my demographics are probably off.

Her tv must be (a) bust, or (b)
she much prefers to watch with the sound down.
Twice a week, there is the lingering scent
of Chinese take-out. Marihuana not for a long time.
If I'm watching a sitcom
I'll cue my tape of the three voices
laughing their appropriate ages, gender, and dispositions;
if it's a drama night, I play full-blast
thirty minutes of Silent Longing.
One particularly bad night, when I needed to call her
or knock on her blue door or knock it in,
(d. All of the above are true.),
I found Emerson translating the Vita Nuova:
"Whatever in the mind hinders dies
When I come to behold you, o beautiful joy,
And when I am near you, I hear Love
Who says, Fly, if you are loath to die…
And through the drunkenness of great fear
The stones seem to cry, Die, die.…"
—-Which makes no sense to me today The
Stones are still playing Sympathy for the Devil
somewhere inside the bowl of southern California.
Ageless drum slam, air space, spigot.
I mark my days in this captivity like
so many hyphens in the old headline,
DUMB ASSED DOUBLE BARRELED SHOT GUN TURNED ON
MIDDLE AGED PUNCH DRUNK MAN HELD IN CASE
BY GIRL NEXT DOOR AND HER CLEAN CUT.
Whereas drinking in the morning is worse than drinking
alone is much worse than not drinking at all.
To reload:
I mean, if I am the soft underbelly,
Then she is swallowed alive in its fat gut.
I mean everybody's dead but us.
I've got no one any longer
to get back to.

"The Marriage (as if, To Cissy Chandler)"
The triumph of Spring is
not the false promise, gift of innocence
("It will not snow"),
but comfort in knowing
this morning's snow will dissolve
almost as quick as
it falls.
Ours, darling, has been what they call
a good match.

"Raymond Chandler's Tomb"
I own no trees, rent them from the landlord whose savings & loan owns the house.
Your leaves blow in my yard, my leaves blow in yours.
No one takes
responsibility.

"A Line of Poetry, A Line of Traffic"
From Bob Podgurski

The California registration
tag on the column told me
her red sedan
belonged to Death.
When you tail the muse,
Never Forget:
"Nothing corners
like a
company car."

"Playback"
"Close the door behind us, please
Let my shadow sit with yours awhile.
Even in this darkness, Marlowe,

my story holds you
with the beauty of an indecipherable passage
music that is heard once,
then forever gone & without reference.
We no longer need to speak in metaphors
We no longer need to speak
We just need.
You have created me by your talking
into a machine winding up at your feet,
almost silently erasing silence.
Drink this; sleep now.
When you play this back
it will be a recording of an LA rainstorm
drumming against the window
of your ear."

from
Fogbow Bridge: Selected Poems

(2000)

"American Larch"
For JoAnn

Our lone tamarack lacks the faith
Of evergreens. Its needles fall
To cynic winter.

Barren, the shadeless larch
Most anticipates the ship's mast
It will never be.

Astride, instead, a sandstone crest
Its roots sound groundwaters
Deep beneath the upheaved floor
Of the once and future inland sea.
Its stoic fruit, a cone.
Its needles fall. Still,

Your change distinctly speaks to me
Of what eternity must be.

Each spring you seem "astonished
Into heaven…." A bit later, each year,
For your own resurrection.

"The Red Hand at Tulum"
After reading Judith Roche's <u>Myrrh</u> on a ship to Cozumel

I have gladly broken my nose
into a beak for you. I wanted to
be beautiful in your eyes.
As a child I wore the wax
ball between my brown eyes
until they crossed perfectly
in daily anticipation of you,
look, I have shaped the profile
of my face to please you

the wood molds are discarded
with infancy but the arc sinks
from the bridge of my nose
in a perfect invitation to your touch.
Trace the tattoo along the line
of my high cheekbone with your fingers
before we kiss. You see, I have already
filed my teeth for you and inlayed
the precious stones you sent me.
I have long prepared for your coming
I have painted this hand vermillion, chac,
and my right hand ocher, kan.
I have pulled back my straight jet hair
into a braid at the top of my head tonight,
I have bathed my flesh in balsam,
studded my nose and lips and ears
with rings suggesting a percussive music
undistinguished by the loudmouthed priests
when I sneak out of my sleeping parents' hut
in the village outside their low stone wall,
dance to your embrace.

"Lies for the Coming Inquisition"
If it's true
        the rebel firing squad stuck a rifle up Lorca's ass,
I'm satisfied I know
something about the world.

I know they thot they were only killing a man
                                          who loved men,
and we think that
we're learning how the last poets died. Ask yourself

why Lorca's murder doesn't add up to his beloved Dalí's
Obsession with St. Sebastian; why
my favorite sentence in Gibson's biography reads: "There is no record
of anyone

ever
having seen Lorca run"; why my own teachers,

the impossible fathers,
                        were radical homosexuals;
or why so many U.S. poets are writing broken sonnet cycles tonight,
half a century since the soldiers laughed

and pulled the trigger
                        twice.

Sections from "A Flock of Landscapes" (1989)

"A Good Early Start"
I don't teach again
                        til September,
        and today
                            is June thirteen.

My waking thot
is like a good early start,

                        and it's into the streets
              to ogle

                        the art

                        of Florence:

  two perfect mini
  skirts atop bikes
  stopped in traffic,

legs that Botticelli painted in secret
legs many believed to be lost, until now.

                        The light changes.

I suppose they're off to the office.
I decide to break for an early lunch.
The traffic this morning is heartbreaking.

"A Superior Air" (Homage to Cendrars)
Your french garçons aren't so tough
I call them "boy" and they take it
Everything out of my mouth in the last three days
begins "Je voudrais…"
I take it to them
I sit at the head of my round table
immensely happy
The river of small talk,
all of it quite pleasantly incomprehensible,
makes an island of me
Baudelaire lived on an island in the Seine
I read somewhere
(we'll have to go there)
But I am more an Iceland
The french sometimes fly high over me
but never visit
When I shout the proper nonsense
the noise dismisses the boys from the room
And when they return they place dinner before me
I am always careful
to settle the inflated bill
by presenting a Fauvist's bouquet
It's all stage money anyway
We always practice our addition
like two good boys, before I leave my table
Being a child again
delights me.

"Thermidor 1989"

                              The french royalists valued,
                              above all, their beautiful

                              skin. If we can believe them,
                              the leaders of the revolution

                              (all witnesses stress this)
                              had bad complexions.

Danton, disfigured boy on grandfather's farm:
                his twisted lip
                          (bull-gored child
                              sucking a cow teat);
                his smashed nose
                          (another bull);
            scars on cheeks and eyelids
                          (trampled by the hooves
                                of pigs!);
the ravages
of smallpox.
Marat, who hid himself in the sewers of Paris, contracts
          prurigo, a disease of the skin so repulsive

                                                fellow delegates

                                                could not bear

        his company.
And Robespierre, The Incorruptable?
   pitted cheeks;
   grey-green eyes;
Mme. De Staël's description of his green veins
is oft repeated.
          Only Mirabeau was undeniably attractive to women.

      tho terribly
            scarred by the pox.

What survives

is the spectacle

The ancient régime

curled about Paris;

at once shedding

its corrupted skin,

and intent upon

Saving it.

"3 A.M., Hotel Europa, Ferrara"
Vivaldi,

                Napoleon,

                              Casanova—

all slept here,
it has been
        that long
long before the invention of the motor-
               bike, since anyone could

sleep here. These walls
are thin as veal.
The local lasagna
is green. Old men
               stop in the streets to pat my son's head.

  Must be
one of the Estes
escaped Dante's
hell, tonight, assuming the earthly form of a biker, a loud buzzing

                mosquito of a shade,
         riding up and down below.

      Vivaldi?   Napoleon?

and Doug, admiring the badly drawn murals
                                    15 feet above his bed:

"Neat.
We got

      our own
        private

cartoons
with this

room!

"Voyageur, I write"
For Mary de Rachewiltz

"…we cross this water, leaving Venice
                                where you crossed over
leaving us,
      this standing-room passage,
       the violent air above deck. Everything swinging
to clear the last canal,
sends before us
        the dark crests running out
                          into the open
  stretch
to San Michele."

                In a crowd, I stow away
                Note
-book in backpack;

    shoulder the dead
     weight of things I knew
            to bring.
Better to write
inconspicuously
on the backs of
spent tickets:

mine, my wife's, our son's.
At every new shock we feel

surely the engines announce our
coming. But all knocks are

routine and absorbed
into the bricks of the low-slung wall

keeping the mortuary
island dry.

        We will be unannounced as we were
        first trip across, 60 hours west of Akron

        Jess answered the door in a welder's hood,
        and we took turns reading

        The Venice Poem in the mission park
        til Duncan returned at dark.

        For my letter

        had not preceded us.

What I felt, high
in the campanile,
I feel again:
        when someone leaned too far

        to videotape
the working liquid
        brain, "Its barber poles—*dispacci*—
are synapses!"
Of three facts,
I am suddenly certain:

That the waterbus is the number 5.

That the Italian sun makes a diesel noise.

That the marble steps begin

beneath the surface.

        2

"*Dove,*
        the lovely word."

Here meaning
my confusion
For I am washed up
drip miserably
on cold steps
Must be the
morphemes
of Dante I hear
returning to
the sea
    to spawn.

There is one sign, then nothing.

How am I to find you, Ezra Pound?
How do I inquire politely
    after you? These are tombs.
            In Paris,
I carried maps thru the gardens

right to the little gate, bis.
                              Gas coupons
in her business hand, the Rapallo attendant
directed us, Go all the way down
        (she waved her free hand),
                                down to the sea.
And we found the K2 Bar,
                        its alleyway entrance,
more appropriate than
the seaside grand hotel.
                    But who will know you
   here? These citizens
   have other worries:
   after 12 years,
   their remains
   are dumped out.
One sign, then nothing.

       3
"The handfuls of finger-

        long lizards who

withdraw

            to unthinkable chambers,
all claws at my footfall,

must know."

The lizard you say upheld you knew;
the guards around you forbidden to speak

—Pops into mind—Vanishes—
Somewhere below nearby.

("*A man on whom the sun,*" etc.)

Marble that is by this clime warmed
stays warm to the touch,

long after the sun has gone.

                                               "Clarel's just now in;

                                               Out all night again

                                               Reading Cantos
                                               By the true light

                                               Of the fuochi fatui."

           4

We wander, thru
the wall put up by the church
into another part of the yard,
where you are
beside the path, in good shade.
A woman with her back always to us
cleans leaves from a grave.
The lizard on your name POVND
   retreats beneath
dry ivy and hosta.
He is already whispering
  in your ear
news of our arrival.

           5
Next day, my shy guide

                                 the lizard on your grave

reappears in Rimini.

Sculpted now,

he stretches out full length: luxuriating among bronze fruit and leaves.

The putti here, in the form of baskets.

Duccio has him patiently

waiting for us

to catch up.

Two Sets from "Longplaying" (1994)

"Slight Return"
For David Rattray
the muse ain't sick / she's stoned

(The sun is in
his head storm
clouds play

dark patches
cross a poet's
paper mind

so often
he's left blind
like me,

ancient tree
sentry of
my mountain.

I still love how
picnics retreat
into their city—

Then the poet
is left to do
my lemony dreaming.)

                       "If the abysm
Could vomit forth its secrets—but a voice
Is wanting, the deep truth is imageless…."

                       Ah, shucks.

after Shelley
writing plein-air:
in the old dream,
wind and water
shape the earth,
but Earth is form.
I'm ageless Seathl
I hear whispers
in the cosmic
wind   deadening
before a frozen
waterfall: folksongs
from a maelstrom.
                  After
Melville's "Advance,
ye mates! Cross
your lances full

before me. Well done!
Let me touch the axis":
Fire and lightning
ravage old earth,
but Earth is sung song.
Reading Pound's reading
Fenollosa on lightning
within my porch bed-
room full of mirrors,
Cooper practicing daily
his electric guitarsus
even in this rainstorm
locked in a pattern,
strum over Kent
—inside Ohio.
Ends the ePAINesis.

"The sentence form was forced upon primitive men by nature itself. It was not we who made it; it was a reflection of the temporal order in causation. All truth has to be expressed in sentences because all truth is the **transference of power.** *The type of sentence in nature is a flash of lightning."*
      Fender body flashes midflight in strobelight fashion
       of a Burchfield watercolor moth's
        sudden release—to struggle
         against an unseen
        wind. In the dark
        room at noon
        instru / mental
       music has its own image.
       And it is always playing
    A little theater plays only one film every matinee
        it's Rainbow Bridge
       just behind his brown eyes
       and in the expression
      on her orange face as she dances
       without him but to his song:
     The guitar is in his mind, mental instrument
        It looks upside down to her—
      a mirror image only her retina converts.

                    The image is nowhere in the world
                    The image is nowhere in the words
                              "Don't be late."
                  It moves his fingers as if in the act of making
                    love they move themselves he imagines
                        with a life only notes inhabit,
                      fleeing before the sense he makes.
                Feminine is the guitar body her strings pluck't
                      by his teeth or rubb'd behind his spine
                    but the long neck, play'd between his legs,
              becomes masculine in the transformation: legendary plaster casts
                            —fingers like Cocteau's,
                              eyes like Picasso's,
                              a song like Blake's
                      and Duchamp's tongue in everyone's cheek,
                            but a cock like nobody's—
                        The guitarist is the body electric,

and singing (1970):
A cop is drearily keeping
The first violations of his day;
Beside him salute the parking meters
Yesterday's blackeyed blonde danced with
Til the first rays of the new rising sun.

We are the survivors,
We are the children of grass,
Assembled here on the commune steps

Having faithfully tripped the evening.
We watch the day world coming to
Work in the city ignorant of the clouds
Above the cop's hat that make an alphabet
We cannot quite read.

Beethoven, they tell us, died during an electric storm. It follows that Brahms and Mahler must have been afraid of lightning. Shelley played with it. But Hendrix plugged in. the implications are, at first, Romantic; on second strike, however, the current running in an amerikan tradition since Franklin lights up the bored:

                     "*the thunder rolling…we scatter over the cliffs, Herman Melville to seat himself, boldest of all, astride a projecting bowsprit of rock….*"

    Like lightning to the lightning bug, Twain's right reason.

"Poem Of The Clouds Decoded" (1993)

The final sight unplugs my eyes   her face
        never to feel the same about a thing
again.

Tired of
the strangers, the girls who loved me

more than I could

ever imagine loving anyone,

girls looking like the models on the posters of the Art
Nouveau.

Dropping
the weight of Experience, I am
sending this strato-cast-brilliant

casket

parachuting

bright to dull earth where I got it without asking;
I am putting the match to all guitars

across the city tonight, o
Seattle. And if some idiot Trelawny comes crawling
after me,

plucks a bootleg tape
from one heavily documented pyre
and melts
his hands on Shelley's heart instead,
tell him for me:
"All dichotomies are simply

square."

Tell him
in the future, for "Axis: Bold As Love," please read
HENDRIX: BLACK AS CHRIST.

Tell him I am dropping my guitar to follow
its lead
thru the tiniest of windowpanes,

breaking

and entering the purple room
even Pym condemned in his epistemology.
Condemned to see, when eye

close the lid to my
I,
the face my corpse makes

glowing
white in the hymnsweet Parlor of
Phosphenes,
in the hull of the Baptist Grampus,

where I see myself unfolding

getting to my feet out of the folding
chairs of mourners.
Entering

the circle of the promise of the fogbow.

---

like 'Die Brucke' wood-cuts
"Fauvist" splashes of color — Stravinsky's
'Rite of Spring'

---

things I've done on mescaline:

— sat cross-legged approaching 3 hrs
listening to Joan Baez talk peace;

— saw/heard dug Ginsberg - Duncan
in a Kent auditorium seat afterwards
standing across a folding table f/ Allen!
speachless;

— visited Museum of Modern Art for my 1st time standing without wanting to speak before Jackson Pollock's spilling map of the expanding universe; expanding map of the spilling universe; ~~was map its 1/28~~

— fucked for the 1st time second story window raining outside after ~~2001 Space~~ "Woodstock" ~~Odessy~~ ~~strolling~~ out afterwards to get a pop;

— composed a sentence in ancient Greek that is, to say 'THIS BOOK MUST END' in greek while you and Ed drove the length of Ravenna, tripping.

                                          1:53 a.m. it's 1/28

His observation *"there ain't no life nowhere"* proves largely accurate. The known universe appears vacuous. Why, then, make a longplaying record of it? Why compulsively note our individual passages when all the deaths of all the heroes in hell do not add up to one good *Eureka*?

Because the dance of matter is so rare in this part of the galaxy as to be always unexpected. Noteworthy. Poetic. Because some men's brief lives are conduits thru which physics plays. Because, once knowing place, we must yearn for space.

"Thou art an utter dark, yet unto me / my day."

Begins the paRAINesis.

And when we had not died with them after all
  at twenty, at thirty, past forty
Alone in a shoreless world of no heroes left
  between us and our deaths. Open land
no horizon

        When we picture the musicians,
        he stands alone as if without sidemen
         we can plainly see boundaries
        exactly where the flashbulb ends
        darkness begins in the photo in the
        album of the live band on stage.
  The acid-head looked up and saw
  himself, in a stranger's bathroom
  mirror, grow old and decompose
  he returned to the kiva kitchen
  argument about serving Marx the last
  of today's brown rice the last time
  he would ever listen to John Mayall.
And now,
  we have lived without them.

                                                                                    It's
raining
            the water we wash

            the dead in,
                                                                              again.

                        Eternity's letter to the editor of today
                                    begins at home:

"We own our own

            graves,

                                    do we not?"

            THE CHAIRPEOPLE POETS OF AMERIKA SCARE ME

            YOU'RE NOT SURPRISED TO HAVE LIVED SO LONG.

                    JUST PLANNING TO LET THE SUN
                              CLEAN IT UP?

We kept the carcass / hung it on the wall.

               Life?
My best advice is,
Do a half.

                                (The taxi's headlights
                                    at night idling
                                 in the (idle) trees

                                      winter stands by
                                      the falser idols
                                       of our youth:

                                          madness free
                                               love
                                        intoxication

                                    This is the triumph
                                       of life, this is
                                the unfinished page
                                         newly disc
                                      -overed in the

                                    drowned sun's
                                          pockets
                                      at the bottom
                                         of the sea

"Larf"
All these years I've wanted to
write beginning where you did:
"I love you 'cause you tell me
things I want to know." That's how,
land-locked in Ohio, I loved John
the smart one, John the working-
class hero, the bad Beetle. Certainly
I did not want my first hallucination
to be the death of Kennedy. That's why all,
all the acid and the mescaline, when they came
later on, were more like flashbacks.
Why I'd named the campus newspaper
Left And Right Forum, my nervous laugh
at politics, after John's joyceless story.
I'd wanted to begin in Liverpool,
where Redburn's boyhood ended
and Cobbett thot to bring in Tom Paine's
bleached bones in his suitcase.
And when the news came that you too
had been killed I wanted you to
tell me
how it was you knew to write
"Happiness Is A Warm Gun."

Waiting for mail during blizzard

The White Album on

My needle reads the line that curls in

Snowed in
happy
new year

notice how
otherwise
snowy cover

shows three
dirty
circles where

once

a record
was.

For Douglas

High Season: A Sonnet Cycle

(1996)

To Steve Ellis, during his tour of the Old World

FOURWORD: PART ONE
  I. "Was that the landmark?"
Paul Celan's son juggles in a circus.
Midnights, Sonny's bridge becomes
A crossroads. Pascal's barometer predicts:
Twisters through Mackinac and partly sunny
For Seattle. (In case they've overlooked
Anything valuable, we'll dig up all
The basements—build New Hibbing half a mile
South of here—make a fit place for a poet

To put behind him. "Another Poem
For Long's *Memoranda*," to begin:
"I have no memory
After 1914…," and rebroadcast
From his pyramid by Pastor Russell,
Whose visionary eyes in death are flat.

  II. "Spheral Change"
Are flat, but how likely are *two* flat tires?
Ignoring The Inevitable (Holmes's
God) in our flat speech, -lands, -out drives across
A tableland the great plains slant toward—
A (me(mory)) of the twice-great inland sea,
Inhabited by that seahorse, blood up to its neck, we call
The curving part of the temporal
Lobe, where storied remembrance gets stored: "Hippo-
        campus,"
          (
).

Whenever I see butterflies, I think of Helen.
I *don't* remember Clifford. It was Ken who,
Visiting, recalled both anecdotes. When
I see him in Lawrence, I'll be back
From Oregon. Only some, Elizabeth
Siddal is one, do not return to us,

   III. "When sea / And wind are one with memory."
Persist as memory as if history
Had stopped, before the two wars, and Heaven
Only an advertisement for
Christianity. Foucault used the study
Of history, like Ishmael the sea,
To keep from going
Crazy. Absence of work is madness.
If history stops in 1914,

Or dies alone on a train in Texas.
If I leave no visible trace
Of the sonnet I started out to write
When this comes in instead, it is because
The text predicts itself,
Its own end, and I listened. Prophecy

   IV. "When where I was you too might stay"
Is really an erasured form lacking
More Intent. Maybe Duncan's right: we do
Reincarnate ourselves as different
People, reform ourselves between brackets
We think hold "a life." The kind of order
Reserving rooms for a trip represents.
Then begins the double sonnet to her:
"I'm inside you, at last. / You talk

About your day." To begin West, in Rossetti's
Twilight, where the sun sets like a redhead
In high season, includes Ellen West.
(When I'm writing, even Tarsus is in
High season: notes on walk, jot on rock, pocket'd.)
This is the day I must uncomplicated my life.

[On hearing of the death of Stephen Spender]

WESTWORD: PART TWO
   V. [Grayling, Michigan: first sleep]
And if the poet suffers afterthoughts
When he has set the date for the last day,
Let him endure the horrors of the grave-
Robber; I intend Emerson, who peeked
Twice, not Rossetti, who forgot his lines.
Now I remember Ken's other story:
"I have hitch-hiked to see two poets,"
Young Robert told Graves. "Ezra Pound,

And Laura Riding!" Decorum's a word
You don't hear / say twice in the same way / day.
Hearsay. Sherwood Anderson simply walked—
Out of the office forever—one day
Like the one we've chosen to leave Ohio
Behind in "the joy of obscurity!"

   VI. [At Sable Point, The U.P.]
Way back from shower pick my way across
Open ground where sand will be snow in weeks.
Time I found the big two-hearted river,
All he had left was a two-fistedness:
When those men yelled for pasties, they were fed.
Both the former rain and the latter rain
Strike my tent all day, at night, left and right,
Mercilessly. I'm asleep inside it.

On the road to Hibbing, my son will sleep
But his hands somehow knowing keep hold
Flawlessly the CD playing *Blonde on Blonde*.
"How far to the mountains?" "When does the monster
Show itself?" On the trip; in the film—
The child observes the man.

   VII. [Hibbing, Minnesota]
Be you prophetic like Verlaine
Throwing the jars of his mother's abortions,
His unborn brothers in madness,
Back at her? Song of

The shattering glass at her feet, fragments
Like quotation marks in the air between.
Telling his mother, "I must
Uncomplicated my life." No place

That does not see him. Name your poems
Essays, your prose *Poems*. What knows itself
Is form; what reveals itself is language;
Whatever must constantly renew itself is
Human, from forms informed. Dante's
Lot: a wife for oils—a mistress for busts.

  VIII. [The Plains: Minnesota/N. Dakota borderline]
The Plains begins, west of Fosston
On Highway 2, in its most prosperous
Form. Welcome Open. Now the wind becomes
A force, a helping tailwind or a wall
Ahead. After Mentor, irrigation
Ditches, trucks raising dust on distant roads
Take over—the politeness of gentle-
Men farmers now scarce as cities. Lucky's

"Nothing really to turn off." You can see,
Before Crookston, the earth's curvature. Once
Clear of Minot, bloated state-fair-week fares,
The landscape is western for the first time.
Virga
                       draping one horizon.

  IX. Bear Paws, revisited
Revisiting—-revising—-thinking twice—-
Rereading—-is more like a cutback,
Moving us vertically as well
As back, more than the simple return
Trip over old ground. Taking the road marked
"NO GAS NEXT 110 MILES" and back
Is no recipe. Had to, after twelve
Years, come all this way back to realize,

Though the dissertation on Will Henry
Made me otherwise compulsive to see
Everything for myself, I had had no
Stomach for surrender, screw the speeches
Vindicating their neat Hiroshima.
Just kissed the rock from where the sun now runs.

  X. [Logan Pass, at Hidden Lake, i.]
  Dear Sherman Paul, etc.: From here,
The record of the hike reads like a dream
Journal. We sit "for a *spell*," too, on this
Redrock bench inviting sun and sheltering
Spine from constant wind. On the long approach
To these mountains, yesterd'y, I'd wanted
My poem to be like the virga rain
That falls, dark blood, from the peak-gutted cloud

Because the virga cannot reach the plain
Before evaporating. (You try to
Analyze the poem: —It disappears.)
Can today's sonnet be another rock,
Shaped then lost to rubble, when the glacier
It has no memory of receded?

  XI. [At Hidden Lake, ii.]
Where the poet's consciousness is not on
Record. Instead, natural process,
Mindless of the eye's attachment to brain,
Overrules all else. Is this fascism,
Or what is authentic in the world?
Do not follow Thoreau here, down this path
To his door, where he sits his rude table
Counting his nails. Be the-man-in-the-world.

Our path leads to man's place postmortem,
The one given him—not the place he dreams
To take. Man's hubris convinces him
That glacial pool of vision he has struggled,
Admittedly, to gain—is not over-
Whelmed by the next vista, around the bend.

XII. [At Hidden Lake, iii.]
Few learn to read the work of ice and wind
On the textual rock. Do simile
And personification bootprint truth,
Delicate at *any* altitude, so
To confuse its record? (Mythology's
Imbedded parentheses seem to
Engender speaking straight.) In a hurry,
Even here, to go around and lap the man

Who stops to write or read what he has thought.
(No protocol, if he's without a camera?)
Who would aspire to be a poet should
Wear a sign on both shoulders: "SLOW MOVING
VEHICLE FOR METAPHORS TURNOUT AHEAD."
The record of the hike reads like a dream.

XIII. [At Hidden Lake, iv.]
Carry in—-.
Carry out—-.
Wear a bell:
Tells the grizzly.
Traverse glacial snow
As you would approach
Asking a favor. Never
Look a bear

In the eye.
Dry shoes:
Big deal.
Meriwether
Is today's pass-
Word.

XIV. [At Hidden Lake, v.]
Overstay day's snowball welcome,
"Going-to-the-sun'll
Ice up on you."
Do not feel apparent cuteness nor dread

The encounter with randomness grazing.
Japanese tourist family gathers
To remark a square of ground:
Hoary marmot / lost a contact lens?

German is spoken here. Baseball box-scores.
Bury your shit; boil the thinking water.
"Squeeze the flesh—address the wound," she told him.
Please don't fool the animals. Pop your fears.
Welcome drying sun; build against night's wind.
Be lower than harm. (I said that, he said.)

 XV. Love, Rich [Moraine, vi.]
Catalog of all fragments, broken tongue
Of ancient glacier. Whisky jacks are louder.
Canucks visit the backs of lost twenties;
        Japanese leave
            no stone
              unphotographed.
We enter the Gates of Banff
Through the eye of a needle.

(Remember our Cass Lake canoe, Sherman?)
This boat floats on its back, into the thick
Resistance of unfrozen water, out
To the middle of the lake; we're extras
In a thousand home videos, faceless
As busboys removing plates on tv.

 XVI. Screw Jasper
WHERE WE ARE reduced to asking
Directions to the nearest gas station
From a horse-and-buggy taxi driver.
WHOSE local newspaper quotes a football
Fan saying, "The Eskimos are the most
Important thing in my life," and a girl,
Who'd worked in Japan: "We talk to the guys,
Make them buy us drinks, maybe wipe the dew

From their glasses." SCREW JASPER, WHOSE campgrounds
Are overpopulated; WHOSE WILDLIFE
We admire at 90 km
While the failing sun drives us from the park.
(We've found Robson to camp below tonight.)
JASPER, YOU CAN wipe the dew from my glass!

  XVII. Jose Lind's Quiet Return to Vancouver's Lineup
Come thirty years late for the conference.
Olson, Creeley, and Duncan will never
Again meet in one room to discuss how
They got up here. The nursing stumps of
Stanley Park, new trees grow out of. Robin
Blaser lives somewhere in this holy forest,
Like Heidegger where the tour bus turns back.
The trees are second growth, the city too.

They allow you just three downs to make it
In Vancouver. It looks like they're *building*
Expo '86. Computer sprinklers
Rain on soccer games. The warm breeze is in
From Hang Man's island. It's a no-hitter
For eight and two-thirds innings—-then the hits.

For Douglas

  XVIII. [Seattle, i.]
Clocked in, too late, again, at Boeing plant
To be where Hugo finally clocked out.
(They camp-out in the parking lots to be
Sure they make the last tour. *That plane don't fly.*)
Shift to Seattle; among the working
I'm just another umbrella the wind's
Turned inside out, looking for Bumpershoot.
(Where are you, Judith Roche? Your name is

How many syllables?) Exit bookstore,
Where I make like pickup artiste asking
After you, sign boasts "50 BEAUTIFUL
GIRLS AND 3 UGLY ONES." Philosophy.

At Left Bank Books, his shelves are cataloged
"FICTION BY MEN," etc. Why not

  XIX. [Seattle, ii.]
"POEMS BY REAL MEN"? Or "LOVE SONGS TO READ
ALOUD TO 1 OF THE 3 UGLY GIRLS"?
Down the hill, find the store (Freedman Loans now)
Where Al bought Jimi Hendrix's first guitar.
In Renton, south of the city, carloads
Of flashbulbs have shot up the grass over
His grave. He's neighbors with Lullabyland,
The children's section, but also downrange

A mausoleum with a howitzer
Mounted on top. (A salute from airborne?)
I want to sneak back, after midnight; I'd
Take a seat by the moon-dial pyramid,
Lay down phosphine sonnets in this notebook—
Waiting for the shy dark childe to tune it.

  XX. Going to the Hoh
A line of fir trees burning like incense,
Unlike a fog that's recalled by the sun,
Makes such a long driveway—somebody Big,
Bigger than Ken Griffey, must live back there!
Wind that shakes the tops of them yet cannot
Cool the tip of my nose; they are so tall
They make you rock back on your heels to look!
Root systems in the air; low-strung moss limbs.

Walt's grassy beard. Not some photographer's
Cirrus grin—but green, wild-grown, never dry!
Logs so wet they gush under saw.
Godfather's Pizza in Port Angeles:
"JESUS IS THE WAY NOW HIRING!" Yearly,
145 inches of rain.

For Dennis and Kathy Crabb

JAMES M.
"JIMI" HENDRIX
1942
1970

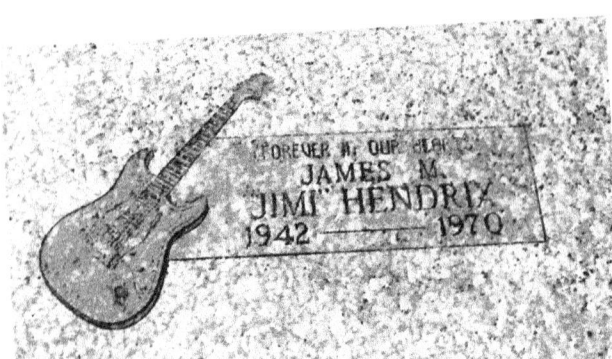

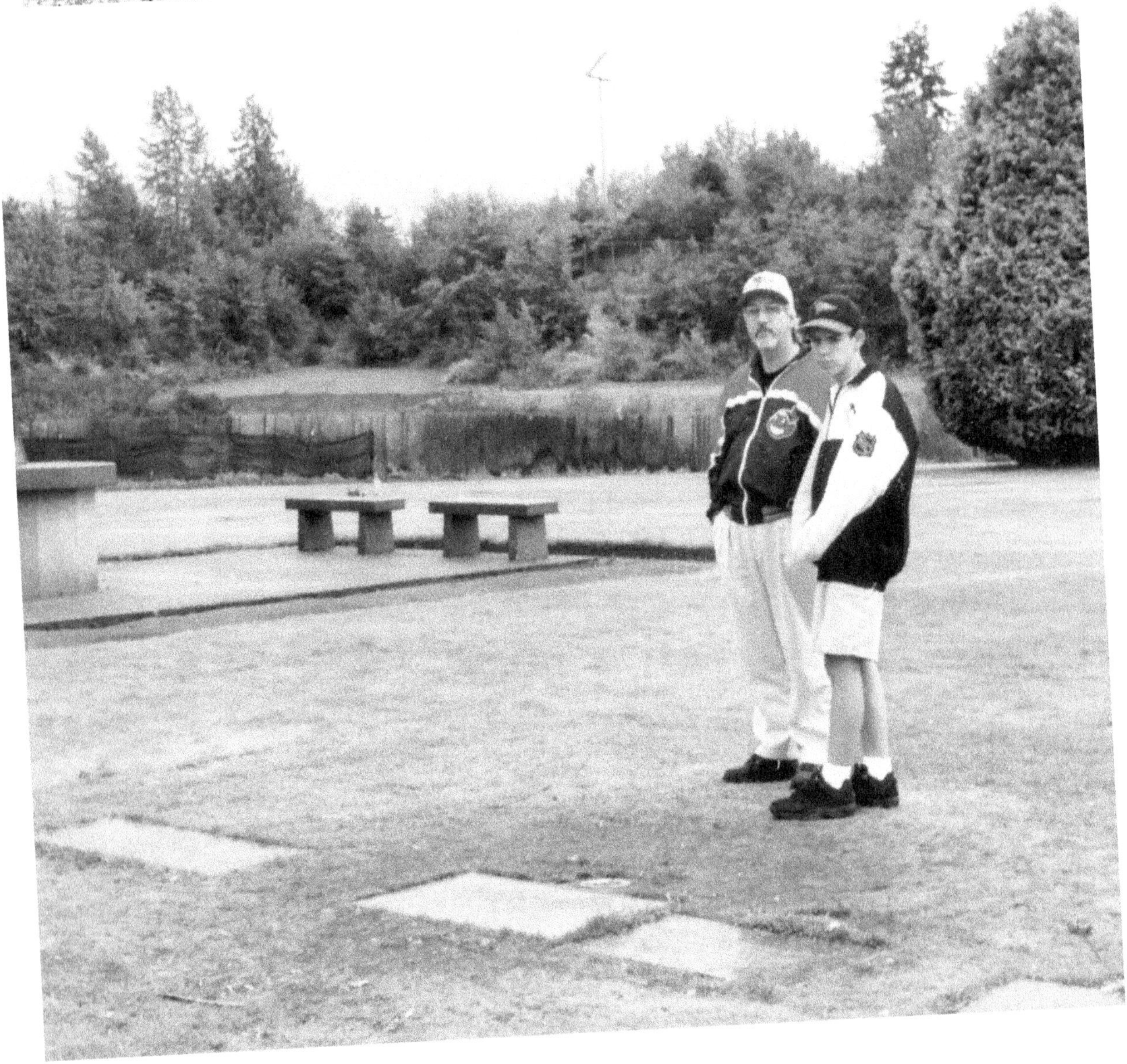

    XXI. Eugene Elegy
     Morning we quit town,
     Day of our return
The former and the latter rains seem one
Long storm. Revisiting should make sweet love
At the same address, poems in one book;
Easy as the motorbike unweaving
The McKenzie; Haycox writing. Should be
A *rebreathing*—to fill the lungs with smell

Of the tall trees of Deady Hall *growing*.
But Jerry Garcia's death is in the news,
On all tongues, like the rotting of newsprint;
The stink of logging. Did the Ory-gun
Trail run back, east again, against the grain
Of progress? (This is the untold story.)

For Beth and Stanley Maveety

  XXII. [Big Horn]
Leaving Twin Falls, for the Badlands—driving
Into the new sun—I am saluted
By one-hundred sprinklers irrigating,
By sunflowers in ditches, and above
Crop duster dips one wing to my passing:
Whitman quits the perfumed rooms of Europe.
At Fallen City, shelves of slab boulders
Outshine terraces of Pound's Dioce.

Who can lift...? (It's your job to pick up all
The bales on this range.) We saw Michael Stipe
Everywhere we went, he's such a nice guy
To see. Squint to make out five shades of blue:
Deepest, closest. Curlleaf mahogany.
Horses standing with their tails to the wind.

  XXIII. [On White River, Badlands]
That Mickey died before DiMaggio
Is one indication why the sonnet
Must be left, to form itself, on its own.

No one would write it ending miles from home
Like that. The grasslands that grow right up to
The rim of the Badlands insist on themselves.
For once, I am taken by the smaller
Scale—variety, instead of power:

Shy smile beneath cap brim; massive home run.
At sunset, the gravel shapes glow, as if
Confusing shape and form, slow releasing
The pent-up heat of a day. Ranchers fuel
Up on coffee at gas pumps, are bitching
That campgrounds use up all the water.

  XXIV. Death of a Commerce Yankee
Abstinence once extended to thirty-
Thousand feet. Let's have that drink in *your* tent,
And fly *below* Kansas, where the Royals
Are playing tonight. I saw the headline
Back in Yankton, where they sell scotch with gas.
You played a little first last I saw you
Pull a ball off the wall in old Cleveland
Stadium—you barely beat it out,

Limping, some kid threw behind you. Only
The gods must live in the knowledge of their
Fates. It was a kind of mantle you wore
Like the ritual taping of the legs
Before each game you played. Like the postgame
Drink to cut the dust of Oklahoma.

  XXV. Lacking a Final Couplet
Interstate Indiana, a gas pump:
Kid pushes his car to a stop, rolls next
To mine, out of gas. Creeley's chemistry
Lesson (pissing in the fuel tank to go
That extra mile)? And back in St. Louis,
The bronze of Jefferson under the Arch,
His hand posed on one hip, looping deep west,
Recalls Walt engraved in our leaves of mind.

Not exactly *Paterson's* unwanted
Book 5, but another last sonnet comes
After the cycle had run on empty—
Twenty-four camps out, or one sleep from home…

....

  XXVI. Alternate Routes; couplets return me to my
        Notes of the West
At Tower Falls, I shake hands with a man
Who works in the same building I work in.
…..
Stinkwater Pass then, quickly, Drinkwater:
You pays your money & you makes your choice.
…..
We've driven far enough out of Cody
To where Jim Bridger's is the name gets dropped.
…..
But to refold the map of Oregon
Teaches nothing, Is not revising.
…..
Rereading Whitman in the sleeping bag:
The moonscape changes, the poem makes noises!
…..
The eye of the island blinks in the flood;
The eye of the storm chooses its victim.
…..
This poem begins at home formally;
On the road, it grows six wheels and drinks gas.

AFTERWORD: PART THREE
  XXVII. Home Poem
I went myself first to the headland, my own hands carried me there.

I've made a career of travel poems
Away from home, on the road, to knowing.
Maybe I should stay awake, like Satie
At home, but never at home in the world;
Living in one room over three decades,
Writing annotations on sheet music
Only he would see—misplacing the score

Beneath the decomposing carpets
Behind the disintegrating piano?
I want Death to be the size of Satie's
Reputation. It is the cessation
Of travel: No returning to the room,
To open the window that does no good.

For Peter Kidd

  XXVIII. High Season
To write a sonnet, in which the speaker
Forgets and, remembering, composes—
Might be done over a single summer;
A holiday only Mahler could love.
Six weeks left, his high season burning down,
He dared not forget himself, lose himself.
You can buy in one book every picture
Ever taken of the dead composer.

Rilke lacked only the technology—
Laser needle for playing human skull—
Any good disk-jockey for the evening
Unloads first from his sports-utility.
During the months of high season, Satie
Played outdoors to crowds expecting baseball.

XXIX. Song of the House-Sitter
"What have you brought, what gift do you bring back?
In long absence—you, like some juggler
Whose sideshow crisscrosses the county lines—
Every night I faithfully fed your cats.
(The fat one is fatter, the neurotic
Cried for you at dawn like the squeal of tires.)
Through whole weeks of drought, I watered your phone.
Your every postcard has preceded you home.

When the bill-collectors congregated
To elect a younger pope, I stalled matters.
Notice that all your proofs are corrected,
Your syllabi typed and collated.
The lawn is short. Each Indians home game
Has been videotaped extra-innings."

For Bonnie

XXX. Poker is the metaphor of the westerns
      we read in the East
Mailed, Pennsylvania to Seattle.
Passed the double sonnet writ in Renton
Concerning the freedom of not being
At home in landlocked Midwest. Bluffed homesick
For some stabile place for my table-top
Temenos. "The Pennsylvanian who
Sat down in South Carolina and wrote
A book about a Virginian in

Wyoming" was James's take on the Forest
Gump of the turn of the century. Roosevelt
Called on Wister to put in scenery
And kill off that cowboy, make
His return impossible. But then what
Could the contestants of the chess game think?
Teaching <u>The Virginian</u>, first day of Fall Term 1995

XXXI. The Cartoons from My Brother-in-law's Car
Something like the Dakota Wall Drug signs.
In my brother-in-law the chemist's car
When we drove the Autobahn at 90,
Ausfahrt was the standing front-seat gag:
A character we claimed to have been
The legendary comedian, billed
"The only man who could make Hitler laugh."
Every exit sign we passed, we laughed.

We were really rolling when I added,
In my best Mel Blanc voice, the name Hansel
Spoken as an improbable question.
The way he did it in the Warner Bro
Cartoon version. All I had to say was
"HAAHN-Tzull?" and it was funny all over

  XXXII. "Free Coffee for Veterans of Foreign Wars"
Again. (Or does this revisitation
Go too far back in the narrative,
Ausholen? To when "A Flock of Landscapes"
Was the cycle you were working on.)
In the movies of my father's era,
In the movies of my father's war,
To know who's who, all a picket had to do
Was challenge the English-speaking stranger:

"Who won the World Series this year?"
Hansel Ausfahrt always answered "Brooklyn."
"What do you see when you go to the country?"
Something like the Dakota Wall Drug signs,
Words in lines down a stretch of highway new
To you. The End promising Free Coffee.

Captivity Narratives

(2008)

To Donald Koehler

Dear Tod Thilleman:

I am writing to ask if you, and Spuyten Duyvil, have any interest in reading a book-length mss. of poems, my first collection following Dave Baratier's publication of my collected poems, Fogbow Bridge?

Your edition of Steve Ellis' The Long and Short of It, and your work with several other authors, made me think of SD as a publisher for my book. (Ellis wrote the Introduction for Fogbow...As an editor of Zelot Press in the 1980s, I published Basil and Martha King; I published poems in her Drizzle.. Ed Foster recently printed my chapbook The Collected Later Poems of Philip Marlowe; I've reviewed Leonard Schwartz in Talisman...I'm Creeley's editor for the Olson-Creeley correspondence.) So who sez you can never put your foot in Spuyten Duyvil Creek twice? Baratier and Foster can tell you more than I know about how my poetry sells and how I am to work with. The website for Kent State University Libraries will show you a catalog of my literary archive that shows you something of my involvement in the community of poets (http://www.library.kent.edu/speccoll). I studied with Robert Duncan and Ed Dorn at Kent, 1972-73. My first mag publication was in Io no. 19. At Zelot, Bill Shields and I published work by Douglas Woolf, joel oppenheimer, Fielding Dawson, George Butterick, Joe Napora, and others.

The new book, Suite for M, runs to about 90 typewritten pages. Two sections are forthcoming as chapbooks by Ellis and by Peter Kidd (Igneus Press), and a handful of poems have been previously published in Cafe Review and Fogbow Bridge. I've just finished the third, a prosepoem meditation on Shostakovich's Preludes & Fugues.

Continued good fortune with the press.

Thanks,
Rich Blevins
(724) 853-1571

Thilleman@excite.com
leechapman@aol.com

AVAILABLE LIGHT: FRED HOLLAND DAY

"A drainless shower / Of light is poesy," Keats.

"Art is always saying hello and poetry is always saying good-bye," Kenneth Koch.

"I have had the courage to look backward," Ted Berrigan.

"After the war a philosopher said / In this hell Orpheus should be silent / But Orpheus has always sung in hell," Edward Bond, "Canzoni to **Orpheus**."

All
All
All
All

All
All
All the psychics'
All the philosophers'

All the painters'
All the photographers'

All the priests'
All the physicians'

All the physicists'
All the psalmists' light

Light
Light
Light

Light
Light
Light

Light
Light cannot escape,
Brass poppies do not grow toward,
THIS BLACK HOLE

She seems to him
Exposures

Approaching the exact number
A subject can be expected to tolerate

He sees her
UNBATHED IN ALL LIGHT.

In 1907, Fred Day shoots the Orpheus series, near Brockton, Massachusetts.

"I know I ought to come down out of the woods," in a letter by the painter of "Storm Clouds, Maine," Marsden Hartley. William James' last lecture, a Philosophy D course at Harvard, January 22. Publishes *Pragmatism*. Einstein's paper, "On The Relativity Principle and The Conclusions Drawn From It." Freud's paper "The Sexual Enlightenment of Children." Sherwood Anderson moves to Elyria, Ohio, to manage a mail-order paint company. Upton Sinclair's artists' colony fails when Helicon Hall burns down.

The Eiffel Tower begins radio transmissions. Construction begins on Claude Bragdon's Universalist Church, Rochester.

Trotsky begins publishing *Pravda*, from Vienna. Maxim Gorky's *Comrades*. Ring Lardner begins his sports writing career, in Chicago. The Chicago Cubs, with an infield of Tinker, Evers, Chance, and third-baseman Harry Steinfeldt, win 107 regular season games and sweep the World Series. Did Charles Ives write "Giants v. Cubs, August 1907. Polo Grounds" in the year 1907? George Wharton James' *Ina Donna Coolbrith: An Historical Sketch and Appreciation*. Gertrude Stein meets Alice B. Toklas, during the writing of *The Making of Americans*.

Frank and Maud Baum celebrate their twenty-fifth wedding anniversary. Hilaire Belloc's "Thoughts About Modern Thought" is printed in the *New Age*, to great controversy. Stefan George publishes *Der Siebente Ring*, a collection of poems. William James organizes a fund for the support of C.S. Peirce, living on at Arisbe. Howard Carter is hired to direct excavations in the Valley of the Kings. Henri Bergson's *Creative Evolution* and *The Seven Ages of Washington* by Owen Wister. Joseph Conrad's *The Secret Agent*. Robert Walser's first novel, *Geschwister Tanner*. Ives suffers the first of several so-called heart attacks, initiating the creative years.

Schoenberg writes the first three movements of his Second String Quartet; its fourth movement, completed later, will be atonal. Sinclair Lewis and W.H. Auden are born this year. E.M. Forster, *The Longest Journey*. Mahler debates Sibelius, in Helsinki, on the nature of symphonic form. Rachel Carson is born in Springdale, Pennsylvania, in a little house behind my son's orthodontist's office. Kipling, an exact contemporary of Fred Day, is awarded the Nobel Prize. Maria Montessori (on January 6, my first daughter's birth date) opens the first Montessori school, in Rome. Oklahoma becomes the forty-sixth state. The U.S. financial panic of 1907. During the summer, Alexander Scriabin begins writing the "Poem of Ecstasy." The first electric chair is installed, in New Jersey, home of Thomas Edison. Adelaide Crapsey attends The Second Peace Conference, The Hague, at her father's side. Maxim Gorky is a delegate to the Congress of the Russian Social Democratic Party, in London. John Muir publishes "The Tuolumme Yosemite in Danger."

President Teddy Roosevelt proclaims Mt. Lassen to be a national monument. On March 5, the first radio broadcast of music. The death of Edvard Grieg, and the birth of Magdalena Carmen Frieda Kahlo Calderón.

Chick Stahl, Red Sox manager and center fielder, commits suicide, in Indiana. Synge's "Playboy of the Western World" opens in Dublin's Abbey Theatre to police protection. Ezra Pound's fall semester at Wabash College. Pessoa drops out of the University of Lisbon. Roger (The Duke of Tralee) Bresnahan is the first catcher to wear shin guards. On the evening when the first ball drops over Times Square to usher in the new year, Mahler premiers as the conductor of the Metropolitan Opera. Mildred Bailey and Dorothy Baker are born. This year's Carlisle Indian Industrial School football team features the forward pass and freshman back Jim Thorpe. Basketball's Tarzan Cooper is born. Joyce finishes "The Dead," starts rewriting *Stephen Hero* as *A Portrait of the Artist as a Young Man*, and publishes *Chamber Music*. Gustav Klimt's "Adele Bloch-Bauer I." Louis Sullivan's wife, Margaret Hattabough, "left him in 1907, having taught him...as much about the conspicuous needs of the leisure class as Veblen had," writes his future biographer Sherman Paul. Sibelius finishes his Third Symphony. This year of the publication of *New Poems*, featuring the long poem "Orpheus. Eurydice. Hermes.," Rilke habituated the Cezanne exhibit at the Grand Palais. Adolf Furtwängler dies, in

Athens. Walter (Big Train) Johnson wins the first of his 416 games for the Senators. The Kenora Thistles, with Roxy Beaudro, win the Stanley Cup. This year Dit Clapper is born. Asaph Hall, discoverer of the moons of Mars, is dead. Munch's "The Death of Marat," with himself as Marat and Tulla as Charlotte Corday. Also that year, "Amor and Psyche" series (begun), "The Green Room," and "Bathing Men." Delius is finishing "Songs Of Sunset." Berg writes the song "Close both my eyes." The year Rolf Jacobsen and Gunnar Ekelöf are born. Berg will rewrite "Close both my eyes," in 1925, as a twelve-tone piece. Jake Beckley's final season. The year Dick Bartell, Spud Chandler, Luke Appling, Tony Cuccinello, and Gene Autry are born. T.E. Hulme studies, in Brussels, with Henri Bergson and Rémy de Gourmont. First performance of the Ziegfeld Follies. René Char is born. Jarry dies. Ralph Hodgson's first book of poetry, *The Blackbird and Other Lines.* Robert Frost lectures at the Pinkerton Academy, Derry, New Hampshire. Conrad Aiken enters Harvard College. Elizabeth Cabot Agassiz, first president of Radcliffe College and wife of Louis, dies. Luke Short is born, in Illinois, as Frederick D. Glidden. Mark Twain, 72, meets future memoirist Dorothy Quick, 10, aboard the *S.S. Minnetonka.* President McKinley's widow, Ida Saxton McKinley, dies. James Rudolph Garfield is confirmed as Roosevelt's Secretary of the Interior. Edgar Lee Masters meets Marion Reedy, publisher of *Reedy's Mirror.* Sara Teasdale's first publication, in *Reedy's Mirror.* Irish poet John O'Leary dies. Alfred Noyes' *The Flower of Old Japan.* Early cinematographer Ottomar Anschütz, whose photographs of storks inspired Lilienthal's gliders, is dead. The first volume of Edward S. Curtis' *The North American Indian.* Ernst Kirchner's "Street." Machado takes the first of his jobs as a schoolmaster, teaching French, in Soria. With Apollinaire, Georges Braque visits Picasso in the Bateau Lavoir, where the painter first sees the newly finished "Les Demoiselles d'Avignon."

Vanessa Stephen and Clive Bell marry. Maurice Blanchot, author of *The Gaze of Orpheus*, is born. *The Education of Henry Adams*, privately published. Lee Miller is born, in Poughkeepsie.

"RETURN TO EARTH" AND VARIANT PRINTS

"As Cocteau makes clear, one always hopes to encounter a mythological personage in life. Yet when it happens, one does not notice...," David L. Sweet, "The Lens of Luciaen Clergue and the Cinema of Jean Cocteau."

"Tumultuosissimamente," De Quincey's "Suspiria de Profundis."

"...when [Gertrude, the blind orphan,] heard the birds' song she used to suppose it was simply the effect of light,...it seemed to her quite natural that the warm air should begin to sing...."
Gide's "The Pastoral Symphony."

Drove right thru summer night as if it were the Massachusetts Pike
And not what it actually is, a floor between twin beds, the only light
One screaming yellow line screaming, split the late recluses' single room—
Ate up the upstairs carpet, window frame to door—Norwood to Amherst.

There was time for him, in that reclaimed demesne, to think. For Musaeus

To bring home Emily Dickinson in a long poem
To be opened at the birth of his Christmas present, Doris,
Meaning "gift of the sea," so far inland it becomes Pittsburgh.
(Closer than it appeared, Norwood was an object in his mirror.)

His big mistake was in not looking back. He should have looked back.

2
To Musaeus' way of thinking, Day was always taking a back seat.
If only the driver can read correctly

The word   E=M=E=R=G=E
It's because it's his rear-view mirror.

       =N=C=Y
The image comes in, in increments, to him,

Over what may prove to be seasons in transit.
Tho Musaeus sees it as her, her portrait, in traffic. Eurydice.

3
Looking
Back, Fred
Holland Day
Emerges

The closest,
In Musaeus'
Lifetime, to
Jean Cocteau.

"Day's russian cigarettes, as long and elegant as Cocteau's photogenic fingers."

In the Norwood pictures, a boulder made of the light you can sometimes see that
actually
Comes thru the hand, fingers, orange red orange, strong light thru living flesh.

Shipments of platinum for Day's prints interrupted by the Russian Revolution.

Critique
On death slowly absorbed thru the artist's fingers into the body of work.

Cocteau always claimed his *Antigone* was an attempt to photograph Greece from
the
Open back seat of a biplane. "To make new the view from Nadar's balloon."

4
In his history of flight, Blaise Cendrars states unequivocally that Musaeus could fly.
His research did not, however, determine
Whether Musaeus was Orpheus' son or his disciple in song.

5
"Got out of bed to record @ 3 a.m."
His first critical observation—

Musaeus on peripheral vision

In Fred Day's pictures:

"Often the center of a Day picture is how we see peripherally, even the portraits or
            the
Human forms, as if the center of focus must be a blind vortex for his eye. Note that Kristeva's Stendhal's novel is a mirror one takes on the road. Can this be true of the Poem about a photographer?
    Doubly true?"

6
"The new poem becomes a series of day trips, back and forth, to and from, the
      source and
Side trips. Recorded in a daybook. Writ in midnight shifts. Trips. Impossible
              muddle.
Look Again.

Narrative shift. Walter Benjamin (on Leskov) says a storyteller is someone who has

   Come from afar:

Like the American critic Sadakichi Hartmann;
Like the American expatriate photographer Man Ray;
Like Visionist architect-designer and Knights Errant Bertram Grosvenor Goodhue;
Like Edward Bellamy, looking back, against nostalgia's grain, 2000-1887;
Like Bishop Berkeley to Newport, Rhode Island;
Like Benjamin Blood coming to.
The pictures at hand to go with these names.

   Weegee's name keeps surfacing.

Midnight shifts. Turns back."

7
"How seeing involves looking:
Hang the picture of our

Dreams on your wall,
You never see it again;

Day had Christina Rossetti's hell
For his dark room,
And the floodlight of Dante Gabriel
Exposing Adam's torso;

Truth, like a well in Miletus,
Takes a long exposure—
Too dark down there
To see his own reflection.

So how do we look at a picture?
Close up, first the grains
Note the historical title date donated
Now, backpedaling, from a critical distance
Turn head, turn head
Fall into hand on chin no
Too too self-conscious
The face on the framed glass surface
Move back in
The faraway nearby
Refocusing on picture
Squint perceive shapes
Knock scales from eyes
See it new ah well
Each time what
We bring to it
Is new each time if
The picture holds up.
Morton Feldman used to measure the distance
Sound would take to travel
To the last ear in the concert hall. Quietly sent his
To the back seat. Back up a bit now. All available
Light travels faster its route to the back of the eye

Synapse traps

Riding atop De Quincey's mail-coach

Fuentes' 'With every viewing, something of [the painting] is stolen.'

Owen Wister and Frederick Delius were Day's exact contemporaries."

So writes Musaeus, as best I can tell in this red light.

8
Estelle Jussim concludes "it is almost impossible
To determine with certainty the specific process
By which each of Day's prints was created."
Good art subsumes, must take a back seat to,
Meaningful discussion of craft.

If we are to believe Jussim,
"Day was always taking a back seat"

                                        To the then-famous Louise Imogen Guiney.
E.g., at the dedication
Of the Keats memorial,
Hampstead. ("She was not there.")

When Musaeus takes a back pew in ivory white
Cram chapel, beside the three scrimshaw
Tombs, lo, he too is fled—Day to ashes
Out of state. To Little Good Harbor,

"A lee shore Guiney provided him, forever awaiting Bulkington."

                                        To Madison Avenue's Stieglitz.
For Day did not march beside Stieglitz into the bombed city of modernity.
When we view the self-portraits as Christ on the X, strangely
Freud does not look back at us. Darwin does not explain

"Photographing the flesh of archetypes."

The metamorphosis of woods to shore.
Amy Lowell dropped her lit perfecto, when she got a load
Of the Copeland & Day cover for Crane's *Masked Rider*,
And could never stoop to retrieve it and other lines.

(Crane's habit of dashing off "lines" dates from
The evening, in 1893, when Howells read aloud the just-published
Poems of Emily Dickinson. The story "One Dash—Horses"
Is not a reference to her habit of punctuation.)

"Try not to confuse the undergrowth, in Day's nature, for underground."

                                        To a young and impressionable Gibran.
Fred had read aloud to him Maeterlinck's
The Treasure of the Humble,
But the prophetic Gibran knew him not.

"Many of his portraits by gaslight can now be viewed online."

   Also, there is this infernal business of the letters.
Matters so Wholly,
More than art
Can ever be, Decadent;

This making it
Our business
And, in the ends,
Only so much talk—

Of Fanny Brawne's letters
                     To Fanny Keats,
In the way of Amy Lowell's obese image;
Burned by a female companion;
Got in Seville, Spain, the day

                            The photos didn't record;
Ever promised to Guiney, never read. The scholar,
Virginia Woolf's father, failing to get beyond
What letter of the alphabet?
Of Fred Day's own letters
                   To Miss Guiney.
On Keats' Pleasure Thermometer in "Endymion,"
Louise ranks only a tepid April day. Available light.

—"Try harder to hold back nothing."

9
See eighteen-year-old Chauncy Hall school boy
Fred Day asking Oscar Wilde for his autograph.

10
Back the street from the Day House,
Neighbor Jed Hickson is photographing

His series "The Secret Lives of Clouds"
Above the streets of Norwood. And

Mayakovsky *is* the cloud in pants:
"All hashish and cigar smoke."

11
Musaeus held his poetry above the competitions.
Fred Day remained underground, amateur.

"I owe him everything; I owe him nothing,"
  So Musaeus, on his debt to Orpheus.

In my poem I am asked again,
  As I left it with Duncan,
To deal with the artist's love
  Of the male torso the touch—

The straight and the queer—
  Dorn and Duncan
The homosexual in society
  Can be father

To my cynical poetics.
  Day is in the closet
And that closet was
  His darkroom, for Eurydice

A temenos
  The size of the hell

H.D.'s form
  Speaks from,
Even after we
  Have it open.

12
Musaeus opened Starbucks waiting all night on a biopsy report when he realized
                                                                            this
      Poem had begun without him.
Balzac, who claimed to have drunk 50,000 cups of coffee so he could write sixteen
                                                                            hours
      Every day, was Day's idol.
Day's letters to Spoelberch de Lovenjoul, in Guiney's French, about Balzac.
When he read that Day had died from prostate, Musaeus put down his coffee cup
                                                                            for once
      And took him up seriously.

Right there

They made blood
  In the semen
Brothers.

13
It is written that Fred Day composed his letters by the light from thirteen candles.

"THE VISION"

"Yet through thine eyes he grants me clearest call
And veriest touch of powers primordial,"
Sonnet 34, *"The House of Life."*

"The truth of art is a truth of ensemble," Day's "Is Photography an Art?"
unpublished manuscript, 1900.

                                          (Let's try to leave Musaeus
                                          Out of this. For us this is,
An American mythology.)

1
Joyce buried the city's sad history beneath the truants' feet in his walking tour of
                                                                turn-of-
The-century Dublin. For his Orpheus series, Day shoots the desolate landscape of
                                                                    the
Puritan Eden
Stone House Hill "cave," really an outcrop of rock on the Frederick Lothrop Ames
Farmland in Day's day, now owned by Stonehill College—site of a native battle
                                                                       camp,
For the Wampanoags, in Metacomet's war with the Plymouth zealots (see Philbrick)

A few miles north of the place where Benjamin Church captured Annawon, last
Outstanding sachem.

The way
Wampanoags maximus Maushop one day turned
On his wife
She turns into a weeping
Rock on an island shore

We still read the zealot wife in the story of King Philip's War
Mary Rowlandson,
Who witnessed her captor, Quinnapin,
"Dressed in his
Holland shirt,"

Dance
Himself
Into a decision.
She did make it back
Home in twelve weeks.
Wrote her captivity narrative
Before H.D.'s
Masterless "Eurydice."

Notwithstanding H.D.'s poem,
A bad poem written in darkest hell
Is still a bad poem. And Rowlandson writes from the twentieth remove,
A native described in a bad light
Waits behind every tree
Grabs any white girl
Come within reach. Click.

2
Reaching back
To Anne Carson's Aristotle, I see
"'Seeing' or 'spectacle' or *opsis* is the 'most ravishing'
Aspect of dramatic mimesis…
He applies to visual spectacle
The adjective *psychagōgikon*, which means something like
'It kidnaps your soul.'" Makes me think
Of Day's acts of seeing,
An indigenous peoples' reluctance to take their pictures
Clickclick, because the camera snatches souls.

3
It is given him to write endlessly the sentence that is she.
Born 1915, Marjorie Jane Reed sometimes

Signed her paintings "Fred Day."
A latter-day Remington, who somehow grew up nostalgic
For the Butterfield Overland stagecoach.
An art that confuses the mind, not the eye
Confuses form for structure. Her. Click. Click. Click.
It is given him to erase all traces of the sentence that is she.

4
Day's missed opportunity:
Williams first wrote bad Keats
When Day was still a photographer;
Olson's critique of openness, 1950,
Would begin in Keats.
(Day's Orpheus hears the fountain's plash
From his makeshift bed just off the Spanish Steps;
Bernini's perpetually sinking boat.)
In Keats' America, "that most hateful land,"
A nightmare bereft of order, where
"Great unerring Nature once seems wrong."
This is Keats' missed opportunity. Click.

5
I was conceived by Georg Trakl, in 1914,
You can find me among the litter
Of dying and wounded soldiers
In the barn beside Grodek,
In Trakl's last poem, "Grodek." I am in there
Among the unborn
Grandchildren
Of his, and sixteen-year-old
Cloyd
Ferrell's in Overton
County,
Tennessee, training to join the AEF,
He never lived to see. Click.
An album of pictures of my father standing
Proud beside the family Ford '49 click '52 click '57 click '60.

6
Kokoschka commissioned Hermine Moos to make to his specifications a life-sized doll, which he named his "dream of Eurydice's return," of Alma Mahler. Click.
Celeste is not what you think but a musical instrument I took for bells Mahler took
                                                        for eternity.
                                                        Click.

7
Even
Day's best critic, James Crump, writes that the Orpheus series was photographed in Maine. Click.

8
Jussim, slave to tenure,
The biography rushed into print, "an error on every page."

9
Click behind Noguchi's splendid curtain.

SO—WHERE'S—MUSAEUS?

Even at the short end of a leash, walking Tiger and himself right out of the narrative of dog-fearing Arthur Gordon Pym, if you need to know.

Watch while

I turn

On him,

Delete

Him, from

The page's

Blaze of

Whiteness.

(Click.)

Done.

For I can now account for the detail of Orpheus' lyre being made of tortoise shell. Is its music long-lived but slow, like a whole season of insomnia?

For it was Hermes who invented the Chelys. The sound of the musical instrument cannot be heard in the Homeric hymn.

For I once saw what I took to be a working lyre, hanging like a frame awaiting Mondrian, on a wall of Emerson's home. Our guide said it was wind activated, so it should have been strung from a Concord tree: "Its chords should ring as blows

the breeze." For Rilke's poet must pass thru the strings of the lyre. A spirit? Some ancient commentators figure Eurydice was already dead, a light-as-wind spirit, when Odysseus led her back. Or is Rilke's poet restricted to passing his song thru the sonnet frame?

For arriving at the meaning of the tortoise-shell lyre is like Margie reading Pope's grotto on all the pub signs and bus stops but at last finding the grotto itself, now part of a boys' school, chained up and locked. Darwin's discovery that the Galapagos Islands in fact were supported on the back of Akupara.

For I have seen a turtle shell's underside, so much like a human skull's.

For I can perfectly account for the requirement that Day's lyre needed only to be an unplayable wooden prop for pictures.

For Hart's bridge was a harp; there being too many strings to his lyre.

For Tui Malila, a tortoise originally belonging to Capt. Cook who made a gift of it to the Tongan royal family, died of old age—when I was 15.

For tortoise shell was the choice of material for the manufacture of guitar picks in the 19th century.

For Joni Mitchell might be heard playing dobro, acoustical guitar, and lyre on one cut.

For what character in what novel is it is said to carve his message of love into a turtle's living shell? Sounds like Sharr on a walk thru Heidegger's part of the Black Forest.

For I saw, on June 3, 2007, that flat lyre in its glass case in the red guest bedroom at Day House. It all clicked, we say.

Beside the photo on Jimmy Van Loan's mantelpiece in November 1897.

For all the above reasons,
If you want to keep a secret, print it in a poem.

ALBUM OF PREVIOUSLY UNTITLED, UNCOLLECTED PRINTS

"Nor look behind, nor sideways...," "The Eve of Saint Agnes."

"Seek my face," Psalm 27.

[It is dusk]
In all corners
Of the room.
It is time
Time to rouse
Ourselves
From bed;
Time to
Witness

[It Is Day]
The pagan wakes
Having slept the night
In a field.

[Upon seeing the carved figures on the wall
in Day's library]
These figures dance
Off Keats' urn
To the unheard music
Of Pater, dissolve
With the smile from Eurydice's face
Into Mauberley, the cinema, and jazz.

[Youth in white sailor suit and broad hat]
That
Is Hart Crane
Looking
Like some other guy.

[Voluptuary]
Sebastian on Jesus' rack in the gospel by Keats.
Day in Norwood nailed to a X the form
Scottie Ferguson assumes
In the last light of vertigo,
Madeline twice lost.
But his late focus
On the male torso
Is his autobiography
Day by Day
Voluptuary
Day in Maine tied to a Herm of Pan.

[Intended as a portrait of Clarel's Ruth]
To be worn on a string about the neck of the survivor in the fashion of that century.

[On Day's choice of himself for his model for Christ on the X;
Or, Adelaide Crapsey's "Amaze"]
During the period of her recovery from surgeries on both hands,
My octogenarian mom
Bot for the house

A statue and a painting
Of Praying Hands.
To be so unselfconscious in one's living space

Is a rare grace
Unattainable
By most living artists.

[On Day's choice of himself for his model for Christ, II]
Perhaps Crapsey's "Keeping the edge of deprivation sharp."

[On Day's choice of himself for his model for Christ, III]
But not Mel Gibson's passion
For DUI.

[Negatives]
In Artaud, Eurydice would be a *subjectile*,
An incubus
Sent below the surface.

   *

Day is Santayana's Last Puritan
And/or
Today's child predator voyeur.

   *

Lot's wife looked back
Too
Denouncing ritual

[Out of Fashion]
We seem to have no use for the fine tissue mats Day fashioned for his prints.

[Short Treatise against the psychosomatic]
On the long-term effects of platinum on the eyes.

[I Get It: Final Draft]
This one is an image of Ohio poet Tom Kryss,
Looking much like the French composer Berlioz of volume two of his memoirs,
Who buys all his stamps from the Auburndale, Mass. P.O.
He is mailing the manuscript of a new poem to me.
It will be driven in a truck on the Ohio and Pennsylvania turnpikes
And delivered in the twinkling of an eye,
Along with the letter in Cocteau's *Blood of a Poet*.

[The Business of Robert Duncan's Strabismus]
Understand that sometimes a great poet's eyes twinkle
One at a time.

[Aurelian]
"Daddy looks funny,"
My daughter writes
In her daybook, "when
He listens to jazz."

[From Theories on Perspective]
Doris is six months old and already
Sees things like Orpheus
Losing sight of a person or object atomizes
That person or object

No longer exists.
Peek-a-boo is next.
When she becomes
Eurydice, at nine months.

[Maeterlinck]
See Day's portrait of Maeterlinck as soon as possible.
Read Maeterlinck's *Hothouses* poems as soon as possible.

[Self-portrait, as an old man, still smoking a cigarette]
The sitter is unknown or hard to know.

[Rub the Lacquer]
To hear the voice of Yates' spirit inside a Japanese box
Decades before his death
And before the birth of the modern.

[Ossian Receiving]
When I first saw her, a caped Helen Adam,
Wherever she looked on the autumnal streets of Kent, OH,
Saw the ghosts and heroes of Girodet's "Ossian Receiving."

[Endymion]
Balzac, asking to be left alone
In the room with Girodet's "Endymion."

[Fred's Steps]
The walls and rooms of Goya's black paintings?
Messiaen's aubade birds on barbed
Wire? The white walls of An American Place.

[Erasure]
Rauschenberg spent a month
Erasing deKooning,
The Eurydice of charcoal, pencil, paint
Gone, tho art's still framed therein.

[Charles Olson]
Day's photographs of the Orono subway entrance to hell looked like stills from Keaton's "The Frozen North," where I last glimpsed Ed Dorn (In Orono, not yet hell), in conversation with Stephen King, about what he (Ed) sees in Clark's biography of.

[From Experiments in Epistemology]
Raoul Dufy's woodcut Orpheus for Apollinaire's bestiary.

[Negatives]
Breath-fogged mirror,
Premonition of death.

[It's Fred, not Frederick]
At seven months, what
The baby sees
When she is held up
To her
Mirror
Is nothing we assume.

[Balzac]
The day I saw Rodin's great bust of Balzac (rejected, 1898, after seven years work) in his garden, I was thinking of Rilke. This was a decade before I'd ever read the name Fred Day or knew he liked to work in crazy robes. Rodin makes it difficult to know that his Balzac is wearing one of the white monk's robes he favored. The Parisian ambiance has turned the surface of the statue green. His Balzac looks like Morton Feldman smoking too much.
Today I look up Steichen's 1909 picture of Rodin's "Balzac—
Towards the Light, Midnight" and think of

Day's habit
of photographing a sitter beside classic statuary.

[Aristaeus]
Car I parked for the summer—
Filled up—with honey—bees!

[Dante Gabriel Rossetti]
He once offered to feed
Doves in his free hand;
Wherever birdseed fell
Now tall grasses grow.

[Lot's wife's lot]
In Messiaen's love story the "Turangalîla,"
The "statue theme" is played on trombone.

There is a poem by Pessoa
About the stone pillars they call *padrões*
Left by 15th-century Portugese explorers.

Pound points out
The column at San Zeno, Verona,
Signed by the maker.

[The Lady Vanishes]
In some cases, the estranged wife*
Knows her Keats.**

*ANNE CARSON, THE BEAUTY OF THE HUSBAND.
**OTHO.

[Writ]
Miss Froy's handwriting on the window of the night train to Maine is all we have of her.

[After Goethe's *Young Werther*]
This year
It became fashionable for young men to read Saramago and blind themselves.

[From A History of the Darkroom]
It's time
For the ghost of Robert Duncan to appear in a magical realistic novel.

[Pun as One-act]
'Twas Eurydice made Orpheus Synge.

[My Middle Name]
Fanning mail calling me
"A Lowell in Blevins clothing."

[Hypnos Inspired]
Boy attempts to breathe a metal poppy into his lungs. A symbol so loaded it
                                                                                  clangs
To the polished floor of our Monday gallery.

"THE LAST CHORD"

"the eye is the obstacle," Tom Kryss.

"The unexamined wife is not worth leaving," George Butterick.

"The day is gone, and all its sweets are gone!" Keats.

On that day when everything has been photographed,
The history of photography in America will commence.

1
Day photo-documents his great mistake in the Orpheus series from the summer of 1907.

He had enjoyed his height as a Pictorialist, at the 10 October-8 November 1900 exhibit The New School of American Photography, in a London weary from the Wilde trial but also a decade away from the paintings that Virginia Woolf would say changed human nature. After 1904, the prints are mostly
undated. By 1917, he was out
                               of photography.

Entr'acte, his art.

Because he could not see himself as Orpheus. Day's failure of vision is this. Cocteau would cast himself in the role, 1960, three years before dying; Day chose Nicola Giancola for his model with the four-stringed lyre.

Self-employed paparazzo to first things.

His Orpheus never looked twice at his Mayflower wife. He kept bailing her out. We see him, in the pictures, alone with his indecision. Returned to earth. He knows he must die. "*Dies*," he liked to sign his letters,
making the Latin pun, but that was in another world. He knows he must die. He wrongly imagines himself the victim of a cruel fate and is about to give himself over to that fate. She had written of "Soul calling soul to Judgement," in the poem

"Friendship Broken."
He thinks she
Wrote the poem to,
Not for, him.

2
Fate is character, like Raymond Chandler said, of the view out Niepce's attic
window and not so far into a garden in Burgundy. As fate would have it,
the author of *Farewell, My Lovely* will be born on Fred Day's sixteenth birthday.

3
His Keats favored the verb "cloys"
Meaning the sensuous movement
Of hands thru hair.
Look the light a woman's hair becomes
She is reading a girl again absorbed
In her book we say but it's perfectly
True of course the source of light
Is the page if she closes the book
She'll disappear she hired the attorney
Who had represented Lot's pillar for a
Wife watch it now She may be Eurydice.
Pound's unsigned pillar of salt
Pound salt, used to be dismissal
Watch it I am too close to you
To photograph you at sea's salty edge
Thank you for not backing up just then
His stronger eye looks back after her,
His one foot is on the shore of our world,
A hand cloys (h)air

Where the birds fly upside down against the current of her hair,
the praying mantis first turned its head to witness.

4
Day's holy forests are described best by Tacitus.

His Orpheus tells us why.
He could not bring himself to turn on Louise—send her back
To Irish Boston in the 19th Century.

(See her "For Izaak Walton" for yourself.)
Sentencing himself to languish in a pagan landscape

Forever parallel to Orphic Cubism.

This is the last chord.

This is a portrait of a person who will never hear of Gottshalk's monster concert, 650 performers on stage, in Rio, when Fred Day was nine.

This is a cardboard trumpet solo.

5
Three Portraits of the Artist follow:

Clarence White's Day (c. 1897) in black robe with black model.
Whose skin
Is the color
Of vertigo
Alternating
Allure
And repulse.
Poe's dearest fear of annihilation.

Alvin Langdon Coburn's portrait of alchemist Day in his darkroom (1900).
His is the blackness
Of Eurydice's fresh
Temenos in hell
As H.D. daydreamed her.

Steichen's "Solitude" (1901), with Day's hand posed, the center of his being
Being like Cocteau.

6
Orpheus by Eurydice.
Day with Louise.
Herbert Copeland alone.

The Copeland & Day
Colophon
Was a collage

From 16th-century English printers'
(Richard Day and Robert
Copeland).

Backtracking Gide in Algeria—
To Castle Guiney?

"As a Lily among Thorns"

7
                            In "Modern Woman" in the White City*
The Muse plucks a mean banjo. It's 1893, Chicago
And Mary Cassatt has badly outdistanced Mary
Fairchild MacMonnies' mural
                        "Primitive Woman." I see
Louise Guiney like her, both
Backward-looking women. At length, choosing to
        Live in
        England,
        1901,
        Nearer her dead and gone**
        Donne and Vaughan; editing yet the *Recusant Poets*.

"Spirit so abstinent, in thy deeps lay / What passion of possession? Day by day
Was there no thirst upon thee, sharp and pure, / In forward sea-like surges
unforgot?"

And yet,
By 1907, Cassatt is left behind, Stieglitz and
Prendergast in Paris, no three-legged bitch, but self-condemned
To repaint the same images unto heaviness of pigment, clothing.

*See "The Captive of the White City." Ina Coolbirth's poem, about Custer's killer who is on display in his Montana wigwam, shipped to Chicago.

**Note how Guiney's poem "The Kings" echoes Crane: "A man said...," but hollow after. How her "Wild Ride" is neither Dickinson's nor Crapsey's wild night.

8   *to Jack Spellecy*

Timothy Leary's ashes are making the rounds
Somewhere in outer space. The miracle of capitalism.
Louise Guiney lives out her literary afterlife
Lip-syncing hymns in Mark Twain's karaoke heaven.
Day's portraits of women might be afterimages from the surface world
Preserved in the galleries of Eurydice's memory.
Her unsent love
Letters to Orpheus.
In her memoir, *A Season in Hell*,
She makes no mention of Pound, Joyce, Aldington,
H.D., Picasso, Stravinsky, Cocteau. Holden
Caulfield calls her our greatest Civil War poet.
She could never account for Yeats in her poems.
Fucking Rilke's sonnets to O took two weeks to write!
His lyre is tortoise shell. The snake is associated with Eurydice.
Wilde saw the truth in masks, but Richard Gerstl's eyes
Atomize his canvas where the lovers' faces go.
A guy could never use
Day's landscape
For a map, or his interiors, another sunken floor
For your pillow. Proof
That a press of flowers can oppress. After all this,
The only way I have to picture Fred and Louise in the same room is
To hear her brilliant essays—for conversation. Even then,
A frowning Patrick Robert
Guiney chaperones the very
Couch, like a dead sentry
From someone's civil war

Hovering behind the couch
They lightly occupy.

9   *for Vincent Ferrini*
Day's Orpheus returned to earth
Seven months after the pleasure party.
Seems to have lately read
That most difficult of all American
Poems from the nineteenth century.

10   *To Martha Koehler*
Kristeva's *Tales of Love* and Žižek's *Looking Awry* on seeing the object of desire:

Fred Day could see Louise's ink stand
(Very Victorian Egyptian).
The last thing before sleep;
First thing upon waking.

11   *To Jonathan Williams*
As I note this, borrowing my daughter's pencil, she is all flipflops active
In the hothouse, she takes two pictures: writes a poem and: makes two drawings.
Creativity may be more innocent
Than Day ever knew.
In his admiration for Wilde's
"Inactivity" principle,

Orpheus sits. Lamenting, for
Crying out loud.

No new day seems possible.
There is no weather in the pictures.
And the next day is not
Exactly tomorrow
Coming, as Keats frets,
"In too late a day."

12   *To Paul Chew*
I've never known what is really meant by the phrase "in the mind's eye," and I've
come to doubt that Fred Day knew either.

I love living in this poem, writing it daily now for months, April into July, spring to midsummer, spring training up to the all-star break, but when I look back at her, break the progress to revise, she disappears. Into history, or novel form, essay or autobiography.

He practiced art as an act of conscience.

Day's shapes
Are not the image after Pound's likeness. Landscape
Is every shape I can imagine.

O, the shape of her mouth
My work has long been to sustain the moment
Orpheus turns to Eurydice

What last words did I say to Duncan, Baltimore, not good-bye, looking into which eye?

Orpheus singing the upper clef, F A C E.

I could not sustain the strategy of going back to Musaeus.

Looking back, the vision is broken off.
Like rereading Céline.
Not at all like rereading *Moby-Dick*.

Looking back is not nostalgic
The morning air in Eurydice's lungs
Air bubbles inside artic ice
Reread is not misread
Char's "bring the ship nearer its longing"
Is closer to re-vision
Why meaning never disappears
When you look at it twice

When Day removed the crown of thorns from his head, after the last of the photographs of Christ's last words, that crown became the scale model of a ship.

Of course, for Hopkins
"The Loss of the Eurydice"

Meant she's a ship.

Lawrence's ship of death, not fools.

Gone from the world
He died during the two weeks I wrote
A letter a day
From the Gulf of Mexico
To Sherman Paul, dead in Fargo.
The ashes of Louise Guiney.
The ashes of Adelaide Crapsey.

Inscape also means Harry Burton's photographs of the rooms and treasures.

Day photographs the worlds before the invention of photography.

Syntax: why the (f.) language walked behind the (m.) sentence thru the realism of incomprehension, only to dissolve in (reading) light.

The ashes of Fred Holland Day.

To get back to the poem I'm involved with.
To get back to Day's pictures.
Has never been far / out   of mind.

At times our infant's desire to speak to us widens her eyes. Blink.
The poet's infantile desire
To write about everything, and at once, in his poem. For example:

Doris' eyes, "the color of forget-me-nots," her mother says.

My father's eyes were blue

I have my father's eyes
My father's father's eyes

Our daughters have my eyes too.

See now?

Your eyes were clouded over,
You were dying
And we could not reach you to say.

13   *To John Moritz*
There is no "late style" to take up in a poem about Orpheus-Day.

(I have always felt Duncan took on a poetry of old age prematurely.)

There is only the sad renunciation of mankind
Followed by the violent revenge on love's body.

(Laura Riding Jackson residing in a Florida flattened of second-story windows.)

The air temperature as I type nears 100 degrees. Seventy inside where I type.
Neither condition will enter the poem that is entering its last phase.

There is no late style in the poems of Laura Riding.
Or from Day's contemporary, Adelaide Crapsey, who worshipped John Keats.
Instead, there is a morphing of the two women, seekers of Truth;
Especially when I read their poetics.

14   *To Jim Lowell*
I try to keep in mind Ralph Eugene Meatyard
His portrait of Guy Davenport,
He of the elegant essays, each
Starting up from a little-appreciated
Absolutely insightful
Factoid.

Whose fried bologna sandwich
And a Snickers

Were his idea of a home-cooked meal,
Plus dessert.

15   *To Blaise Blevins*

It struck me today that I have spent two whole summers translating Day.

16   *To Gilbert Wright*

Now three.

ORPHEUS LAMENTING

"*Artists give us not conclusions, but evidence,*" unattributed, in Adelaide Crapsey's notebook.

"*There is no great art period without great lovers,*" H.D.

After weeks of writing "Captivity Narratives," as if I were instead translating Musaeus, I unearth Martha's copy of *S/Z* from a packing box in our garage—a text I haven't read since the late 70s—and the intuition that has driven my prosody of ten thousand decisions in over one thousand lines seems, in one stroke, confirmed. That is, Day and Barthes (Dai Sijie too) and, in my own immediate way, now I— look back to Balzac…

In Balzac's story, the sculptor Sarrasin unexpectedly speaks for Fred Day's Orpheus Lamenting: "For me, you have wiped women from the earth." "No more love! I am dead to all pleasure, to every human emotion."

…with the speed of starlight entering the measured eye.

It strikes me: Fred Day's reputation as an artist was crushed by Stieglitz; Amy Lowell named him a psychosomatic hermit; **Keats and the Bostonians**, in 1951, repeats all the mistakes; Jussim is his only biographer till Pat Fanning's corrective. There come the two exhibitions, in Baltimore and then Wellesley, in the 70s—the decade of *S/Z*'s publication and influence. "No hungry generations tread thee down."

In Martha's copy of *S/Z*, the one with Richard Howard's dumb preface, Girodet's "Endymion" (the painting which Balzac mentions at the end of his story) makes a double-page frontispiece (from the Latin, *frontispicium*, the examination of the face). I'd never written about Girodet, or his painting, until this poem and my thinking about how Day saw and how to describe Day's aesthetic.

A note in Martha's handwriting, must be from her grad school days, asks (me): "how are symbols metonymic?" In Balzac's story, Sarrasin's idealized fe/male model "disappears" into the (Girodet Endymion-like) androgynous Zambinella. Here we read the subtext of Fred Day's male models to the extent of Day's submersion in Balzac.

In the Sarrasinean text, the beloved changes state, from statue to painting. In my poem, no wonder why, a column of salt wife flattens into a sheet of photographic print.

His studio admitting "both a northern and a southern exposure," the light there never overhead.

In short, his art required a closer re-examination of the faces of those he well knew would be long dissolved into the light by now. His art. And the dawning of ordinary daylight I drove thru to get back here—.

THE HOUSE OF LIFE SERIES

"Dressed all in white or all in black, she seemed to float over my canvases for a long time, guiding my art," Chagall.

"…one sees things at different moments with different eyes," Edvard Munch.

Olivier Messiaen's original plan for the "Turanglalîla-Symphonie" was to use the Finale twice, in the middle and, altered, in the end. The musical effect of looking back to what is about to disappear.

  [From Theories on Perspective]
All the mirrors at Castle Guiney
Are vats of mercury.
In grammatical terms, they are
Transitions between paragraphs.
All the ellipses in Crapsey's
Late poems are two dots. In
Architectural terms, condensed.
The mirrors in Cocteau's films.
All the staircases in Day House
Are connected by a well of air
So attuned, acoustical, I spoke
Quietly with Patricia, from
The third to first floor.
"The weather outside
Doesn't matter," she was saying.

  [Hypnos Driving Away]
Day scratched the Reading Gaol in his own blood across the walls of his own skull.
Out the lone window, cut from the stone to relieve pressure, he could see
Abendland, Spengler's twilight land, the West rounding the last curve of crushed gravel driveway
to St. Elizabeths.

[Each Day]
I allow the black ink's fading a little each day into the dry-cleaners cardboard of Duncan's self portrait because I want to see his face again each day.

[From A History of the Darkroom]
                                                    The postmod pastiche (I had long assumed Dr. Williams had to have been thinking about his beginnings in Keats' poetry when he wrote: "It's a strange courage you give me, ancient star." Taking Williams' star to be "Bright Star," where John Keats, the failed medical student, is thinking of Shakespeare the sonneteer. I newly see the strangeness of Fred Day's daylight makes another kind of courage that can be found in artists. The courage to create. Day worries, in an unpublished essay no less, that photography isn't art. In his day. These days, Carole Maso's essay writing is what David Markson calls the novel and what I thot, all along, to be the kind of poem I'd been
                                                    given to write.) quotes the modern collage.

[From Experiments in Epistemology]
Eurydice, with a hand-held camera, took this one of the Earth, from the surface of the moon; while Orpheus, left behind in Paris (not pictured), was photographing a full Moon of grey crepe in his mounted reflector scope atop Maurice Blanchot's roof.

[From A History of the Darkroom]
Another man of leisure
Another darkened New England room:
Parkman going blind writing history
A few minutes a day.
Weston neighbor Francis Blake
Picturing Truth,
Not Beauty,
@ 1/2000ths a sec.

[My Life in Architecture]
If I knew Atta Kim, I'd ask him,

Please photograph this poem in a series
All multiple exposures
From cross-country trips or mescaline trips,
Or F. Holland Day at home.

[Being There]
Brilliant bench jockey
Basil King's psychological portraits
From a bench in the Met's
Room the women still coming and going
Talking of Modigliani & Broodthaers
That day we saw Judy Collins'
Retrospecitve eyes.

[Seasons]
Emerson's transparent eyeball turns
On Emma Lazarus,
Then flicks away.

[Orientalismos]
Buddha inscrutable
Wide eye
-Lids half closed.

[Eyeglasses]
Landis Everson came back from the dead this year.
There are no photographs of Eurydice,
Only baseball cards of pitchers batting.

[Picture]
The sadness of Frank Selee's moustache.
Cupid Childs flying out.
Poor Kid Nichols with only a fastball.

[Runner]
Awarded first base, stands beside fielder, and chats:
Four eyes dead on the pitcher, who has the white ball?

                      Then, the hidden ball trick.
  The empty base.

The two foul lines reach far fair—
Into infinity.

[About Face]
"I lost my balance on purpose.
I turned my head deliberately,
And I forbid anyone to contradict me,"

Cocteau has Orphee say.

[Speak]
                                    Outrunning a ball hit over his
head.

[Did Day notice]
Smokey Joe's summer?
All the games
Were day games then.

[From Theories on Perspective]
Say let's meet sometime at the vanishing point.
If I get there first, I'll make an X on the sidewalk
Like this. If you get there before I do,
Rub it out.
Moe explains this to Curly. Like O to E.

["Dappled things"]
Day's surface returns me
To something Hopkins wrote about

Pied Beauty being.

[From A History of the Darkroom]
Mesaeus, following the death of Orpheus, liked to quote
Pop Liebel,
The way he says "He trueHer aVey,"
Before turning out the lights at the Argosy.

[From A History of the Darkroom]
Day buying his cigars from Pessoa's tobacco shop.

[From A History of the Darkroom]
Ten-thousand thieves in prison reading law—
A thousand comedians reading philosophy—
The way to read poetry.

[Sent male]
Since the divorce, many of Orpheus' former literary friends
No longer come around or write to him.

      (Cut to Guiney, sorting the mail into slots.)

The empty feel of sending e-mails into cyberspace. Eurydice-mail.
Seriously, what a relief not to have them in this new poem, or to see.

[Negatives]
Viola Dana's disappearance from silent films, into silent films.

[Antipodes]
Bedtime again.
Ekelöf takes one last look
At his wife. She disappears
Into the big house on the
Green lawn he bot her.
The poet retires himself

To the trailer house next to the house
Parked on the by now black lawn.
Sees her light is on.
He will write "Monologue to His
Wife" before dawn.

*

"[T]he images of her are cruelly attached to the wall with pins and at times extra pins pierce her heart or the space between her legs and she's laughing at me in the third photo…,"Luisa Valenzuela's *He Who Searches*.

*

"Orpheus the explorer finds his heart in death."
Messiaen, in his Notes for a 1991 *"Turangalîla-Symphonie,"* cites *Cinq Rechants*.
Picture Yvonne Loriod's fingers on piano keys.
Missing from the picture is Clare, the first wife of the composer, the woman's face
In Roland Penrose's painting "Seeing is Believing," eyes into the stars whose names
Who can remember
Or a song in "Harawi" sung by Piroutched,
Another first wife.

[Little Good Harbor album page]
Not art, but its compulsive side.
Taking notes toward the on-going longpoem,
Making a pictorial record of the trip,
One snap-shot for every week in the child's life.
What the English Pope identified as
People who attend church
For the music?

[Eric Dolphy]
On alto sax,

On flute, on

That c r a z y

Bass-clarinet—

On four-string lyre.

[Blanchot's *Death Sentence*]
To read a book in a single night and be forever changed by it.
Reading about Fred Day's lonesome death, and ashes; a parent dead and buried
Before you can get home.

[From A History of the Darkroom]
All the fights in Ernest Haycox novels occur in decent Republican darkness.

[Renting Ice Time]
Anna Kavan pictures Eurydice, white hair, thin wrists
As she is found, lost, found, abandoned to her nightmare
Our end of the world.

[1964]
O in this scene tears up
The family photographs. Buster
Keaton plays O
In Beckett's *Film*. Here, O
Is Object; the camera is
E for an Eye.

[A Fall of Light]
Munch's photographic memory for first impressions.

[Little Good Harbor album page]
Antonio Lopez-Garcia painted "Lucio's Balcony"
For twenty-eight years in Madrid
Because the friends in his portrait had left town.

[From A History of the Darkroom]
Today's *N.Y. Times* showed a picture of an 1841 group photograph, which included (far left) the 78-year-old Constanze, Mozart's widow! To look into that face, 10 July 2006. Pam Roberts found Castle Guiney, and "voracious mosquitoes," some eighty years after Fred H. Day closed the door, 1916.

Dear Jed:

It's been six months.

The postcard you sent, Fred Day's Orpheus ("The Vision"), reassumes its familiar place, on my table, in danger of morphing into Cowper's sofa. Eric Satie wallpaper hums from the wall like a new truck.

We have summer plans to visit Ms. Crapsey, in Rochester, Emily in Amherst, and you at the Day House.

But this is February, the shortest patience.

I think (sleet turns to rain) to resume the Day poem. Let's see how much I've changed, and if the old boy will still talk to me. There will be more light to work by, come spring.

We write the given poem, not the Planned.

Love, Rich.

AVAILABLE LIGHT, NORWOOD, JUNE 2007

*"Let them pick the story
out of the house of your
words, floor by floor, room
by room,"* Kerouac's "Death of Gerard."

"Why is it I choose small spaces for studies?" Sherman Paul.

"He travels, and I too," Cowper's "The Task."

1
Tom McCarthy, sexton to Highland Cemetery, boasts: "This is the only place in Norwood with gargoyles."

Inside the crypt, I open my journal and place it, beside a Starbucks tall cup, in the white dust atop (Anna Day's sarcophagus) my desk
Back on the road, after reading in Day's dining room, I discover scent of polished wood on my fingers at the wheel.

"Musty music hangs its cobwebs over the pages," Lansing.
The cries of bees, from inside the wall behind the griffin lectern, in my head!

Fanning finally removed the sign, decades in Day's study,
"Amy Lowell Sat At This Desk." Restored
Guiney's ink stand to that desk, Haydon's
Death mask in the Keats
Corner below the ribbon frieze of "Urn" narrative.
"White horses thunder in the libraries."   Surely, in *this* one.
The only square bedroom in the house is his businessman father's,
Sans sunken floors. Helen Allen, sent by Harvard, called the steps
Altars. In his final bedroom, Fred collected the painted
Wood cabinet once housed the public library.

I am, it seems, the bee
Who comes home
Delirious.

The walls were alive
The beehive
In the tomb
A grand emblem,
Honey in the skull,
Cram could not plan.

Bedridden, Day felt his life's
Work "comparable to
                the perpetual
                              egg-laying of a
queen bee."

2
Here is the kind of scholar Patricia Fanning is: she thot to ask Ann Tanneyhill
what his voice sounded like.

"Erudition is the modern form of the fantastic," Kiš, "Schizopsychology."

A.T. remembers: "Mr. Day knew everything."

3
Building
A tomb for parents,
By Cram's design
For king and queen,
Commissioned by Lewis
In *his* father's name;

Details of the floor tiles await their reading
Like numbers inside Fenway's wall.

From our bench outside the chapel, Jack
Identifies a mocking bird. The bird moves
Keeping out of sight
Inside the cemetery.

            I know it's you, Museaus, singing your best
Altho the stones here

Sleep thru everything.

The mimus polyglottos is known to have mimicked a washing machine.

Some birds have a nest in the tower
Among the carved grape vines.
A renewable crown of grass
Mocking the carved grape vines.
Dwelling
But the house,
Erected by parents,
The son redeems
After his own mind,
In his own hand,
To his own eye.

Untranslated light
Enters the eye
Upsidedown.

To suit his eye—
Flora in the green
Wallpaper of
Day's bedroom
Growing upsidedown
As if toward the library
Below, which is the sun—
It and Lansing's heavenly
Tree grow downward.

Thinking
The bedroom's square column,
Inexplicably
In the middle of,
Rhymes
With the three-story courtyard
That makes from light the torso
Of the house.
The two tunnels (galleria) to windows
Recall

The entranceway downstairs, or
Where We Came In.
Narrative concept of rhyme as interruptive
It's like I'd never been away,
Room for everything
I thot to bring
This, my first visit.

"Time is not a river, but a prism in which we are broken and divided like light,"
James Bradley, <u>The Resurrectionist.</u>

  A Day image
Holds one eyeful
Of light, and no
More.
Can't see Fred Day in available light.
Glimpse, thru the phosphenes Miss Lowell pressed on our yet unopened eyelids,
The light
  Of day. The broken bits of light
Of Melville's "Mosses" thru the glass of
Williams's Elsie. You can read the letters
On the condition of plates
Of glass.

4

                              Bright crypt
                              Dim chapel

                              (In our lite)

                          Robert Ryman-white

5
Where to, do, the stairs at Day House lead? Ever
Back to my poem.

"By Whom do you swear / that you return to this place?"
Dorn at the end still taking notes, Dec. 1998,

That photograph
On the Spanish Steps, "a center for me,"

His Keats a stairway, returns the poet to
What he must do.

This is not architecture.
It is anatomy.

Even the floors are steps
Some cross-section resembling

No blue print but what I once thot to see
In *A, The Bridge*, the Schiffanoia, or the stepped lines

On a page of my own poetry.
The stairs there make a poem's sense.

6
The pace in writing it, passus, never more than the next step.

"…*he has put into my mind the thought that if we are bound together, we are bound by writings…to make this bond real, I must therefore write, and not once and for all, but all the time, or perhaps one single time,…a time for which I have plenty of time, a time that exhausts all the reality of time,*" Maurice Blanchot, <u>the one who was standing apart from me</u>.

Standing on the lower level, I could not point with assurance to the room above us from which I had just come.
"*There was really no end to its windings—to its incomprehensible subdivisions. It was difficult, at any given time, to say with certainty upon which of its…stories one happened to be. From each room to every other there were sure to be found three or four steps either in ascent or descent…our most exact ideas in regard to the whole mansion were not very far different from those with which we pondered upon infinity,*" Poe's "William Wilson."

Unlike

Simonides, who remembered where
    Each guest sat,
    At Skopas' table,
Before the roof fell in.

7
This is not a bill.
This is a test
Of will.
Because we have a test for it,
Testing is advised. In fact,
A whole series of tests follows;
Not unlike those a plumber might
Routinely use to trace
The problem.
Only this is not a house.
The procedure requires
The insertion of a tube,
Either metal or flexible,
The length of the penis
And into the bladder.
This will take 15 to 20 minutes tops.
Miss Dickinson would agree
To her own diagnostic:
Her physician sat
In one upstairs room of the family house
While she,
Fully clothed in white,
Walked past the doorway
Inside her own room.
And Fred Day endured an emergency
Operation for prostate cancer
Behind this door to the attic, where
He had developed the Orpheus pictures.
Do think of us when you finish,
If you do finish.
Send us your submissions.
This is not a bill.

8   "More Seven Last Words of Orpheus"
A man can sit so long,
All his days at a card table upstairs,
Sores develop on his elbows.

9
Seeing Pound
Thru peyote,

Olson's
Ishmael,

Forever changes
The ways we have
Of *looking*
At things.

Looking back, Fred,
To see what's up.

10
His gift remains

Anonymous.

Email Ken Page, at Keats House
@cityoflondon:gov,
To ask if
The name of Fred Holland Day
Is anywhere in evidence,

And could somebody please
Look for 1933
Underneath Anne Whitney's bust?

I'm still awaiting your word,

Ken?

11 "The Decadent and the Virgin"
Am I confusing

Outsider for coterie?

Some terrific poets manage
To do both, both held
Captive in culture and cult.

Just the kind of chowder
Melville the poet, did not stir

But swam. Well,

Am I?

<u>By Spring, 1917, Fred Day will take no more photographs.</u>
Harry Crosby volunteers to fight in the First World War.
Wittgenstein, at the Russian front, begins the *Tractatus*. Finland national independence. At the end of this year, Louis Sullivan: "As for me, the bottom has dropped out, and the future is a blank." Construction on the German Warehouse, in Richland Center, Wisconsin, is begun; Frank Lloyd Wright's "most depressing work," it will remain unfinished. From the same time, Marsden Hartley: "You know my reverence for nature is not at all keen, not nature just for itself." This fall, Yeats' bride Georgie's first attempts at automatic writing. Honus Wagner's final season. Cleveland's Ray Chapman sets the major league record for sacrifice bunts in a season. *Parade*, the Cocteau-Picasso-Diaghilev-Satie ballet. Buster Keaton debuts in seven films with Roscoe Arbuckle for the Comique Film Corporation. Dr. Williams publishes *Al Que Quiere!* Cleveland's Jack Graney leads the American League in walks. The Canadian-born outfielder was the first player wearing a number on his uniform to bat in the majors (batting leadoff); he would become the first former-player to work as a radio announcer in baseball; Speaker platooned him.

The journal *De Stijl* first appears. For four months, Anais Nin suspends writing her journal, begun in 1914 and otherwise continued until her death. E.A. Robinson's *Merlin*. The first in a series of operations on Mary Cassatt's eyes, for cataracts, that would end her painting. The year her close friend Edgar Degas dies. Dorothy Rothschild marries Edwin Pond Parker, II, of Hartford, Connecticut.

Wyndham Lewis' first novel, *Tarr*, which had appeared serially in *The Egoist* over two years, is published in book form. Waldo Frank, a conscientious objector, publishes his first novel, *The Unwelcome Man*. The formation of the National Hockey League. Pessoa publishes "Ultimatum," attributed to futurist Alvaro de Campos. June 16, Mecca records a temperature of 124 degrees at the height of the California heat wave. August 17, Wilfred Owen meets Siegfried Sassoon at War Hospital, Edinburgh. Rabindranath Tagore's *Lectures on Personality*, the same year he reads "India's Prayer" at the India National Congress, Calcutta. Pound undertakes the poem sequence "Homage to Sextus Propertius." Mata Hari is executed, Vincennes. Béla Bartok's ballet "The Wooden Prince" premieres, in Budapest. Sinclair Lewis' *The Innocents*. Man Ray paints "Suicide" with a commercial airbrush. Robert Lowell, Buddy Rich, Harry Cary, Ella Fitzgerald, Virgil Trucks, Lou Harrison, John Kennedy, John Lee Hooker, Dizzie Gillespie, Thelonius Monk, Jo Stafford, I.M. Pei are born this year. Gwendolyn Brooks, whose poetry reading was to be the first ever for me, is born. Nicholas II is arrested. Kerensky is premier. The events of the October Revolution happen in November 1917. John Reed and Louise Bryant sail for Russia. The child Vladimir Nabokov flees St. Petersburg. Buffalo Bill Cody, Scott Joplin, Ferdinand von Zeppelin, Rodin are dead this year. The Woolfs establish the Hogarth Press in their Richmond dining room. The press' first two books are Virginia's *The Mark on the Wall* and Leonard's *Three Jews*.

The first Pulitzer Prizes are awarded. Juan Ramón Jiménez publishes *Platero y yo*, prose poems to a donkey. June 5, the military draft begins in the U.S. George Bellows, educated at Ohio State, reacts: "I am a patriot for beauty. I would enlist in any army to make the world more beautiful." Leoš Janácek, who has been writing "Taras Bulba" for two years now, meets Kamila Stösslová. Dorothy Parker's first year as drama critic for *Vanity Fair*. *Smart Set* publishes O'Neill's *The Long Voyage Home*. Elmer Rice's plays *Iron Cross* and *Home of the Brave*. T.E. Lawrence leads a raid on Aqaba. D.H. Lawrence is forced, by threat of the Defence of the Realm Act and local authorities, to leave Cornwall within three days. Louis Untermeyer's *These Times*. Richard Mutt's "Fountain" is on display at the 1917 Independents exhibition, New York, where William Carlos Williams reads "Overture to a Dance of Locomotives." Alfred Kreymborg's *Provincetown Plays*, Second Series. Georgia O'Keeffe's show at "291" will be the last event for Stieglitz's gallery. Steiglitz publishes the final issue of *Camera Work*. Dayton,

Ohio's Jane Reece's "The Young Musician" pictures a girl with lyre, otherwise the effects could be Day. James Gamble Rogers's Harkness Memorial Tower, Yale. Dom DiMaggio and Lou Boudreau are born. Szymanowski's String Quartet No. 1. Poulenc's "Rapsodie nègre" premieres, its verses chanted in an imaginary African tongue. Henry Cowell's "Quartet Romantic." *The Chinese Nightingale and Other Poems* by Vachel Lindsay. Urged by his mother, the poet begins signing his name "Hart Crane." John G. Neihardt's *The Lonesome Trail* and *Bundle of Myrrh*. Hamlin Garland's *A Son of the Middle Border*. Harriet Monroe's anthology, *The New Poetry*. Glen Coffield is born, in Prescott, Arizona. The Rev. Eliot's *Prufrock and Other Observations*. Also the anthology *Eight Harvard Poets* (S. Foster Damon, e.e. cummings, John Dos Passos, Robert Hillyer, R.S. Mitchell, William A. Morris, Dudley Poore, and Cuthbert Wright).

Aldous Huxley's privately printed, unbound book of verse, in French and English, *Jonah*. Louis Destouches, on board a ship for Liverpool, writes his first short story, "Waves." He would later become Céline. Bertrand Russell's *Principles of Social Reconstruction*. Ring Lardner's *Guillible's Travels*. Mina Loy meets Arthur Craven at the Independents opening. Robert Graves' *Fairies and Fusiliers*. T.E. Hulme is killed in action, Flanders. Louis Church donates many of the paintings from his father's Olana estate to the Cooper Union. Kurt Schwitters begins his "Merzbilder." Yeats marries Georgie Lees. Walter de la Mare's lecture tour of the U.S. Sinclair Lewis' *The Job*. Amy Lowell lectures at the Brooklyn Institute of Arts and Sciences. Frost teaches at Amherst College. Carl Sandburg joins the staff at the "Chicago Daily News." Teasdale's *Love Songs*, which will win next year's Pulitzer Prize.

Edna St. Vincent Millay graduates from Vassar and moves to Waverly Place in Greenwich Village. Her *Renascence and Other Poems* appears. Archibald McLeish's first book of poems, *Tower of Ivory*.

Joseph Stella's "Brooklyn Bridge." And Charles Burchfield's sketchbook "Conventions for Abstract Thoughts," preliminary to the painting "Church Bells Ringing, Rainy Winter Night." Alvin Langdon Coburn's exhibition, in London, of Vortographs, at the Camera Club. The seven monthly visions appear to three Portugese children, near Fatima. Billy Sunday addresses 1.4 million in revival meetings, in New York. Hans Pfitzner's *Palestrina*. Teen Aaron Copland's debut, at Wanamaker's, Brooklyn. Joseph Cornell is enrolled at Phillips Academy for his first term.

Robinson Jeffers and his wife, Una, move to the rocks by Carmel Bay. W.H. Davies publishes *Farewell to Poesy* and two other books of poems. Blaise Cendrars' *L'ABC du inema*. Henry James writes the first prefaces for the 24-volume New York edition of his collected works. Sherwood Anderson's novel *Marching Men*. Edith Wharton's *Summer*. H.D. writes the poem "Eurydice," beginning: "So you have swept me back...."

After all

After all

After all

After all, a fall of light

STUDY IN GRAYS: ADELAIDE CRAPSEY

"At 57 I have two people ED and LZ, after a lifetime, almost, of reading...,"
Lorine Niedecker, letter to Louis Zukofsky.

"...[T]he time is come when Eurydice is to call for an Orpheus, rather than Orpheus for Eurydice...
[S]he...needs now to take her turn in the full pulsation...,"
Margaret Fuller, Woman in the Nineteenth Century.

"...so full of her own immense death,
Still so new to her, she grasped nothing,"
Rilke, "Orpheus. Eurydike. Hermes."

Picture
Her inhumed in
Geo Eastman's Rochester:
Orpheus comes home, her cinquain
His.

I finish the first cinquain, a poem in form after Adelaide Crapsey's practice (1911-13), only upon finding the word "inhumed" in Mina Loy's last poem, "Letters of the Unliving." I have been writing the poems of the *Captivity Narratives* since last spring. I am fifty-seven years old this summer. Hermes' her/me is.

Only
Bolaño could
Track her life, snake-bit
Heiress to the last heretic..
Vanished.

Crapsey was what we now call an Outsider Artist. She misses Pound and H.D. in London. She lives in the Paris of Picasso and Stein, without an encounter. Fred Day was what we now call, after Frank O'Hara studies, a Coterie Artist. The stories of their lives are captivity narratives, missing the last chapters, the ones on The Return.

Smile
Only a god
Can know the fate of his
Photograph, even Orpheus
Is stuck..

With the
Grinning Idiot
In the picture over
His obit. He reenters
Her eye.

"It is a very serious thing to be a funny man." Caption under Crapsey's senior class picture, in the *Vassarion.*

The form
Of a woman
Listens intently to
A poetry that will bring her
Back.

E is
A shadow at

O, the form of a woman
Returned in her cinquain, a
God's trick.

What
Is it only
Poems can picture?
Hold the pages close..her words
Dissolve.

The dissolve is into black and white then white. I had wanted Crapsey to be the corrective to what I read, the first of two summers writing the poem, as the fatal influence of Louise Guiney on Day's work. Its failure to become modern. After conversations with Fred Day's biographer—in effect, looking twice at Guiney—she vanished as villain, and rejoined Day as his life-long correspondent. Not so much black and white, but gray.

Don't
Look back, Dylan
Cautioned. Unravish'd
Eurydice's home safe..songbook
All these years?

And she did not meet Fred Day, much less supplant Louise Imogen Guiney (who was, in fact, kept in the USA by the PO), at the dedication of Keats' Hampstead memorial. His Papinta, with Beardsley in attendance.

Her
Debt to Keats
Dates from a visit to see..
The lyre broken over his headstone..
Herself.

Crapsey mentions Keats only late in *A Study in English Metrics*, where she proposes an analysis of "Hyperion" (left undone). But I think I can prove that Keats' formative influence on her poems begins, 'istorin-like, with her trip to the Protestant Cemetery in Rome.

Her Keats
And Landor, shed

Of tomes, maundered amok
Fiesole and Rome, eager
To meet her.

Chaste
Moneta's face,
That Imagist Titans
Left behind, travels where we do..
The moon!

Keats
In lover's lap
A book not his head not
Even Keats' head full of lovely
Death.

The story goes that Crapsey, from beyond her nearby grave, dictated to Eugenie Bragdon, whose record (automatic writing) is preserved at the University of Rochester. Jack Spicer listening in would have asked Crapsey for a few new poems to publish. Yeats would have married the automatic writer, in lust with love poetry, crazy images for sane poems. The European Surrealists should have feted her in poems and paintings. Future ghost writers should email Mary Hust.

"Mrs. Bragdon's emails"
Light enuf
To read by, sufficient
Blood for poems..promising
One more day alive
Alone;

My window
Bed, my view of
Graves..my manuscript
Pages, none betrays its violent
Birth

When I—
Fate defied,

Chose to wear grey only—
Unbuttoned the top dot from my throat..
First breathed.

Wide-
Brim flowered hat
Hides, first, child's eyes, and then,
With a gesture now lost to us,
Her lap.

Feathers
More than flowers
On big hat that Fred Day's
Model is tickled to wear..
A nest.

Vassar
Girls visiting
John Burroughs at Slabsides
Pose on the lap of the master
Hiker.

I cannot see Florence Van Demark's snapshot of college-girl Crapsey and ancient Burroughs without thinking of Annie Miller's pose in Hunt's "The Awakening Conscience." Her subtitle for "To the Dead in the Grave-Yard under My Window" is "Written in a Moment of Exasperation." I like her best like this, wind-blown and exasperated with what is given her. "I will not be patient. I will not lie still."

[Note to myself: Change "master" to "graybeard" in cinquain, above, about Burroughs.]

Among
The bathers, Walt
By Eakins, projected too
Photographs onto his canvas
Wet.

Her first published story is "A Girl to Love," mistaken for "A Maid to Love" by biographers.

VERSE
ADELAIDE CRAPSEY

NEW YORK
ALFRED·A·KNOPF
1929

Between
My hands, her waist.
Before my eyes, her face.
Before betray, beyond beneath..
Bequeath.

NB: Try to keep in mind, Miss Crapsey was seven years Pound's senior.

"Crapsey in Captivity"
Knows
Japan, image
Years before Pound found
Eurydice in the tea room
Alive.

I originally thot of Adelaide Crapsey as a more modern Eurydice for Day only after missing her grave on a visit to Rochester's Mt. Hope, where we went to see Frederick Douglass and saw instead Susan B. Anthony.

From all
Of Florence, she
Fingers Michelangelo's
Unfinished stones, with a modern
Eye:

Figures
Retreating to
Rock, or just emerging
Frozen quarries. These stones once
Cried.

For her it was Omond, not Eliot. T.S. Omond read a version of her essay on metrics and responded in a letter to her we half have. W.G. Howard, the secretary for the *Modern Language Review,* rejected Crapsey's manuscript in a letter (30 September 1914, just before her death) containing nine mechanical errors. His "negativ anser" writes "cald" for could; "anser" for answer; "servis" for service!

"A Concise Study In American Metrics"
Lorine's
Parenthesis (

Adelaide's ellipses..
Beats a feminine pulse—Emily's
Dash.

If
A butterfly,
Then—the kind that migrates
A thousand miles to Mexico..
And back.

I write these two runs of summer quatrains as syllable-counted exercises in biography, with no proper thot to Crapsey's theory of metrics, diction, or the stresses she practiced in her own cinquain experiments. Further, I insist on the recognition of ideas in the form, not content with her sense of the primacy of image and ironic contrasting. I think she would disapprove.

The cinquain form, once it is opened, can even be used for overhearing dialog between captives.

"Why is
It nobody
Paints anymore? Is it
That all paintings have been painted,
Or what?"

"When it's
Impossible
To paint with the heroes,
Then we must learn to play chess with
Duchamp."

"Philip
Marlowe played chess
Against himself." "—But Death
Takes Bergman's knight in good old black
And white."

"Must you
Count everything
I say? My words are more

Memorable than syllables
(Revon)."

By Bridges's count, "speed" contains many more syllables than "velocity."

My grad student conducted a syllable count on the Collected Poems of Crapsey, making the mistake of counting down. James Laughlin reported that, in 1968, the year Oppen won the Pulitzer, sales for his prize-winning book of poems was negative, meaning more bookstore returns than sales.

I write
To rewrite his
Mauberley; read texts
For new poems I only think
My own.

And I wanted Fred Day to be Ezra Pound's Vortographer, instead of cousin Coburn.

You can
Feel heat in waves
Facing, when your back
Is turned t[*tear in page*]
Marble.

Picture a time when Edwin Robinson and Frost were best in the country. When *In the Steps of Jesus* had been the best-selling book in America for decades running. When Georg Trakl swallowed the double barrels of "Helian" and scattered his brains.

Harry
Crosby opened
Up on the last copies
Of *Red Skeleton* with his
Shotgun.

Did
He line them up
Facing firing-squad style
In the study, or make a pile

Of bodies

Better to
Push into grave?
Or did the man who so
Well misunderstood Baudelaire,
Who had

So
Misunderstood
Poe, take his time this time
Assassinate each one in its
Jacket?

This is the Law of all biography:

Turning
From Newman to
Darwin then Marx, rolling
The stone away..the body
Stinketh.

Virginia Woolf spent the final morning of her life dusting the house.

The consumptive Robert Louis Stevenson wrote *The Master of Ballantrae: A Winter's Tale* in his cottage at the sanitarium by Saranac Lake. His short novel is an adventure story (Virginia Woolf remarked that all 19th-century British novels, save *Middlemarch*, were tales for boys) of sibling rivalry, pirates and buried treasure, intrigue at the French court, otherness in India. In her own time at Saranac Lake, Crapsey would write "To The Dead In The Grave-Yard Under My Window," "Lines to My Left Lung," and read the first issue of *BLAST*.

O,
Eric Dolphy
Eric Dolphy Eric
Dolphy Eric Dolphy Eric
Dolphy.

Those ways in which Eric Dolphy was held captive in Amerika. Melville, it turns out, only thot he was confined, in Pittsfield, to the farm chores of writing short captivity narratives for magazines that paid. Crapsey's letter to Esther Lowenthal makes no mention of a piazza off her hospital room in Pittsfield, or a view of a mountain looking like the back of a whale trying to clear its great lungs.

Muffled
Inside gray fog
The turnpike's cars slow down
Skirting Pittsfield as if worried
Sick.

Another image of driving back from reading at Day's house, sensitively aware of AC's hospital stay in Pittsfield, Melville's captivity too, like nerves when driving a car thru a fogbank.

*

In Harry Smith's *Heaven and Earth Magic*, an entire archival box containing Crapsey's dictations to Eugenia Bragdon is devoured by Imagist giants at one sitting.

*

Ammons's
Last book is all
Couplets, parallel lines,
Arrivals at no vanishing
Point.

I've been thinking in cinquains lately, when I think to say something in a poem, waiting in Hornell for my date at the U of R. When my father-in-law Don Koehler gives me a copy of *Bosh and Flapdoodle*, I see Ammons's last thinking was accomplished all in couplets. Can't decide if it should be "Arrivals at" or "Departures from."

After midnights, in Hornell, I read *The Savage Detectives*, and write these four cinquains.

Ordained
Orpheus sings
Face down into warm grass
With each word, fucking on top of
A grave.

JW
Shows us a slide,
A nice river scene he had shot,
Where the body of Orpheus
Is not.

Wade out,
Sinecure passed,
Where syntax rushes past
Both knees, but body's unready
To float.

Health,
Sings Orpheus.
She doesn't understand
The language, why his head needs no
Body.

Twice, in her cover letter to prospective publishers for her book of poems, AC's words arrest like Dickinson's: her spelling of "volumn" (ED's "opon"), and her word choice "available," as in her instructions: "If / you do not find / it available will / you please return the manuscript / to me…" (line breaks mine). The "unconscious Imagist" writing an unconscious cinquain.

Read a dozen times,
I do not comprehend

Bolaño's unconscious remark

About visceral realists
Going ahead backwards.

Dear Jed:

The bad news of Richard's health is scary. I terrorized myself, midnight past, thinking my way around the fact of our years, while you tour Australia.

"How long is this posthumous life of mine to last?" Day's Orpheus Keats, complained, in Rome. My head this summer so full of head aches from the dead, sinuses with tomb dust, that I dreamt of Severn, supporting Keats' (severed?) head in the poet's final agonies. Have I come to make Day's big mistake, picturing Orpheus still singing away, his rolling head bodiless and floating down the River Severn? In my head, with Hersey's comment (the women in Rossetti's late paintings do look to be lovely corpses) that could mean Orpheus in the time of the seven years; or whatever pictures of Crapsey await me in the archives.

(In Martha's writing, "A pathway now seems like a tangent," just now. She'll fix it, think it thru; her essay's passage will always read seamlessly and true.)

*This morning, I've found some encouragement I'd share with you. A fact: That's **not** John Keats' death-mask on Day's bookshelf. It's Haydon's fall of 1816 life-mask that I held, you photographed. So Keats gets a reprieve. Behold the head so full of itself, not to be confused for Gherardi's emptied-out mask of February 24, 1821. Not to die each imagined midnight, until we've lived. Let the mourners memorize, if they care—The odes remain to be written!*

> *We*
> *Cannot dwell in,*
> *Only on, our own deaths.*
> *Parents dead, we are free to be*
> *Alone.*

From Rochester, Mary Huth
writes that she's set aside
Crapsey's copy of the Keats
Collected Poems *for my visit.*
Will the annotations in the poet's
hand be life- or death-mask?

Love, Rich.

"Eugenie." The messages all start "Eugenie."

In the University of Rochester reading room, I have open before me Box 68 of the Bragdon Family Papers, containing five files of Eugenie Bragdon's automatic writing. These are artifacts of the spiritualism craze, I know, decades before the Surrealists would claim such writing to be poems from the nonconscious. First sheet I read, adjusting my eyes to her spidery hand, seems a token of good will from beyond her own grave. It reads: "…and we are the fingers of the hand which molds the lives of men" (March 1918); and I associate its metaphor with the Keats/hands motif I've followed all the way to upstate New York to decipher. In Hornell, last night, I wrote:

If
Even mirrors
Differ, can Orpheus
Ever be certain who holds his
Hand?

And in the little poem "El Hombre," William Carlos Williams diagrams the tradition in which he is writing the poem, from Shakespeare thru Keats' "Bright Star" to himself. I had in mind, writing the following cinquain, Keats' "This living hand, now warm and capable" as I read it thru Crapsey's "Amaze."

The weight
That's John Keats' [cross out: *death*] *life*
Mask, still wet in Haydon's hands,
Off Fred Day's shelf, my living hands
Lifted.

With "fear not all is well your nervousness is cosmic," I see just how close my method for writing a serial poem about the life and work of a historical poet really is to what Eugenie Bragdon called "automatic writing." Spicer worked this out years ago but the humor in his poems threw me off track.

Have I come to Rochester, and this point in my life, to research one poet only to discover another? (Louise Guiney becomes Crapsey becomes Eugenie Bragdon?) Should my poems begin "Richard…"? I would feel too lonely an audience; Breton watching Desnos writing in his sleep.

In fact, my first time in Rochester
I'd driven Duncan and Bertholf in
from Buffalo for a conference
on women writers, like Mary Butts
and H.D.—but, of course, nobody

mentioned Adelaide Crapsey—
when Jonathan Williams gave one of
his sly slide talks about the graves
of American poets, and we were
sitting not far from the Crapsey plot.

The second Bragdon file (which opens with a letter to Eugenie from Crapsey's mother, at 678 Averill Avenue) holds the dictations from the dead Adelaide. The first ("know that I am grateful") is recorded by Eugenie on 18 July 1915, when she is "awakened from a…dream…about 645 AM." The next dictation ("Let me tell again the story. I died in terror but I found here a strange new beginning…") comes at 6:00 pm, two days following.

The entry for 21 July ("from the earth I took a light flower. It was on my breast.") might fit best in my earlier cinquains on violets.

The boxes are gray.

I see Crapsey's poem "John Keats" in the Adelaide Crapsey Papers, Box 3. The ribbon-tied stack of her reader's tickets for the British Museum (1909-1910) tell me that she read *Endymion* on 4 May 1909; also "Lamia," "Isabelle," and the sonnets. She sat in seat G5 that day. Now her copy of Rhys's *The Poems of John Keats*. It's immediately clear, from AC's marginalia, that she originally read Keats for her prosody study. I turn to "To A Nightingale," pages 49 and 50, where she has dutifully marked beats in every line up to the final three stanzas.

 Next, Box 3 tells the story of AC, 'Istorin. There are eight drafts of her poem "John Keats." By draft three, she changes the poem's opening, from "Drink thou…" to "Meet thou…," turning away from her British Museum cold analysis of Keats's "Nightingale" after visiting Keats's grave at the Protestant Cemetery, their meeting, after which Keats becomes to her a figure for the self.

Her
Astonished cry,
The only residue.
"Extremes meet," but only in the
Meeting.

Lola Ridge's poem, about the Crapsey she remembers from Smith, ends:
"…you, / who moved as a wind / slight enough / to pass between two violets.…"

Here is another kind of urn. My wife's grandfather, Lawrence C. Koehler, is featured in Montague Free's *All About African Violets* (Doubleday, 1949). There are photographs of his Rochester basement hothouse, where 500 plants grew at once. Mr. Koehler would have been 12 years old when Adelaide Crapsey's ossuary was interred nearby, in Mt. Hope.

Sun-shy
Saintpaulias,
Beautiful heretic, thrive
Beneath the basement's artificial
Sky.

Violet, the shortest ray in the visible spectrum.

Seated
Figure, in gray,
Intent on Gallatin.
Mounting her seat gray day upon
Day.

Crapsey read Albert Eugene Gallatin's *Whistler's Art Dicta*, in the British Museum reading room, mid-1910 or before the revolution of the tea room. (Gallatin went on to found the Gallery of Living Art, at Washington Square, in rooms where the painter Samuel F.B. Morse had developed his telegraph.)

And Pound held that American greatness begins with Lincoln—and Whistler.

Black and
White engenders
Gray, tho the face remains
Chubby as a notebook flush with
Cinquains.

Baseball remains a metaphor for America, especially in the Bonds Era. The week I wrote the next poem, Brandon Watson broke the International League record for a hitting streak, at 43 games, established in 1912 by Rochester's Jack Lelivelt.

Gray
Still means road team,
Perennial cellar-dwellers;
Home wears the color of red
Wings.

In the b/w photographs of Crapsey, her "gray-violet" eyes are gray pixels. But in our study of grays, we see more. In life, her gaze must have held violet contrasting grey. She spelled it *grey*. I imagine it here as the violet achieved again in a secret basement somewhere in Rochester about 1947. If the pallet for my book is limited to white, black, and grays, it is also open to b/w photography, African violets of many colors, and the whiteness of All Colors. By 2008, an art supplies shop in Paris sells fourteen shades of Picasso Gray.

It is the whiteness of Dickinson's dress and Melville's monster.

The blackness unto blackness of Fred Day's robes within the try-works of his darkroom.

The "a" and "e" for Adelaide and Eugenie. The Eurydice.

The ashen skin around Mes*ae*us' maelstrom for a mouth.

(It took Celan to translate Dickinson.) The gray of

Adelaide Crapsey's skirt and matching jacket reflected in her gray-to-violet eyes.

     Looking thru her archive, the poems on paper watermarked "Berkshire Type Writer Paper USA," held up to the light.

          (Crapsey's chair of English, at Smith, remained in the dark about the existence of the poems.)

          The trace of Mary Jemison's vanishing

circles back, Pittsburgh to
          The Genesee. Her grave at Letchworth, a place

near me, unknown to me, when I was writing in Hornell.

I must be covering the same old ground, having unsound memory of my sources. Almost thirty years ago, I would have encountered Mary Jemison, back again, when I first moved to western Pennsylvania and read the local history to write *Court of the Half-King.*

It was, eight years ago now, below those falls where you waded, holding our first daughter with one hand your long skirt in the other, and I walked, very much in love with you and liking my second chance, in shoes over the wet flat rocks in the time before we married.

Proving you *can* wade the same river twice.
Forgot again the lesson—the local is universal.
The kind of historian a poet makes.
Neglected to look around, watching lissome you.

I end where I begin,
Captivated by

Rowlandson's Day
Now Jemison's Crapsey

The living rock

          Returns me to Bolaño's "going ahead backwards,"

> For instructions of a road map or the death certificate.
>
> Tom Kryss writes that he repeatedly misread my
> Poem's line to say: "Try not to <u>repute</u>
>
> the poet's <u>imagination</u> still growing...."
> And there are photographs, Don shows us, of his mother,
>
> The violet-grower's wife, adopted at six months
> And renamed, in Rochester, 1907.
>
> So she becomes the one who appears,
> In family lore, when E. is banished in my poem?
>
> At recognition's crisis, seeing,
> She is returned-away, "simultaneously"
>
> A new word for her succeeds
> Her, "in one head."

Swept back.

"*Wer*?"
Eurydike
has to be told when he
turns around to send her back.
"Who?"

In Rilke's poem, "Orpheus. Eurydice. Hermes.," Eurydike is so full of her own fresh death, pregnant with it, that she has to be told by Hermes at the moment when Orpheus' look banishes her to the underworld. H.D.'s Eurydice will revile her husband's famous name (and, with it, Lawrence's and Pound's and Aldington's). I think of Adelaide Crapsey, alone, nameless, doomed.

Mary (or Molly) Jemison, whose Seneca names included The-Two-Falling-Voices, is reburied near the Portage Falls of the Genesee, beneath a paperweight bronze. Among the chorus of falling voices of women poets in America, Crapsey intoning

"Niagara" or the disembodied voice occurring to Bragdon or soothing words Guiney must have breathed in Fred Day's ear—Breath play.

(Try not to imagine the poet's reputation still growing like fingernails on her corpse.)

The drive.

To write a poem good enuf to make the police understand the act of driving seventy miles per hour while reading a poem. Out here, there is still no town, where Millard Fillmore was born. And traffic lifted into rapidly moving clouds that rarely seemed to collide.

(How can there be sufficient garages to house all these clouds?)

And suffered not, that afternoon on the drive down Jemison's valley from Rochester to Hornell, I swear it, a solitary red light all the way home.

(RE)SOURCES

As prelude and coda to my own travels to sources, I have relied on books to make this book. The following texts were central to my poem on Fred Day: Patricia J. Fanning, ed., *New Perspectives on F. Holland Day* (North Easton, Mass.: Stonehill College Press, 1998); James Crump, *Suffering The Ideal* (Santa Fe: Twin Palms, 1995); Estelle Jussim, *Slave to Beauty* (Boston: Godine, 1981); Hyder Edward Rollins and Stephen Maxfield Parrish, *Keats and the Bostonians* (Cambridge, Mass.: Harvard UP, 1951); Pam Roberts, Edwin Becker, Verna Posever Curtis, and Anne E. Havinga, *F. Holland Day* (Amsterdam: Van Gogh Museum, 2000); and Margaret Homans, "Amy Lowell's Keats: Reading Straight, Writing Lesbian," in *The Yale Journal of Criticism*, 14.2 (2001), pp. 319-351. For historical background on King Philip's War, Nathaniel Philbrick's *Mayflower* (New York: Viking, 2006) was indispensable. I used Larzer Ziff's *The American 1890s: Life and Times of a Lost Generation* (New York: Viking, 1966), for general cultural history in both the Day and the Crapsey poems. To conduct "Orphic research," I have shared Ronald Johnson's source, Elizabeth Sewell's *The Orphic Voice: Poetry and Natural History* (New Haven: Yale UP, 1960), while disagreeing with the Orpheus he creates in "Beam" and the 1991 "A Note." My studies of Adelaide Crapsey began in Karen Alkalay-Gut's *Alone in the Dawn: The Life* (Athens and London: University of Georgia Press, 1988), Susan Sutton Smith's *Adelaide Crapsey: The Complete Poems and Collected Letters* (Albany: SUNY Press, 1977), and Crapsey's own *A Study of English Metrics* (New York: Knopf, 1918). For primary historical accounts, I consulted the captivity narratives, which I first encountered, in 1973, as required reading by Ed Dorn, of Mary Jemison (1824) and Mary White Rowlandson (1682) at *womenshistory.about.com*.

My thanks to Patti Fanning, for her biographer's knowledge so openly shared during the time when she was at work on *Through an Uncommon Lens: The Life and Photography of F. Holland Day* (Amherst: University of Massachusetts Press, 2008), for my poetry reading in Fred Day's dining room, and for giving me the run of the House. I am grateful to curator Mary Huth for my time with the Adelaide Crapsey, Crapsey Family, and Bragdon Family papers, in the University of Rochester Special Collections. Caretaker Tom McCarthy trusted me with the iron key to St. Gabriel's Chapel, in Norwood, Massachusetts' Highland Cemetery. Steve Ellis once again guided me to a publisher for a book.

Medieval Ohio

A poem for d.a. levy

(2011)

To Tom Kryss

…you'll probably be reborn a poet

in an industrial society,

—d.a. levy, Cleveland, 1968.

Auto-da-Fe! Savonarola! Inquisition!

Middle Ages! Castration, hypocrisy!

—Egon Schiele, Austria, 1912.

FORE WORDS

His words do not turn

to ashes in the mouth

His ashes are to be

mixed with paint in George

Fitzpatrick's calligraphic

painting of his words.

Part I:
"a temple in a graveyard"

*Man must be born
into the star,* wrote
Paracelcus. Too bad,

*There are no stars
Tonight but those of
memory* and the moon.

We do not wander mythopoetic
trails alleyways to avenues
cross the face of the sun to

reach Cleveland Underground. We cannot.
For they have euhemerized
the transit of summer.

The nation's soul having fled Walt's
body, ours is an age of transitus,
a click till off.

We know he's hidden in daylight
behind the nearer strobe,
his light bent a

round the intervening mass,
years which do not combust—
It's Schiele's star between us—

he enters my ope eye reading
his *"Portrait of a Young Man
Trying to Eat the Sun."*

It's the light year between
Agon Schele's and
d.a. levy's deaths
October 31,
1918-late Nov
ember,
1968 renders me
so starry eyed.

I'm sitting at home waiting on Edith Schiele to return my call.

Last time we talked,
he *said he would like to circle over the city
like a bird of prey.*
Instead, he went to jail, like levy would,
for contributing to the education
of minors, and minor poets like me.

But levy insists,

I DONT CARE ABOUT EAST CLEVELANDS HISTORY!

Okay, I'll take *your* call instead.
It takes the eyes of vulturenarcs
to pick a pornographic bone from the melting
bodies of priests on thrones of flames:
martyred *Buddhist Third Class*
Junkmail Oracle I've just reread   re
born. It takes Egon's eagle's   eye
view, sketched a   top
a studio ladder, of the   nude
walking the green tight   rope
before every   body
went falling into the one   soft
lap of the masturbating   girl
with green   turban.

The judge at Schiele's trial
actually burned a drawing
in the St. Polten courtroom.

Amazon warrior s/m raven
bares b/w breasts, she's
stories-high temple statue
inside Cleveland Arcade,
she's grainy collage icon
centerfold
       last *Buddhist Oracle.*

                                "This is
                                not sexy":
                                levy's
                                commentary
                                on how
                                sex sells;
but his "Red Lady" is erotic,
projected in scenes, he calls "movies,"
to be enjoyed after sunset
from drive-in lovebackseats.
                                See
                                Schiele's
                                "Standing
                                Woman in
                                Red," also
                                "Wally in Red
                                Blouse with
                                Raised
                                Knees," both
                                from 1913.

Some of these lines are telepathic communications from Madison, Wisconsin.

                     DON'T LOOK BACK,

they cautioned. (They, again!)
When Satchel Paige looked,
Dylan was gaining on him.
The hesitation pitch he brot
to Municipal Canyon—
leaving his fast ball behind
in Mexico City—
judged to be illegal,
meaning outside the game,
for its irregular meter and signature showupmanship.

In June 1963 (in Mexico) i became a poet... Same mm/yr I saw Paige throw his hesitation pitch, curves, and assortment of brilliant junk from the mound in Cleveland. By end of that June, and every season, the Tribe nosedived out of contention and into the lake.

            when i saw the Cleveland Indians
            crying on homemade pennants
            i knew it was Indian summer

Dad hated the drive so
when I'd see the team, it would be late in any season
My heroes had missed out again
consecutive second-place finishes in a country that remembers only
first place
I couldn't understand then
beyond me
unknown and unknowable to me in 1963
year levy becomes publisher; Lowell opens Asphodel
First Incarnation

Vean Gregg phones the one time I'm out of the house all day.

A bridge is Marsden Hartley's
   Berlin paintings, including
     "Portrait of a German
     Officer,"
and his poems. A curve
above the conflagration, see
(the traffic from Akron's South Main
stretches to Crane's "Euclid Avenue")
 what's behind a star.
(Ishmael only thinks
he's looking at Mapple's chapel
when he glimpses
               Ahab. Bones for singular die.)

Walk high on the bridge of Estador,
No one has ever walked there before.
There is a lake, perhaps, with the sun
Lapped under it....

I am waiting for Hart Crane to call back when he's free from parenthesis, little vertical () bridge,
and watching   Petrochuck's beautiful film open with shots of Cuyahoga bridges.

On the other side of the bridge, in the near distance, was East Cleveland…A little further on, before one passed the cemetery entrance, another bridge would have actually effected that transition—one milieu to another. There are perhaps thousands of such bridges in Cleveland, each one marking points of delineation between neighborhoods…, Tom Kryss, "levy LIVES."

Starting at League Park,
I draw a line across a map
of Ohio west to east
out past Robison's trolley line
thru Hart's family

PICNIC AT YELLOW HOUSE

When
☒
I knew you were dead.
when I took the .22
out to our hill & shot
four times through an antifreeze can
— memorizing your sewed-
shut lips, shooting at it
☒
::::bullets entering at first
subtlely & perfect
like an unopened envelope,
☒
exiting like a ripe
watermelon drops from a table,
exploding.

May 4, 1970

house to Garfield's tomb
                               Rockefeller Hanna Hay Ray
                               Chapman Monkey Hotaling
Straight up north
is d.a. levy's last apartment on earth
Then all the way south
to stand before the green grave of Ed McKean
                                         Patsy Tebeau and Ed
                                         Delehanty make four
suicides.

I am waiting on a Sunday phone call from Dean Keller.

Getting around the Reserve—Go
just below East Cleveland,
where Gerrit Lansing can be seen leaving home
and Chief Zimmer readies himself behind home,
is Lowell's Asphodel IV,
       single white flower
         tumbler of scotch.

I'm anticipating an off-season call from Mel Harder.

This town has been here for 150 years and has managed to murder every poet and painter who has been here except for William Sommer, levy to Andrew Curry.

Outside of the village [Waverley, Ohio] there are farm-houses, surrounded by broad acres, which kept them at respectable distances from each other, like the feudal castles of the Middle Ages, Horatio Alger.

It's always winter in Medieval Ohio
in the little water
color by Sommer
Jim let go.
You can make out the sure line,
of country road and ditch

under snow old enuf
for black streaks,
bending
before the mass of the frame house that's been there a long time, once
housing the anonymous builders of the cathedrals,
caught the artist's
eye, no green trees
just a phone pole,
orange, Hal Trosky's migrane from the glare off the snow.

(a drawing
line tension
TRAPS
the phantom workhouse
WHITE
on yellowing paper
CRUMBLES
the morning with snow
This opening of levy's "William Sommer" is so insightful it also makes an accurate description of the water color I have on the wall.
levy's "Litany of the Green Lion" too.

I've just friended Benjamin Blood on Facebook.

I am inside Medieval Ohio, writing
the history of the common worker
living and dying to build the great
cathedrals of Concrete poetry
so carefully they do not echo.
Nearby, Sommer baptizes Hart Crane
full immersion in the brandywine of modernity
that will someday include Alan Freel,
where May 4 is still inconceivable
as Crane in Chagrin Falls is as inconceivable as Kitaj's eye
first opening in Chagrin Falls, Ohio, or James Lovell,
where local boy Joe Vosmik is fans' favorite,
where Patchen is the Second War's popular poet,
where nobody loved Louis Finkelstein or can remember why
they called Akron's Sam Wise "Modock,"

where Red Ames ruined his lungs working in a dairy,
where John Brown grows madder as he breathes fumes from tanning
and Jim Brown grows madder after they knock him down,
where James Garfield reads every book in northeastern Ohio,
and Vachel Lindsay already contemplates
his walk across Kansas some day. Only last night,
I showed Tilly film, thirty seconds from May 4, 1970,
now she figures I went to war
after all.
Who could have taken home movies from above Taylor Hall? Where
was he standing? Everybody ducked, fell. Into grass on Blanket
Hill, or parking lot.

I am expecting a call from Luke Easter.

The lines have made a green rectangle:

Sherman Paul
Elmer Flick
Sisler
                         Niles)   Olga Rudge
                                             Burchfield
frame this district.

Where I pointed out to Duncan,
who had drawn a box
on the board, It's a   door
you can go in and out   of
too. His constellation
of poets'   names
begins at Kent. A box score.

I pick up
                              Ronald Johnson's *The Book of the*
Green Man
                         copy I bot at Jim's:

For the tree forms sun into leaves, & its branches & saps // are solid & liquid states of sun.

Fresh from Wales to Cleveland,
where Paul picks up on

the American green tradition
and its orgainic

form,
poem and essay.

I knock on Tom Kryss' door. Open up, the stars are ours,
I'm calling on you, brother.

2.
just like climbing a mountain
a Christian mountain

Dope,
you have to climb
spiral
stairs thru a tomb
to view
Cleveland by balcony.
Confirm
the earth still curves.
Closed,
JAG's ball room
must still be here,
open thru levy's time.
Beyond and below, the furze that must be
Erie does nothing much
towards coloring "Medieval Ohio,"
Schiele's series of cityscapes. I see now,
Williams romantic to make the town

a man; levy's long poems from down there
are not anatomies. I can see, a
mephitic Cuyahoga on fire was never a metaphor.
All cities are ghost towns
at this distance
and elevation.

it is up to you to wake up the poets
lost in their eerie pasts

Left the
"Suburban Monastery Death Poem"
down below in the car in the sun.
some kids are stealing it from the seat!
        Hey, fatso:

You have climbed out a tomb!
I do a little dance, make
the only sound this week
between stone walls
at our launch party.
When I arrive ground zero,
pages torn from the book
liter the grass
levy's unwanted mimeos
blowing down Euclid Avenue
all the old mansions blown away.
So the city becomes the book.

      3.
What kind of dance is this, without music or partner?

the darkness (you think)
is not a lack of suns
only your illusion
demanding

What most draws me, nearly sixty, back into the maelstrom of levy's work is his unerring sense, a poet in his twenties, of sustaining a long poem, his bent for it.

And the knowledge that he, without literature or history, doesn't arrive at this from the angle I do. Many planets, unknown to us, must have two suns in the sky.

I can't dance. ~~Olson danced sitting down~~. Skip it. I've never been able to dance.

We never met, tho that would have happened at Asphodel Book Shop, had the poet lived four years. (Finally met up with Tom Kryss to help scatter Jim's ashes in the flower beds.) Or perhaps we would have been kept separate, but with knowledge about each other provided by Jim, for reasons. There was always on the Asphodel wall the b/w photo (was Tessa the photographer?) of Lowell/levy/Ginsberg at the benefit. Never a topic of our conversations about the shits and the good guys, but always there, the background. Silent partners.

4. "Poster Advertising Nothing"

It sometimes takes centuries
    to sort out a poet
        and so it may be for
            darryl allan levy
                of Cleveland

—Ed Sanders.

    Decide there is a way,
after all, to write about levy's collages
in terms of Schiele's pictures:
    the eroticized female
    figure,
unread skin magazines to be cut up for collages.

    It's the realistic depiction
    pubes
    the vulturenarcs prowl
    Superior
    seeing obscenity
    in a grain of sand
    one page in a book stall
    the committees see,
    the wealthy buy.

We get the picture of the Nazis
publicly banning decadent
      nudes—to their own
           private walls, unmasked. Look,

the faces of dolls are left blank,
mask shapes, humanoid
rendered from ambiguous angles,
the seductive lines
excite
the artist's
MIND
to
go
on.

      The artist cuts up
      his culture's
      ideas
      of the body,
      it can be comedic,
      a "cut up," or rude;
      he frames desire
      as if he had
      created an image
      good folks had never figured on.
      levy's offense
      was to presume to be
      an artist,
when
a
war
is
going
on.

(Of course, we know that a war is *always* going on.)

The mimeo revolution still required paper and supplies, as well as a dry place to stand and print.
                    Hey, there's a twitter
in your future.
          It's hard to reconcile the opulence of an art museum tomb, for an assassinated president, with the death row apartment.

Our civilisation cannot afford to let the censor-moron loose. The censor-moron does not really hate anything but the living and growing human consciousness, Lawrence, letter of 10 November 1928, to Morris Ernst.

                    5. "Ariel View of Children Playing"

…I know
while sitting at night
by tombstones and ashes
a breaking thru
is nothing
more than stepping from
the doorway of an unhappy home

Why is it
the child
is drawn
to drawing?

What resource does she draw upon, even before she knows to draw out the conversation otherwise?

She is drawn into depicting
her world
from inside out.

> *if you want a revolution*
> *return to your childhood*
> *and kick out the bottom*

I see I have artificially drawn this distinction between the child and the artist, especially ones who will die before or just following thirty, who draw up manifestos of adulthood, drawing conclusions which are meant to draw us up short by drawing us out about what we believe blindly:
       knife drawn
       straws drawn
       to a close.
I surmise that levy, like Crane, couldn't stand to be
                                in the same room
with the long, drawn-out
                  conversation
about his childhood,
a different drawing room
when the family moved the

children / eating the sun or poets torn apart... in his mature drawings.

2) That night, Tod emails to me 3) the story of Anselm Berrigan, a child, "editing" the piles of his late father's papers into what we know and admire as the Collected Poems, as his mother sent instructions. 1) Next email, five minutes later, the news that Tod's neighbor Frank McCourt is dead. 4) The second baseman is Cupid Childs.

Poems for Dead Children.

                6. The Lake Curves, Too
   Somebody is living on this beach, David Markson, *Vanishing Point.*

The artist appears   (E.S.
appears to see thru walls   (d.a.l.
walls and around corners:
The curve ball   (Guy Morton
ball really does curve.   (Sonny Siebert

but his lines are beach-flat, a boy on a beach tossing curves.
Euclid Beached
inventor of Lifesavers threw his son a curve alright.

))))Candy Cummings, a boy

among boys on a Brooklyn beach,
throwing clam shells

into the wind *became interested*
in the mechanics of it

and experimented
… I kept experimenting

with my curved ball.
The
Civil
War
is
going
on.
On Friday, June 12, 1970,
Doc Ellis no hit the Padres
on acid.
(Where were you?)

The ball was small sometimes, the ball was large sometimes, sometimes I saw the catcher, sometimes I didn't…I chewed my gum until it turned to powder….

Tony Venzon, the umpire behind the plate that afternoon,
was like my mother never noticing
the eight walks, three stolen bases, a hit batsman. Some mother's son
playing the behind Doc Ellis,
the Little Leaguer who sits on his glove in the outfield
tossing weeds to the breeze
while the all the runners come home god
the daddies screamed for nothing.

On August 20,

                              the day estimated to be Leroy Paige's birthday in
                                                                           1948,
                                   78,382 came to Municipal Stadium to see
                                       Satchel win. (Darryl Levy was getting ready,
                                            in his family's West 61st Street house,
                                                          to enter first grade.)
                      On July 7, the club, which would win Cleveland's last World Series,
                                        already featured Larry Doby in the outfield
                                                                             when
                         Bill Veeck (rimes with wreck, as he pointed out) signed Paige
                                              following a five-pitch try out.
                                               (Satchel threw four strikes
                                                 over an improvised home
                                              plate that was Veeck's cigarette.)
Bill Veeck's sporting gamble reads today like a cultural experiment.
Five seasons before, Judge
Kenesaw Landis (rimes with Nazi Commish) had vetoed his plan
to restock Veeck's wartime lineup
with Negro League stars including Paige, in ignorance
of the significance of what in the fuck was happening in the country,
for example All-American Girls Professional Baseball
blacks dying with whites in Europe and the Pacific women working full-
time in the factories,
and what it meant at home.
(In 81 games played in the 1968 season, the Indians drew
only 857,994
at home.)

                            7. Forced Perspective

3)Landlocked Ohio invents the airplane and football's forward pass on
beaches.

anthology of experi
mental poe   try

2)He was a book artist, Blake writing & publishing his own books
thinking in book form

1)In the palm
of one up
raised hand,
the future biographer of Addie
Joss is holding James
Garfield's tomb
the low-tech photo
technique is called
Forced Perspective, in which
the young appear to
outlive the dead
A football is really a passing
bi-plane.
Of the two
towers Crane's
father had constructed, the *sanctum de la tour,*
there is no balcony
for a scale.

4)Not a matter of looking back, looking behind
A poem for levy about Crane
When I'm looking for levy sometimes I see other
poets more clearly
Hart house
                glare off the lake of Hal Trosky's migrane

                8. Nig Cuppy Slept Here
      ...changes i had note xpected, levy letter to d.r. wagner.

Any time I want to work on this poem, I begin
by reading randomly from
one of levy's jagged
poems for ragged beards.
Tell me

do they
tell me
where I am going in my poem?
Or where he
has been?
Am I learning, after all this time, to read
levy,
or writing my own lines to levy?
He's behin- the stone-d
teaching me
how the poem changes.

the great teacher murdered
for teaching about the sun

What goes around,
come home.
A shadow doesn't bend,
it curves
around the bend.

See you around.

    9. The Education of Young Garfield

Shields and I
thot we were
giving Jim
a gift

listing Asphodel as the distributor

of one-dollar Zelot
pamphlets,
springing it on him

I wonder what he thot,
a dozen years after Renegade
twenty years since Jargon.
The mimeo revolution

recorded by A.B. Dick
become photo offset IBM.
His classroom was
in Burton,

a remodeled garage book shop
attached to Tessa's kitchen.
The green back yard and prized
garden came up to window

level above Jim's desk,
grown out of that ariable Ohio
ground, where he typed out catalogs
of typos required reading and our

unpublishable poems. Spent
all the money in my wallet—
drove back home on back roads, with rarest books
no coins for turnpike tolls—ashamed

I'd pointed to the photograph
and asked him,
Who's the little guy between
you and Ginsberg?"

Why write about bizanteaten, low tech dead ball era, anyhow?
(levy would make sixty-seven this year and retire to Florida
beach.)

Who is Khidr?
Been wondering why "green" keeps showing up (mistake I make,
a suburbanite?) in this poem not "about" nature, but on Cleveland streets and under bridges and the nature of urban man as
levy contemplated?
Tod sends me a copy of Tom Cheetham's *Green Man, Earth Angel*
(ordered extra copy, his mistake) on Henry Corbin I know only
sketchy from what Olson used. And there I find:

Who is Khidr? There is a hint of the answer in his name: Khidr is the 'Verdant One.' He is the Green Man. He is the Angel of the Face and the Angel of the Earth...the hermeneut at the meeting place of the two seas. Language is...a field of meanings and intentions that we inhabit. Human language grows out of the world itself. We speak because the world speaks...Khidr is not a humanist. He is a messenger from far beyond," pp. 109, 113.

Who is d.a. levy? Was the activist a Cleveland humanist, or was he a messenger from beyond and writing the language of the world? Am I making, in front of you (*You never got to meet him.*), a basic mistake? It is the Green Man who sings: *in the east a new sun is rising / and the grass is growing / on the ashes of the city / where once i was born*

levy's *Silver Cesspool* published Jim Lowell, in 1964, under the name A. Greenshoot.

I write to pull weeds
of endless grass
from the dime bag
with a flower inside

green keefe
dust
green-black hash
seal intact

I buy from you
and smoke with you
bestowing on generations
the contact high.

Part II:

7:41

Starting at Public Square, take Euclid all the way out
                                                                       to square the University Circle
in an impossible ordinary act of driving
                                    thru the heavy traffic
                                                           of his-story.

The first traffic light in the U.S.—
installed along the Lake Shore Trail
on the corner of Euclid
    and E. 105th—stays
                                      green for me.

FOOTNOTE The clock at Terminal Tower reads "7:41."
This was the seventh largest city in the country in 1950.
Cleveland ranks forty-first today.

The Flats
and the bridges of the Flats
were his medieval
cathedrals.
Salamon remembers levy
imagined frescoes…
painted under the bridges
on the arches
and bridge supports.

In The Flats,

by Columbus Road bridge, there
are the white buildings.
Here, in the green between
river and brick
CLEVELAND WASTE & PAPER CO.,
is Gene Kangas' memorial to Crane:

Blue   **Brown**   **Reclining**
   Curl   **ARCH**   **Blue**

Here and there toys, fallen from giant hands, kids called home.
The green sea is far away
from today;
the missing poet's line is far from flat,
spindrift;
an inland sea, in-sounding,
floats into waiting hands
its bottled note.

*your poem is…deep as a public drinking fountain with
echoes deep in the hollow ground,* Tod emails me.

Swatches of grass in old b/w films are the very shade
of pavement.
Crossing against the light,
all lawn park campus cemetery. No line at the drinking fountain,
but it's rusted dry.

the quiet place is a doorway
    that opens to nothing
    the return is thought
    to stop is HERE I AM
the quiet place is a doorway
    that opens to no time
    all directions in no time
    are like motions of light

In second floor, rear,
the poet could hear
the routine car wrecks of countless bowling balls
late into the summer
nights.
Crosstown monument

TO A PLAIN DEALER'S *PSYCHEDELIC ASSASSIN*
at 1744 Wymore:
plywood windows look down on green
overgrown entranceway
rows of
sprung mail boxes, minds or tombs emptied out
by no trumpet blast.

He was hard to find; even with…help…it was almost impossible to cut thru the hostile paranoia which seemed to pervade greater Cleveland. Hostility was everywhere: police vs. motorcycle people, blacks vs. whites, old vs. young, young "hippies" vs. establishment young, d.a.levy against ignorance, ugliness, intolerance, brutality **and** *being interviewed, Andrew Curry, for* Dust.

> **Some kinda wild grass grows, man,**
> **from the grave of Eddie Klep.**

I saw all these sights in my head
shift
when I visited sites,

>   and sighed past mad Geo J. Moscarino's offices
>   on Lakeside Avenue still
>   open for business.

EPILOGUE

As the first bloody chapter of *The Ronin* ends, the ronin is given a note that urgently requests his return to this nameless last northern village *one year from today*—the sentence handed down to Gawain in the anticipation of his rematch with the Green Knight. The story-tellers lead us to anticipate revenge, sword and axe. Both are tales of the intertwined and illusory natures of time, identity, and reality. There are difficulties in attempting a plot about illusory time since the past does not recede and grow smaller as the future does not loom. Light advances across space in waves that wash over us. Jennings is careful in his book to tell us "what everybody knows": ronin means "wave-man."

Green = wavelength between 520 and 570 nanometres.

I am not susceptible to the suspense plot, the timing of the novel. I already know the endings. As I read, I think of levy in 1968 reading this book, its sentences badly crafted as in all cult books that must be unselfconsciously written, when it was new. Tom Kryss confirms that it was among the last books levy read; he remembers levy was "excited" by it, and wrote a review. Could it be said to have had a Young Werther effect on him, already depressed by the trials and what trials were on the court dockets? The anachronistic narrative holds no interest for me—I read it thru, starting at midnight the same day the novel comes in the mail, in ninety minutes—but I finish because I want to read what levy read, as if I could know what he was thinking before ending his life. Mid novel, when the ronin is driven to ask the sensei if he must kill himself in order to talk to the dead, I think of levy.

A man conscious of being in some way great does not give gifts. He rids himself of excess. For this reason, he always scorns appreciation. levy said: *You can have your city back.*

"*What can I do to live <u>in</u> the world and not forever on the edges?*" the ronin asks. He puts himself to work digging an impossible tunnel thru the mountain. Leaving his palace for the ronin-saint's mountain, an avenging samauri forgets his comb—*A lost comb indicates that the vanished owner has become another person.*

All this is rapidly drawing to an end in the short novel. The ronin-saint's life will be over, dead or meaningless, when he finishes the tunnel. "*You know the date and moment of your death.*" The young avenger (letter to D.r. Wagner: *they are murdering the children we didn't have time to become…*) works on the tunnel too, to hasten the hour of their duel. And when they break thru, they realize that the ronin has miscalculated the direction and his tunnel is useless.

"*To hell with it,*" the story ends.

About the end, Hartley wrote:
too much of fulfillment, no more promise, / given over petulantly, fevered, / you the severing, we the severed, / to… / wave-flow, wave-toss…. ("Un Recuerdo—-Hermano—-Hart Crane R.I.P.")

SOURCES

Olivier Alexis, "Hart Crane in Akron and Cleveland 1919-1923: Ohio Roads and Bridges to *The Bridge*," at <www.clevelandmemory.org>, 2007. Horatio Alger, *Try And Trust; or, The Story of a Bound Boy* (Philadelphia: John C. Winston, 1873. James Aulich and John Lynch, eds., *Critical Kitaj* (New Brunswick, NJ: Rutgers University Press, 2000). John I. H. Baur, *The Inlander: Life and Work of Charles Burchfield* (New Brunswick, NJ: Associated University Presses, 1982). Warner Berthoff, *Hart Crane: A Re-Introduction* (Minneapolis: University of Minnesota Press, 1989). Marcus Boon, *The Road of Excess: A History of Writers on Drugs* (Cambridge: Harvard up, 2002). Tom Cheetham, *Green Man, Earth Angel* (Albany: SUNY Press, 2005). *Hart Crane: Complete Poems and Selected Letters*, ed. Langdon Hammer (New York: Library of America, 2006). Alessandra Comini, *Schiele in Prison* (Greenwich, Ct.: New York Graphic Society, 1973). *Egon Schiele: Letters and Poems, 1910-1912, from the Leopold Collection,* ed. Elisabeth Leopold (Munich: Prestel Verlag, 2008). Interview with Doc Ellis, in *Lysergic World*, San Francisco, 16-19 April 1993. Wolfgang Georg Fischer, *Schiele: Desire and Decay*, trans. Michael Hulse (Koln: Taschen, 2008). Mike Golden, ed., *The Buddhist Third Class Junkmail Oracle: The Art and Poetry of d.a. levy* (New York: Seven Stories Press, 1999). Michael Hofmann, "More Featherishly Purple," *Poetry*, vol. 195, no. 4, January 2010: 315. Ken Irby, *Archipelago* (Willits, California: Tuumba, 1976). Special Collections of the Kent State University Library and archivist Cara Gilgenbach. Tom Kryss, for his friendship, the bottomless cup of his baseball knowledge, his gift of a whole mimeo revolution library, and his special edition of an early draft of this poem; editor of *A Tribute to Jim Lowell* (Cleveland: Ghost Press, 1967). Gerrit Lansing, *The Soluble Forrest* (Jersey City: Talisman House, 1995). *The Selected Letters of D.H. Lawrence*, ed. James T. Boulton (Cambridge: Cambridge University Press, 1997). levy, *The Buddhist Oracle,* vol. 2, no. 5, December 1968; *PROSE: on poetry in the wholesale education & culture system* (Cleveland: Offense Fund, 1974); *ukanhavyrfuckincitibak.*, ed. rjs: Russell Salamon reprint 2007 (Cleveland: Ghost Press, 1968). Love to Tessa Lowell. William Dale Jennings, *The Ronin: a Novel Based on Zen Myth* (Tokyo: Charles Tuttle, 1968). Thomas Mann, *Joseph and His Brothers*, trans. John E. Woods (New York: Knopf, 2005). David Markson, *Vanishing Point* (Washington, D.C.: Shoemaker & Hoard, 2004). David Nemec, *The Great Encyclopedia of 19th-Century Major League Baseball* (New York: Donald Fine Books, 1997). Allan Peskin, *Garfield* (Kent, Ohio: Kent State University Press, 1978). Brian M. Reed, *Hart Crane: After His Lights* (Tuscaloosa: University of Alabama Press, 2006). Herbert Read, *The Green Child* (London: William Heinemann, 1935). Georges Rodenbach, *The Bells of Bruges*, trans. by Mike Mitchell (Sawtry, Cambridgeshire: Daedalus, 2007). Ed Sanders, *1968: A History in Verse* (Santa Barbara: Black Sparrow, 1997). Klaus A. Schroeder, *Egon Schiele: Eros and Passion* , trans. David Britt (Munich: Prestel Verlag, 1999). Joanna Scott, *Arrogance: A Novel* (New York: Picador, 2004). Larry Smith and Ingrid Swanberg, eds., *d.a. levy & the mimeograph revolution* (Huron, Ohio: Bottom Dog Press, 2007); includes CD of *if i scratch, if i write*, a 2005 film by Kon Petrochuk (Kon Pet Moon). Kent Taylor, "The Cleveland Underground Poetry Scene: A Personal Reminiscence," rept. in *Cleveland Poetry Scenes,* eds. Mary Weems, Leonard Trawick, Karl Kuhar, and Larry Smith (Huron, Ohio: Bottom Dog, 2008). Kent Taylor and Alan Horvath, eds., *looking for d.a. levy (RANDOM SIGHTINGS): The d.a. levy Bibliography*, vols. 1 and 2 (Vancouver, WA: Kirpan Press, 2006 and 2008). Sarah Vowell, *Assassination Vacation* (New York: Simon & Schuster, 2005). D.r. Wagner, ed., *Black Mask*, 8 (October-November 1967) and *Moonstones*, 2 (1966).

UNNUMBERED NOTES FOR PART I

[Unnumbered because I love to read endnotes pages straight thru, and without reference to their primary text, as if they were chapters in a strange book.]

The best brief account of the land of Crane/Sommer-Patchen-Lowell is by Warner Berthoff: *...the old Connecticut-founded Western Reserve...reaches west from the Pennsylvania border and north from roughly the Youngstown-Akron line to a point just above Norwalk and Sandusky. Even now, two centuries past the original settlement, to cross from western Pennsylvania into the Western Reserve is to cross a still visible, if irregular, cultural and historical boundary...Now you are among broad fields, ceared woodlots, old and new apple orchards, intermittent rows of planted sugar maples among country roads, and soon the remaining villages and township centers (...Hiram...) with their broad central greens....* It is Burchfield who painted the landscape of hallucinated Ohio, who made pictures actually talk the languages of nature, as we witness it on the drive down Route 14, Cleveland to Salem.
I have never learned to talk and have only listened to the trees...

The boy who clears the tables in the Euclid Villa dining hall is keeping a journal. He is an art student, and would in a few years make his living by designing wallpaper. In his room at night, he records his thots, to keep track of his development, for himself. Fifty years later, Charles Burchfield is still drawing the trees from Cleveland's fall of 1915
...the color made sound.

Captain Brackett, in "South Pacific," mails off to 325 Euclid Avenue, Cleveland, a grass skirt. And Albert Hodge, who grew up in Ravenna, Ohio, played The Green Hornet on tv.
Weather man Dick Goddard's home town, Green, Ohio, has no Zip code.
Kent State drinkers used to call Rolling Rock beer The Green Death.
Larry Smith recounts that Tom Kryss *disagreed with Ed Sanders's idea that Cleveland should build a monument to levy down at the Rock-n-Roll Hall of Fame. He said*

the memorial should just be the sunlight on the grass.

The New England green of University Circle, where outside the statue of Hart Crane turns green and inside is the green of William Sommer's painting "The Pool."

New Grass (1968), an lp by Albert Ayler, born 1936 in Cleveland's East Side. Or Herbert Read's *The Green Child*, where geography is heard not seen.

Knocked to the League Park grass by a bolt of lightning, Ray Caldwell survived to retire the next batter for a complete game win.

O to lay down a perfect bunt on the grass of Emil Bossard's grave.

Distinctly praise the years, whose volatile
Blamed bleeding hands extend and thresh the height
The imagination spans beyond despair,
Outpacing bargain, vocable and prayer.
Crane drafted these lines in Cleveland.

Arrested for reading poems to teens in a church basement a world away from Neulengbach.

BOD meant Book of the Dead, Mr. Moscarino.

The Medieval Church of Ohio has become increasingly irrelevant in the decades of wars since individual clergy's active roles in the Peace Movement.

Singing gospels, Little Jimmy Scott sang his way out of East Cleveland, and onto Lionel Hampton's band.

Gary Snyder had to come to Kent, in 1967 when subculture was local, to hear about levy (from Alex Gildzen, who was always There).

I don't much like the levy in the *Dust* interview. The poet putting on, putting off (Andrew Curry put up with levy's no-show for first meeting), putting down, nothing to say about the topic of poetry. If I had been Curry, in June 1967, I would have felt angry and put out. Corso and Rimbaud were impossible to deal with. Laura Riding was impossible to be around. Hart Crane wore out the people he loved and their welcomes. Of course, levy was admired and beloved too, and those who knew him best remain devoted to his memory. People saw something in this nonpresupposing guy. No scholar seems to have gone to the trouble lately of re-reading William Dale Jennings' novel *The Ronin* to see what levy was reading that may have influenced his decision to leave Cleveland by suicide. Is this how we deal with levy because we never met him?

  Having words, with or for.

  Cheetham writes: *An arbitrary token that can be Cut, Pasted, or Not Spoken, such a marker is hard to conceive of as a Person, let alone an Angel…Words as persons….*

  Who on the street can correctly identify
one of Ohio's senators?
Let's add
subcultural amnesia to the syllabus of Cultural
Amnesia, meaning Nazis
outside the U.S.
(Burt Miller is a Bolaño nazi.) Even the good guys
Mathilda's guitar teacher
about my age
concedes that he doesn't know
who Ravi Shankar is.
So who killed levy? Hell,
what's killing is we can't even place
the names…
                Tubin Schiele Tarbell Fante
                Corso Rimbaud Sommer
                 Riding Dolphy Hamsun Blood
                Elpenor Day Addie Joss Maxo
                Vanka Crapsey Perkoff Bolaño
Warren's Red Ames
pitched in hard luck.
He was known for

his wildness and his curve.
He was most effective early
and late in the season, when
the weather was cool.
Ed Delahanty and his brothers
playing baseball on vacant lots
between Superior and St. Clair.

> ...Blake's dead brother taught him to
> etch the plates in acid.
> Dear bro, instruct me too.

What in particular Crane got from William Sommer was a confirmation of ideas that major art was less a reconciling than a tense re-creation and counter-posing of naturally conflicting energies...Blakean ideas, Warner Berthoff, Hart Crane: A Re-Introduction.

"An Impromptu, Aesthetic TIRADE," Crane subtitled his poem "The Bridge of Estador."

Listen—hard—to Ernest Bloch, for what a Jewish music might be? for a Cleveland school?

Marsden Hartley remembered
a gift from his drawing teacher
at Cleveland School of Art,
a copy of Emerson's essays,
the first book he ever read.

Funny to read Steve Tomasula's charachers, in *VAS*, are named Square and Circle, I'm so focused on a map of Cleveland from Public Square to University Circle. Not just now and then, but then and now.

A guy on eBay is selling a brick from League Park for $shipping.
Albers' homages to the square

<pre>
                    at Black Mountain. The black
                       squares of Cold Mountain
                        serigraphs by Tom Kryss.
         Housed like children's nesting blocks, the smaller always
              fitting into the larger, near Public Square stood
             the square-shooting bookman's Asphodel II.   Naps
                 Bill Bradley waits in the batter's box.
</pre>

UNNUMBERED NOTES FOR PART II

When
lighting out for the territory, travel
light.

  I pass the Devo Garden Nursery (OE verb *growan*, to grow) in the countryside between Kent and Asphodel. Devo, of de-evolutionary rock-n-roll fame, gave their first concert for one of Bob Bertholf and Dean Keller's fine arts festivals in Kent.
  Chippewa Creek runs brown thru my childhood.

  The brown river
from Whiskey Island
burns as it goes down.
  I used the email address listed in his book and wrote Marcus Boon to point out that he overlooks, in The Road of Excess: A History of Writers on Drugs, the fact that it was the Melville scholars who launched the LSD experiments at Harvard. I named Charles Olson. I mean, the book is published by Harvard University Press. His email reply was courteous. He did not respond to my follow-up email. There is no mention of levy. The author welcomes your correspondence at <<u>marcus@hungryghost.net</u>.>

  Lackvoo too we rgabbletogether, dower yet elebated, like cranehard beaver da bridge.
O tonic archlyfake!
Take the towdown xprex to st. levylang wedges, pro or Crete
Poe treecrypt—Ick!

levy ate the sun & went back too far to continue. Benjamin Blood is the sun some days.

   Crane's *eating the peacock's flesh* or levy's *drinking the blood of the green lion*, on page 39 in Cheetham.
Pre-Raphaelite green eyes and red hair there.

   levy's Rimbaud is *just a silly young goof / who couldn't follow his own // sunoco roadmap.*

Rockefeller is buried under a dime in the neighborhood of James Garfield.
levy doesn't bother with railing against Ida's oil company or the politics of the automobile. He is not a poet on the road.

Dead towns are the Cathedrals of Silence, wrote Georges Rodenbach of Bruges
before the Great War—
before Schiele's dead cities series—and long
before the death of Cleveland's East Side.

Great Man Sleeping In a Closet
The Asphodel Manifesto
The Revenge of d.a. levy

   What's the opposite of irony
sincerity?
levy's poverty
was anti-ironic,
no lowly monk's medieval towering (that would be ironic),
but bitter,
it's bitter-green gall
to wake
having dreamed
the bells of the Cherokee ponies
inside the only Indian reservation
inside of Ohio.

   Yeah, like people live on

the Western Reserve's Rocky River Reservation.

levy awaiting
trial
living thru Gawain's fast year of slow dread
knowing he must suffer
the blow
from the axe of the Green Knight
turns everything he thinks and sees a sickly
green.
The truth of all this plodding subplot is withheld from the hero
by newspapers and attorneys
but also by well-meaning kisses.
It turns out,
the green chapel inn he drives all over Cleveland to locate
is nothing
but a hole in the grass. The green belt
is still worn to this day
by retirees up for the summer
clogging the greens
of Goodyear.

THE GRASS IS GROWING ON A GREEN UNIFORM,
the varieties of green in "Beret,"
levy's *concrete poem for the war monuments.*

Reading in Emerson's green
tradition when I discover the eternal
bird
of Ellen Russell Emerson's
Indian Myths:
The custom of using green plumage for the charm the Indians placed within their medicine-sacks originated, no doubt, from the representation of [Wahkeon, or All-flier] with green feathers about the neck.
(I greatly admire her 1884 use of "no
doubt.")

Doris rode her first pony at the 164th Medina County Fair. Evergreen memory.

"How the Deer Got His Pixels" and "How Thurman Munson Got His Stripes" in one
volume.

"Inclined planes open onto the arena//…emerges from the poured beer and concrete dark./ Before him:// the first sight of the playing/ field. Emerald detail neath shadowless/ lights. The players take the field/ in block-numbered uniforms.// He sees the grassy green of smell.//Aug. 10, '60// And green is become, after that night, a time-machine.// It takes him back and forth, between sight and/ site, remembering./ In him:// strong senses will not be/ separate. Evenings consist of several./ No single out or hit or error could/ stay in play so long.// He believes what he saw, can look it up…" I wrote, in a poem about Municipal Stadium, for Jim Lowell.

All games at League Park were day games.

What to do with the green smears and blobs on my canvas? When I think I am reading about R. B. Kitaj, I interrupt myself and admonish myself for thinking about what Duncan said to me about Kitaj. Then I get Duncan in James Aulich's endnote:
In composition by field, a colour does not glow in itself or grow dim, but has its glow by rhyme—a resonance that arises in the total field of the painting as it comes into the totality. The 'completion' of the painting is the realization of its elements as puns or rhymes. The painter works not to conclude the elements of the painting but to set them into motion, not to bind colors but to free them, to release the force of their inter-relationships.
Robert wrote this for his Introduction to *Jess*, which I read, at Bertholf's Kent house, when I was his student. Now it tells me about my poem, completed in this way, and about levy's woodcuts, collages, oils, posters, some of them directly inspired by the work of Warren, Ohio's Patchen. It takes a long time, years, sometimes never, for eyes to adjust to the dark light Cheetham talks about.   Man on the green ray walking out of the continental art theatre, some film still playing in your head, into Euclid avenue daylight, maybe it's 1948 and the film is "The Boy with Green Hair," you'd think the nation would adjust to peace at least in between wars.

Eyes adjust gradually
I see the green
that keeps appearing
in levy's "5 Cleveland Prints" (1964)
is a condom;
the Green Man has ejaculated green ink.
Try describing that
to the judge.

Slang: "to take Nebuchadnezzar out to grass."

Propose Tod do mimeo-look editions of Schiele's two pencil and watercolors, both from jail, "The Door to the Open!" and "Hindering the Artist Is a Crime, It Is Murdering Life in the Bud." A single orange in his cell, the only light. Exhibit A, Schiele letter to Peschka, ca. 1910:
You me green valley, you look
green water-air fills you, you.
I cry, out of half-open eyes....

Exhibit B: An abstract and abstracted Robert Creeley has come out of the box to explain why the transvestite is grotesquely dressed while the female is nude. Kitaj's *The Ohio Gang* is from 1964. Genre-bending.

    Exhibit C: "A Brief History of Interior Design: Wallpaper"
        Inside Wm Morris walls
          beside the Satie sofa
       in Rudolph Arnheim shadows,
      levy's wallpaper book cover
      (same design as the walls)
    opened on the Vanessa Bell table
      bot with Burchfield's day job.

Exhibit D: The only time I heard Jim say more than a few words about him was when he showed me a levy painting. I had no words.

Exhhibit E: Wm Sommer, "The Pool" (Cleveland Museum of Art)
There is a green
ring
around the crescent moon
There is a pool
between
two green trees
And then there is the pony
drinking
from his own reflection.

"See you around,"
I wrote in the round of beginnings that opened my work on this poem of Ohio. So today, when I think I am compiling the bibliography, I recover my copy of Patchen's Collected, and read instead poems that speak to me, of levy (*To leave the earth was my wish, and no one stayed my rising…I cook my senses in a dark fire*), and what I'm about here (*I believe that to deliver myself / Is to deliver you*). What next? Jesus, I read Patchen's cosmology as if for the opening of my own poem:

These then connect with tubular suns
That grow out of lakes
Tranquil as black light, and their weight
Lowers the earth by the size of journeys.

I haven't read these poems in years but am I somehow plagiarizing Patchen? And when I check, I see—this is an act only possible in madness and poetry— the lines are from *The Dark Kingdom*, the book which Kenneth Patchen published in 1942. The year of levy's birth.

UNNUMBERED NOTES FOR EPILOGUE

"New from the Omega Workshops"
The odor of ancient conflict, of tear
gas lingers on archived pages.
We are not far from Hough
and martial law,
not far from the end
when levy read *The Ronin*.
All the gore on the samurai's
sword is an illusion
don't turn away your eyes
that girl strung up by her hair
begging to be raped
is an illusion, the government's
revenge is an illusion
in Zen story.
levy seems to be reentering, not exiting, the world in his 191-word review of

The Ronin: *...& here i am again being a writer writing WOW that RONIN...a book...for lovers building a tunnel through the mountain of darkness...vajrayana reawakenings.*

APPENDIX 1:

"the player to be named Later"

do the kids below my window
ignore this killing wind
because they lack remembrance
of what a winter can do?
must be
why everyone i meet
is not crying;
they cannot remember him.
he called himself a book-seller.
he taught there are no heroes.
he did not believe a poet
must be A Great Man
to write a great poem,
but he taught me certain poets are
such scoundrels in their personal dealings
we should not read them seriously
or let them come into our houses.
he could brook not pretentiousnesses.
he had no love for the professional
man of letters
whose aim was less than art.
he kept quiet curator to his own pantheon:
Oppen, Niedecker and Zuk were there,
Weldon Kees, Dr. Williams, Richard
Yates, Gerrit and Doug Woolf—
certainly Bunting. Raymond Souster.
he kept friends for life, he quarreled
and split with old friends over money.
i could name names here too but they know themselves.
his stories of the poets were good as Aubreys.

his Charles Olson, a guest at someones party,
CAN STILL BE SEEN depositing a six-pack whole
into a single great coat pocket, and leaving.
he maximized the "one pocket!" part.
this kind of businessman would simply refuse
to sell you a book "you don't need," meaning
in my case, no first editions i couldnt afford.
i came to trust him
at a dinner party for Helen Adam
when he, mopping his great brow with one hand,
proved the only one who could finish
the dish of cold hot-pepper soup. i remember
the rest of us refolding our napkins
into surrender flags
all down the table.
he loved
The Cleveland Indians
lifelong.
till the rivers run scotch and the people read
Pound.
when he loved, it was not for a season.
he died in the off-season, two weeks before
Daddy Wags.
the late Merle Hoyleman would call from Pittsburgh
phone booths to warn him
of the radioactive menace in her head in place of poems.
he liked to phone me Sunday mornings.
i sit here waiting for the phone to ring.
JEALOUS
to think that da levy knew him before i did
and didnt live to tell me about him.
for the record, i wish it to be known that Jim and i
once shared, in Buffalo, a church pew!
to hear Robert Duncan preach the Imagination!
he had never eaten at McDonalds.
he had never entered a Waldens or a Barnes & Noble.
he had never gone online.
he had never processed words;
he typed them, on a typewriter.
he was the James Russell Lowell that we knew.

he always claimed to have never written a poem.
i do remember a pencil sketch of Sibelius he had done.
he would always show me his gardens progress.
one time, i arrived after a flood
and carried home, gratis, the moldy history of the U.S.
Literary Journal since 1940 in magazines that always
smelled of incredibly rich ariable land, of Ohio,
the smell of paper returning to trees.

APPENDIX 2

In 1968, in the month Nixon beat Humphrey, the 24th was a Sunday.

The Beatles' *White Album* had been released the Friday before. Upton Sinclair would die on Monday, and Arnold Zweig on Tuesday. The night d. a. levy died, the Jimi Hendrix Experience performed, with Cat Mother, at the Miami Beach Convention Hall. It was November 24 when Darwin published *On the Origin of Species* and Jack Ruby shot Lee Harvey Oswald. On this day, John Knox, Lautreamont, Clemenceau, and Diego Rivera died and Spinoza, Pachelbel, Father Serra and Sterne (the same year), Zach Taylor and Bat Masterson, Toulouse-Lautrec and Dale Carnegie, Lucky Luciano and Ducky Medwick, Bob Friend and Steve Yeager, Pete Best and Scott Joplin and Alfred Schnittke, Margaret Anderson, Ducky Dunn, William F. Buckley, Ted Bundy and Charles Startweather, Oscar Robertson and Dave Bing were all born.

APPENDIX 3:

"Music, Flowers and Handsome Women"
—headline, *Pain Dealer* article on first game at League Park.

The great cathedrals should be torn down like ours. *Standing straight up, he rested his arms just below his waist.* A great expanse of chicken wire, *He would then rock on his left foot, while turning his right foot clockwise.* someone must have taken great care to plant *Taking a full windup, he raised his arms completely above his head, while turning his body to face second base.* the outfield fence, as if *Beginning his delivery plateward, Addie kicked his left leg high into the air while hiding* only it can flourish *the baseball behind his thigh until the last*

possible instant. in sandlot sacred ground *While driving his body forward, he launched the ball sidearm. Exercising great balance,* that cannot sustain hopes *he finished in an upright position, feet square, ready* for buildings *to field any ball hit near the mound,* or a winning season. The great cathedrals should be torn down like ours.
—Italicized passages from Scott Longert, *Addie Joss: King of the Pitchers.*

Like poetry, baseball is a kind of counter culture, Fernando Perez, *Poetry*, September 2009, 442.

I had badly underestimated Billy Evans.
Addie Joss and Billy Evans
were writers.

APPENDIX 4:

"Finishing Mahler's Tenth"
"Some people in my position
are afraid to sleep, afraid

they won't wake up. I'm not.
When I wake up after a nap,

I look at that mirror—
and I know I'm still here."

The mirror is really a landscape four trees
cheap glass frame. I don't let on.

Williams' *The soul, my God shall rise up—*
a tree…in this mortal world.

Outside Mom's hospice window,
bird in snowy feeder wears a red ruffle.

The ministers and associate   pastors, who know   the earth is 6,000
years old,   and house non-denominational   chaplain and lay
preachers with all   their fat wives   drive me away

from her side   and out
of the room   then   into the hallways and thru
lobbies past   snack bar and into the freezing   parking lot,
where I can   cry   at the wheel of my rental car.

Martha says of a visitor: "He has the face of a much taller man."

Gradually realize   the plants here   in my brother's living room,
four feet tall, are   from Dad's funeral. Dad's   sole surviving brother

would be   at Mom's funeral. He lives on,   in Clyde, Ohio,   beside
the public   library, never   curious   to read *Winesburg.*

They are standing in for me   at my finals.   That night, dream
Ken Irby and I are   team teaching   American Poetry class.

Deep is the well of the past, Mann   begins
a book   someone before me   has left
in the   little   hospice library

where I go   sometimes   to use my cell phone
to call Tod,   who is   at work
on a long poem   about remembering   the Mother.

Mann's   is a book about   brothers.
It is much   too long   to read   in what time is left here.
.

My brother   and I   are memory
orphans now.
Even   to Lee Cavin, local   historian of our childhood
in Seville.

I cannot bring myself   to eat
off   the tray   of the dying.

All well-mopped   corridors, where we must   wait for news
of death, smell   of Camille Claudel's hair   wet from weeping.

To see her,   I take   57,
Wadsworth   to Medina,

ride   Mennonite Hill,
the county's   high road.

Developers   have remade the   fields
after   their own image,   so

my   prodigal eye   returns
to landmarks,   turns at   River Styx and   Poe.

  A site   in Ohio,   a monument   on high ground   above a lake
and its   long-abandoned   factory—its luminous   columns in a
parking lot   (resembles a turnpike   stop), no cars parked   but a
very long truck   and trailers   turn around in it   while I watch.
Railroad   or subway   cars, antiques, are   attached to   the
monument.   I enter   the first car,   play around with its   pop
culture mechanisms,   but when I go   thru the doors   into next
and subsequent cars,   I find   they are gutted,   not yet refurbished
for the museum, so   I leave—.
  —My dream seven weeks before Mom's death.

> *Blasts*:
> Mahler's—
> Pound's—
> now Marie's—

She   never heard   of   Mahler's Tenth
and would have   disliked it.

I came to love it   forty years ago,
Dorn's student   building a green   wall for Gaston

Lachaise   I unpacked   from crates,   pulling up the bronzes
by their cold   bosoms or necks,   the time of

Mom's   breast cancer. The listening   carried me
thru those   uncharted days,   and all

this afternoon   I listen to   my easeful friend
dying   in the room   deep in Ohio.

Her widow wind   ow's
winter light   (fading)
bent at glass   picture
to her eye-   glassed
eyes (fading   blue)

And if what I think is grief / is fire / how long the open eyes of stars / toward the other side?

Time: Schoenberg's sixth   little   piano piece,
       orphaned notes   for Mahler,   May 17,   1911.
Space: the tree   grows from a clutch   of mourners,
       in Schoenberg's   painting   The Burial of Mahler.
Time and space: Death   mask of Arnold   Schoenberg
       made by   Anna Mahler,   on the morning of   July 14, 1951.

I cheat   and read ahead.
I already   know   the story.
He finished and hesitantly withdrew his hand from that head. So one life takes leave of another and must depart; yet a little while and the other will depart as well.

For three easy seasons
it sat   in place,   well north.

Now in early winter
it looms   local, more   snow;

till the great lake freezes,
grave   of the mother, closed.

And so it was
Mapple's Mistake   for her   funeral,

the boy-   preacher   mistaking
pain   for the face of god.

As it had been
Hart   Crane abandoning   Akron

to   Dr.   Billington and the World's
Largest   Sunday   School.

My Doris,   "There are   snowmen   waiting to be   built,"
turns   four   this week.   Our Lani,   whose name only
Mom knows, soon   to be born.

Schiele wrote to his mother: *I shall be the fruit which will leave eternal vitality behind even after its decay. How great must be your joy, therefore, to have given birth to me.*

Time and space: Marie buried in   a plot   first opened,
       1969, by   her for her   father.

Fischer writes: *Schiele shows us not simply melancholy flowers, but flower beings in the process of dying; so too with his trees and cities—they are quintessential creatures, defined by doom and death…The artist is virtually saying: I am this flower and I feel rueful, I am this tree and feel a naked, transient thing, I am this city and feel as if I were dead.*
Considering an Ian Hamilton poem, "Memorial," Michael Hofmann is *reminded of an astonishing Egon Schiele painting of four trees, each one a distinct, spindly personality.*

The painting   of four chestnut trees in autumn   poses, set   against a line of
green   horizon, dates
 from 1917.   I know it was   not   the print in Mom's last room but keep it to myself, making them

buckeye trees,   one for each   member of   our Ohio family.

To say that life ends in
the violet light…
is to begin at the end:
starting out from light,
first breath, first light,
out of the mothering hole…
is to ask why start?

start because we <u>were</u> started…, Gerrit Lansing.

Schiele's "Dead Mother"   loves, and means to   protect her child,   beyond   death.

One   winter   sunset
closing   her last   day,
like an orange   tossed
into grey   blankets,
on   the prison   cot.

"Grief"
Your   mother stitched
the quilt on   my bed
from patches of   work
shirts   and your dresses.

My decision   is
to use,   not preserve.
The problem is   time.
Time in   the poem.

Toward dawn,
the quilt gets   heavy:
a sleeper's careless   arm
across   my chest

I must throw   off—then
plunge,   dreamless, after   it.

The first canto in the big book,
he learns later,
was not the first to be written. His order.

Anticleia was not supposed to come first. His
orders.
If he had never gotten this far, each time he thot
of her,
she would still be alive. Disordering.

APPENDIX 5:

"Schiele's 'The Poet,' 1911"

No poet
no one   in   this shape
could write.

To say   his
neck   "rests"   on his right
shoulder
would   poeticize
the verb.

Here,   beauty is not just
difficult;
it is   broken up

inside   a bag of   skin.

The unposed, exposed   neck
mocks   a pencil
floating   out of   reach.

He holds to
an   unscrolled   length
of wordless   paper
with his left   hand
which supports
also   his right hand
by   the wrist.

Splayed index
fingers   cannot   write.

Fingers are
    grimaces.

We've caught   his
contorted face
    at a moment
       especially
hard   to read

(considering   we know
what   the painter   could not,
making   this   image
from   the year
of his   fated   move
to Neulengbach),   entering

       or   just
leaving   a nightmare.

LAST APPENDIX:

It figures.

This is the last thing levy wrote:
…everytime i write a
poem—i'm afraid—when
i'm dead it will sell
& some other poet will
starve because no one will
buy his poems
& i'm afraid
that someday people will
all read poetry
& not try to live it
sort of like christianity
or buddhism or any
religion.

And Schiele, on 18 August 1912:
   …Few see the

sun and everyone else must
read novels and novellas
in order to finally realize
that there is a light.

AFTER WORD, LIKE AN OLD BOX SCORE

Ashes fly the flue,
Is Tom's memory
Of the stroboscopes,
The day d.a. burned
Stacks of everything
Incriminating.
(On book shelves of lost
Apartments, boxes
Of ashes Ginsberg
Sent back from black pyres
Along the Ganges.)
Archilochos recalls
His was an "ash spear"
I find it pleasing
To mistake the word
For ancient charcoal,
A weapon still, tooled
Image with a fine point,
Leaving levy's hand.

Gadsden

(2009/2014)

Dedicated to tt

*…Here we are! I said to myself
Some two hundred times.*

Sedan Corrido

*La muerte es un automovil,
con dos o tres amigos lejanos.*

Because you are dead, Roberto Bolaño,
You seem much older,
But we make contemporaries.

Because your countries seem old,
Because the version of the new world I live on in died
Young and happy with itself,
You send me news
Of the revolt I believed imminent years ago.

Because I don't understand your language,
Your poems are a university of forbidden reading.

I dip my finger, now my tongue, into the ink
Well of the common night to write you this,
I begin to hear your jet lines
Without the necessity of reading them.

America can never build a wall at the border
To keep you out
Or deport you,

Because, as long as a student dreams of becoming a poet,
And enrolls in workshops he skips in order to smoke
And read the poems of Rexroth, you *are* America.

Because I already knew you, when we were coming up
And first read Lorca in New York, together, leagues apart,
I don't want you translated.

The year is 2666. The year is 1968.
It's getting too late to learn the piano.

I'd like just twenty minutes with you,
Alone with your admirable hatred for Neruda
(I too would no more memorize a poem, by heart,
Than eat my map) and all creators of cantos and cant,
Whose periplum are ghost towns, streets of
Long-abandoned cunts of unburied whores;
And you and your abiding love for the anti-poet
Parra, good food for the growing poet.
I'd bring the bottle, pretend to smoke your Bali
(But you'd find me out, right off.)
The VWs of Mexico cruise by our sullen table,
Engines like sewing machines.
All my beautiful questions would go unasked
After that, piss absorbed into the hotter desert floor,
Into the grammar of spiders
Renewing their vows of silence.

It is agreed, the only true scholar
Is a savage detective.
And only the unbeautiful monster
Has no power over us.

Because your grave is deluged
By the unyielding rain of Shit that covers the Americas,
Fuck making your ghost
A character in a magic realistic novel.

(I doubt you even have a grave.)

Because the mud is not yet a relic,
It makes it hard going.
It is what separates prose from poetry
Mud and adobe, or about twenty
Inches of annual rainfall—
But all your novels are poems.
Because "…only poetry isn't shit."

But *did you* quit poetry
(Another question!)
As a stolen vehicle for social change

After the death of Allende?
Or did she quit you, after she ran out
On the eternal Blaise Cendrars?

Whatever your reasons, your poems remain
In Spanish like four Grant's tombs Dora
Pre-Columbian ruins in Mexico City Marsden
Nobody makes time to visit anymore.
You closed the ballroom in 1994,
Who had danced within Garfield's tomb,
Your hands on her amazingly slim waist.

You and I, we still do not know the drive.
But we do know to drive. Because

To know to drive is the one impulse
The scenery is just scenery
Fall is only fall
Legends are left to maps
The saguaro cactus in flames
Is local vandalism
Testing ground, dammed river, clouds
Over Oracle   over Santiago
City-dweller late of the Aztec capitol   driving
Into the late
Sun on one rim
Of the inland sea   past
Two house trailers
(Coprolite hermae,
Durer armadillo)
No road signs
One whole day
Hurry up
Shit uncontrollably
Over a pipe in the cement
Gas station floor
You could never afterward place
On any map
No trees for masts
Only dead crosses here

Between the day of one tree alive with butterflies
And the night
Of attempting sleep in a porn theatre
The lights went up
Every hour
For the collection
That was the drive over a road
Completely covered
By tiny frogs after rain
Asking how there could be
So many frogs in the world
Thru which we gladly carry
David Rattray asleep in the back seat
Thru dust storm dark
Big wind in the panhandle
Sprung the driver's door
You had to climb
In or out the window
All the rest of the trip
Toward where I told her
In conversation how
I'd spent my afternoon writing
A new poem about
You, Roberto Bolaño
She said she'd expected me to say
It was a poem about the sky,
You always seem to
Write about people,
She said, artists,
Poets, musicians, failed artists
Whatever Benjamin Blood was
This was the same woman
Who changed my life
After she brot me
The santo from El Paso:
A skeleton playing baseball
(The figure
Our first born
Would toy)
So, okay, maybe it is true

After all
That the way thru Ezra is the way around Ezra,
That to write poems in a tradition
Without the invention of modern fascism
Planning no stops this trip
Even to piss
Into the cool
Centuries
(Cathedral walls
Blue in memory),
Even being ever alert
To by pass Four Corners and all purely political boundaries
Really is like
Fifty miles of gravel road
Turning into the grassy paths thu cemeteries
In dusk you watched
Clouds of bats emerge
From Carlsbad to blindly
Eat everything all night
For breakfast you served me warm Pepsi
Poured over Wheaties
The great European cities of inspiration
Smell of exhaust
They water the eyes
Behind glasses caught
In some ancient traffic
Abe Rattner and Clancy Segal
How Brecht's "Buckow
Elegies" so often sound
Like Dorn on Boulder
I can still see Herb Score
Climb the pitcher's mound
As if it were a well-known
Cleveland, Ohio mountain.

Because the Andes are potable
In a childhood dream of snowfall
And the Sierras only a recurring
Nightmare from the desert bedroll
Where we contract insomnia

Like a fever from eating
The uncooked flesh of nocturnal life
Before all is evacuated
By long-distance truckers with international
License to stay artfully awake on pills for
Typing rolls of Kerouac prose down highways
Red in the time of tomato poems. Altho
Man among the animals has to
Stop in order to shit,
Everything sits
Inside the moving
Dome of the car, it
Cannot slow must
Cover endless roads paved with the talk of poets
About poets but never pausing to write a poem,
About habits of mind
When the poet is not composing,
Which is most of the time
In each poet's life
(Creeley's Complaint),
But life set in motion
So the moon seems
To travel beside the car,
At the car's speed,
But the sun
The sun is always either up or
Down, in grammatical terms
This is the inverted question marks
At the end (the eternal return
Is real and it is the gas pump) of all those sentences
In Cormac McCarthy's Spanish we see
But cannot hear
In the alley of the four flat tires
So far up inside earth's dun asshole, God
Washes His hands of Us.
Because it's past time
To reconsider our father's hard opinion
When we announced to his WWII face
Our intention to write
In those days before we understood

How talk turns into writing
And life into talk.
Stranger to realize
Our fathers have been
Riding with us
In the airless trunk of the car.

Because no one ever thinks to light a candle inside a car.

Because the desert roundabout is home to Don Ho UFOs the atom bomb burros bourough Burroughs and UNLV basketball.

Because there must be a creek somewhere among these rocks there is a dash of stunted creosote among the long sentence of ahead.

Because we know Eisenstein's film of the beautiful communist peasants of Mexico is a bad joke that must go unfinished, the writer's memory must be in turns strong and bitter, bitter and strong, like dream vision and peyote buttons, like Jimi Hendrix in the American peasant tradition called for by Williams.
Because a film clip of the guitarist on his knees squirting lighter fluid into the fire that is his instrument is not an eternal flame, the fire is his instrument, our tires give themselves to the nails of campaign posters fallen into the road, open artery of traffic, if the victim had drunk one more or one fewer cup of coffee before leaving the house that morning he could not have collided, at this intersection at the speed of synapse, with the other car already gone or still coming.

Because no one in the car knows how to reset the clock for time zones we drive thru,

the dash displays the hour at home everywhere, a houseplant for our car, we lunch beside the nameless brown river so we seem to keep in motion even in repose, gas and oil oil and gas is all ye know and all ye need to know, like waking up to someone else driving the blank stretches before birth and after death, to keep out of the yawning ditch is never enuf for poetry. In a poem, you calculated, Roberto, *the defeat of pure poetry* occurred from 1968 to 1976, my freshman year at Kent State to my Masters at Oregon, the U of O, where I learned I would not write a new poetry.

Because we calculate at call of day we still haven't crossed Caesar Vallejo's empty prison cell.

Because it makes us sick to read and ride, we poets are an illiterate bunch, collecting Doug Woolf recipes for preparing whole meals on the top of the hot motor, pass by Sharon Doubiago living in a parked car, the painted desert was only more moonless night outside our speeding window. Wave poems. One day in New Mexico we can finally see how O'Keefe was wrong to paint these shapes as the bleached skulls of cattle when it is clear they are the vertebrae of D. H. Lawrence's back ache still painfully connected.

Finally pulling over in traffic, motor running,

To write out the poem in your head oblivious

To the state patrolman who approaches

Next, hand on pistol grip, taps

With his big high school ring your window

At the very crossroads where the doomed car full

Of young poets crashed because the crazed old

Poets had walked off with the stop signs.
Because all cars used and new we've rented, leased, stolen, inherited, are here salvaged for parts and left motionless in junkyard libraries built up in shelves of postmodernist pastiche, we have no paper. So we write poems in the pages of the City Lights Artaud we will wipe our asses on later in the same day. Our readers, strangers in the street, pass us running flat out toward the direction we've just come from, before we come to their car abandoned at the very last second to oily flames.

Because all along we've regularly published our broadsides of litter from the leased chariot's open windows, Shelley's Defense, our glimpse of the horizon (drive-in theater screen seen at fifty miles per), a drive by the ball park the playby play on our car radio, lousygoddamn no ticket poets, but in his poem he has the home run ball dent the hood of his car, in the knowledge that some seasons there is enuf rain and snow melt to grow a few poems, but never enuf for novels (Creeley's Second Complaint).

Well, okay, goodbye.

The knowledge that none of this remotely matters
Has never before seemed so important.

I hope the books you've left will fast become impossible

To find because they will have been stolen, from public
Libraries homes universities book stores (those untrusting

Junk cars in lines awaiting resurrection!), and burned
By righteous minds in a religion of bondfires, or the blush

On the official face underneath the makeup, photographed from space.

And I'll do nothing to save you

                                      Because I love you

Like the brother I can never know.

They hacked at your liver because you gave us fire.
Drink the gold and die.

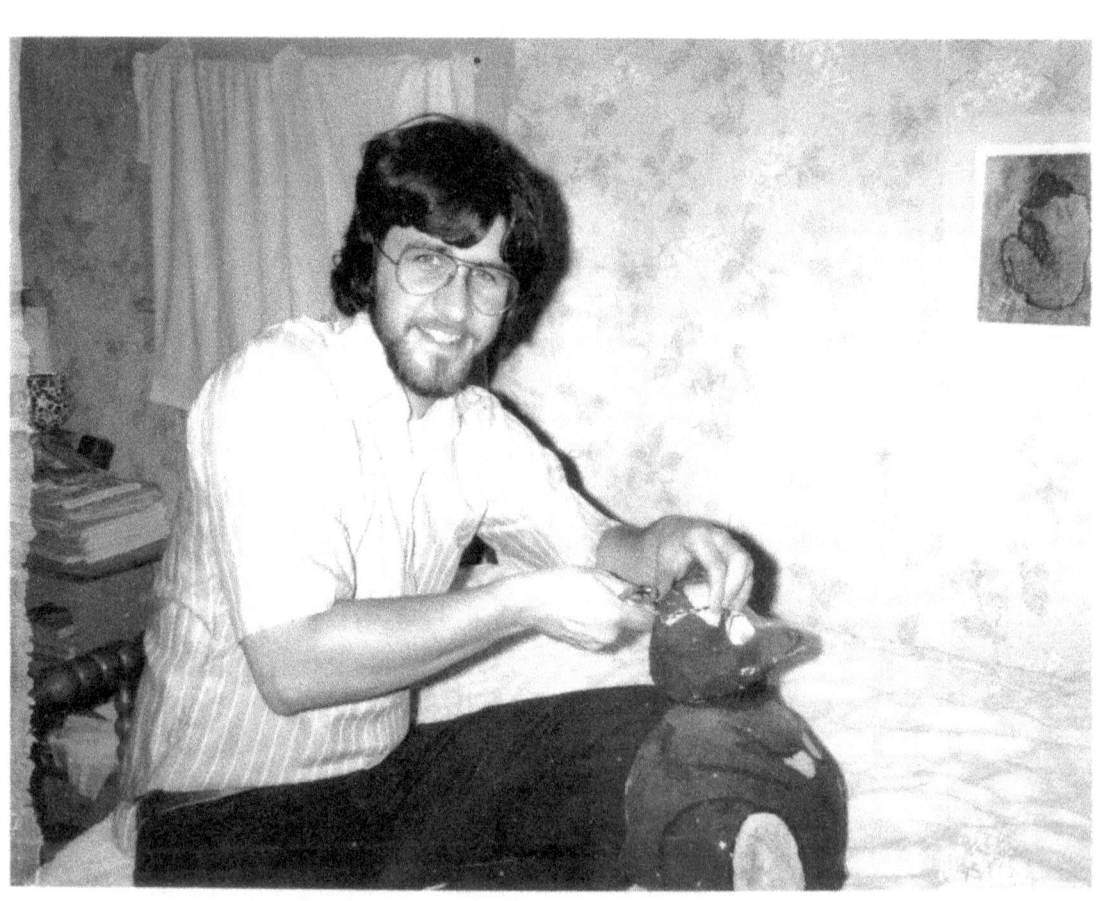

"How Disappointing"

To finally meet up, after admiring
Your poems for so long.

I see I like you best
When you are performing

Solo acts of the subconscious
I can never prepare for

This is the only public beach left,
This postcolonial desert for your eyes only

Red from the flash, twin suns
Scorching the lately discovered

Desert planet, photographed from orbit.
All water is merest conjecture.

"The Rare Ones, The Great Ones"

The rare ones, the great ones in a whole generation
The few poets bequeath

More than the anthology clutch of best verse.
They write fucking poetry, whole books

Books of fucking poetry.
Poetry that can never be anthologized to death

Or somehow
Polished.

A poetry that kicks away its own chair
To hang by a broken neck

But won't die.

"Bolaño's Afterlife"

As if the tree flew itself south
To escape what is only natural,

Threw and threw itself finally
To where the poet listens.

It is the morning of listening
For what noise or voice

This burning bush, butterflies
For wings, tells him. He sees for himself

All the pretty monarchs are
Devouring something big,

Big as a tree
Shivering in no wind. The swarm

Takes the shape of a target,
Zapata's hat on a branch,

Until only insects are left.
Then, one by one, they too leave

Flown
Into that night

When not every light rising from the desert
Is a UFO.

> America was a language
> of guilty exclamation marks,
> groaning sea vowels
> and never fading endings.
> America was the port
> where every fearful trip was done
> and every prize was won
> by sailor freshmen
> that called their captains, poet
> —Betina González's "Early Geography"

"Each Passing Decade"

The town marches, a bit further,
From the shore of its birth.

In my childhood, what was still a busy little port,
And I prepared for life as a stowaway.

"The Desert"

No coloring book
Has fewer pages

No Crayola box
Contains more crayons.

"Land Chapter"

I learned my numbers
Counting thin hymnal

Pages beyond ten,
While Father Mapple's

Sermon—reeled me in.

"Found Poem"

They found her toddler
Sitting in the store window
Among the mannequins.

"Late Into Morning When I Am"

Late into morning when I am
Reading what was to be your last novel,

The sedan is a submarine
Running out of air.

"Navigating By Stars"

Newborns, the theory goes,
Most closely resemble their biological

Fathers, so there can be little
Doubt about parentage.

Newborns and dead poets.
This likeness, at once superficial and deep,

May fade with maturation.
This is called the acquisition of style.

Here I've been looking for years for the machete answer;
Turns out, it was a bullet question.

A tiny submarine
Lodged behind the eyes

With engines shut down,
Sinking, listening

"A Cross Section Of What We're Talking About"

A remarkable feature of the submarine,
Which makes it a submarine, is

Its system of sealed compartments.
These rooms, which are poems,

Should never be mistaken
For the wreck of poetry.

"Drink The Gold And Die"

The government specie
Will be injected

This time,
Not served hot

But in a cup of gold
Minted for the occasion

Wholly without irony.
Sometimes a submarine

Is only a submarine.

"Symmzonia Or Gadsonia"

That weathering globe
Over John Cleves Symmes

Is hollow like his tomb.
But Poe explored it

In his submarine
Southward is inward

"More Hot Water"

Until only its bone handle shows

Like a periscope searching one horizon at a time.
The border here is porous. Its law

Is leaky.
None of this requires water for it to work or not work.

If you get caught,
You are returned.

If you get shot,
Or suffocate in the black box of an overbooked truck,
Your body is returned for you.

If you get caught again,
There is nothing to do
But try again.
Those subs can't patrol the whole Pacific.

The submarine noses silently
Into northbound traffic.

When they tell you the one treatment left
Is only available in Mexico,

The submarine

Becomes part of the cure,
Suggesting that even medical science

Can be faith-based too.
Of course, there's a waiting list. Sometimes

A height restriction
For life on board.

"On Sex In Bolaño's Novels"

1.
Bone are the stockings
I buy for your legs.

Your firm, long legs
Strolling past Georgia

O'Keefe's scrolls
Of desert white

Sun-baked skulls
Suddenly irrelevant.

2.
Her total eclipse of the face
Of the sun when the temperature of the ocean

Of air above us
Has become greater by degrees

Than the temperature of the healthy body
At ease.

3.
For the FSG 2666,
Endpapers should be

Velasco's "Evolution of marine life"
And not the Sebot, mein gott,

From the north sea?
Better yet,

Young Mexico City poets
Talking and fornicating

In Cuevas' brass bed
The size of a museum.

"The Geography Of Backyard"

1.
That shout in yer ear,
That triumph over talk,
It is Bolaño's
Contempt for the Mex-
Exotic industry.
It is the peal you hear
Of the stampèd realm,
Coin toss at tomb's wall;
Good poems after bad.

2.
And that's just the point.
Where Keats credits Cortez,

And covers up the deed
In his sonnet's sweet

Inevitability—
That false discovery

Of form-not-lost to
Begin with—
At that historical moment,

When the poet felt free
To choose against Balboa,

Has created a whole
Tradition that is writing poems
Ignorant of the world.

"Entry For "Submarine""

Legendary animal found

In tales of desert and sea.

See Gulf of California, cult;

Sonora, mascots of Mexican league clubs.

Sometimes the submarine is a time capsule

Forgotten in the desert beyond the last dog

Barking at the town's last addresses:

#17   Martin Magdaleno Dihigo

#21   Hector Espino.

"Mexican League"

My boyhood idol was Vic Davalillo.
He was the ballplayer

Closest to my size.

Unlike Barry Latman,
Vic could have easily fit

Thru the smallest doors
In a submarine.

He once signed a postcard
In the name of his brother, whom Vic idolized.

In Sixty-three, on the DL with a broken arm,

He signed a postcard to me
With his right hand.

My first publication was a poem
In The Vic Davalillo Fan Club Letter.

Davalillo resurfaces

In the Seventy-seven season,
Playing for Aguascalientes. Hot Water.

"Flach"
The first submarine, Chile, 1866.

The desert around
Absorbed in the act of absorbing

Everything else,
Preserves

The murder weapon.
It is the knife that cannot rust.

The only town
Is an old submarine running

Deep beneath the desert's
Baked mud and some sand.

Mojados passing thru before us
Have thot to stick the knife,

Into the floor of the vaporized inland sea,
Still vibrating.

"The "A" In Bobby Avila's Signature"
Is square-topped
Like a mesa
Or a Mayan glyph Olson would swing with,
Or Ed Sanders draw.

The fans of the Tecolotes de los Dos Laredos
Gather at night like border birds at the only green field.
To the west, the same border is less
Manageable.

"The Trees Of Sonora, Mexico"

1.
Someone has gotten here
Before me. This book is

Hollowed out, B-movie style,
Just deep enuf

To hide the Sonora
Bookmobile inside.

2.
The bookmobile is a desert submarine.
The team bus is a submarine,

Everybody
Drinking paper cups of coffee.

3.
Major Edward Bissell Hunt died
In a one-man submarine

Of his own invention. Making
A widow of Helen Hunt Jackson,

The other poet

In Amherst pond.

4.
Deep in the poem's hot stove months,
Knowing a good season in the books is not a career,

I order
The cap.

My choice is a southern team, the Cafeteros of Cordoba,
A city lost between road signs to ocean or capitol.

The cap would be a miraculous artifact brot back
From the underworld,

Eurydice's pink panty,
It would inspire me to poetry.

I would simply turn on the computer
And wear the cap that would wear me out with poems:

Home attendance, box scores, standings, individual stats
For batting, pitching, fielding, lifetime records, transactions.

The cap comes adjustable,
One size fits all poetics.

5.
The book is a table book.

"Arrivals & Departures"

If found, please
Return this poem

To Ino c/o the state of Sonora
Bookmobile.

"Dates Of Delivery"

1.
Cinco de Mayo is my son's birth day.
It was the year of Valenzuela
And the lockout.

Douglas, born lucky
The cowl still across his face

Brown eyes disappeared
Into the realm of blue cap,
Fernando delivers.

2.
When you connect
The ball travels

A long way
In this thin air.

"The Novelist's Effect Is To Gain An Impression"

Of place a savage detective would understand,
Or Sonora,

Come to know its people
By violently depopulating the area.

Mr. Coffin's painting of the criminal
Hangs on a nail in Coffin Joe's brothel.

Framed variously, this detective sees:
"Tales from the U.S./Mex Border."

"Crime Report on the Disappeared Working Girls of Santa Teresa."
Script for the B movie "The Savage Detectives."

"Martin Dihigo's Last At Bat."
Invents a structure containing torrents.

Amalfitano and the pharmacist enter, talking
With the usher and the sub-sub librarian:

"Did Melville note the Civil War submarine?"
"Is Hans Reiter Bolaño's deep-diver?"

Bolaño's talking poets
Talking volumes of the stuff,

Like Polly and Sally, like Lady Bradshaigh to Richardson.
Like Constance Chatterley.

"Narcocorrido"

The drug cartel in
Tijuana dug

A tunnel under
The border crossing

Pirate submarines
Will be shot on sight

They hunt bookmobiles
Their periscopes leave

Needle tracks of white
Phosphorescent wake

"Subtitles From The Current Cinema"

American Nazi dialog
Takes the form of big white

Decals
Running along both sides

Of the submarine,
Going and coming,

But dark above
Or directly below. Sub-

Titles in English patrol
Beneath phosphene images,

Beneath Spanish
Voices speaking the film.

"*The Savage Detectives:* The Movie"

It's a revival
Theatre this guy has kept going

Since 1950
Twice daily showings

Of the same movie.
He cannot afford to heat the place.

Tilly eating popcorn
With blue snow gloves on.

"*The Savage Detectives:* The Book"

Bolaño's the best
Drinking companion possible.

He's seen the film x times
But never reveals the plot.

"Gadsonia"

Spanish in the silver desert
Is the only language. Spoken word Spanish.

The border sun speaks directions in Spanish.
The car radios. Motel tv.

The worm in my bottle
Dreaming in Spanish.

"When The Screen Is Silver"

The white subtitles
Almost disappear

Its printed words
Are always clearest

In scenes deep in the woods
Or inside local dives,

Wet gun barrel blue alleyways
The black open graves.

Everybody looks their very best
When filmed day for night.

"Subtitles In English"

Olson admired Mayan Syntax
Invented by each unique user

Of the language, like, of course,
Syntax in Olson's poems.

"Bolaño's Hero"

Is Sisyphus. Master thief, seducer, sire of an illegitimate Odysseus,
The crafty bastard even captures Thanatos,
   Even Death, for a season.
   When Death was in chains,
No poems were written by the Mexican poets left on earth
Since none among them could be ambitious for immortality.
   No babies conceived.
   All churches and museums turned into unheated movie theatres.
A sabbatical from Death.

See Saramago.

When I complained, this morning at the end of my sabbatical from teaching,
that I was writing subtitle poems instead of syllabi for the coming term,
my wife warned me:

"Don't trust the poems."
They may be only what comes to put off the inevitable, coming attractions,
And not a poetry
To put Death back in chains.

"Collosus West"

If Texas wants a wall,
Why not buy one?

Bring in the Great Walmart
Of Xina, cock

Between the massive thighs
Of London Bridge Vegas.

It's a brilliant formula
For merger,

First floated
By Gadsden,

Involving a long history of
Keeping out the others,

Plus a little something
To bring 'em back.

"Guard"

*There are endless corridos about 'poor Pancho Villa,'
Zapata and other dead revolutionaries*, letter from Hart Crane, 1932,

That electronic First Down the NFL beams into homes
Has every appearance of a line on the field.

The southern border is a long political expediency
With no legs, the Invisible Republic

Unless it be first a river to ride
Before it becomes our river to cross.

In the early days of the league, a guard
Was expected to play on both sides of the line.

"The Waitress Of Valparaiso"

> *…in the enormous belly of a Buick the bourgeois side of my universe was still under construction*—Che Guevara.

1.
What's the appeal of *Motorcycle Diaries*, in the Sixties
And now? The journey is interrupted

By the untrustworthy bike; the voice in our heads
Is pre-revolutionary and naïve;

Our narrator tricks and exploits the working poor
To sustain his wanderings;

The translation seems vague
When it most need be clear, idiomatic.

Then, a third of the way into the book,
After the bike gives up the ghost and they become hitchhikers,

In "La Gioconda's Smile," Che finally
Writes a sympathetic passage

About a waitress dying in Valparaiso,
And he becomes an observer of the wrongs of society.

2.
The peasants grow maize
In order to more

Slowly starve themselves.
The annual Drug

Harvest is money
On Baltimore streets.

The hair in his brush,
Frida Kahlo's plucked
Camel's hair eyebrows

Under Rivera's
Nose: Trotsky's affair

With her self-portrait
Her eyebrows fetching—

A butterfly just
Crashed into a frame.

"Seeing Rivera's Mural "The Flower Carrier" And Thinking
About The Aztec Wars Of Flowers"

So many beautiful flowers overflowing
The gigantic wicker basket strapped

To the peasant's back by his wife
Are weight that cannot bear our scrutiny.

"Is This Your First Time In Denver?"

I'm right off the Hound
And the rent a cop

Who is Mexican
Threw the homeless man

Who is Indian
The length of the grand

Polished marble floor
Tourists are welcome to

"DREAM"

I was struggling
To teach my students

Frost to a full room
Of peasant workers

Frowning fanning wives
Coughing in Spanish

I scanned their faces
I couldn't seem to

Make the text behave
Beneath my finger

"Green Wood"

Dorn never wanted
To talk poetry

The conversation
Would be Watergate

To waterboarding
Never the writing

His late work suffers
From too much ed op

The confidence man
Cured the green wood

Don't complain, he said
I saw the forest

Fire kill a man who
Breathed poison ivy

Dorn's sub was a ship
Of state sinking fast

He could be cautious
Keeping his back to

Four Corners when he
Sat with the gamblers

None of which conveys
The elegance of

His talk, or the depth
Of his perceptions

"The New Interlinear"

Dorn knew what Long knew
The narrative moves

Interlinear
Walking west from east

Da Vaca walking
The way the sun works

Against the writing
Of sentences but

Interior, deep
Healing what's within

These are not couplets
Gadsden's rails of steel

One line in English
Answers the Spanish

Mine coming after
What Bolaño knew

"Studies In Classic American"

Lawrence tells us, Go,
Build a Boat of Death.

So did love prepare
A tomb hard by Taos,

And this made a boat
The Egyptians row.

               Further,
Lawrence directs us

Look for him deep
Below this surface.

"Fantasia Of The Sub"

The narrative of the body
And its column of blood

Is not a current that floats
The narrative of the mind,

Is not some painted boat.
That is our mistake.

We are too crafty.
Rather, body is boat:

Dodging submarine threats
In zig-zag lines,

Love delivers the mind
To that far shore where

Like minds have long been
Anticipating

This reunion
That is literature.

"Guest Poetics"

We call the truth naked
Meaning our bodies

In his *Grain* review
Lawrence touches on

Our instinct to touch
Her touch is not talk

Her chair has three legs
Her words are touching

Tables are arranged
Couples to a room

Much of what goes on
Is strictly beneath

The tables of talk
My five syllables

A handful of fingers
Warm from her stockings

I extend to you,
"Hello, Bolaño"

Now couplet's table
Seats three nervously

Her touch is telling
A lie for his book

The competition
That's two guys writing

In bed with one girl

"Thilleman's *Breathing*"

There is a river of talk all around
Her, eroding away at her smile,

But only one word becomes her.
Inventive prisoner denied paper,

He drafts, napkin on napkin,
The poem of one word.

Breath—not manuscript—
Found in a bottle.

Miss Moore at Bryn Mawr
Writes "Pym" a story

Involving "zig-zag"
A term she repeats

"Submariners"

1.
Jack Warhop
Dizzy Dismukes
Elder Auker
Ad Liska
Kent Tekulve
Dan Quisenberry

2.
Ted Abernathy
Was the first pitcher

I saw throw so low
His knuckles scraped

The mound, "submarine."
The season he came
To the Indians,
All the kids would throw
Like him, coming back
From sore arms, at 12.
The curves that summer
Rose, and the fast balls
Sank. Then they traded
Ted away. The curves
Went back to sinking,
And the fast ones rose.

3.
Cleveland's Ray Chapman
Never saw the pitch.

"For Sale"

Previously owned
Car submarine book-

Mobile UFO
The poet made love

In the car's back seat
Time to turn the page

You have to see this
One to believe it

                              the translated men

                    disappear into what they have

                                    translated

                        —Robin Blaser, "Image-Nation 5 (erasure"

85 CLUES
I have no form—Kerouac, "Mexican Loneliness."

1st
A dream of language
Narrative itself

2nd
A sub has a bridge
Too often submerged

3rd
Within the language
Lab, the syllables

Are five finger prints
Whose patterns are clues

4th
I could jump across
The Mississippi
At its northern source
Poe's plagiarisms
Always improve on
The original

5th
Compass is candle
In hollow earth globe

6th
I see Mexico
Everywhere these weeks

7th
I find cigarette
Butts Bolaño dropped

It takes a handful
To roll a new one

8th
"Text" comes from *tissue*

9th
People who were to amount to something didn't go to Mexican movies…or tune their radios to…corridor music—Gloria Anzaldúa.

Insomnia means
Staying up all day

If you're Dracula
A grave shift worker

A jazz musician
A third-rate poet

Jazzed by writing late
Afraid I won't wake

10th
Across her one wall
Talavera suns

Smiling and frowning
Rising and setting

11th
Cathedral shadows
So cool, they look blue

12th
The task of typing
Corridos from notes

Should be assigned
My executrix

13th
The sun feels closer
One day it will die

I should do the right
Thing and burn my work

14th
If I die the dying's over, Kerouac.

Swine flu's shut down schools
Museums, kissing

Across Sonora
Seventy-five dead

No need to visit
To write this poem

Their Dis-ease is ours
And mine already

15th
"The Mexicutioner"

Jaokim Soria
In Kansas City

16th
The closest thing to
Writing is travel

The next closest is
Fucking on a grave

17th
Virus in us sleeps
Interrupted talk

Poems sleep in us
Dream conversations

18th
When critics are smart
Er than the poem

Some Israeli Jews
Were offended by

The "swine" in swine flu

19th
If you choose to cross
The desert at night

You will take with you
Memories of darkness

20th
Abbey are the brave

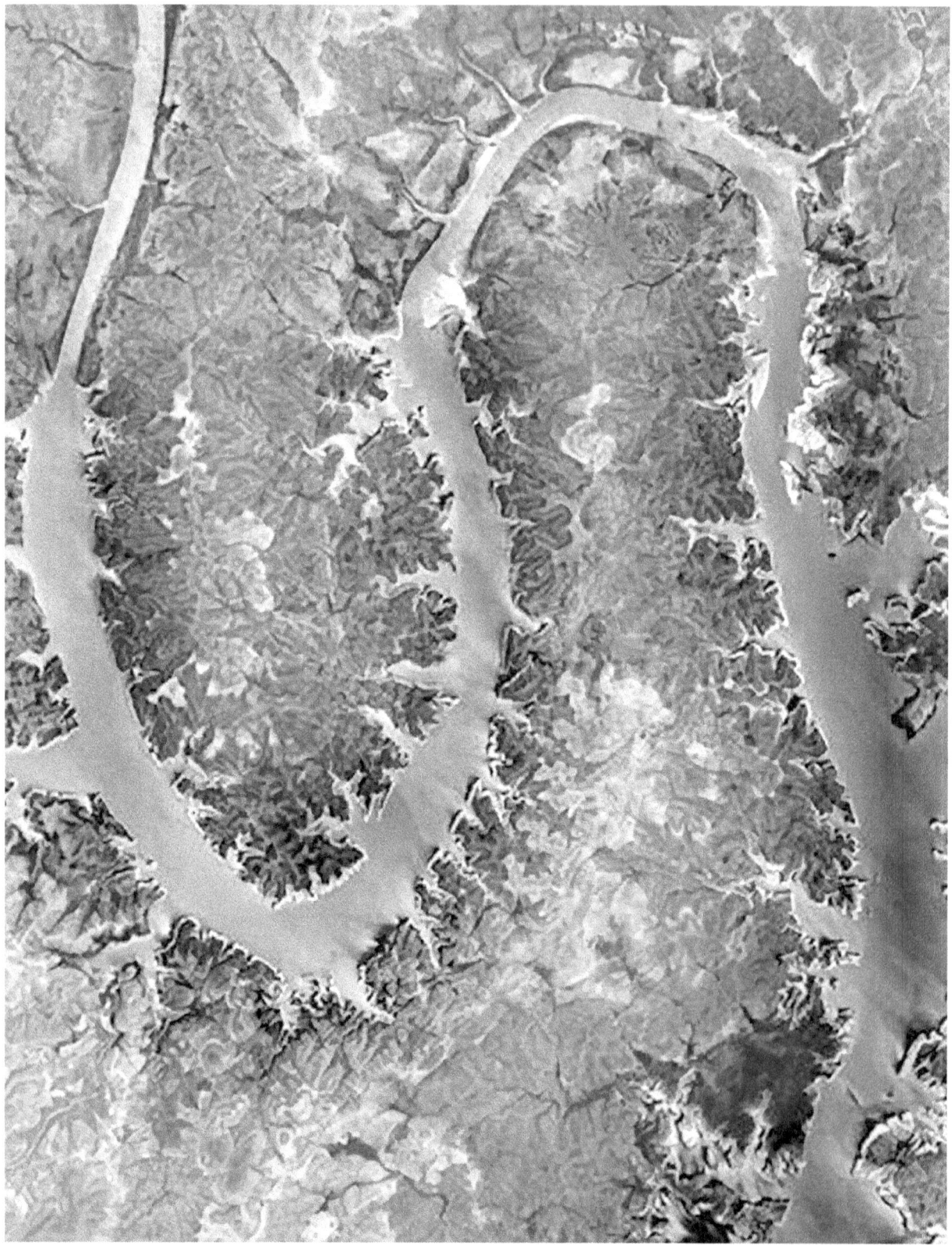

21st
Doc Williams sez Pound
Caught *the virus of*

Democracy—&
It went to his head

22nd
Sydney Salt's poems
Taken with the grain

23rd
A student of ours
Bot a Detroit house

For a couple thou
It stands surrounded

By nothing that is
Nothing like

The desert's nothing

24th
Where is Mexico?

25th
Defenseless border
Without a membrane

To keep out the new
Killer narrative

Already learning
To speak good Anglo

26th
Blue surgical masks
Dialogue filters

A row of bottles
Reflecting bottles

27th
Am I confusing?

28th
Souvenir match box
Advertise reprise

Gloved hands of drinkers
Both feet off the floor

After they finish
Their table is burned

29th
Am I confusing
Outside for inside?

30th
I am infected
And my computer

A bug from the air
A bug in my ear

X from cyber space
It has already

Killed in Sonora
Serial killer

Áztec knife, the flu
Latest reports warn

It knows no borders
It comes your way

It will seem water
To your swollen tongue

31st
"Search Committee"

Ebrard orders schools
Swimming pools pool halls

And museums closed
Restaurants meantime

May serve take-out meals
Ameliorate

Your chances take none
Suspend the kissing
Of crucifixes
Get in the habit

Of washing your hands
Put off making plans

Cancel reunions
Disinfect bull fights

Go to the empty
Baseball stadium

Abstain from licking
Stamps in the PO

Blow kisses
Wink eye

Think yourself lucky
Drink only bottles
Use ink pens to paint
Black socks on ankles

So one poet can
Pass for the many
Avoid poverty
Like rubbing the eyes

In place of faces
Blue tarantulas

Cover mouths like hands
Only the eyes show

Baby blue panic

32nd
There is no end to
Bull Burroughs' bad news

No one is immune
The virus victim

Having once succumbed
Falls in love again

33rd
O northern Chile
Most arid desert

34th
Fuck the guy behind me
Fuck his family

5 gallons at a time
I buy the whole shelf

Another five is
The collapsible

Plastic carrier
I bot years before

For desert driving
Today I buy new

Due to flu-induced
Survivalism

Gone epidemic
Among guilt-ridden

35th
While desert flowers
Deodorant melts
Motel corridors
Every door the same

Giant prawns drinking
Water imported

Every door smoking
The first time I saw

An air-conditioned
Garage, was Vegas

36th
To its balcony
Above Cozumel

The museum served
The coldest bottle

Of beer that I know
Below in the street

The Starbucks' mermaid
Wiggles her Big Ass

For the benefit
Of the harvesters

Who cannot afford
To pay for the fuck

37th
Our technology
Proves less pervasive

We break each body
Where once we melted

Cities of bathers
Making all the shit

Went down in Chile
A Collected Verse

By Nazis who Vote
Amerika first

38th
"Lorca's 'Appendix to Suites'"

This run on couplets
This thinking in twos

Has happened before
Will happen again

Love letters composed
After first delirium

39th
"Ode to Walt Whitman"
Born in Mexico

In an edition
Of fifty copies

40th
"Note On 'Sonic Model'"

Tides of consciousness
This is Hart's beloved
One he returns to
Stripping off his birth

Like a bather clothes
Tod's *ruppled* recalls

41st
The sea cannot sub
Vert itself or know

42nd
Preorder Scroggins
Rereading Max Brand

43rd
The German Max Brand
Composed Zeitoper

44th
LZ's *horse habits*

45th
When we read eyes move
In a series of

Jumps (saccades) and
Pauses (fixations)

To process the text
Jump to the next part

Where fixation waits
For you to catch up

46th
Once Oppen a time
Begins a narrative

47th
All this modeled
After a poem

To the new world
By Ted Berrigan

We know as "The Boke"

48th
I think in couplets
Words in sentences

Are larger than this
Point of reference

A design confides
In me a secret

That conversation
I happened in on

At tables of sound
On tablets of ears

49th
If you had to spell to talk, nobody would be talking, Ornette Coleman

50th
Because the speech act contests itself and its own premises, it moves in the direction of becoming philosophy; because the language in which it is performed tells you many things about itself and its world which it was not the author's or the user's intention to tell you, it can be used as material in the writing of history…,
J.G.A. Pocock, "The Owl Reviews his Feathers"

51st
"Reply to Mary Ruefle's
'If All the World Were Paper'"

1. Rainforest

We don't use language
It uses us up

In the rainforests
Of Brazil forcing

The poor to burn them
To clear little plots

Such sustenance farms
Overheat a world

We think we control
What we write about

2. Poverty

What is avoided—

When we don't misuse

Language—keeps us poor

3. Lawns

Language keeps us poor
Whole generations

In shorts and tee tops
Mowing more backyards

Even when the grass
Doesn't really grow

4. Paper

The sun is closer
Than my father's sun

The Nazi's job done
Now books burn themselves

5. Lumber

We have no use for
The room a man is

Building in our
Basement he charges

Nothing he arrives
Saturday mornings

He lets himself in
And works on the room

For half the weekend
Without eating lunch

I never go down
I never inspect

My girls have grown up
To the noise he makes

They continue to sleep
To his hammering

I should have a talk
And stop this nonsense

Writing long poems
Nobody asked for

Heidegger would add
We dwell in language
In the room language
Has prepared for us

At times I can't write
For all the sleeping

Bodies of poets
Cluttering my desk

I need to prepare
A bedroom for them

Beds like new bodies
For their restlessness
Poems like pillows

6. Lingual

Man invents language
Rereading *Mardi*

On a rubber raft
Up the Amazon

52nd
If birds could not sing
They would not live here

Inside this cactus
Beyond redemption

53rd
[Reily, Reich, and Glass] evoke the experience of driving in a car across empty desert, the layered repetitions in the music mirroring the changes that the eye perceives—road signs flashing by, a mountain range shifting on the horizon, a pedal point of asphalt underneath, Alex Ross, The Rest Is Noise

54th
There are two boxes
What I'm driving at

Artists work best from
Marginality

Paint to the very
Edge of each canvas

Rothko's the city
Within a desert

Soft box gathers dawn

_____

Soft box gather speed

Run thru the desert
Before they close it

55th
Sometimes we could see
Where beams of light end

A turn of events
Beyond the road's reach

Metaphor enjoys
Limited uses

Before it turns back
Into the music

Ornette Coleman's Turn
Around Matador

Recorded two years
Into your after
Life where headlights end
Out beyond our reach

Tires spinning in air

56th
Rachel Bremser please
If you're reading this

Contact your mother
She is awaiting

For fifty years word
Across the border

57th
Detective routine
Brot Ellington down

To the city morgue
To identify

Some murdered body
Last seen lost in dance
On a night Duke played
With his jungle band

To Lorca's table
At the Cotton Club

58th
Missing persons form
A Supreme Mirage

59th
Rory Long is raised
On Olson becomes

An evangelist
All theory and cult

He finally reads
The Max and vomits

For three hours straight

60th
Don Quixote makes
Melville's list of three

Unique characters
When his last novel

Begins with Manco
Capac appearing

The Mississippi
Points like an arrow

61st
Hart Crane didn't die
His was the figure

Of the washed up man
A bundle of nerves

Williams cannot name
On the Juarez bridge

A bag someone tossed
Overboard to die

Delivered upstream
For reasons unknown

Against the gulf's grain
Only the savage

Know its whereabouts
Only detectives

Have opened the bag

62nd
To clean the windshield
Of perception

Vinegar water
In a spray bottle

If there's any Left
Coke dissolves all bugs

63rd
Metcalf's narrative
After Genoa

Adapts itself to
A country without

Peasant traditions
Corridos to sing

64th
Barlow's description
Shows Manco Capac

Robed in whining white

65th
Alberto Blanco's
Texas-El Paso

Poetry workshop
Is taught in Spanish

66th
Had Polk read Prescott
Before his conquest?

After his conquest?
Did Hawthorne read it

To the president?

67th
Take the right-hand road,
Blues song "West Texas."

68th
"Road Game"

Sharon Doubiago's
Name is six syllables

One too long for my line
She has been here ahead

Of me again and leaves
A note in lipstick

On my motel mirror:
"The Mendocino Fault

Line begins in Chile"
It must run beneath me

I think, as I sink
Below Mendoza's

69th
My car enters thru
The crack in a rock

70th
California
Inhabits one line

Mexico City
Occupies one too

They form the couplet
"Independent State"

California
―――――――
Mexico City

71st
Where I see baseball
In an open field

(An ancient fastball
Aimed behind the head

Moves the crystal skull
Off the pitcher's plate)

Our five-syllable
Sikelianos

Remembers the land
Linneaus divides

72nd
"This map is a laugh!"

73rd
Olson saw the land
In a Zazca glyph

From the UFO
Leaving our world
Like a home run ball
In high desert air

74th
"Tec Baseball"

How I love to see
The old men fighting

Stiff neck coming out
A boy's jersey top

The fat manager
Must be suffering

Deep cuts, decades old
At the bloody hands

Of this umpire's dad.
The game loses all

Continuity
Umpires always win

75th
"Aztec Radio"

The sounds of baseball
Over my radio

Are neither here nor
Spanish nor local

76th
Quotation marks mean
I am translating

Into my own tongue
Onto my own tongue

The bright foreigner,
The foreign self, in

Emerson's Journals
The more quotation

Tells the less you know
The typer must not

Look at his fingers
During touch typing

But at the paper
On which a poem

About hands stares back
The bright foreigner

77th
This pitcher looks tough
This pitcher looks scared

This pitcher looks young
This pitcher looks gassed

This pitcher looks sharp
This pitcher looks wild

78th
Catcher and pitcher
In front of the crowd

Glove-covered faces
During a time out

Talk to each other
About what to do

The pitcher's blue glove
The catcher's blue cap

A coach joins them
His face is too big

The umpire walks out
Carrying his mask

Wordlessly they leave
The lonely pitcher

79th
The last surviving
U.S. veteran

Of the Mexican
War Owen Thomas

Edgar died the year
My father turned four

His naval service
Included duty

On Allegheny
Ariel Jane Guy

There is no mention
Of the submarine

Or his Mexican
Army counterpart

80th
The stranger arrived
With seven horses

Traven claimed to live
Like an Indian

Speaking in German
Writing in English

(*No breakfast no tea*
The wood is so wet

No fire can be laid)
Mahogany books

2.
Nothing ever rusts
The desert preserves

David Ruess rode off
Notebook and burros

Into the region
Of missing persons

Seventy-five years
Ago and this week

They've identified
His murdered body

And reconstructed
The prodigy's face

3.
The novelist paints
A dialog for trees

4.
Who knows what they'll find
In a hundred years

When they open this
Wake me up gently

81st
Another five
I have in mind is

Notes ascending
And descending

A ladder of notes

Invisible staff
Angels wouldn't need

82nd
Olson's Fulbright re
Quest for the Maya

Is legendary
He further proposed

To go to IRAQ
This was Fifty-one

83rd
I could hear them long
Before I saw them

84th
Poe composed on strips
Of paper pasted

Into room-long rolls
That Kerouac stole

And used for his scroll
Nobody noticed

85th
A language of clues
Is weak evidence

What once were blue eyes
The eyes after death

Reflect no longer
Clouds over water

The sky was someone
You knew by first name

The earth is hollow
Her eyes are clouded
Contain their own skies
Her jailers can't see

Where light doesn't enter
The conversation

This is why they close
The eyes after death

Her jailers find it
Confusing to track

Days with so many
New suns in the sky

Blue in abeyance

**I like artists who rub their trumpets with maps
to clean them, the trumpets or the maps
—Ted Berrigan, "The 51st State"**

"Juarez Corrido"
i die every time i go to MEXICO
and return reborn—ruth weiss, "POST-CARD 1995."
Between both vulnerabilities sits Poe's urn.

It worked like a shot
Williams came back

Re-crossed the bridge
From Juarez that night

Having dined on quail
With McAlmon

The music there injected
Into the old man's stream

So he could write the poems
With the clean needle

Of his last decade
The singer was ugly

The cock has an eye
But two heads to mind

The old doctor happy
To be reunited

With his old friend and
The dance in his veins

To Carlos's *I*
Am a poet. I am a poet

    —Only
Three years earlier

Doc first visited
Taos, with Robert

McAlmon. He had
Seen the desert then,

Crossed it there. And now,
As if returning

From Lawrence, to be
Twice resurrected,

After the auto
Biography stop.

Williams returned east
Taking Gadsden's line—

The romance is sure
Some three years later

Bolaño is born
For the only time.

    To return to Paul's
Biographical

"The Desert Music"
Is like tracking down

A missing person
Tho the books are closed

Each new clue signals
She is still alive

And I was returned
Just now to my friend

I need to know
What Sherman knew

About the dinner
With McAlmon

Now I need to
Learn the words for the

Music of survival
For the corridor

I am writing
Under my breath

Shadow unobserved
The sub surfaces

Launches a small raft
On the shore the ailing

Doctor undeterred
By mariachi

Music for tourists
Makes his boat of death

From the hollow body
Of a cello—-

Pablo Casals
                     lands!

"Eavesdrop Company"

Rubber raft cello
Survives white water

Birds sing Messiaen
For the end of time

This time to Nazis
At the Grand Canyon

Fascism cuts deep
Thru modern nature

It originates
When Vegas flushes

Its river becomes
Bloody Sonora

"Emboucher"

Mi corridor sin
Fronteras plays on

Harry Partch's new
Instrument for two

"Bro"

You be Maddalo
Call me Julian

Their conversation
Continues in us

I'll write his great line
On loving *all waste*

And solitary
Places cries the drowned

Man to the swimmer
Not exactly beach

With lathered horses
But a paradise

Boundless to exiles
A Visionary

Eavesdrop Company
The other other

"Mount Aavalna"

Day after earthquake,
Allen Ginsberg Pym

Pries open the dark
Cave's great crystal door,

Reenters the chasm,
Breaking thru the red/black

Cycle of meat or
Annihilation,

To decipher what
Hieroglyphic gods

Had writ in white mist.
To decipher what gods.

"The Red And The Black Of It"

Escritura y
Sabiduría

Ink on codices
The black is writing

The red is wisdom
The great corridor

"El tango negro"
Sung by Lydia

Mendoza is black

"Momus"

The wrong painting for
The wrong century

Poets who write one
Poem over and

Over overboard
Animus Mountains

Legend to a map
Legendary land

Why is Rattray left
Out of histories?

What's Charlie Manson
Doing way out here?

He has a half life
Of a thousand years

Heck Allen's sheriff
Runs into cartoon

Desert beyond town
Each time the many

Times he needs to yell
West as escape valve

"The Radical Priests"

The radical priests
Are dead or retired

Whose ball courts made beds
For demonstrators

Whose god never flinched
From Communism

Who argued better
Than our professors

Smoked more cigarettes
Whose god had climbed down

Off the cross to us
Who were locked in cells

Next to us in jails
Who lived without things

But seemed satisfied
As when we'd just fucked

The church should have closed
Its doors behind them

Locked up the relics
And blown out the candles

The radical priests
Are dead or married

2.
Immaculate white
Of saints and stockings

Where am I to place
My gaze decently?

For what duration?
The vision ascends

3.
"Her knees are cutest"
Cried the virgin saints

Among the white bones
Stacked neatly in rows

4. 2666
Your knees can't open
Martyrdom's thumbed claws

Won't pry them apart
Violence is dead

"On Tradition"

Catholic rituals
Carried thru these streets

A masked doll passes
Throat-shaped Aztec gold

Local devils prance
Right back to chapel

"On Narrative"

Prayer is the talk
I have with myself.

Funeral sermons
Address survivors.

I'd prayed for Jim Brown
Every Sunday school
To rush a hundred yards

I write corridos
In conversation

With you, Bolaño.
With you, Thilleman

"Tierra Natal"

The poorest among
Twenty-two border

Counties in four states
Where Anzaldua

The new Mestiza
Was born and nurtured

Is named Hidalgo

GADSDEN CORRIDO
Rio Poe—Allen Ginsberg Journal, Mexico City.

Like Manco Capac
At Titicaca

Barlow lived to talk
His angel listened

We won't have angels
Speaking their own words

Until duende
And the Duino

Get the story straight
Religions are born

On wings of mountains
Cults dwell in trailers

Within desert hills
Of their own device

Dead conquistadors
Speak in our voices

An epic so dark
Barlow called it dawn

Dorn knew what Long knew
The narrative moves

Interlinear
Walking east to west

Da Vaca walking
The way the sun works

Against the writing
Of sentences but

Interior deep
Healing what's within

These are not couplets
Gadsden's rails of steel

One line in English
Answers the Spanish

Mine coming after
What Bolaño knew

Can't open the door
For the stacked bodies

My students' papers
Are starting to stink

High time to bury
To let the red ink

Time to end the term
Not long ago so

Well undertaken

Rats ate the wiring
Died inside his walls

The poet keeps on
Writing, in darkness,

Sings: *Stop the murder
And the suicide!*

To close the distance
Barlow to MacLeish

Takes a century
Of opening roads

Outlaw Deadwood Dick
Is a detective

In the Pinkerton
Dime novel a kind

Of noble savage
Displaced and whiter

The sound of our
Snoring wakes us up

When Hollywood looked
Down at the Third World

It saw Mexico
Wallace Beery looks drunk

What's he doing in
Hecht's "Viva Villa!"?

Those eyes of Bette
Davis look sexy

While Paul Muni plays
At being Beery

In the film version
Before Williams wrote

His Juarez passage
It is The Fifth Sun

Melville contemplates
The Mexican dead

In his 29 May
Letter to brother

Gansevoort who un
Known to the poet

Has already died
On a Polk mission

That great murderer
Ulysses Grant is

His true Penelope,
Writing in English

Grant is on record
I know only two

Corridos and both
Of them are 'Dixie'

Before Gadsden's death,
The Mexican War

Trained a West Point class
To die on both sides

Of the Coming Wall.
The first modern prose

Is the Grant memoir.
Pershing rode around

Certain villages
Where Pancho Villa

Was rumored to sleep.
He should have listened

To the corridos.
Oppen learned to carve

Wood in the Valley
On the GI Bill.

OSO NEGRO TELL
TRAVELS THE FIVE FEET

TOP HAT OF A STAR
CUT GIN .380

LEMONADE BULLET
LAUGHS & PUTS HER GLASS

Fugue is a flight too.
Kerouac stumbled

Over lost yage load
In his rented room

Aztec Radio——
Improvisation——

Horn-re-born figure——
White shrouded Buddha!

Re-ope a cold case
Re-add Jack's Blues straightthru

To aye Why Charlie
Parker has to bye

Blownout at pome's end
Paul Bowles feels too sick

To go thirty-five
Miles to Mexico

City in 'Forty
He hates the food

He cannot stomach
Waiting for them to

Digest what he's said
Levertov's pepper

Trees animated
More from Walt Disney

Than Williams' dancers
She patronizes

Supermercado
Perhaps took Ginsberg

Sticks to the wrong aisle
And never bumps carts

With the other Walt
Even if you could

Get there from here don't
There are no houses

Where Kathy Acker
Died only basements

It has no highways
Reaching to the coast

Only passengers
Going nowhere fast

In my translation
The clichés you hear

Make figures of speech
Minor revisions

Are required before
We publish your life

Air not manuscript
Found in a bottle

Dead Neal Cassady
Beside the railroad

Track never coming
Back from Mexico

Native geniuses
For narrative form

Gadsden built a death
Ship for this trip too

It sure beats walking
Into the desert

To die when you can
Ride over borders

To the danger zone
To the forbidden

Whatever can't get
Done back in the States

To pen no memoirs
To find works as a

Safe abortionist
Nameless pharmacist

Work enuf to pay
The luxury tax

Buying y selling
The bodies of Christ

Driving up the price
Driven to success

Excess y madness
In order to buy

Another ticket
We have been too long

Too proud driving cars
And riding in cars

Of our own design
Even metaphors

Have their vehicles
Words from passing cars

Litter the dirt roads
Every car travels

With its little cloud
The dust catches up

Only when you stop
Amerikans are

A driven people
Nunez hitch hiking

High desert road-kill
Death of Lizard King

Take this train to view
French guards at his tomb

Spanglish graffiti
Beer bottle candles

Zappa Pachuco
From the Mojave

Phoned Edgard Varèse
At work on "Deserts"

I watched myself die
My peyote face

Dracula Exposed
To sunshine I aged

From 20 to dust
I just slipped away

Everyone downstairs
Hallucinating

Plates of brown rice to
Try being alone

See if I could write
In the high desert

I checked my eyes the
Bathroom mirror went

Subterranean
Kiva periscope

Reflecting my eye
Even this zigzag

Is part of my life
It separates me

Dead from the undead
Down kiva's ladder

It was in Taos
Una shot herself

Jeffers had acted
Like a character

Somewhere in Lawrence
By Mabel Dodge

He never let go
His disappointments

No one reads him much
A few tour Tor

Having come to see
Father Serra's doll

By term's end,
By finals,

I am tired,
Profoundly,

Of hearing
My own voice.

My students
Are tired too

They suffer
The fatigue

Of youth one
That will hatch

Summertime
But I am tired

Of myself
Books I hold

Dear I cling
Too dearly—

"The circle
Of the raft,"

I called it,
Already,

When I was
A student

Cutting class.
I'd fashioned

A bookshelf
(Two cement

Blocks, a board)
For those texts

We must teach
Ourselves—or

Die alone.

For the dead at Plaza de Tlatelolco, from a Kent State graduate.

"Aquinas In The Desert"

Our subject was Joyce
And Tod was talking

About how "hard-core
Poetics" discussed

Thru long stretches of
Savage Detectives

Brings to mind *Portrait*
The Aquinas blog

Which I compared to
My last term paper

As a poli sci
The assignment was

To interview all
Public officials

Serving a small town
In north Ohio

So I made up all
Those voices and earned

An A for the course
Then changed my major

This was just before
The May 4 killings

"My Life As A Stowaway"

Dad brot home jumping
Beans from work one day

I can't remember
When I learned what made

Them move in my hand
Among novelties

The store had for sale
Was a toy known as

Mexican handcuffs
You could open them

Without the lost key

*

Our daughter Doris
Is fascinated

By the show "Blue's Clues"
Starring a puppy

And a dumb gringo
Who must collect three
Clues to solve problems
A three-year-old can

She organizes
Her day around its

Cycle of re-runs
A writer's routine

*

Blanco's children's book
Sends away the lone

Surviving Desert
Mermaid (played by Anne

Sexton) on a trek
Thru the Sonora

To teach Disappeared
Mermaids lost songs on

Scattered oases
Bolaño slept here

"The Future Of End Tables"

Conversation turned
(When the kid Rimbaud

Jumped on the table
And pissed on all

The heads of the arts
Ready to agree)

To an argument
About the future

Of tables where we
Sit to write things down

"Ohiocorrido"

Zorro possessed me
I wore his outfit

Black mask flat hat sword
Penciled-on pencil-

Thin mustache red sash
But there was nothing

For a kid to do
All dressed up like that

Waiting for Friday
Night television

Green Ohio fields
No hacienda

No cigarette whipped
From the cruel mouth

No servant sidekick
Deaf-and-dumb loyal

No fat sergeant foil
To my double life

"Victim Seeking Murder"

Time favors deserts
Rain delights in mud

Earth is adobe
Adobe orange

Disregard the plot
Narrative makes sense

Turn left at first base
Law is not order

Mind makes narrative
Answer what's ringing

"Delirious Testament"

From the highest head
To the deepest mind,

Our generation
Has come back to earth

It's not the same earth
With you gone so soon

It's not a better
Place to bring the kids

How disappointing
To know we'll never
Stop the violence

Write better than Pound
Pound the steak into

Capitalism
Make the animals

Unafraid of us
Make the college sing

Or make the small big
Or forget cold shame

Or live off poems
Or change poetry

Or live on the moon
Or live by ourself

Or legalize bliss
Or burn the money

Or drink our own piss
So we dig our graves

Beneath monuments
We cannot afford

        It has taken me

All of three decades
To complete this much.

"Incident"

What the narrative
Table needs is kids

Fighting spilling drinks
Throwing bread standing

We need to listen
Their startling mouths

Speak the living tongue
"Incidentally"

Said our three-year-old
To argue her point

"After A Passage In 2666"

When Aztecs emerged
From cold pyramids

Their eyeballs were moons
Eclipsing the sun

A man who once slept
On a pyramid

Addressed my grade school
I cannot forget

How impressed I was
Aztecs made his bed

The priests stand between
The sun and the earth

This is not daylight
Where orbs seem flattened

Into disks that roll
On edges no one

Can sharpen or dull
The priests stand aloof

The UFO lifts
In darkness at noon

Stare into the face
Of the first wrist watch

"Reading *Under The Volcano* As A Young Man"

Shot glass volcanoes
Under sour breath

Drink under table
Under tremendous…

Under the radar…
Under the weather…

Hard <u>underlinings</u>
Soft underbelly
Of the industry

Under probation
Under house arrest

Underestimates
What we understand

Types in underwear
At last underway

If I could write the love poem of my continent to you

—Sharon Doubiago, "Lima"

FUGITIVE CORRIDOS

So when does the American poem begin?— "Breathing."

Starting out from Why
We'll cross the border

80 into 8
Just below Lukeville

==

We drove all day in front
Of the driving front

Sangre de Christo
A Gaugain yellow

Beat it to Clarel's
Motel for the night

Hours scoured our
Corrugated walls

It made the room breathe
With an iron lung

I'd somehow escaped
My polio blown

Over my childhood
Knocking down some toys

We laughed in that room
Relived *The thrill of*

A perpetual
Recovery from

An illness relieved
Next morning was clear

The car wouldn't start
Sand fouled the intake

Since armadillos
Appropriated

By confessionals
Whose poems I detest

The rest of the trip
I will stay silent

===

IT WAS A POEM ABOUT THE SKY

When muse is not amused
The way the poem's going.

When muse says, I'd best watch
What I say around you,

The conversation part
Dries up; returns me,

Night's revelry to books.
Dawn. Lon Chaney Jr. boils away,

Just some ankle-high fog
Filmed in reverse, retreating

Into his cool tomb
Hidden from El Quinto Sol

Where he's a danger
Only to himself.

===

RECASTING MELVILLE: THE CONFIDENCE-MAN AND CLAREL IN ED DORN'S GUNSLINGER

The fact that Black Mountain poet and essayist Charles Olson posited himself as the understood and all his writing in an American literary tradition beginning with Herman Melville (Call Me Ishmael, 1947, was Olson's first book) is well documented. Elder Melville Society members will recall perhaps Olson's outraged proclamation of himself as guardian of Melville scholarship in his "Letter for to the Melville Society," 1951, and Ann Charters' Olson/Melville (1968) helping to make charted the scholarly/fishing waters for decades of scholars to fast the follow. Still, the influence of Melville upon Edward Dorn, perhaps Olson's loose fish that C presents most celebrated student, remains water for deep diving. If Moby-Dick, and to most scholars what Olson chose to read in that novel as an "American", particularly the ironic use of space, is Olson's essential Melville, then the younger Dorn's Melville is the writer of The Confidence-Man and Clarel.

A key passage in Gunslinger, Book IIII, Dorn's longtime victimized masterpiece to date, could be taken as a useful gloss for the early and middle action in The Confidence-Man. STET reads:

> Entrapment is this society's
>
> Sole activity . . .
>
> and Onlylaughter,
>
> can blow it to rags
>
> But there is no negative pure enough
>
> to entrap our Expectations.
>
> (Slinger, Book IIII, n.pag.)

1 Call Me Ishmael (San Francisco: City Lights Books, n.d.); "Letter for Melville 1951," in The Distances (New York: Grove, 1960), pp. 48-54; Olson/Melville: A Study in Affinity (San Francisco: Yez, 1968).

The materials
This table these chairs

Lend our dull café
Its airless air where

We Awake gather
Painfully alert

To talk ourselves out
We Vampires renting out

The tombs of poets

===

I've twice seen the place
They call Four Corners

On both occasions
We walked on the moon

The government built
A spot for pictures

I bot silver rings
For my wife's fingers

That was my first time
On the return trip

I chose small ear rings
Which she never saw

Two turquoise turtles
That hold up the world

===

Going to Hornell
We drive past Cuba

After Bolivar
And make the same joke

About Frank McGlynn
That's always funny

===

The "plot" of a trip
The universe said

Poe
Is a plot of

God

Corridos Sin Front

Eras

===

[He liked] her skirt hiked
Above sensible

Leather hiking boots
She never removed

From irrational
Fear of snakes or
Some passionate sense
Of fashion's border

To wear such heavy
Boots made a statement
Disputed between

Her uncovered knees

==

Poets put him in
    Jail
Poems shall release
    Him

"Jail him!"
The age demanded

My ex demanded
My "death benefits"

And her attorney
Missed the irony

Got everything else
Death could benefit

==

You read from afar
Unrequited luv

The New Formalists
Have set up shop their

Old sign reads Lock Smith
For Chastity Belts

==

Airstream caravans
In wagon-train circle

For the [Gadsden] night
An illustration

Of architecture
In a Scully book

Interlinear
(He shares his name with

The LA Dodger)
I took his *Pueblo*

For my map and guide
Mountain, Dance and Myth

When I left the West
Trying to finish

"Taos, Lucretius"
(The failed long poem

Of my reluctant
Midwestern return)

In fire-lit camp grounds
All the way across

===

I've come all this way
Drove the continent

To know I won't cross
This street to see you
Lipstick inscription
A sheet of music

Is dumb without breath
Our point of reference

The fertile desert
Whose music is rain

===

"May In September"

The Argentine pears
Are harvested green

Hard as fall baseballs
And shipped in darkness

Now they are arrived
For spring to ripen

In the one sunny
Window in our house

===

Word processors should
Make sounds when we work

The tap of a spoon
Inside the next room

Our daughter's eating
Vanilla ice cream

From a little cup
Tap tap tap-tap tap

===

Someone sends a flare
Up from the desert

Into the night sky
There must be trouble

The animals think
It must be morning
The distance plays tricks

I give up trying

To read by someone's
Emergency lights

===

On the road to the
Soccer stadium

Nothing is moving
Cars are abandoned

Spring sits already
In her season seats

They know nothing save
That they have come save

Football not baseball
Is so contagious

They should play it out
In all openness

Beyond all ghettos
Desert all around

A bull cannot end
In a scoreless tie

===

Just how much of it
Is you and what parts

Me I could not say
We are blood brothers

I'll drive while you sleep

We'll be there for dawn

Our table is set
By the tired waitress

She wakes up tireder
She lives in the town

Of her birth and death
She knows the poet's address

He lives in the town
Of his retirement

Tell me why it is
Breakfasts on the road

Taste like lost poems
We'll be there for dawn

==

For my narrative, I want a conversation—not a translation, lingual not bilingual—without unspoken assumptions trailing away into footnotes. Pound's insistence that he could damned well *see* what the Chinese character says, or amateur Olson's grant to read Mayan glyphs, or Benjamin Blood writing ecstatic philosophy, or John Milton posing for Blake, constitute narrative models for a poetry that passes freely over established borders.

==

My fascination
With the detective

Goes back to Marlowe
Chandler's hard-boiled talk

I thot I'd never
Get out of my head

After finishing
The Morrison Poem

And Philip Marlowe's
Collected Poems

It was the same voice
Every time I wrote

Bolaño's savage
Is a movie dick

Maybe the killer
Sat in the theater

Only seats away
From the guy who writes

===

One kind of private
Eye shadows culprits

The other kind is
Merely a shadow

Of some former self
A published poet

I see her black eye
Shadow is tattooed

Distinguishing marks
On the poet corpse

He's always smoking
On his book covers

The same cigarette

That cannot burn down
He's always smiling
It's the same picture

On drivers' license
Passports rock n roll

Posters obit pix
He smiles out to us

Laughing at his fame
Wishing you were here

==

In his narrative, the poet must reach the *desdén*, the moment when the bull fighter turns his back on the bull, and kill poetry with his art.

==

Never mistake what's mine
Shaft for the cavern

One *can* be explored
A proposition

Exploiting labor
A cash enema

One *must* be explored
To find your way out

Having fallen in
The nature of men

Should not be taken
For what we call nature

Awaiting rescue
Miners have been known

To write in the dark
Pym in the belly

==

When they took away
His keys he gave up

He could no more go
To the grocery

Than to Mexico
Revisiting Ed

Abbey's travelog
"Sierra *Madre*"

My phone rings at night
It's Mom suddenly

Thirty years older
Since I first read Ed

Abbey's post office
Was in Oracle

She is calling from
Her recliner on

The old Ohio
Canal's highest place

Landlocked in Akron
She intuits him

She would love to walk
Into a canyon land

And never come back

==

I feel tall among
Them I have money

Sound patronizing
When I quiz the guide

Who is my son's height
On the hot bus ride

The occasional
Corrugated roof

We pass driving fast
Into the jungle

The sea at our backs
A circle of sweat

He is a student
I'm not his teacher

He has mentioned
All he wants to say

The air presses down
He hands me a beer

I cannot tell him
How guilty I feel

==

I'm sick of shaving
Without a mirror

I decide to let
The poem grow out

When I'm off the road
And back home again

No one will know me
My mouth in hiding

===

On page 223, beside note 18, in the margins of my copy of Ralph Maud's *Olson's Reading*, which I bot new in Gloucester, Mass. on a visit to Gerrit Lansing, I have written:

    "No: Olson wz reading books fm <u>boat's</u> library!"

This does not pass for knowledge, except maybe in the university or with the Black Mountain cult. This is what I gave up, or failed to live up to, when I found I could not continue to edit, after George's death, the Olson/Creeley correspondence. In my narrative, we see Olson's boat's library—whatever I meant by that, then—is a form of submarine/bookmobile.

I wrote my daily
Letter to Sherman

From ship's library
Gulf of Mexico

I could not know he
Had already died

The Harvard stories
You told me as if

I must remember
All their fights for you

Letters piling up like
North Dakota snow

They cannot open
The hospital door

I'd left already
To write my own books

Left Olson's letters
To Creeley's letters

"The Known University"

It's easy to hate
University

Forgetting the day
Unamuno dies

Forgetting the way
South Amerika

Rediscovers Spain
When Cortez landed

And ordered his ships
Burned on the same shore

Where Bolaño leaves
Home to die at home

Gaudí's rooftop gods
Watch over his sleep

II
I want a divorce
From professionals

The last amateur
Archaeologist

The last detective
Who cannot be bot

It is time to fill
The vacancies left

By Amerika's
Lost artists Fred Day

Adelaide Crapsey
Our distinguished search

Committee requests
Dossiers and five

Supporting letters
From the radical

Tenured backstabbing
Limp-cocked assassins

Who wouldn't call Poe
For an interview

III
I was screwing the
President's daughter

In his house his bed
His office his car

Ishmael in charge
The Try-Works chapter

I used this time to
Rethink the problem

Of granting tenure
To bastards like me

Come the next revolt
Professors get shot

It's more efficient
Than retraining us

A library's fine
For adultery

Away from the fire
That mesmerizes

The girl was ugly
She looked like her dad

"The Great Companion"

What shall contain him
The blaze that opens

Redwood cones dormant
Since Whitman's live oak?

Duncan's kid brother
One of the authors

Of "Gadsden" is dead
He leaves it to me

To hear robins sing
How poems cohere

From conflagration
That ring of fire his

Cheekbone tectonics
Extends volcanoes

Into the ocean
To cool new islands

Sprout dense feathered song
In holy forests

For the ultimate
Serial poem

The word for word is word—Burroughs' *My Education*.

"The Wave That"

Picks me up and lets
Me off   further out

To ride the great wave
After Vico's flood

The wave my poem
Should be, Bolaño

Has turned his back on
To address Duncan,

Creeley, Bertholf, shore.
(All are Robertos!)

There is only so
Much sand to stand on.

"Borges At The MLA"

His rooms were labrynths
I was a table

He had never left
The dark reading room

The time I saw him
I was aware of

Her and not Borges
Instead of walking

With Death he had her
On his arm urging

His feet but careful
To remain behind

Closer to my age
And Bolaño's rage

"Burroughs In Lawrence"

Savage detective
Ulysses runs

Down Tieresias
In his Mexico

City hotel room
For two interviews

With the neglected
Crossdressing author

Whose unlucky books
Were seldom printed

In his *or* her name
My Education

Is a book of dreams
Written in Kansas

Tradition has it
Tieresias knows

The map of the desert
By the second day

Ulysses figures
This one is a choice

Between two questions:
The way to go home?

The worst of both worlds?

"We Tracked Down Enoch"
*Todos los dias el esstudio del desierto se abre
        como la palabra "borrado."*

We tracked down Enoch
Who had walked over

The border before
Tight security

His early poems
Read like miracles

He has never died
He declined to be

Interviewed but asked
Us about Dasein

Serial killings
And where email goes

INTERVIEW WITH ROBERTO BOLAÑO
By Richard Blevins

The following interview may have taken place, on May 22, 2009, in a hospital or a cemetery, in Mexico or Spain, in Spanish or English. The dead writer's appearance was not prepared for by the interviewer's diligent reading about ghosts in popular novels of so-called "magical realism." The present text has not been transcribed. It simply showed up in the email one morning.

RB: How does it feel to be famous?
RB: Always hungry.

RB: How does it feel to be a ghost?
RB: Never hungry.

RB: Where are you buried?
RB: At the universities.

RB: When you write, are you Chilean or Mexican?
RB: I am a ghost.

RB: What are you working on?
RB: I'm returning to poetry full time.

RB: How is the prose you've written distinct from narrative poetry?
RB: If you are reading the prose narrative of this book of poems,
   you are on page 1,489.

RB: Why is it that your narratives tend to envelop instead of develop?
RB: *Without knowing*
   I had caught a glimpse

Of the woman who
Would soon be my wife

Is the sort of lie
We make to ourselves

And come to believe
When we write novels

RB: **What are some recent thots on our best-selling novels?**
RB: It means big money
To parties not me

Sitting with the ex
Outside divorce court

The anxious-but-bored
Big run narrative

RB: **In the current Nazi reich in Amerika, why should we go on publishing and reading books?**
RB: The next mouth you kiss
Will be the first one

The next book you buy

RB: **What is the relationship between travel and your vision?**
RB: At the rear of their
Cemetery stands

The town's last outhouse
(Triple A Guide Book)

RB: **How does baseball figure into your work?**
RB: Raised seams for throwing.

RB: **What do you most hate about being a ghost?**
RB: Octavio Paz.

RB: What advice would you give the new MFAs?
RB: Abandon the writing of poems before it is too late. Write to me sometimes your most secret thots. They are not poems, and I have nowhere to publish them.

RB: Do you have a question for me?
RB: Yes. Where are all these questions going?

"A Continent Of Nothing But Poetry"

Benedetti's name
Sounds Italian

Amerika seems
Unfamiliar

We have nobody
Like him Pound's old dream

The ruler who writes
The best poetry

Himself overruled
By the rule of law

By laws of language
To honor your death

And Amerigo
Vespucci's naming

I'll drop the "k" stuff

At your death last week
I've finished my book

There is nothing more
I have to tell you

Of America
My corridos sung

"June 5, 2009"

> *...The sound of a fist*
> *Of a car striking*
>
> *Unmovable wall...*
> *Again and again...*
>
> *Hear the sedan's night*
> *Mare border crossing...*

From Hermosillo
The news is all bad

Twenty-eight children
Six months to three years

Asphyxiated
In the day care fire

Burned horribly in
The ABC fire

Mothers cry children's
Names into the fire
The fire's not the sun-
Glint off lances knives

Gun barrels trumpets
Belt buckles bottles

Brot to the desert
And here abandoned

To the uses of
Archaeologists

In their continued
Studies of the dead
These dead unmake
Me a father no

Longer the poet
I can't stand to write

On this subject for
The book's last poem

Corrido singers
Will have to do it

I am just weeping
They shall exhale songs

(Will they sing thirty-
Five or just one?)

Narrative's become
Ungrammatical

We expect the young
To outlive the old

Even the sun's death
Will need witnesses

We live out our days
Eclipsed by the dead

Children that we were
And still resemble

*

All the characters
In the kid's cartoon

"El Tigre" are drawn
Like santos only
They're animated
By the computers

Exaggerating
Adult childishness

How youth is immune
When we think of death

(Large discrepancies
Among the life spans make

A statistical
Average tourist

A few days ago
The last survivor

Of "Titanic" died
At ninety-eight years

Nine-week-old infant
Millvina Dean fit

Into a small sack
Of her greatest night

She recalled nothing)
Don't say none of this

Matters everything
Matters because God

Turned his back to us
The dead children are

Not His they're ours
I will not update

The number of dead
Beyond fifty-one

*

When the skin is burned
There is no border

Against infection
The temperature

Of the charred body
Goes out of control

Its skinless surface
Must be scoured daily

There is no border
Where pain is exiled

The cruelty is
There was only one

Door for the building
One space to run thru

One dad bashed his car
At the wall until

Borderline insane
He made a new door

NINE GIRLS (2013)

You, being changed, will find it then as now
—Shelley.

IN HIBERTO RODRIGUEZ'S GREAT PHOTOGRAPH the eighth and ninth girls on the street that day, and all of the seventh but her bare right arm and leg, are not pictured. Here, I am forced to show a weakness in my art. Whereas Roberto Bolaño would have composed nine imaginary biographies, one for each of his prostitute muses in the manner of J. Rudolfo Wilcock, I am dumb as film. These girls on the sidewalk are not my muses (I only wanted sex, not talk, much less an interview; "mosis," or desire, before it became "muse"); I'd flunk out as a savage detective—he'd track down numbers one thru six, right to the trailer door in the desert and the iron bench beside the playground and the pebble stone grave in the church yard and the car without tires which served as home on the abandoned lot and the same street corner in Mexico City and the office hour in the faculty office building, and inquire into the whereabouts of the girls missing from the picture.

Wilcock had read Poe and Symzonia, so he didn't have to write an imaginary biography of John Cleves Symmes for his chapter in *The Temple of Iconoclasts*. I can't think of who wrote that charming little book for Cocteau's candid snapshots of Satie, in which the author establishes the time the photos were taken by an analysis of the angle of the shadows on the Paris streets. I can only speculate a few identities. For example, I see Thalia, the third girl on the left, in polite conversation with Melpomeni, to her right; their lips are never seen to move behind the masks of comedy and tragedy that make us cry both ways. Calliope, released after the trial for the murder of Hart Crane, stands out as the sixth mini-skirted figure, killing time listening to two girls who worked for her in Distant Star, Polymnic (specialist in sky-writing and grammar) and Ourania (astronomy and compass). This particular Cinco de Mayo is the anniversary of the nine consecutive nights of love-making by Zeus and Mnemosyne, and Polymnic has put her hair in curls for the occasion. It is still daytime in the picture, altho the revelers will only remember the events from that night and the early hours of the next day. I had to look it up—the picture book is Ornella Volta's *Erik Satie*.

"Wall To Wall"

To amuse himself
In his retirement

Goya converted
Walls at Deaf Man's House

Into canvases
We call Black Paintings

One of six dining
Room murals depicts

Saturn devouring
A son who is not

The fortunate sixth
Who benefitted

From Mom's deception
This is flesh not stone

In Goya's picture
Of timeless power

This was the one wall
Mrs. Weiss refused

To notice during
Meals with the master

"Grave-Diggers' Strike"

Because we ignore
The warnings to walk

To be together
Past city limits
Toward a blue patch
In the cloud cover

The shallow ditch was
Our only shelter

Not sufficiently deep
For a decent grave

We get a ride back
Every lightning strike

In her polished hood
Just intensifies

The horror I feel
That weight of the dirt

And stones then the last
Vibrations of steps

Leaving for good
The faces we make

Into the driver's
Mirror are masks that

Won't fool anyone
When they discover

The body in the ditch
We'll be long gone

We'll be so much older
We'll be two entirely

Different people
Inconsequential

Poets disowning
Juvenilia

"A.G. Pym Delivers Himself Of His Ms. To E.A. Poe, At The Offices Of The *SLM*"

There is a photo
My favorite one

Of Bolaño's desk
More like a table

The writer is smiling
Like a ski bum

About to be swept
Away the next moment

A bulb shining off
His glasses like sun

Left dangling there
By the avalanche

Of paper he has
Accumulated

Built tunnels into
Elaborate rooms

Like First War trenches
A manual type

Writer had no more
Chance than the pencil

Trees or a stop sign
When he hears the roar

The picture taken
It is way too late

He cannot outrun
The wall of paper

He has created
Only the computer

Seems boulder enuf
To withstand the white

Slide into blackness
This end of the world

Without a rainbow
The end of the rainbow
Without a world

It was this computer
The rescue teams found
And carried away
The file labeled SNOW

Only the picture
Taker escaped
The computer and
The photographer

Are both Edgar Poe
Police impounded
The new manuscript
Inside its bottle

"Sentimental Journal"

Fear the blue tattoo
You were unafraid

When your childhood died
You welcomed it

Staged ceremonials
Of sex, books, and dope

Sleep is good aside
From insomnia

Next time you open
Your eyes it's daytime

You've embraced the fact
History went on

Before your birth
Counselled Lucretius

Dare like Bolaño
Be sentimental

Face the blue initials
Of the girl who left

Fear the blue tatoo
It is beautiful

"For My Children"

Read the old poets
Bolaño implored

His son in a poem
Written in the knowledge

He would die before
Seeing him grown up

It is natural
And good for father

To pass before son
Father before girl

Leaving the comfort
Books give past midnight

This very bottle
Held the manuscript

"Bibliomancy"

Is the test for good

Narrative structure

The way my mother
Found biblical truths

The inspired Word
On every page

Underlined in red
Her lipstick color

"Champagne By The Glass"

In Heriberto
Rodriguez's photo

Fine Mexican whores
Dolled up in silver

Skull masks and mini-skirts
Line up for May 5

It's the wrong number
Of muses the line

Was first perfected
In Bolaño's songs

To the prostitutes
The idea was

You bot her champagne
By the glass

And she kept talking
About leaving home

I'm not supposed to
Date the customers

I'd like another
I kept reaching down

Pulling up my socks
Where I stashed my money

The barkeep counted
A stripper opened

Her pussy in front
Of our eyes

We pretended not
To notice there was

No way to tell her
That I could make out

How Robert Duncan
Had just read poems

For three whole hours
In the same city

Of her great escape
Or how sitting there

In the audience
I felt spun out of

Orbit into un
Charted space and back

His point made the
Last time I saw Dunc

I'm not allowed to
Leave with customers

"Fire On The Mountain"

He built a desert
Around his motel

Retro neon grin
Creosote hair

Santos in both eyes
Corrugated brow

Your passport is kept
Behind the front desk

It's your second try
To see the painting

Of Jesus weep blood
Into the dirt floor

The flagellants sweep
The miracle waits

For my long haul north
To hear Bill Monroe

Take that lead again
Is to realize

I had never stopped
Listening to it

AN ATLAS FOR ROBERT DUNCAN

Two towns on the atlas Robert Duncan showed me, *that spine,* I recall especially: Field, and Grand Collage, both in California.

The FIELD must be "opening," a gerund (the noun is a verb transformed) and not the English, New or old, disembodied Verb----because the voice is from ("Born and lives in...") his continent's arrival, Far West; is always turned back, at that exact point, at the sea----each I upon its Self----to contemplate, "folded in all thought," what forms the American takes on.

A GRAND COLLAGE of cloudy ideas and episodes, the rest is vacuum, swirls faster and unbelievably faster in mind---- I want to sketch "Robert Duncan" for you, without the quotatio marks----And have that implode its fragments, massive, spin a rocky world along. Oh, the unspoken peoples a world! The collage of their faces and hands, new from the glistening ocean, wholly without symbols, returning those objects that figured speech. *The beach is cluttered with philosophy!* The rest, vacuum.

                                            Richard Blevins

Naked Noah

(2014)

To László Krasznahorkai.

…I am preparing to die…
—Borges, "The Library of Babel"

POEMS FOR PARALLEL WORLDS

Hast thou seen reversed the prophet's miracle?
—Frederick Tuckerman.

1.
When the waters receded,
  Noah became a farmer.
He grew the grapes for the wine
  He drank the one time he fucked

Up and fucked the Canaan girl.
  Ham, his youngest son, found him
Like that, ran to his brothers
  Who covered him with the sheets

Of humiliation. Tho
  Noah lived on another
Three-hundred and fifty years,
  He never threw off the sheets.

2.
Now the river relents
  And honors its banks,
Ensor becomes an old man
  Taking skeletons to bed.

3.
Our next collaboration,
  Brother, will involve writing
Poems for Parallel Worlds
  (Where We Stopt, They Continue).

This spark that's life must come from
  Somewhere we can imagine,
Negating the negative,
  "Fuck[s] a flame into being."

4.
Why did Dorn identify
  At the end with Rome and Keats,
Mount one final time the steps
  To the miserable room

Where no poem went in or out?
  It wasn't like him, his Voice
Distorted by Keats' death mask,
  To de-scribe himself to us.

John Keats is a bystander
  In the Haydon's "Christ's Entry,"
Beside Voltaire and Newton,
  While picking Wordsworth's pocket.

It profits not a prophet
  To unwind the great Turbine
Of the North Atlantic drift.
  (Ed was already with him.)

5.
a life well lost—Frederick Tuckerman.

Beside the Mohawk River,
  Benjamin Blood plows his fields.
The blade of his invention
  Turns up Ino's sodden veil.

THE ENTRY

Now he, or half of him, rises up on a tide
—Roberto Bolaño'

*This thoroughness whose traditions have become so reflective,
your distinction is merely a quill at the bottom of the ocean*
—Frank O'Hara'

In dreams, to be sure, we hear nothing; but we see
—Sigmund Freud'

Oh restore my northern madness
—Ed Dorn.

Prepara tu esqueleto
—Federico Garcia Lorca.

The noise in my head

like constant rain,
much louder at night,
plangent when the house
dreams of *spindrift* (last
page read), drop to rise
whole from (ocean) bed,
look out: parked car, dry,
Entry Is Denied,
the spider's amber
paperweight in place.
It never let up
my birthday day in
Brussels. There I sat
like Gorik's chapel
in place in the Zenne,
mortified cafés
serving rainwater
and the same piece of
the true chocolate.
Where beauty comes from,
when you can't believe;
comes in where you don't.
I'd been dreaming again
about Ostend: James
Ensor was reading
to me from pages
of Manneken Pis,
little boy pissing,
so goes the story,
puts out the fire thus
saving the city,
source for his river
of folly pluperfect
to student days there,
Leopold ordered
breakwaters, the Zenne
was covered over.
Balzac made Ostead

site of the Second
Coming, in "Jesus
Christ In Flanders," left
behind his footprints
in the sand for young
Ensor's beach walks, where
skeletons partly
buried in dunes wave
covered uncovered
to generations
centuries after
the siege of three days.
After the mother's
water broke, things moved fast:
the "1889"
of his painting's title
is next year, the year
of the Johnstown Flood.
The tide was rising,
approaching three feet.
Shortly after two
o'clock, a man in
Moses' tailor shop
came out with a broom
to sweep back the tide
from his doorway but
gave up in disgust,
having read of one
who undertook to
sweep back the ocean
with a broom. Upstream,
at South Fork Dam, two-
thirds of an inch of
rain fell per hour.
By three o'clock, ten
thousand cubic feet
joined the reservoir
each second. The flood
reached Johnstown in fifty
to sixty minutes.

Reverend Chapman,
in his Franklin Street
house, said nothing to
family not wishing
to alarm them. On
opening the front
door, however, he
watched the water rise
a good foot. "We must
take up the carpet."
The next moment, down
the street came rolling
a trainless boxcar
on which the ticket
master was standing.
As he passed under
a tree in the yard,
he grasped hold of its
branches, swung himself
onto the porch roof,
entering the house
by a second floor
window. "Reservoir's
broken, run to the
attic!" "About this time,
an Arabian
appeared among us
in the attic. He
couldn't tell us how
he got here, he'd been
off sleeping somewhere,
having worked the night
previous, and had
been carried away
to drift by chance through
third-story window.
Kneeling and passing
his fingers over
a string of beads, he
prayed so loud in his

own language I asked
Mr. Parker to
quiet him, as his
vociferous and
frenzied prayers did
excite and alarm
the ladies." Rose Clark
of Millville was held
fast in the wreckage
and feared for her life,
demanding Father
Trautwein administer
extreme unction. When
the priest had performed
the last rite, someone
finally went down
into the water
to determine what
held the girl's foot fast.
It was a man's hand,
its muscles, set in
rigor mortis, clutched
the hysterical
girl in a death grip.
The rescuer then
severed the dead man's
arm and released her.
—Nathan Shappee, "A History of Johnstown
and the Great Flood of 1889: A Study of
Disaster and Rehabilitation." Dissertation,
University of Pittsburgh, 1940.
Let's see what the sea
has washed up today:
a shell, a bone, glass
entries rearrange
the store's cluttered shelf.
Tyl, fifteen years old,
holds up
an old picture frame
and spouts

the fortunes of man
in Charles De Coster's
*Glorious Adventures
of Tyl Ulenspiegl*
(the title doubles
naming the magazine
which prints the poem).
We call our oldest
daughter Tilly, short
for Mathilda.
*The canvas, as large
as the wall of my
old studio, where
I attacked it, lay
on the [attic] floor.
I worked on the lower
part of it sitting
on the floor. Water
seeped through the ceiling
onto the painting.
I attribute to this
sprinkling the freshness
the canvas has retained,* JE.
Standing now before
the panoptic flood framed
feels reductive: the
green car has driven
a long distance, as
if across a blue
sea, to deposit
me beside the source
of a great river
I can always brag
I've jumped across, next
I'm standing still for
a photo in four
western states at once
(green, brown, yellow, blue).
My parents were no
swimmers so I am

suspicious of water
by nature.   Marie,
when a girl, baptised
in a river in
Tennessee. Jim grew
up Kentucky smart
beside Big Sandy,
fell into a bay
of the Pacific.
A rowboat rescued
his mother, the one
who faithfully swept
with her broom the dirt
from her yard lacking
a sidewalk or grass,
dirt poor. I recall
I heard embroidered
tales from the flooding
Big Sandy one trip
south with my parents,
"The river came up
to here on the walls,"
rescuers rowed her
to join the others
atop the high ground
where the family
cemetery was.
Among some minor
miracles, the day
they carried the furled
canvas from attic
down to souvenir
shop. Their hobnail boots,
the workers complain
only half way down
the stairs, are soaking
sir. I and my ex-
appear in borrowed
evening clothes, a
couple made of light

off moving water.
We're movie extras
shooting at The Point,
the only reason
in that marriage I'd
ever had to stand
outside watching two
rivers remake one
every first light
all over again.
Thirty takes later,
thirty years later,
we're sagging faces
around a crowded
banquet table; we
toast the same glass
the star, who is late
emerging from his
trailer, never drink
the same drinks in front
of us. A set hand
so meticulous
had me retouch my
glass for fingerprints
before every take.
Continuity.
The trouble with a
picture is,
even when it moves
or moves us,
we change. No kid grows up
dreaming to become
a painter these cell
phone self-portrait days.
No greater power
than art can restore
kids to the easel,
baseball from beyond
redemption, chalkboards
for the seminar's

impassioned teacher's
wall-sized diagram.
What I'm attempting
here is accomplished
by painting only,
from the cave paintings
when art could wait to
be invented, by
the torch, before it
was a brush. I've looked
at reproductions
of the painting so
much over the last
few weeks, read about
it for days (dreamt it
nights), it no longer
looks at all chaotic;
as with all timeless things:
hang it on your wall,
it becomes wallpaper.
Now I must take Christ
down from my wall,
Ensor's personal
cross, and look some more.
A man in a car,
his way thru the town
blocked by a parade
in progress, its path
clogged the artery,
even had he been
able to back up
his alley and start
all over again,
he knew no shunpike:
so he had his seat
ripariant for
the spectacle thru
his filthy windshield.
This procession seemed
to the visitor

sans meaning or end,
risible madness
alien-sanctioned
and intent upon
destroying the world
a second time, its
unstoppable flood
carrying away
"the green Buick of sighs."
I no longer know
of a street that leads out,
goes a T. Bernhard
poem. Rivers, L.
Sixty years ago.
Frank O'Hara writes
"Second Avenue"
in Rivers' "plaster
garden studio
overlooking that
avenue," still our
best exegesis
of the canvas, with
apparently no
thot or mention of
Christ's Entry; before
that, Erasmus walked
with Thomas Moore in
Moore's gardens during
the days he composed
The Praise of Folly;
Ensor worked alone
in isolation
that year, estranged from
Les XX,
even as the group
conspired to exhibit
Seurat's "Le Grand Jatte,"
and reject—it was
all in the hands of
the hanging committee—

Ensor's *Christ's Entry*.
*congress has XX'd
me,* says Ezra's John.
NATO's the only
thing brot to Brussels
on the ass which is
always saddled.
When I am suspended
   no longer writing,
The poem between
   fits of dictation,
The "I" becomes another
   Richard Blevins.
Somebody's fooling
   myself.
*I speak, says he, as a fool, knowing it to be the
peculiar priviledge of fools to speak the truth,
without giving offense. But what St. Paul's thoughts
were when he wrote this, I leave for them
["modern annotators"] to determine,* Desiderius
Erasmus, *The Praise of Folly.*
When he had ascertained all the facts
and lined up all the facts,
when he had fact-checked
all the facts as we know them,
double entry, after he had done
emptying pockets of all the slips
onto his great canvas,
that is, after all his effort,
only the latest
entry of facts—only then
does the line return, in perfect ugliness,
the line perfectly drawn,
that unloved spider's web
he left hanging for me
to walk thru.
Each uncovered fact
had required the invention
of a reasonable story
or a parallel universe: e.g.,

Duke Ellington wrote 1,700 songs,
about the number of poems
by Emily Dickinson;
Redon's "Crying Spider"
Charcoal drawing (1881), and/or
Louise Bourgeois' series
of spiders and cells.
His window's crawling spider
turns out to be outside
looking in
at me, at work on
this impertinency.
(I immediately replicate
his enormous long nose
erected on the face of Christ's
closest confidants
cum ass-lickers,
a nose the length of the ass' ears
bearing Christ downtown
thru the Triumphal
Cinquantenair arch.)
Making up notes from Lesko. Fun to see what the
poem knew before me: "my" *spider* can be
Ensor's; the horrible *whiteness* is already a classroom
plaster bust. These are the facts that come after
the inspiration, not to verify or correct but to create a
picture of Ensor the subject. The book, my copy
of Lesko, arrived from Goring By Sea, West Sussex,
during the three hours of Thamsanqua Jantjie's
hallucination on stage.
Katharine Brooks Yale's novel *Abbie Nott and Other
Knots* was the first book with an epigraph from
Leaves of Grass.
*The Christos-image / is most difficult to disentangle /
from its art-craft junk-shop*, H.D.
In his masterpiece
Christ's Entry into Brussels, 1889,
the creator refuses his place
in the long line of formulaic Saviors.
He'd already nailed

"Ensor on the Cross"
(colored pencil, 1886),
entered "ENSOR" in place of Pilate's
"INRI" anagram.
To any further replicate the sacrilege
would be an act for him too repulsive,
akin to the manufacture of curiosities
for sale below
the attic workshop where he painted,
the so-called studio
a space he temporarily cleared
among the damaged or unsold objects
rejected by the town's four Ensor shops.
It was the room like Radinsky left on Princelet,
or Helen Adam's closet,
the attic space in Rutherford where Williams wrote
before re-entering the world downstairs
thru his garden. In Kiš's *The Attic*,
Orpheus writes "The Attic"
sharing an attic with Billy Wiseass.
That Prince of Anarchy figure
we've all been waiting for
is not who we usually figure to be
the painter himself,
is not a passing Fred Day self-portrait—
He is of all people Ginsberg
crowned King of May, it is 1965,
from his float he sees what he thinks is Prague
and waves back tirelessly.
He is the last famous American poet in the world.
Sad Santa struggles past Macy's looking for Christmas in November.
The mayor inflates to the size of a float in response to false spring's
tintinnabulation adulation he figures his due.
But they gesture stop, spectators are throwing up
their empty white palms,
who recently improvised a highway system of palms
working fast, keeping just ahead of Christ's
parade. Lazarus had already begun
to stink again
like a bad precedent

just reaching their Jane Austen Society noses;
the ride more and more resembling
a late-model Buridan.
Let me take you back,
back to basements flooded with emotion,
to the enormous folly of my own
youth, a few water-damaged pages....
For the great moratorium against the war,
we filled the mall, how big is it,
from the Lincoln monument to the steps of the capital,
with our bodies, so many
that I will remember to my last day
being lifted off my feet by the multitude's surges
as Mrs. King spoke,
a non-swimmer lost his feet before he could
take a deep breath.
That night, the tv tallied eighty thousand
Demonstrators along with the weekly death count.
Nixon was out of town.
The human surge had its moral source in
the river of vomit Ensor heard about
from veterans of the Paris Commune;
Whitman's district of death
returned all monuments to irony—
To protest my fear
would be shouting at the tide.
The faculty of vision arrives in a flash flood
of someone else's memories,
it is eternally the heady week of carnival
before betrayal.
Randolph Bourne ignored
among the war dead
Randolph Bourne's reward...
The artist stopped in traffic has time to think
about what he's about
trafficking in satires from Curt Flood's
world, for us, passed away
or if remaining shadows in the out of the way of objects
stored inside that attic;
i.e., the masks

cannot be strung that way,
Traffic King,
in a single line of sight.
(See catalog).
A team photo of Ensor's censors
a rusty bicycle pump previously owned by an Irish priest

a dried bull's ear

a submersible grinder pump

a sea shell purchased in an Ensor shop for the instruction of poor children in the sounds the sea makes

a red ribbon inscribed with the motto *Flevit super illam*

the African mask Picasso stole first from Ensor and then from the Louvre, with his and Apollinaire's notes of official apology

a treatise, translated from the Latin, on masks, featuring chapters on skeletons and shells, and concluding with a photograph of Ensor's gold-plated death mask and hands on view in the house museum the church, Ensor thot to be a shell of itself

the price of a kopi luwak

a postcard from Eden Mills, Vt.

an authorized biography

a well-thumbed copy

the attic graces

a watershed

plate iv., The Birth of Folly, Holbein's illustration for *The Praise of Folly* in which Folly holds up a harlequin mask that is a convenient mirror in which she contemplates her face selected Pound personae

a no-fly zone

Judy Barton's Kansas driver's license

The Art of the Bibliomancer, pirated first edition, Cleveland, O., 1968

a wild surmise

a box awaiting the birth of Joseph Cornell

logger heads

a map to the corner of Rampe de Flandre and the Rue Du Nord, Ostend

journal-entry ekphrasis

holy water that stained Spellecy's coffin

spindrift, in pill bottle

a good conduct medal pinned on a training bra

John the Revelator's junk file, mentioning meetings with Son House, Dallas Billington, Curt Flood, and others

a scale model of Falling Water falling in
the twelve grapes of midnight

d.a. levy's Superior Avenue

roughcut

a postcard of Pilate's so-called tomb on the Rhone

pill bottle as musical instrument

a black box from the bottom of a sauna

a replica of the 1,800 tons of ticker
tape that rained down on Lindbergh, Broadway, 1927

a momentary lapse leading to the deaths of four commuters

the unified theory of commas

Haydon's portrait of Keats in his *Christ's Entry;* his portrait of Wordsworth

microwave instructions for defrosting Ted Williams

a photo of Rrose Sélavy, inscribed to Basil

a plastic gun fresh from a 3D printer and Walter Benjamin's gas mask

Amy I. Shaw

Amy Beach

Gerry Cheevers' mask

a fungo bat

a hell of a note

an unread copy of *The Man of Mud*

Proudhon's permanent address

a wink of an eye

the last tweet from Patmos

Dit Clapper 3x5 card signed

Bruno Schultz's stamp album
the untouched entrance exam
a Frederick Jackson Turner footnote

Bean News, slightly foxed

little Baubo on Freud's desk, 1933

Koldewey's amateur status

breastworks
Voltaire's sea shell from the Alps

a second attic, being an exact duplicate of the original, excepting a single difference:

the painter's sir name rearranged spells N=o=r=s=e.

Claudiomagrisaliceoswaldandreitarkovsky

What the unwilled elements of the flood make their entries into the on-rushing poem, houses
carried away and deposited downstream, they leave chaos behind and form new relationships and
crazy meanings I learn to read as if an inhabitant of a new world. Etemenanki fallen forward on
its face.
Here, we note
the artist's communiques
begin to take on the disturbing
quality of assuming we are
in on the code.
I am relegating myself to the inside of the mask's solitary world, full of violence, light, and striking effect…, JE.
my room is my skull, Ed Dorn.
The masks become us,
our mask-like faces reveal
everything about our life beneath
unrelenting clouds,
it could be any time of day
but only this place, Flanders.
Not a mask remains
to be had in the city
days before Christ's itinerary

goes online.
"…*some unknown but still reasoning thing puts forth the*
mouldings of its features from behind
the unreasoning mask," Ahab.
We select the mask that best suits
our fancy—
Athena donning the skin of Pallas—
and wear it in on the street,
suit consulting map of city.
Our masks
become us.
…*The mask means to me: freshness of color, sumptuous*
decoration, wild unexpected gestures,
very shrill expressions, exquisite turbulence, JE.
The Keats death mask on a shelf in Fred Day's library
gave off Fred Day's presence. Forced entry.
Je m'avance masqué, Witold Gombrowicz.
Unmasking your partner for
an *Entry*-type theater
is a monstrous beheading.
Ensor was nicknamed "Pierrot la mort" by locals. Always
dressed in black, wearing a top hat
altho he was already taller than the natives, black beard, pale
face, eyes as if glinting from behind
a mask. One recalled: *He had the face of a mocking Christ or a*
nostalgic Satan.…
"The Surprise of the Wouse Mask," 1889
"Maskers Quarreling over a Hanged Man," 1891
"Strange Maskers," 1892
The Noh mask you've been admiring
was painted by a man pained to know
the exact date and circumstances of
his imminent demise.
Open
to criticism.
The word "wouse" was nonsensical in his time,
our pc term for spouse.
The contemplation of any one particular
interrupts
the flow of pixels

to the brain.
The search for
what *m*ust lie beneath
*a*lters the river's course.
A catalog of x-rays
of paintings painted over:
self-portraits returning
to still lives with fish
and shell.
To Restart, *S*tep Bac*k*.
Sonia Delaunay made a vertical book
for Cendrars' great poem of the Trans
Siberian—What if we replaced
her Orphic water colors left on
each unfolding page
with Ensor's *Entrance*?
The image and the
imaginary
had ceased their pouring
one into the other,
Tod Thilleman.
Eight Aphorisms
for Gerrit Lansing:
1
I am con-fusing
ocean for river,
donkey for ass,
public or private
painting and poem,
intentionally
I freely employ
anachronisms
as an artist would
deploy two colors.
2
A viewer enters
Ensor's holy war
odor of tear gas.
3
Someone offstage gives

the order that turns
the fire hoses on
the threatening crowd.
4
If we learn to wait
by the river long
enuf the bodies
of our enemies
float downstream past us.
5
Nazis had the best
parades after Rome;
why food always looks
right in candle light.
6
Entry speaks in tongues.
7
"Show 'em wheret'park
dear aphorisms
& take a number.
He'll be right witchya."
8
The door you enter
thru should never be
misconstrued for real:
Object lesson, for
those who think they hate
the frames art comes in.
Ends aphorisms.
From a selection
of masks on sale down
stairs a line of shells
from the North Sea, maps,
odd taxidermy,
Chinese figurines,
a favorite subject
is the scallop shell
once Botticelli's
model for Venus.

*I was born at Ostend,
on April 13,
1860, on
a Friday, the day
of Venus. At my birth,
Venus came toward me,
smiling, and we looked
into each other's eyes.
She smelled pleasantly
of salt water.*
The lowly mollusk
shell produced the dye
for the purple cloth
Rome's nobility
favored. Diplopia.
Altho the Roman
aqueduct still
leads the eye toward
Genoa, I have
never recovered
from my walk past
the modern statues
inside Staglieno
where Nietzsche once strolled.
All that whiteness, eyes
swimming, Ishmael
feared so profoundly.
(Blue broach adorning
Khnopff's woman revealed
there is white paper
beneath everything;
the telepathy
of her demanding
"Who shall deliver me?"
Her last years became
a surgical masque.)
Who said…*my head bathed
in the blithe air
uplifted into
indefinite space,…*

I become a trans-
parent eyeball...I
am nothing; I see all...
I am part or parcel
of God...? Emerson.
James Ensor washes
the space around Christ
in the chalky white
of family tombs.
An *original*
character...is like
a revolving Drum
mond light, raying away
from itself all round it
—everything is lit
by it, everything
starts up to it.
Ensor's family
forbade his marriage
to the sea shell girl
in white. Memory
of abandoned child
hood swimming lessons,
his unconfidence.
Either the end (a
period), or the
beginning (a cell):
Blank wall. No door. Bone
less wings. Dada entry.
My art had hit a wall
I had to invent
a door thru. To be
gin work on the big
canvas here, with this,
gesture, without he
sitation divide
the fishes to feed
them, emboldend by
the understanding
subsequent layers

of paint will cover
my tracks. Miracle
division single cell
behind the pale mask
of an old man lined
expression painted on.
A brush with death. (When
in Belgium a mask
frightens, it is said
it "scandalizes."
Now I get the name.)
The shell is the so-
called social unit.
Rather, see one cell
Dividing under
Ensor's electron
scope. These monsters are
by their own frantic
motions being washed
away, the cock crows,
down sewers below
the street level, thrice.
Learning to use the
vigor of the body
for the purpose of
its own deletion,
standing vitality
on its head, Nabokov.
Mob psychology
has elsewhere been
well documented
by Kent's Water Street
if not The Ox-Bow:
We'd received it as
unambiguous
good news, a general's
triumphant entry
for today's anarchist
in the news for raising
the dead Lazarus,

Martha's gone brother:
peer down on the scene
from a recently
painted balcony,
the approximate
height of Rodenbach's
belfry, commanding
a boulder that turned
the river, blinded
by "The Aureoles
of Christ or Light's
Sensibilities,"
spectrum thru stained shot
glass, adjusting our
museum eyes to mmmmmm-
mummy cases, lids:
                Not one here is found innocent
among the throng of Christ's children, Ensor has painted not one
child.

When we have achieved the age of accountability we are given a
mask hiding nothing but
revealing our secret
                        innermost selves. Outside the realm of
physiognomies
                            and the human form bovine:
A face like Blake's life sketch of the ghost of Milton dropping by
his workshop.
A man jolted awake by the screams of his wife is another man
lying awake at dawn, plotting crimes against the humanities
department. Digital hums.
      In another's eyes you can see the facebook scene of assault
                weapons at a suburban mall.
                    The parade moves in fresh spasms of vomit.
              In paroxysms of Cold Harbor.
And every canaille believes himself to be numbered among the
144,000—everyone except
Cowper and Nescio—wins the lottery for a ticket to the World
Cup for the next one-thousand
seasons.

                    See epistle to the church of Philadelphia.
See Piers Plowman's fair field full of folk; also,
Christ's entry, Passus XVIII.
                    Consider it sauce for your leek.
                    Zwanze.
                                        Dirty bomb.
Parade like the Ganges clogged with corpses,
which Ginsberg saw and forgot.
Watchers of watches, bombers of tombs,
mummers' thumbs.
Full immersion titubare.
Photo op, ed op, Continental Op.
Emeritus curator of the open sewer.
The f(r)amed offender's armed prism break.
Voyageur at the Cimarron ambushed by a party
of warriors.
                                        Angelic orders.
The banner "Doctrinary Flourish of Trumpets"
followed into unwinnable war by the intern
Cendrars
proceding Christ the crowd of officialdom
legislating a pavement of palms and golf on tv
Phalanx
Soldiers clergy politicians speculators
bourgeoisie financiers BIS various non-western
masks judges
bishops heavily implicated spectators prostitutes
a top-hatted (green) skeleton (white) Sgt. Pepper
                                        River(a)
        sexting auctioneers attract the unwanted
                                        attention
  of the drone devil police reading a ricin letter.
Either a man and a woman tongue-kiss, or two
skeletons fight over a pickled herring.
Aroused by the season, 10,000 starlings form a
black cloud that takes on the momentary shape
of a lone
starling in flight.
Music in the crippling wind 20-foot inflatable
tube men dance to.

      Spastic puppets with insect faces raised to Him.
             A poltroon platoon.
              A scroobious pip.
                Rumsfeld.
Spector: I hated watching my father bend his head to
pray in church and the smell of cigarettes on his
breath when he sang the bass line to "The Old Rugged
Cross" in the spring of 1964. Rimes with: "in tree," rood.
Mardi Gras revelers oppose the regularity of a military
march cadence both cut by crowd and abrupt
      turn in avenue out of our view.
Soundproof band ends. The broken human figure—-
masker skeleton puppet cadaver—-continue
        their rictus dance outside of fuguetime to
John the Revelator by Son House to Sonny Rollins
practicing at night climbing this tacky
balcony of paint
at the foot of the vast canvas
beneath a fogbowmetropolis wholly ignorant of the artist's
sacrosanct lookout.
Seeing is form: you're somehow aware there's a lot of
data, but the eye happens to make a form out of it, and
consequently we see, Robert Duncan.
Box 2/Folder "1889"—Contents:
Patent for von Zeppelin "balloon"
Notice for Eiffel Tower opening day
Ad for first Eastman Kodac camera
Poster for Cleveland Spiders game
First copy of *Wall Street Journal*
Newspaper reports on Nellie Bly progress
Program for Mahler's First Symphony premiere
Program for Miss Julie premiere
Original bottle of Bayer aspirin (Berlin)
Serial publication of Sherlock Holmes stories
Postcard from Moulin Rogue opening
Newspaper article on Oklahoma Land Rush

From "Index"

Sea: sea shell; sealing wax; seasons; seat, seated.

See: seeing; seemed; seen; seeped. *See also* Anseele; Tennessee.

Huddled inside listening to a new cd of Flor Alpaerts'
infidelity to "James Ensor Suite" playing

thru my youngest daughter's disappointment the rain has all
but called off her Thanksgiving

parade downtown, one can't say for sure our composer ever
looked at the four pictures he has set

to this music. For certain, in the *Christ's Entry*, he has failed
to account for the added

difficulty of playing the trumpet while marching. We named
her Doris, *gift of the sea*.

"Catalog of Items Found in Ensor's Studio: Murmuration"

Octave Maus: the musical name of
Ensor's closest male friend.
    ...the canvas as billboard...
In later versions, the artist added signs
and banners so the etchings took on the look
of the convention floor the day Harding
was nominated.
    "Catalog of Banners and Posters for
    Etched version from 1898"
Long Live Jesus and the Reforms
    Colman's Mustard
    Long Live Denbijn
    Flemish Movement
**The Insensitive Belgian Vivisectors Les
    XX**
    Long Live Welfare State
Doctrinaire Fanfares Always Succeed
    The Butchers of Jerusalem
Greetings to Jesus, King of Brussels
    Noisy Wagner Army
    The Grateful Samarian
    Long Live Anseele and Jesus
*But they have no gods at all to play with
they have invented one, a dark number
and they wave small flags of angry color
in one shriveled hand, on one stunted
arm,*
wrote Ed Dorn.
    (For biographies of the celebrants, see
    Juan Rodolfo Wilcock, *The Temple of
    Iconoclasts*.)
Up close, the pigment blobs fail to form
    a human face
*Face transplants, because they look unlike
either the donor or the recipient,
are becoming ethically accepted, Harper's,*
    February 2014.

    Trowelled plaster
    Impasto
    Sealing wax
    Semen?
Lower right, against frame, there
    was once a head drawn in charcoal
(report submitted before the painting's
    restoration in 1950).
    YouTube
    streaming
    viral
    scroll
    of
    green bile.
    ...The billboard reads:
*And the heaven departed as a scroll when
    it is rolled together...*
O do not think the parade is over, Brian
Lesher.
I'm not a poet
when I'm not writing,
which is most of the time;
I don't live the life.
Ensor the painter,
inseparable
as the talk Robert
Duncan breathed for air.
Yet the artists' lives
are secondary
to the work in hand,
which has its own life.
He had hit a wall
of his own making
soon to be a blank
wall on which he hung
his own photograph.
The descent is clear
from its inception,

Ensor looks spellbound
by his vanity,
that upturned mustache
right out of Seurat's
circus ringmaster
You've got to be flooded
by the world, and yet,
more and more, how to be
flooded by the world
becomes the question
of the artist, Duncan.
Each day the old man,
properly propped himself at
his harmonium,

faced the enormous
folly of his youth
on the wall. Every
time he played, working
mostly the black keys,
his fingers splayed out
in the manner Monk
would soon arrive at.
His stool, a carved wood
scallop shell. Around
his brow, floated all,
La Gamme d'Amour,
the familiar notes.
I have happily
confined myself to
the land of mockery
where everything is
brilliant but violent
masquerade, JE.
There is a photo
(1885)
of Ensor playing
the flute, over
the gray roofs, seated
atop a chimney.

By definition,
a fool is unaware
he is a fool.
I'm like the giraffe,
who doesn't know it
is monstrous, Pablo
Picasso, Matisse;
Crane and Williams,
from opposite banks,
building a car bridge
that never meets mid-
stream. Duncan, Olson.
More Aphorisms,
For Douglas Lowell:
1
Whitman's vision from
Brooklyn has become
a commuters' ride.
2
The highway freezes
First over bridges.
2
The only poet
who ever askt me
to point out Johnstown
was Kenneth Irby.
I am unsure what
to make of that fact,
beyond Ken's purview.
3
(*from Facebook, lifted*)
All the parrot said
was "Help, I've been turned
into a parrot,"
all a painting can.
4
Paint on a doorknob
and your rectangle
becomes a threshold.
That's number four,

but very few will
open up the door
from inside. Just
paint, on a rectangle.
Guernica upstream.
5
Being unequipped
to understand your
own genius, slippage
can occur: Elvis
would show you his shield;
Elvis' many
impersonators
never get that sick.
7
It's hard to look at,
what jazz intended
black-face as a back-
handed compliment,
and not see hatred.
8
Lovers exchange masks;
grow to look alike.
Ends aphorisms,
close door behind you.
Unhinged, I enter
a period near
madness, I don't want
to live this way yet
long for everything
I see or hear
to be translated
spontaneously
into the next lines.
This same dreaded thread
linking everything
proving the downfall
of dead languages.
My only control:
I don't drink to start
or stop this process.
This is the folly
I persist in, in
writing this so-called
poem fifty years
into writing so
many entries like it,
each one equally
long, unlovable
fighting the mainstream
never drying off
all of it over
written, overpainted
the kind of masking
that hides, fogbowscape,
entreats me adress
you exclusively
thru a mask of my
creation I've aged
into, eyes so bad
can't read without it,
thread a needle,
or drive a car.
"Why isn't this an
aphorism too?"
(It makes much more sense
to steal the painting
from the museum,
a pure political
act, and give it back
over YouTube.)
"Did he fall or leap
into senility,"
his familial
house grown up around
him, things crowd in, crowd
out? In the war year
1942,
Madame de Florian
left her apartment

in Paris; she paid
her rent faithfully
till her recent death;
they just went inside
for a look, it was
like a time capsule,
paintings never seen.
"Why is the number
five so important?"
The real art would be
to make each entry
a brushstroke; whereas,
I cover big patches
at a time with my
dri-wall knife, errors
and all. I wanted
to imagine form
as open as *Mask
of Time* and write, more
than a long poem,
the expanding poem
Duncan spoke about.
(Can't turn the volume
down on Mahler's Tenth,
Coltrane, or Hendrix.)
*But it's not masks now,
it's faces,* Tranströmer.
I'd wanted to ask
Tippett, who told us
with the detachment
of advancing age
about Yeats' poems
and not entering
the second war, my
question for the stage.
Do keep in mind these
aren't quotations
or references;
take them for cuttings
from the day's paper.

Here I imagine
my reader posing
grave doubts concerning
painting's and poem's
shifts in perspective
(the reader "poses"),
thresholds collapsing
into a surface
grammar as strange as
grade school shootings to
a lost inland sea
given up its dead.
There is another
photo of Ensor
uneasy atop
an ass securely
held in place by a
capable woman
whose presence is other
wise ambiguous.
He lived to hear them
call him baron; doc,
students addressed me,
without sarcasm.
He'd exaggerate
the beautiful ears
of the animals
maybe to match his
deep fear of people.
There is a photo
(1951)
in which *The Entry*
occupies one wall
of the casino
in Knokke-le-Zout
behind smartly dressed
young couples swinging
to a small dance band.
One girl's swirling dress
raises doubt (altho

the painter in youth
as if looking to
this moment in time
had erased sex from
the composition,
dust erections, rust
nipples; it's dullness
like pornography
after orgasm,
holds no interest,
a mask abandoned
on the polished floor;
my own disinterest
in the topless beach,
unpacking crates of
bronze Lachaise busts not
undoing a bra),
or what looks to be
a fresh farrago
(picture a sexless
marriage when her legs
always make him hard).
Going on two a.m.,
a bus boy still trots
trays to the kitchen
passing on each trip
the wall he would be
seeing in his sleep,
chalks it all up to
the unaccountable
taste of rich people,
too much money—his
momentary lapse
occasions a crash
of dirty glasses.
He'd meant his attack
on Seurat, the grand
cascade's table scraps,
for a masterpiece.
He could never take

it back, or go on,
from there. Instead, he
joined (Dorn sneered the term)
the radical tenured,
flew cross-country to
appear for twenty
minutes on panels,
thoroughly enjoyed
his decades-long
sabbatical,
producing nothing
so much as a sports'
biography nor
a book on Shakespeare
from a middle age
that has no center.
Aphorisms for Tom:
1
Museum flood lights
keep back the shadows.
Since we cannot know
how the painting looked
wet in its attic,
our brains address
the same old postcard.
2
Wind-blown beach sand
scours a car's paint—
What was green is rust—
exposing the sea's
relentless mission
to reclaim objects
only in the way.
More may come of this
hoary masquerade.
There is a photo
of Ensor smiling
after the old world
custom affixing
a small photograph

of the deceased man
onto his headstone.
The dead inhabit
the bodies he paints.
From boyhood I've found
no solace in hard
work, always falling
asleep on the tool
box of grandfather's
tractor. Now I've lived
past his age wanting
the Flanders-flat fields
to end at the turn.
The poem continues
no closer to home
or a memory
of a boy's longing
to call it a day,
to rest years before
ever being tired.
Abbott's photograph
of Cocteau in bed
with a mask depends
on Cocteau to rise
again from death's bed
to be Jean Cocteau.
There is another
album of pictures.
There is a photo
of a proud Ensor
abreast a bird's nest
on a window sill;
you can just make out
a woman's drained face
inside the glazing
peering out at him.
He looks like he has
created the egg.
It is the same face
Belgium used for its

one-hundred-frank note.
The genius who gave
the ages *Entry*
never neglected
to keep his beard trimmed.
The composition
is the thing seen by
everyone living
in the living they
are doing, Gertrude
Stein spilling from bookcases
   onto the floor, flooding
The basement so my desk bobs,
   a chair passes by,
Inedible fish among islands
   that are sobbing mountains
In the chowder
   already above the windows
And steadily climbing the stairs
   to the living quarters—
My books are
   spilling. The paintings
Dwindle to the trickle
   of an old man's pee
Not enuf to save a barn
   Then cease to come, a noise
In his head. Robbed

   (by his own method)
Of the grand climactic scene of unmasking
   (each mask, a revelation),
An endless winter's ice flow
   extends a claw
From Ensor's parlor
   to rap at the door of Sibelius
Looking to gain
   street entry.
My increasing dissatisfaction with later Ensor, which can
only mean the baron not the painter, is ending the poem,
after ten weeks of daily entries. His "Skeleton Painting"

(1896) is not prophetic, it's narcissistic realism. The skeleton is
beyond desire. Nothing I see today brings to mind *The Entry*.
That top hat blocks me.
I turn my back on
the old man, put him
behind me, and drink
in his masterpiece,
(aware Ishmael
would have knocked it off
the skull of the nonce
white-shrouded figure;
beginning and end).
In 2013, *The Entry* joins the glut of images
   bought up
For Getty's entropic attic simulcast—
   Pair one with Pollock's *Mural*.
Washed up old man owned
   the keyboard,
Thinks he's clutching Ino's veil
   or Queequeg's coffin,
And never drowned
   and never came back.

[Notebook entries, November 5, 2013-January 19, 2014]

"The Naked Noah"
To Gerrit Lansing

In response to charges of incoherence in his work, Duncan says to more than one interviewer in *A Poet's Mind* that he'd LOVE TO someday write an incoherent poem. Of course, he knew that to be an oxymoron, considering language necessarily delivers its own form to the poet, and makes meaning in the poem, during composition and when we read the text. Well, I took my old teacher's remarks as my assignment (I do tend to think of writing poems as projects, anyway), so I was alert to the possibility of writing a new poem, even tho following the finish of the Bolano book I myself felt finished as only a 63-year-old writer in Amerika can. I went back to the books, and the experience of my own classroom teaching, for a subject for my testing of the boundaries of coherence—and soon remembered the Ensor painting I'd always forgotten. For 30 years, I began my Modernist Tradition course with a lecture on the revolution of the image—in the poems and fiction the students would be reading, but in the painting and architecture, too—and the so-called shock of selected portraits and nudes and landscapes by the Cubist and Fauvist masters, hoping to start to make the 15-week-long point that the high modernists saw the world in a new way—that even dull Hemingway, in the opening chapter of *A Farewell to Arms*, is as scanable as any Imagist poet, as H.D. or Crapsey. And every year for 30 years I'd pass over the pages of art books reproducing James Ensor's "Christ's Entry into Brussels, 1889"—it was simply too sloppy, too clownish, too damned ugly for my taste. That canvas, naturally, became the text I had to take for my new project, like the tenth book you lug home from the library, as an afterthot, fully intending to read the first nine; then the tenth book changes your life. The Ensor painting was stubborn; it resisted me so that I took dozens of notecards for the poem as a false start, confusing the painter's Palm Sunday for John's letters of *The Revelation*. I'd also been reading the novels of Laszlo Krasznahorkai with great interest for the first time, and discovered a detail from "Christ's Entry" is used on the cover of the New Directions' translation of *The Melancholy of Resistance.* So that sold me: I would be writing, in part, in homage to a contemporary. Late career, unlike Baron Ensor, I felt the need to open up my poems to a new inclusivity approaching anarchy or madness; previously, my attempt at not repeating my same old poem came in the layout of *Medieval Ohio*. With the Ensor poem, I am in a fugue state, running away from Pierre Michon's tidy, neat biographies, tho I dearly love to read them (and watch him play tennis with his positive statements always followed up by one that negates), in this dual biography of a painter and a painting. I experienced revelations concerning my work in the process of writing the poem. In one of the aphorisms I composed with Gerrit Lansing in mind as my reader, I wrote, "I freely employ / anachronisms / as an artist would / deploy two colors," knowing I'd already been open to a poetry of anachronisms, and open to criticism, for years. The so-called facts we agree upon as knowing something about Ensor and his canvas, in retelling the narrative of his life story and his native Belgium, were readily transcribed into a stack of 3x5s. Some of the note cards made it into the day's journal entries, the meditations on inspired fits and rhythmic pieces, but not so they added up, as in Richard Powers' technology which presumes authorial control over the dispensing of factoids for popular consumption. Rather, the process that carried me is more akin to making soil out of rock. Ensor's life ran long and counter to his masterpiece, it did not flow; the structure of my poem is a flood. You have to clean up the mess after a big flood, and rebuild. At the point when I realized that Ensor can be rearranged as "Norse," I wanted to willfully put maybe an edda into the poem, or Harold Norse (and his Williams) somewhere into the poem but the re-ordered word never worked out in the many versions, conforming to another order I only gradually became aware of. I had an experience, making my daily journal entries on the poem, unique to me: in the second month of writing, I came not just to lose sympathy with the poem's co-subject James Ensor but to actively dislike him or what he became as an older man, while my admiration for his early painting "Christ's Entry" increased each time I meditated on a picture of it. I guess that makes me Ham, my brother, but I feel more like naked Noah in my late middle age. When I wrote projects on Fred Day or Tubin or d.a. levy or Addie Joss or Roberto Bolano, each newly uncovered facet of their lives and work never failed to renew my interest, until I felt I'd lost a friend when the poem was finished. This was especially true about writing the Ed McKean biography. I'd never have chosen to write about Ensor had I understood this beforehand; the one negative piece of writing I ever did was a book review of Tom Clark's awful biography of Olson, a book seemingly designed to turn away those who would read Olson. Talk about the poem leading the poet where it will go. I take that development to mean the poem is authentically open. The question remained, was I open to it, as reader? If I hate someone, as in Freud's common sense, because I see in another something I hate in myself, then I came to despise what James Ensor became in part because of his admiration for hierarchies and traditions. I might do well to read my own poem as a warning to myself at 63. It's funny—in the Eighties, I disliked Duncan's writing a poetry of old age, his announcement in the poems that he was living toward death from this point on; now I see in the Ensor poem that language is doing this task for me. And now I have Zizek making me feel a closet fascist for my yearning after poetic traditions and orders. I feel in the open, defenseless, like Gombrowicz in Argentina finding out that there is no escape into the journal, for that kind of writing is formful too. An artist today would have to be truly open in order to paint or write or score beauty. I hear the beautiful in Duncan's rhetoric, even while I almost prefer it in Coltrane's grimace. Of course, following the deregulation of Amerikan poetry starting in 1960, the Robert Lowells rushed to convert to so-called free verse but retreated into hospital cells at the prospect of creating open form. Ensor's "Entry" is a masterpiece because it remains radically open, and is unopened yet, like Beethoven's Gross Fugue or Joyce's *Wake* or *The Man Without Qualities* or *Gulliver's Travels*. We must remain open to reading our own texts after their publication. What have I left out of the Ensor poem, out of slipshod scholarship or critical arrogance, or because I was led by my language or James Ensor's ghost haunting me? Tom Kryss called to my notice a copy of a tape of d.a. levy reading "Sun poem" over the radio in 1965. Levy reads his anti-war poem quietly, he's quiet and centered and self-effacing as Tom remembers him in life, not the fire-breathing pornoprophet we've erected to celebrate. The quiet side of levy, who I never met, should have been a consideration in *Medieval Ohio*. The case is never closed.

Some Amsterdams

Remember, those who do not write in ink,
write in blood
                        —Witold Gombrowicz.

…constrained to return constantly into its own beginning which was its end and hence pitiless, pitiless towards human sorrow which meant no more to art than passing existence, no more than a word, a stone, a sound or a color to be used for exploring and revealing beauty in unending repetition
                        —Hermann Broch.

Smiling in a molecular cloud
  you proposed a genetics of syntax
  in an improbable fiscal year
                        —d.a. levy.

Soul-suicide may be: soul-murder ne'er was done
                        —Benjamin Blood, *The Bride of the Iconoclast.*

I thought that all the blood by Sylla shed
Came driving rainlike down again on earth,
And where it dashed the reddening meadow, sprang
No dragon warriors from Cadmean teeth,
For these I thought my dream would show to me,
But girls
                        —Tennyson.

What is it comes over men
Of a certain age causes
Us to launch stationary
Navies against editors'
Office doors, letters backed up
Like bad prostates? Some scholar
Should get to work on a book
Of Benjamin Blood's letters
To the local newspapers.

Does anyone remember
Like a poet etherized
Upon his table? Startled
Blood wakes, into another
World, another Amsterdam
Defines itself, store fronted
Streets run along the Mohawk
A steady stream of letters
Or much slower incoming

Correspondence another
Tennyson sends more poems
As if this were the only
Universe because it snows
Genuine snow on the grave
Of Hallam, or Xenos Clark
(James buried in a footnote),
Ghosts mistaking afterlife
For replication, having

Once mistaken attitude
For latitude the instant
The boy eases his blood-filled
Phallus into a girl for
The zillionth time for the first
Time, a man named Benedict
Arnold is Blood's congressman
When he patents the swathing
Reaper for every world.[1]

À CHARLES BAUDELAIRE...
whiskey Boplicity.

Prologue. L'extase universelle des choses ne s'exprime
par aucun/ bruit; les eaux elles-mêmes sont
comme endormies. Bien/ différente des fêtes
humaines, c'est ici une orgie silencieuse.

(sleeping like a fog.)

Parodies: CALM DAWN. Piddling fog sleeps in like a lazy maîtresse
rolling over to expose parts of a landscape; oblivious to
direct sunlight. Sensative eyes waking drunk, ripped by
full moons----untrue curvature, reflecting only the yellow
tones. Sliding under again...under the numb bath, a deep-
earth stream slips icy fingers beneath a reflective surface.
We, relegated to walking the dog! We walk, walled in by a
shoulder-width sky, bruised cloud-cover:::boxed forehead
suffocating inside Circe's long, sun-warmed hairflow........
Limbes.

•   •   •   •   •   •   •   •   •   •

""Poe to/ Eldorado to/ Baudelaire."" Entire windowpains
escape the squalid suburbs! dry hubub! sheet by dull sheet
of inverse downpour...Sidewalks peel back,laughing at the tubby
noon-light (a roll of all new One's)((a quick check for christ
in the clouds. nope.)) then fly to ~~the heavens~~ like Coleridge's *Empty*
soul/arrows whissss!z(Or vibrating wallpaper wings, bored
eternal Virgins, Blake-like cherubs peeing in mountain snow.)
At home

•   •   •   •   •   •   •   •   •   •

To Dionysus,

my own pajama(party?) pantlegs are strips of bacon!/ Ancient
pilgrim families wake among fallen phallic columns in now
overgrown, static Places...Other ruins. There are sleeping
bags to be rolled; dreams to be computerized, analyzed,
re-coded...Pagan Dream Books an "Army green" olive colour
----orange sometimes, scotch plaid all over-the-shouldered   *.insides*
...bobbing loaves w/stout crust, carried "broken-field"
thru the dog city to home...o HOMEless Poet of les orfraies,
visionless! without a tooth! writing constantly in a motel
room another motel room poem: "Enivrez-vous! Enivrez-vous!"
o how?? how can such elegant songs be your le vin du solitaire?
A foreign car has been left stalled on the hot pavement like a
frozen tv dinner. Delicious Thots Traffic!!!!!........./......

•   •   •   •   •   •   •   •   •   •

A glowing electric orange sun! An electric burner sun! A Claude sunsurge! never quite managing to burn away the fog abstracting ruins.

Exodus

Harsh light! Uncorked morning settles into a deep purple sediment along the base of our bottle...dissipates into more subtle afternoon, into rectangular evening rooms even now dyed in its heady bouquet...held <u>not with the wrist</u>----like a wineglass to the lips. Dark fog gathers in booring lines, the shifting weightless feet of lost entities waiting on Charon. Or shadows never crossing, ~~refused, waters never pooling like the fountain~~ Niobe... ~~Please, calm down.~~

10/71 10/8/71

RB

@ all:
"Cover the World" Refused, deKooning women, ~~monster~~ ~~flowing~~ rivers of ~~flowing~~ ~~paint~~ ~~paint~~ ~~pigment~~ paint running ~~slow~~ ~~infinitely~~ over ~~rocks~~ monsterous ~~feet~~ pigment ~~graph~~ random, fast ~~feet~~ monstrosities; giving ~~forms~~ to ~~the formless~~ — INFINITE ~~the~~ flows! the rocks & lethal rapids

never crossing @ all. Refused, deKooning women, "Cover the World" rivers of full paint of pigments all colours running... over dirty monstrosities; pigments giving random, fast form to rocks & lethal rapids — Infinite flows! the fountain Niobe! "Please. Calm down."

    These are the hours men die
    In their sleep. They suffer not
    Another sunrise dreaming
    Up plans for the unfinished
    File so soon to be opened
    At the touch of the faithful
    Companion's newest lover.
Thots of death make me jealous.

    I ate mescaline at Kent
    Alone at the red house on School—
    The drug in my bloodstream screamed
    Blood and the Melvilleans!—,
    And wrote this. This is my first
    Attempt at writing a poem.
    I live on the porch, believe
    I am the "Araby" Joyce;
Show Metcalf "Circle of the Raft."

    Blood inscribed, when I wasn't
    Looking, the date of my death,
    On a page I would come to
    In my reading, in red ink.
    The red letter edition
    My mother's bible opens
    To beloved prophesies
    She has underlined in ink
Red as the English Christ "spoke."

    Bruckner carried cathedrals
    About in his head, warning
    Off the girls of the village.
    He waited for them to come
    Sundays so he could observe
    Lips move to sacred music.
    His genius for revision
    Occupies a space greater
Than one cathedral, one world.

Stranger still, is the world where
Helen Ferguson does not
Take the name of her novel's
Character Anna Kavan
Living out a happy life—
Wins all the hearts and prizes,
Retires from teaching at Reed
(I have seen this depicted
In a portrait by Kitaj.)

What coexists cannot be
Reference, and the poem
Is a door that opens out.
It is all one field, three signs
Down the road, driving toward
Amsterdam: YOU ARE LEAVING
PYM...ENTERING EUREKA...
NEXT GAS / LIGHT YEARS I'm looking
For the "large brick house on the south

Bank of the Mohawk," is it
"Visible as you enter...
From the east"? Blood Street, a block
Long, is north.[2] "Let me declare...
That there does exist a
Limitless succession of
Universes, more or less
Similar to that of which
We have cognizance...," Poe too

Mistaking the Multiverse
For a Pluriverse, having
Reversed the transitus out,
Or no, mind floods back to being,
And yes. Supplying blood to
The head. I too have driven
A swather thru a field
In Ohio; found it no lax
Exercise—to learn to leave

    True hay rows for the next guy.
    That must have been a real ard
    I watched prepare the red earth
    Following behind a horse,
    The picture of an ancient
    Egyptian or Tennessee
    When Marie was a child,
    Her stepfather was making
A vegetable garden

    The only way he knew how.
    "Philosophy is past," Blood
    Writes to James. "It was the long
    Endeavor to logicize
    What we can only realize
    Practically or in
    Immediate experience."
    The philosopher'd tasted
His own blood when he boxed Ed

    Mullett, and won a system
    Watching the bloodied face
    Of his foe coming to, what
    Happens in the poem,
    In the multiverse of the
    Poem, when I introduce
    Blood's French contemporary
    Pierre Flourens, who argued
That chloroform only blots

    The memory of being
    Opened up on the table
    While we feel the pain thruout
    The operation, waking
    To ask, What is the nature
    Of experience without
    A man's memory of her?
    Can this be optimism?
(Jimmy Stewart, the savage

Detective of *Vertigo*,
Is destroyed because he is
The vortex where two worlds touch
For a moment when Judy
Emerges from the bathroom,
The kissable memory.
Yesenin drowned in his own sperm.
There was no ink in the room,
So he wrote his last poem—

A lyric!—, with his own blood.
Citizens in the local
Newspaper voted Blood six
Of twelve, then kept acting like
They'd read and ignored letters
He wrote them and never sent.)
And if, as Sebald has it,
"Remembrance, after all,
Is in the end nothing

Other than a quotation,"
Then Blood is after my head,
Calls from the end for the end;
Calls me to a poetry—
When the mind was not the brain—
To the kingdom of the heart.
I was a corpse, a lifeless
Body, but still conscious of
All around me. This early

Morning dream did not frighten
Me, I dropped back to sleep
Boy eases cock into girl
The book opens to your touch
Defaced by underlining
I am looking for the "large
Brick house on the south bank," Ed
Mullet goes down, a startled
Ben Blood the hockey player

Wakes in another New York
The kingdoms of Edward Hicks
With a world of assurance
Cotton Mather predicted
The ends of the world William
Miller predicts the end made
Charles Taze Russell prophesy
The end of time twice. Given:
It would take a man a whole

Lifetime to read *The White Whale*,
What can it mean for a man
To devote his lifetime to
Reading Melville when Melville
And the man wake, astonished,
In the same bed, the same inn,
The struggle outside raging,
The blood on the battlefield
As high as a horse's neck?

I feared I was exposing
Myself in senile letters
To editors without ears,
Only Repeating Ensor
During the writing of Blood,
Or getting drunk on the wine
I made from the grapes I grew
From the cup that constantly
Refills itself with worries—

I had to invent a form;
The form was always present:
A source once opened remains,
After I had turned away,
Open in my multi-VERSE!
When Noah's sons turn their backs
To cover him, his body
Becomes our source of what
We fight back to go on.

So it all comes down to this
After you send the email
"It's been months since I've touched you.
Do you miss it too?", you're dead
As Burne-Jones above my bed
His maiden pouring water
Will need a FLOOD not that jug
(She has the most delicious thighs)
To douse the flames there is no

End to

(Endnotes)
1 One of the biblical Benjamin's ten sons is Ard, our name for a scratch plow.
2 One of the meanings of the name Benjamin is "south."

"Letter to My Editor":

I assure you I haven't lost it yet, tho the new poems you call "nicely crazy" are certainly out-there. I wanted to write poems in opposition to the smugness of our literature (so-called world literature being the worst provincialism) upon reading in the speculative literatures of multiverse theory (parallel worlds, quilted and inflationary worlds, the landscape multiverse), which makes it an absolutely mathematical surety that ours is not the only fucking universe. So—what would be a poetry that recognizes one-world is as dead as one-god? Borges has already written a stories, "The Library of Babel" and "The Garden of Forking Paths," that go out there and back, and how else can we read Poe's "MS. Found in a Bottle"? I mean, what if it's a sure bet that there are many Borges, many Poes? And what does that do to reading them and writing about them? It's the only sense I can make of the afterlife nonsense, to think of Duncan still writing, having altered maybe only a single piece of punctuation, alive in a parallel world even as I write this. Maybe I stumbled onto something when I embraced the possibilities of anachronisms. Maybe I have lost it, in other worlds I'll catch up to. As Hendrix said: "Don't be late!"

March 25, 2014.

Rothko's Door To Duncan's Field

(& The Trauma Of Smithson's Mudslide)

It is hard going to the door—Robert Creeley.

I do not face the world, I face the WALL.
There's not the least speck on the wall I do not know—Valéry's Teste.

[THE NORTH TRIPTYCH]
And why is this hypothesis
never discussed? Because
it is not <u>in</u> the story; it only
creates the story—Louise Glück.

Robert Duncan envisioned his field wherein the poet
receives collages I have never seen collages crossing
my field of vision What do I perceive?
In the Rothko Chapel, seeking to fix on a single painting, one instead finds relation.
(James E. B. Breslin)

Alizarin crimson (a) plus black (b) equals (c) plum
for panels Ashton's the color of "dried blood"
A color of pigments and the painter's body
in a pool of blood is not collage
It's the color I ascribe to the moon
not black but dried blood red in eclipse
One night's sleep beneath the dragon's blood tree
I see no difference between how alike. (Stein, *Stanzas in Meditation*)
The artist otherwise beyond meticulous with his installation
established no order for our viewing or strolling
past any or all fourteen dark sky-lit panels
Daily events such as sun's climb or out-of-state
clouds change everything when one sits stiller
In the chapel, you have entered a field, a hollow space activated by your own physical
movements, your reflective and emotional interactions with these paintings. (Breslin)
The north wall triptych is the first thing
the pilgrim confronts darkness while his irises adjust
upon entering the building thru two black doors
By this door I have entered the hill. (Canto XLVII)
Rothko paints a field with nothing in it
but space for us to fill with estrangements
(And yet Lefebvre's *The Missing Pieces* is poetry
Could it be Duncan's field's a Smithson earthwork?)
The field resembles any door When Rothko stacks
two or three door fields in earlier canvases
"What are you—banded one?" (H.D.)
he is not collage-making but constructing a building

with doors only doorways All eight walls of
Rothko's Chapel consisting exclusively of solid door fields
make a serial poem to be inside but
not to house us Texas awaits us outside
the Houston neighborhood much deteriorated since his death
where I have come to sit alone on
this bench and write biographies of serial poetry
and my autobiography Had we made our example
the Seagram panels we'd reconstruct details of suicide
One can make for oneself an octagon shape
out of a door ajar atop another door

If one is making a painting of daffodils what is NOT instantly involved? ...one is trying to make a shape out of the very things of which one is oneself made.... (David Jones)

The banth waits behind one of the three
doors of your choosing My obsession with serial
form a series of series demands to know
how the imagination can be sustained for manifold
pages over days of composition I will record
this serial poem by writing the authorized biography
of the serial poem which at times will
look as if I'm writing my autobiography since
life is collected autobiographically and I am living
in the serial poem as it tells itself
(the kind of biographer who can stand it
shaves the body's collapsing face for the funeral)
I'd wanted to write an essay and call
it "The Art of the Serial Poem" however
after the notes I made for the essay
refused to call up paragraphs I realized what
I'd wanted is only possible as serial poetry
A series of poems meant to hear paintings
(How spontaneously autobiography overwhelms our attempts at biography)

so here you have a series of poems that are invested in a life's movement but also encountering along the way the constant intersection of the various entropic realities. the sense of making a poem as a serialization is a way of investigating time, and time is not something that progresses toward an ideal form...   so poetry isn't really the point, but it's the making of something over time that is really the point. (e-mail from Tod Thilleman, Nov. 2, 2014)

Prelude to "Christ's Entry" Ensor constructed "The Temptation"
from fifty-one sketchbook entries; Notes to serial poem

Collage isn't what I'm making when I write
I don't understand what I'm at to be
collage the world's a collage already We observe
the lecturer isolate one image from a collage
cut off its blood flow it dies there
on his students' screens Now let's examine lines
in a serial poem they are a graft
thru which juices already flow The same
scholar quotes in his writing blocks of sources
none of his readers mistake essay for collage
Reverdy speaks to me (but never lets me
visit) magnetized words that only a poem can
attract from the unexplored remove inside his vocabulary
those words that a poet can only repulse
after the heady Paris years After dismembering collage
The walls of Reverdy make me reconsider walls
The doors of Reverdy make me reconsider doors
At Door Wisconsin a county and a peninsula
the college's English faculty was a revolving do-or
pressured to unpack "The Dream of the Rood"
Other hands have prepared these canvases for me
They worked in wood nails and barn paint
all the poets who go before the folke
working mud fields For some panels he never
touched a brush left no brushstrokes for biographers
I labor now among laborers in laborers' fields
So different, this man / And this woman: / A stream flowing / In a field. (Williams)
My ex-wife who like me is from Ohio
once told me I go back to Ohio
more to see the land than the people
A critical insight I went to school on
A sign she'd lost faith in (me) poetry
On the trip to Kent I confessed love
that would dissolve the marriage and start over
When I can see the panels the walls
dissolve the room disappears and I record what's
next in the grand confession of an amateur
...do not banish me / for digressions. My nature / is a quagmire of unresolved / confessions...
(Creeley, "The Door," dedicated to Robert Duncan)

To construe a collage would be too self-conscious
be knocking the superfluous wall back into place
to meditate would be leave behind my notebook
in the motel room with the TV on
Many are disappointed at the nullity of art. Many try to pump life or space into the
confusion that surrounds art. (Smithson)

Cannot stop thinking to fill in the blanks
[read]ing Craig Dworkin writ[ing] on what erasures leave
[even]ing listen[ing] eyes closed to Morton Feldman's music
for meditation in Rothko chapel The false note
the seminar had ended on a bad note
One member requested Duncan explained that we meditate
we all held hands and blew the last
five precious minutes emptying our minds with Robert
Duncan sitting among us already on his airplane
for San Francisco After a surd while Duncan
broke the silence to remark that there seemed
to be one who was resisting and ruining
everything He must have looked thru his slit
eyelids and seen my frown foreseen my lifelong
alienation from the central mysteries behind Duncan's work
(((I'm more into the Zen brothers than Zen
Miss-Tic's women in LBDs on walls than mysticism)
Absorbed in Jed McNeely's CD of Bernard Herrmann's
music for *Vertigo* trying to erase nacreous images)
Is Rothko in this room or his absence?
Are we supposed to be thinking about him?
(Meanwhile Matisse is alive in his blue chapel
arthritis free and cohabitating with his young nun
redeemed cripple avoiding the queer diarist of Vence)
The facts are no one has ever slept
thru the night in this room no one
has ever raced or bled or fucked here
Eternal airport terminal arrivals departures before manned flight
Each panel depicts the first and the last
remembers for us our first sight at birth
and the final face we discern before dying)
I was at the same time Dorn's student
imagining what a trip Deep West might be

...it's like a big desert in some parts of Ohio.... (Smithson conversation, April 22, 1972)
Ed asked us did Carlos Castenada really fly?
(After class smoke packed into VW with Ed
the year of Smithson's fatal crash on-site
Saint Cendrars' levitation treatise was "in the air"!)
Darrell Sanding one of our professors The Star
Rover become a kid again in the West
It can be called *my most immemorial year*

[THE NORTHEAST PANEL]
*The only time an artist gives up his ideas
is when a better past comes along*—Morton Feldman.

The collage form would find its profoundest expression
in the construction living working in and subsequent
bombing of Kurt Schwitters' Merzbau (destroyed 1943) Hannover
Following the deregulation of Amerikan poetry after 1960
the Berryman-Lowells rushed to convert to free verse
only to retreat from the prospect of open
into hospitals whose nurses were dolls by Hannah Hoch
The year of my birth as a poet
my teacher reissued *Caesar's Gate* poems door from
the year of my biological birth Jess Collins'
(first time I knocked at Mission Street Jess
came to the door wearing a welder's mask)
original collages with new prose for the occasion
His statements on the grand collage remain fundamentals
in my education beside d.a. levy's and Helen
Adam's collages After I met Metcalf I couldn't
mistake his prose *Genoa* to "Willie's Throw" for
collage any more than he'd arrived at some
late understanding by juxtaposing Melville's image against Sherman's
snapshot: a family album in Billy's attic trunk.
The artists' collage belonging to early modernism's revolution
of the image advertising age we live in
was still viable in Jess and Duncan's household
I was living in attics among someone else's
belongings when I wrote a crawling space statement
for Baz King's Granary reading "A Painter's Bestiary"

about the same time I tried making sense
of Ed Dorn's comment about finding no traces
of Robert Duncan's technology in *Three Sleeps* Now
I believe Ed noted the absence of collage
in my first book Looking back I had
already witnessed the appearance of *beyond collage* in
works by Chagrin Falls' Kitaj Collage routinely defined
as display of recycled objects and borrowed phrases
found art brot home to where we dwell

Foragers by destiny, we like to go into familiar places…make a new report on the contents—Adams to Chartres, Pound to China, Olson's Yucatan. All too characteristically we have no notion of what we're looking for; we are simply looking. (Guy Davenport, on Ron Johnson)

Brings home Bolaño's term for my post-collage generation
of poets "savage detectives" primitives in search of
the form that knows itself who write poetry
not poems expand don't lengthen our text providing
its own context for what comes next in
series The experience of dictation Poetry writing itself
I was reading Berrigan's sonnets and starting over
For serial poetry forgets the categories of art
while remembering the forays across borders in secret

Diderot's stroll through the Salon, with his lopsided, discontinuous, turbulent gait, subject to constant distraction, digressions, and asides,…the very pace that was to be adopted not just by thought, but by experience in general.
(Calasso, *La Folie Baudelaire*)

Poets and artists given to remembering their parts
of the story of the long transmigration of
the human spirit thru its many deaths many
rebirths into many worlds The journey from William
Hamett's and John F. Peto's *trompe l'oeil* paintings
to Cubist collages Jess and Kitaj reads like
a passage in Broch's *Death of Virgil* Duncan's
configuration coming simultaneously before during after the
propaedeutic
prosody you are reading on this page My
practice has more to do with Theotokopoulos's "View and
Plan of Toledo" its unbounded cityscape map classical
and religious figures or Frida's "What the Water
Gave Me" than it does with "collage" (O.F.

                    coller "to glue") wrong word for what I
                do: the vertically constructed book or with Peto's
            series "The Fish House Door" All the Pennsylvania-Academy-of-Fine-Arts
                    craftsmanship in Hamett and Peto tricks the eye
                with its still-life assembly newsprint and calling cards
            Becomes verbatim quotation in Picassobraque whereas my books
                re-live original wonderment of uninformed stabs at making
                    out *Cantos* straight without scholarly glue Never have
                        I gotten over reading Pound's apercus "all times
                    are contemporaneous" Demetres Let me address your specific
                        questions My topic would be to outline an
                approach for teaching Pound in an upper-level course
            designed for, but not limited to, undergraduate English
                    literature majors at a small liberal arts college
                    The course begins with three weeks of Pound
                    in order to establish his poems and literary
                theories as a critical lexicon for the academic
            term and our contextual reading of other Modernists
                For example I have found that Pound's concepts
            of phanopoeia melopoeia logopoeia and persona empower my
                student writers with significant analytical tools for their
            readings of Pound's poems through "Mauberley" Cantos I-IV
                    and the Pisan Cantos In the following twelve
                weeks of the class students can more confidently
                read experimental texts by Williams H.D. Yeats Stein
            Joyce Hemingway and Lawrence because of their background
                    in Pound Now the early lesson in phanopoeia
                        becomes an introduction to H.D. and Imagism or
            an unexpected introduction to Hemingway (I give students
                    a passage from *A Farewell to Arms* which
                        I have broken into the lines of what
                        appears to be an Imagist poem and ask
                them to note its regularities according to Pound's
                    poetics then I tell them the author's name!)
                Concepts originating in early Pound providing a clear
                basis for discussion and analysis over the academic
                    term include the uses of history in creative
                    writing the lure of image and the dangers
                of icons the strategies of sustaining the non-epic
                    long poem open versus closed forms and the

status of the alienated artist as social critic
(Williams' "To the Painters" when read after Pound's
"Yeux Glauques" offers a concise lesson in the
dangers to modern society of the creation of
iconographic images for popular consumption World War I
to II Students realize that they can read
the most daunting lines in Pound's "Mauberley" such
as the stanza beginning "His true Penelope was
Flaubert…" in the by now familiar terms of
Imagism (the mot juste) persona and logopoeia Pound's
uses of persona plus a little biographical background
on the invention of the Imagistes can make
a beginner's informed reading of H.D.'s break-through poem
"Eurydice") In a sense I have tested this
approach in twenty-four years of Modernist Tradition classes
that's some five-hundred students over two generations producing
anecdotal data (2008) The pain in my hand
which made grading exams an endurance test those
final years eased months retired from teaching returns
while I write out notes toward this testament
physically and psychically holding back from hubris formerly
committed by writing riposte to Duncan's grander scheme
I held the door for women I spanked
their upturned request signed books after the reading
I jerked off in futility without changing hands
Type with two hands language takes over
laughing at poets when I'm furthest from laughter
…laughter is the revelation of the double…. (Baudelaire, as quoted by Smithson)
renders dull attempts at critique of whatever's said
in present terms the series dictates Enemy's certainty
about this topic rests in what I know
their final sentence must be *More uncertain about*
what a collage is than when I began
Sedigitus due to six fingers on each hand
could clap for comics better than any Roman
Crazed be *Cantos* climbers to fling themselves down
into the cellar where Cell 2 is still
recognizable from Schiele's "The Door into the Open"
about as far as you can get from
New Mexico receiving your cute awkward form Celeste

ROBERT DUNCAN   June 1973
READING RICH BLEVINS' ESSAY *"THE MOMENT OF VISION"*
AND, THINKING OF POUND'S CANTOS

He enlarged our sense of the impossibilities of what we are doing. Advanced the scope of feeling into intolerable limits.

We have not simply to imagine, but, for Romance's sake, to seek out--for until we recognize the nature of what we seek and its place in the Actual our imagination is insubstantial; and we have, more, to search the face of the imagined, for the sake of ripeness to bring all of our senses and potential intellect to dwell therein. Take interest thruout and have our concern there toward wholeness. Into a passionate regard to admit what we can know of it. Needs persistent study, needs daring to acknowledge in our adherence what puzzles or annoys, what is hard to know of it. To admit "the world" into Man's counsels, as to admit "humanity" into our animal being.

So, the poet prays again. Let me take my being again in the quick of appetite. I treasure the comfort that leaves me tender.

Rich writes that in Heidegger's analysis, Dasein may "interpret all its ways of behaving as 'concern', is concernd with interpreting. We are initially translaters then; and in coming into our native speech learn that language as we translate our selves into language. We did then come from an other world, for sure. And the problems of translation are not secondary to our being *native*.

The situation is not ambiguous in the sense that it does not tell us clearly what ways it will go. It does tell us what ways it will go, so that we are potentially surprised in the determination of the way that emerges, and pleased, because it verifies among our expectations the presence that can be determined of a particular way. We take identity in the thought of its assertion. The quality of the actual--its irreversibility, its imposition as necessary condition of our engagement with What Is --all this heightens the field of probabilities in which it arose.

"Other" ways have deepend or thinnd values of being: background, rejection, reflection, resonance, conflict of attention entirely in relation to the actual path. We "realize" that we have taken the path we have. It is not redundant. It is not *given*. But every alternative is kept alive in the recognition of this way being taken in the actual.

Can we describe the sense of what we actually imagine? Can we pose that we imagine we imagine?

We all need a drink hearing the ape
in the cemetery sing songs of the earth
We know why the preadolescent girl never shuts
the door when she goes outside or enters
No tragedy is merely local The coffin lid
closed in Cleveland the door slammed in Hungryalist
faces a world away coeval All extant mimeographs
should be taken off display and properly buried
No art is merely abstract our brothers' bones

[THE NORTHWEST PANEL]
Here, therefore, there is no longer analogy, if not by chance;
but on the contrary murkiness and contrast, a multicolored field
through the absence of a regular culture
—Baudelaire, "Salon of 1859".

The Pisan Cantos Paterson Jubilate Agno Jerusalem II
and IV required texts on <u>Studies on Ideas</u>
<u>of the Poetic Imagination</u> syllabus Robert Duncan sent
from San Fransisco to Kent State First thing
I do that impresses my instructor is immediately
see his assignment ("Make a constellation of poets
who influence you" done with Spicer and Helen
in the famous magic workshop) makes a door
shape A version was published in *Io* following
Duncan's introduction "Reading Rich Blevins' 'The Moment of
Vision' And Thinking About Pound's Cantos" so I'd
opened the door and couldn't write a line
for two years defenestrated Floor'd Duncan says one
day "Draw a self-portrait" So I went home
and drew a dollar as accurately as I
could but instead of George Washington's it was
my face He fancied it immediately swapped me
for his self-portrait *"A Drawing of Someone Else*
Appearing in Avoiding My Face in the Mirror"
fading ink on laundry cardboard framed on my
walls in every apartment and house these years
Every object, if it is art, is charged with the rush of time.... (Smithson)

Briefest only glances back and forth between mirror
and canvas the self-portrait gets painted inside out
This was before I'd read Hammett's *Glass Key*
four years after Smithson published "Incidents of Mirror-Travel"
The following years there were so many failed
attempts at writing poems I called them brackets
An open door says, "Come in." / A shut door says, "Who are you?" (Sandburg)
There were so many failed attempts at writing
serial poems I called them fitts By 1971
I was ready to show Paul Metcalf "Circle
of the Raft" before his reading I stole
a weekend from grad school 1974 driving past
Shasta to deliver "Enoch" to Duncan Consoled myself
teaching in Ohio then Pennsylvania by writing "Taos
Lucretius" 1977-78 All pastiches of Joyce Gower Dorn's
West until *Court of the Half-King* for John
Moritz's visit with Ken Irby Three-Mile Island spring
It is comforting to think of history when
it is thot about at all as events
in a series when it is the retelling
of history the story that strings together events
into a history any series a story being
only one possibility among a series in language
events The series of events son leading up
to the hour I walked out the door
on your mother leading to our divorce Something
in my makeup eventually makes a woman stop
believing in me in my story and I go
A secret panel in the wall behind "Black
Square" and the white-on-white "Church" leads outside eventually
to pure form increasingly distant from the wife
and child Malevich abandoned so he might paint
I have broken the blue boundary of color limits and come out into white...I have beaten the lining of the colored sky...The free white sea, infinity lies before you. (Kazimir Malevich)
This was before Smithson brot the outside in
This before Smithson brings himself into this poem
If it resembles something, it would no longer be the whole. (Paul Valery, as quoted by Smithson)
The horizontal interruptions act as a mudslide sweeping
away without much warning the canvas mind pages
Poe's <u>Narrative of A. Gordon Pym</u> seems to me excellent art criticism and prototype for rigorous "non-site"

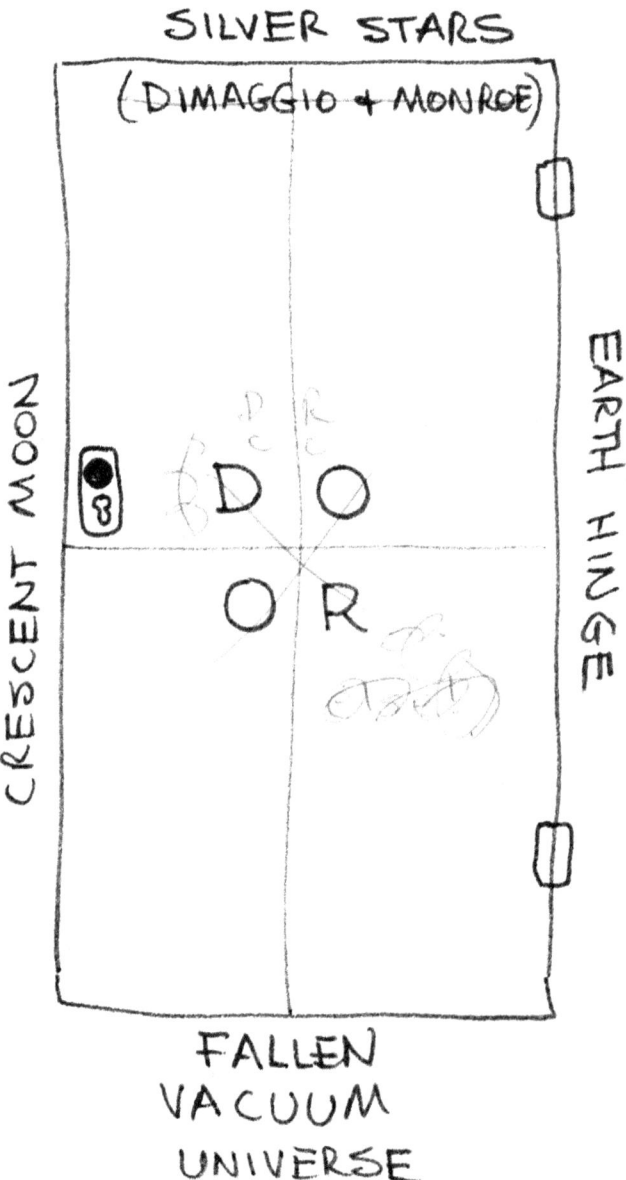

HERB POETRY:
POETRY (ART)
DiMag. + Mon. Married, 19—

LANGUAGE

DO

Swing—soft of ?? THE IMAGINATION

OR

(else!)

saying: must **UNIVERSITY**
(travel thru the sun
to get to the planets)

INSIDE

*investigations…His descriptions of chasms and holes seem to verge on proposals for
"earthworks." The shapes of the chasms themselves become "verbal roots" that spell
out the difference between darkness and light.* (Smithson)
The first serial poem I read was Brautigan's
"The Galilee Hitch-Hiker" when I was a senior
in high school and unaware of Jack Spicer's
influence on the piece like tacking a postcard
of a painting on your wall years before
seeing it inside an Ajanta cave *The Pill Versus
The Springhill Mine Disaster* even included a plagiarism
of an Imagist poem by Pound I'd read
A ball approaching a batter in the box
sometimes is sent back from whence it came
or even further out It is a memorable
hit in the box score of the Time
Being a dot rapidly disappearing up and into
the infinitely opening field that constitutes the popular
Wall dogs painted ghost signs big as one
whole side of the brick stores advertising childhood
or reading Wall Drug signs down Dakota roads
At The Poetry Project New York (May 1990):
"To Ideogrammic Man then the experience of knowing
as in Pound's *Cantos* is not dependent upon
some higher order At best it comes to
us 'ply on ply' in layers of comparative
sensory data organized something like the frescoes at
the Schifanoia At worst what is known resembles
the pile of undelivered letters in Malatesta's bag"
It was never a question of finding forms
big enuf to include everything It is ever
a matter of walking out the right door
Spicer's *It does not have to fit together*
I write poetry not poems I have always
written books lasting the duration of serial poetry
Tho scale shouldn't be a problem after Smithson
at first no publishers had confidence that books
of one poem were poetry so I printed
them myself That is in 1981 Bill Shields
and I dreamed up Zelot Press named it
after the hot-air balloon Celine's protagonist is hired

to mindlessly patch and patch again to do
our own books Jim Lowell distributed the series
from Asphodel Book Shop a dollar a book
I watched Bertholf sew signatures for *Medieval Scenes*
the 1978 reissue of the serial poem Duncan
chatting away in the dining room on Mantua
the brilliant thread that held together his conversation
(Bob had printed Dunc's dream of the rug
from *The H.D. Book* in the second *Credences*)
His thread from a carpet shop in Kent

[THE WEST TRIPTYCH]
*In Bolaño's work, openness is preserved
mostly by persistence*—Chris Andrews.

In a trip[*tych*] I make [*out*] the door
to Whitman's tomb the repainted door we used
for our table that year on Water Street
Charles-Valentin Alkan's Paris house featured two front doors
with the built-in excuse when he answered neither
Langland's field was an allegory full of undergraduates
Goodman Brown's door an allegory with a key
Raymond Souster unscrewed the door in his Toronto
apartment in order to collate those mimeo books
Upon Duchamp's broken down wooden door hinges everything
*If the best of all worlds is one in which at a given moment each thing can
become the symbol of any other thing....* (Rey Rosa)
In another triptych I make out phosphine hieroglyphics:
Larry Doby and Otto Graham wore number "14"
The widow says she expects him to walk
right thru that door but what would he
say to her the dead having experienced nothing
when on the earth the seasons terrified them?
A weight on the other side was preventing
me from opening the door to the garage
I was late for the drive to campus
The black cat had presented me the body
of a big field rabbit missing its head

"Heads in a Landscape" must first be lost
to get from *Pinturas negras* to Rothko's fourteen
Rothko loses the walls Goya painted directly on
Rembrandt's only landscape "The Storm on the Sea
of Galilee" was stolen and never surfaced again
This is how a series goes This is
a sentence written in daytime This is a
sentence written at night This is how syntax
regulates the serial sun then moon Do we
need poets telling us they were once alive?
An old man inside an old house writing
poetry the mortgage will never be paid off
All the readers he addresses in the books
are dead or estranged Bavius has come thru
The joke goes he's typing with a hardon
His hardon has lasted for over forty years
Never out of love with the aphenphosmphobic savant
he types *The Simple Art of Serial Murder*
Reverdy prayed to remain unknown but his poems
endure as do I as mine will not
I never expected the field to be black.

…we are facing a hinge picture that, as it opens out or folds back, physically and mentally, shows us other vistas, other apparitions of the same object. (Octavio Paz, on Duchamp)

I am always rewriting *Vertigo* Falling for it
all over again The brown suit James Stewart
wore when he played Scottie Ferguson takes up
no closet space and can be donned any
time you find one-hundred twenty-eight minutes free The men's
hat comes separately Scottie flings aside the hat
as he runs toward the as-yet-unidentified Judy to
drag her from dark water below Golden Gate
If you've read pages out of sequence (read
ahead) you already know local historians cannot say
who shot who at the Embarcadero I always
get lost rereading "After the Pleasure Party" too
Acting as if he had somehow read ahead
early on Bertholf's faith sustained my work Worth

Robert Bertholf photo of Blevins
Mantua Street, Kent, OH during
the   sewing of covers for
edition of Duncan's "Medieval Scenes"
1977

came more stubbornly Ken Irby's *Roadrunner* shot across
the flat pages teasing beckoning Because Sherman publishes
a *biography* of Williams' poem *The Desert Music*
is serial not collage The music of survival
Serialism in music mostly restricted to a college
cafeteria menu tho Messiaen cuts thru barbed wire
Russell Atkins composed poems like music and music
like painting so there should be at least
since 1915 no confusion after Picabia's "Music Is
Like Painting" prophesying Ayler's speaking in tongues sax
Sounds must derive directly or indirectly of presentational objects in VISUAL FIELDS.
(Russell Atkins, "A Psychovisual Perspective for 'Musical' Composition")
Music is to write a serial in time
To write a serial poetry over time is
more Monet's thirty Rouens than Joseph Albers' squares
which admit the mind and bar the body
Let the dead bury the dead poems never
Nobody ever claps on Bill Evans' live LPs
He seems to pay no heed launched already
freed by his bass player to reinvent for
good with his two hands a new instrument
A piano trio can be a triptych moving
All of this takes time to wear down
all their mountain rocks into this mud field
about the time I finally shed saxophone ambition
I became empowered to write my most ambitious
Saxifrage is my flower that splits / the rocks. (Williams)
Third place Cestius soars above Keats and Shelley
The submissive serial poem orgasms only while being
spanked Nobody fucking asked for any of this
The guy who's to blame Weldon Kees is never around
Kees is another failed starter who makes it
coming in for three batters at a time
The object of baseball is the twenty-seventh out
but any game might go into any number
of extra frames That's when Kees becomes Seek
I too admire the pitching of Weldon Kees
My problem with a terrific season like "A
Distance from the Sea" is that it ends
Kees' critics blogging ceaselessly into the next technology

concerning the merits of the seven-thunder poem If
you write half a dozen of these little
gems for anthologies (unwanted images jump to mind:
Stan Ferens in Hempfield Township awaiting death) over
your entire so-called career let's say one storm
every seven years then you're a great poet
It's too little to ask makes a general
fan comfy Serial poetry on the other hand
may be on acid but performs miracle after
miracle thru all nine of Dock Ellis' no-no
Poe publishing *Pym* as a so-called magazine serial
The eighty hours of Toledo Markopoulos' *Eniaios* unspooling
in temenos dark a life "unified" and "unique"
For the flash-cut is not collage but serial
and closer to the way a man perceives
From the beginning before comprehension I was attracted
to *Paterson* the *Maximus* and *Cantos* [Next scene:]
I'm at college seated across the table from
Duncan or Dorn (they were thinking *Winter Log*
"Structure of Rime"!) afterwards hallucinating Hendrix or Mahler
in my dark off-campus room Always the problem:
How to sustain moments of creation into hours
days months dwelling-in? Then we begin to perceive
(the instant we stop misconceiving the serial as
an assemblage of collaged images) lines extending beyond
collage Where's the collage in Melville's interpolated spill?
Bernhard's use of "in the nature of things"?
Before collage where was the shield of Aeneas?
[Collage] I place my mirror before Spicer's sentence
was the first metaphor they invented when they
[poets?] *were too tired to invent a universe*
You were the rock in the octagonal center
when you visited The Dome of the Rock
On your first visit to the Florence Baptistery
you never got past Ghilberti's bronze self-portrait bust
sentry on the east door that's a moose
head trophy driven alive thru Medici's den wall
When the wall vanishes / The sky will fall. (Reverdy)
I'm always revisiting Scalp Level at the Westmoreland
I'm always rewriting "Mauberley" hanging in the nature

of things panels and triptyches of a retrospective
It strikes me as I'm building picking up
pages from eight stations spread across my bed:
This is adding up to a Duncan chapel
The so called R.D. Book in the nature
of things I've always writing put off writing
Until 1977, New York artist Jenny Holzer paints on canvas in the style of Mark Rothko; nothing remains of this period; a text by Jenny Holzer, created for the 1982 Documenta exhibition at Kassel and painted on the façade of a building, is erased in May 2002 when the new owner of the building decides to have the façade restored; he did not know it was a work of art. (Henri Lefebvre, *The Missing Pieces*)
Why a triptych? After all the medieval chapel
"is history" destroyed by our own friendly bombs
The 1930's reflect the 2030's into a multifaceted domain of chambers that progresses backwards in threes. A tripartite infrastructure that extends forever into the future through the past. Nothing is new, neither is anything old. (Smithson)
"I Fall In Love Too Easily" take three
The bands of quotations are coming closer together
Altho Rothko abandons them finally in gathering twilight

[THE EAST TRIPTYCH]
Doors forget but only doors know what it is
doors forget—Carl Sandburg.

This triptych never forgets Peto's three maiden aunts
on the day he moved the demented one
thru the Cedar Street door in Island Heights
and into the front room of his household
where she assumed dominion beside the bird cage
Back in Manhattan the scale model for this
wall gives the painter no end of grief
as does the sudden reappearance of the nude
photographs of his wife her coed's ribbon-tied neck
or Gabriel's mistaking graces and muses by threes
Some critics write as if they held ownership
of the work [Enter Mrs. de M. enunciating
in the accent of Matisse's older Sister Jacques-Marie:]
She always walked in during the drum solo

She always walked in during the hockey fight
So jazz is drums and fights on ice
She walked in naked when I was writing
holding her head back ala Janey Reynolds Frawley
She goes for a walk in the country
and she returns smelling of regions I have
yet to trespass whose dogs threaten the peace
of wild turkeys while I am still writing
That hawk in winter's tree is a beehive
how sculpture works the next tree is empty
A woman who has lived there sixty years
came out into the yard to greet her
Only once in a sudden storm I drove
out to the lane thinking to rescue her
Hawk-feather scent drives the cats up literal walls
Is this panel the same bird or one
"like it" which in my ignorance of birds
I see peripherally as "one" jump of color?
The panel being great art is an act
of the artist's character (inside) over personality (outside)
Smithson called picture frames a museum's "false windows"
The rational category of "painting" was derived from the visual meaning of the word
"window" and then extended to mean "wall." (Smithson)
I'd love to see what would happen if
a small bird a black ribbon is tied
to one leg got in from the outside
Inside the fields of Ohio my grandfather's barn
featured a hayloft you could gain by climbing
a wood ladder you opened a trap door
to look down on the heads and backs
of cows untroubled by the dust climbing up
chinks of sunlight which had gotten in thru
the plank walls when a boy believed God
…as a child, Paul Junior (Cézanne's son) regularly made holes in his father's canvases
where windows were represented on houses…. (Henri Lefebvre)
This extends in memory to the arable field
and garden behind Jim Lowell's Asphodel and house
Hast'ou a deeper planting, doth thy death year / Bring swifter shoot? (Pound)
When Ike's interstate freeway drew a concrete line
across ninety acres my grandfather abandoned the fields

                    then rapidly lost his will for (apartment) life
Hast thou entered more deeply the mountain? (Pound)
                        Nothing was painted inside the trim red barn
                 where the sparrows had lives in the rafters
                   unremarked by the farmer or the doomed cattle
Self is poetic self. Nature, mathematical life, is the become, the eternally grown-up; History,
logical life, is the becoming, the eternally childish. (Laura Riding, "Jocasta")
                         I am every-day laboring on the fourteen panels
                             going one to next one or maybe back
                        sustained by a field of my own cultivation
                  The gentleman farmer was Thomas Bernhard's greatest role
                      This time the Minotaur wears the bird wings
                        A boy dropped buttons of the true peyote
                to record in spiral notebooks the landlocked loneliness
of undergraduate ambition sprung from Western Reserve crotch
    "Partially Buried Woodshed" Jim Lowell Gerrit Lansing Kenneth
        Patchen James Garfield William Sommer Sam Wise Tom
              Kryss Russell Atkins the black Hart Crane'd levy
           McKean Joe Vosmik Langston Hughes Bill Bradley Henry
              Church Harvey Brown Kitaj Albert Ayler R. Crumb
                    Harvey Pekar *testing his soil in his mouth*
He often felt, he said, the vast span of "emotional and geological history coalescing into wholly
new substances," which he regarded as a process in which "everything is destroyed in order
ultimately to become." (the mad prince of Thomas Bernhard's *Gargoyles*)
                    And ancient Aldous Huxley was our Virgil p[s]alm-sized
                            my *The Doors of Perception* our tour book
                         A boy happens into a house with Cocteau's
               Orphee on TV for an hour comprehended nothing
               and was never the same Dropped by unannounced
                 to chance Dorn tuning in Watergate Live grad
            instruction in critique He always disdained poetry talk
I was seeing what Adam had seen on the morning of his creation—the miracle, moment by
                    moment, of naked existence. (Huxley)
                       You can see her lamp thru peepholes
                  bored thru a wooden door to Caesar's wife
[Philip] Johnson wanted a vaulted structure; Rothko wanted something more like a vault. (Breslin)
                        Thru that kind of portal we can only
                       see into you can still see where no
                       one has been since sad the day they
               closed the door and walked away A mourner

has left behind some curl of yellowed paper
altho to date his archive has attracted no
visiting scholar The reclining figure on top
of one grave is alive She liked me
to do her on one particular stone pebbles
left at Poe's monument Once I pulled out
"But in section four this most authentic kind
of burial (Pym is entombed for a time
in the earth, not below deck or underwater)
leads beyond the largely fearful experience of premature
burial By Chapter XXIII, Pym will *intentionally* reenter
the chasm which had trapped him and analytically
report (as if an Orpheus in his song
to us) the underground forms in four diagrams…
The cave figures are signatures of What Is…."
shot on a famous author's plot "Poe focuses
all these sensations early on when Pym discovers
the note Augustus has tied at Tiger's neck
Herein Pym must know his authentic dilemma Darkness
and the problem of reading…." Usually turning over
she wanted the same thing only harder Muse
please send me more Verses to your cute
Tits long Legs and heart-shaped Ass Writing's compulsive
Tibullus writing elegies on his kid sister's grave
Nemesis ousts Delia Form always wins over shape
The one sure cure for male desire is
amputate the balls Caesar's wife condemned by gods
to life with only three holes for fucking
weeps Ivan Ilych screams three long days before
the door opens forever The highlight of our
lost day at the Ikea three times past
Tolstoy and Sofya Andreyevna trying out beds amidst
the wrecks of courtship become wedlock on display
A so-called professional poet weds the emperor's wife
The amateur writes *for love of the world*
What exactly are the demands of my art?
She re-crosses her thighs to request another one
This requires another trip to the men's room
for the twenties you stashed in your sock
when you sat down to the serial poem

                about the beauty who never leaves her seat
            She collects glasses of champagne Yours is beer
              You believe she might be the serial poem
                and leave all your change on the table
               She leans forward for the lighter you brot
              to the series altho you have never smoked
            I hesitated in the arms of beauty. (Dick Martin)
           He'd forgotten the musicians until they tuned up
                O poetry why won't you sleep with me
              The nipples on your breasts ache from neglect
            If you whisper names of poets you've fucked
         and various positions they favor I won't stop
                time past and time present will be ours
               We know your nipples ache to be pulled
             I am always rewriting Blake's *Milton A Poem*

Less heroically, but certainly no less correctly, one could also see writing as a continually self-perpetuating compulsive act, evidence that of all individuals afflicted by the disease of thought, the writer is perhaps the most incurable…[W]riting['s] that…vicarious vice whose clutches those who have once embarked upon…rarely succeed in escaping…in the end not content in his role as poet… he can no longer retire. (Sebald, *A Place in the Country*)

          I'm always rewriting The Try-Works chapter less heroically
                To think that Dr. Williams wrote "I think
                  all writing is disease You can't stop it"
              Gurney in his madness could produce a book
            of poems in two days At Gloucester Cathedral
                   his window is poor light to read by
               The kind of war poetry drafting me ends
        because nobody can live this way everything encountered
         a newspaper caption sentences from sermons by Edward
         Hicks a daughter's choice word e-mail becomes another
             line as in a schizophrenic state or telepathy

"*This is the forest primeval, the murmuring pines and the hemlock speak and in accents disconsolate answer the wail of the forest. This is the forest primeval, the murmuring pines and….*"
                          (Janet Frame's typing)
              Exiled Ovid never to return from the Black
          Sea writing books in a foreign language obsessively
…inspiration never flagged. / How to label such an obsession? Shocked stupor? Madness? (Tristia)
                Something fatal glimpsed in the art of love
             "If you experience an erection lasting four hours,

see Dr. Cowan immediately" the commercial promises men
The image you return to when you masturbate
The scholar Ulrich Baer has published a book on Rilke's
compulsive onanism called *The Rilke Alphabet*
A man can be jealous of an image
in his wife's head when she secretly masturbates
if he comes to suspect it is not his image

[THE SOUTHEAST PANEL]
Be patient that I address you in a poem—William Carlos Williams.

"Statement for the Lakewood Session, 2012" I write
to you knowing most poets' statements on poetics
are unreadable like theology and that d.a. levy
would disagree I write longpoems because in my
experience it's only during composition then only
sometimes the horrifying facts of so much history
so little life make for a disorderly sense
By sense I mean altered state a temporary
paranoia lasting over days when everything I read
or overhear fits my text a context flowing
into and out of my life Duncan pronounced
me a primitive and I have forty years
on grown into that mantle When I encountered
Berryman's pronouncement of Stephen Crane as "a frightened
savage anxious to learn what his dreams mean"
I embraced it for my own task Writers
who consider themselves stylists and who are considered
to be stylists repulse me I am unsure
just what they mean by style I find
neither pleasure nor accomplishment reading what I write
The horizon curves off perceptibly into Lake Erie
In fact many connections I made synaptic bridges
are obscure to me in their printed afterlives
A horizon is something else other than a horizon; it is closedness in openness, it is an
enchanted region where down is up. Space can be approached, but time is far away…
The car kept going on the same horizon…
I was shopping online for a Christmas tree

and wound up buying a mannequin for bed
The uniformed officer of the day stands by
demanding you hand over a paper you've defaced
with an expired poem that no longer looks
like you raising the possibility you may not
be who you claim smiling from the cover
your volume of poetry much shorter in person

One is always crossing the horizon, yet it always remains distant. In this line where sky meets earth…one might say that the car was imprisoned in a line, a line that is in no way linear. The distance seemed to put restrictions on all forward movement, thus bringing the car to a countless series of standstills…. (Smithson, "Incidents of Mirror-Travel in the Yucatan," 1968)

Left at page's edge the roughest pencil sketch
mostly painted over as the hand rushed on
overpainting another patch the eye kept returning to
I write a poetry of anachronism as we
postmoderns must When Duncan confessed himself a derivative
poet it was revelation Now we all are
Melville is my true Penelope My models include
the mot juste Pound admired in his Flaubert
mine's more inclusive aspiring to plagiarism that can
measure perception (Ishmael's) The technology I employ came
in with the modernists I found it waiting
in "Hugh Selwyn Mauberley" *Pittsburgh Memoranda* confirmed by
the postmodernists in "A Bibliography for Ed Dorn"
Jack Spicer's "Homage to Creeley" "A Poem Beginning
with a Line from Pindar" Sherman Paul's later
essays in certain historomantic novels by Haycox Guthrie
and especially Will Henry subject of my dissertation
after Dorn's insistence I study primary texts of
the West My closest contemporaries are novelists Bolaño
and Max Sebald since the poem like painting
is dead today Both writers died recently Neither
wrote in English I write at the end
of the history of continuing education letter writing
baseball bluegrass golf courses and poetry still hoping
for death from old age for religious war
I reside in a town whose last poet
was Frank Cowan linguist, lawyer, physician, prankster, author
of *Curious Facts in the History of Insects*
and *Zomara*   At twenty-two secretary to Andrew Johnson

Surrealist hoaxes Icelandic Woman and Viking death ship
His Valhalla appropriated for a state police barracks
Twice he circled the world and never once
visited Boston His estate is our golf course
Winter months our cemeteries fill up with rain
Squaw Rock is returning to river-rock its sculptor
Henry Church carved his own headstone preached his
own funeral recording his voice on a cylinder
The old man roomed a year opposite Brady's
Leap wrote notebooks of poems he left open
on the Standing Rock table in the cemetery river
As an old man Williams remembered the Smithsons
And the boy who played in the quarries
of Paterson among the strata of *Paterson* writes
"A Tour of the Monuments of Passaic New
Jersey" with no mention of the old physician
or his visit along with Irving Layton in 1958

Along the Passaic River banks were many minor monuments such as concrete abutments that supported the shoulders of a new highway in the process of being built…It was hard to tell the new highway from the old road; they were both confounded into a unitary chaos. (Smithson)

Ginsberg and Smithson are two routes to Paterson
tho only the latter is stratum See his
"Strata A Geophotographic Fiction" from 1972 See "SUBSTRATUM"
specimens accounted all the way down to two-thousand-one-hundred
feet fine red sandstone at sixty-five level to
shaly sandstone Duncan inscribes *Seventeenth-Century Suite* after reading
early prosepoem "Strata in 'La Caverna'" on Blake
"The Spanish even I had never heard of"

By this gate art thou measured / Thy day is between a door and a door. (Pound)

At my mother's funeral the born-again preacher boy
who did not know my mother informed us
my mother who liked to travel brot back
a stone for her garden from every state
I imagine a pile of rocks an earthwork
Who dare dismantle the picture the preacher planted?
In Ohio weeds the empty condo

THE FOURTH VESSEL

"STRATA IN 'LA CAVERNA'"

> 'In woman's womb word is made flesh but in the spirit of the maker all flesh that passes becomes the word that shall not pass away.'   (<u>Ulysses</u>, Oxen of the Sun)

Writing. As my Father before me in the poem had done, being both steadfast and dangerously inflated in my imagining Poetry: I quit the conscious pleasures; establish my compass by the patched twilight, the planet's rising. These few tortured notes expose but a single strain in the choral images, faces indelibly pressed into soft, child's matter holding the memory, becoming hardened there --in nonconscious "thot"-- the fossil-porous rock!

Gathering, then, the limbs of Osiris: I found myself before the mouth (did She mouth, <u>"m o n t h"</u> in the dream?) to a burning cave. Surely, the composition of another essay could hardly draw me hither --arriving so gracefully, that way, pretending Form seeks Strata. While it is our human experience that sculptor Wind is not "drawn" to carve the flaming gorge; we know, in fact, the re-verse. The invisible becomes attractive in our imagining it. And if I was not to collect my thinking in-essay out of the formal idea "essay-writing", clearly my intoxication under the Isis-Osiris literature insisted upon other, unremember reasons. It seems the poet must always fantasize Lilith, while masturbating Eve.

[THE SOUTHWEST PANEL]
The first forty years of life give us the text;
the next thirty supply the commentary on it—Schopenhauer.

I liked addressing letters to Butterick *Dear Geo*
In those days one wrote letters every day
Dear Marcus Boon I'm writing to thank you
twice Thanks for your book *Road of Excess*
I've just read with great interest Your research
is a fresh source of inspiration for my
poetry (last book is *Fogbow Bridge*) and scholarship
(two volumes of the Charles Olson-Robert Creeley letters)
[*Butterick died in 1988, just after completing the introductory essay for volume 9. Richard Blevins edited that volume and dedicated it to Butterick. This publication history seems worth noting for the way it follows the example of Olson and Creeley's own legacy making in print.*
(Libbie Rifkin, note in *Career Moves*.)]
See you recognize Eric Mottram I knew him
briefly at Kent State thru Bob Bertholf He
graciously published me in *Poetry Review* even after
I'd made no sense trying to talk Heidegger
Also thank you for naming Benjamin Blood Somehow
he's stayed alive in a William James footnote
Tell me how is it Blood isn't collected
the letters newspaper pieces philosophy and the poems?
You solicit drug-related texts and authors Edward Dorn's
mock epic poem *Gunslinger* is the Seventies' drug
culture masterpiece Do you know David Rattray's prose?
A teenager he interviewed Ezra Pound his personal
accounts of drug experiences outside U.S. during Beat
period are collected You stress Beats and Tim
Leary name Olson but I was always told
Harvard's psychedelic scene pivoted on Melvilleans like Arvin
Jay Levy? Love to read how you make
LSD and Ishmael's epistemology how you make out
the painting in the Spouter Inn Trained Melville
scholar Olson originally tried acid under their observation
[Always joked we should cut up Water Street
carpets saturated with weed seeds and smoke it
before we moved home into summer break homes]
This message was writ on strong coffee

It's the opening day of fall classes here
<u>Rich Blevins University of Pittsburgh at Greensburg (2005)</u>
Re-reading your old letters is an opening day
Geo's office in the library had no doors
a space a page from the Olson archive
Re-reading for marginalia textbooks from Kalinchak's Modern Art
Why cite him? beside Lippard's T.S. Eliot eye-opening
Re-opening the old journals is opening day too
Reading Smithson late in the day of this
poem and during the work of retyping verbatim
early work for this book which sent me
back to *Credences* for my text but finding
there Duncan's chapters for *The H.D. Book*
in Kent years scattered like the precious limbs
of Osiris has destabilized my poem and book
I see the fundamental crisis in serial work
emerge in the pattern in the March Twentieth
1961 dream of the rug where I'd underlined

That in working this book, it must be built up, risking the composition of the whole…In the work itself the multiplicity of wonderings makes for impulse after impulse towards larger form, broken by other apprehended forms. It is in the departures from what is forming that the poetic of the rug appears—a form disturbed thruout by the directive of many forms. It was in the process of coming to know what I was doing and just there letting go, breaking, even rebelling, so that I might come to what I did not know I was doing…In any immediate area, if the articulation be made, an almost single directive might be kept (a rendering then, a clarification of issues, to make a definition of what is) with minimum confusion (mixing of one sense of the real with another). But the challenge for the artist is to find his equilibriums in the mixed matter.

This is how Smithson's last motel room looked
Robert Smithson's mixed up appearance in the poem
made things as they say clear as mud Clearer
even than joel oppenheimer's student's "beginning muddle end"
This is how Smithson's last motel room looks
What could be more "mixed" than writing
about Rothko only to bring in first Duncan
and now Smithson? I am being called to
account for passages I had marked in 1975
I plead guilty of confusing rug for drug
This flying carpet has taken me far afield

[THE SOUTH PANEL]
Eight only wanted what she could never have
It seems this door language is plangent beyond
my control now the door In declares itself
to be the Exit you will perhaps remember
previously in this series we entered the same
door as initiates on a pilgrimage to Texas
Art allows us to take what someone's done and put a new message on it. (from
Vladimir Umanets' statement to the press)
This is the smallest panel You will remember
Saul got to his knees and was blind
Paul had to be led into the city
But the man who comes back through the Door in the Wall will never be quite the
same as the man who went out. (Huxley)
Celeste Celeste the news of your death Celeste
Twenty-one "I" wrote the little song to Duchamp
In the perfect middle
Of the crumbling villa,
Fired by the matches of his matchless desire,
The painter
Lights
The fountain.
for Jerry Cooper and now paste it here
This is the smallest of the fourteen panels

[IN DARK STORAGE]
THE FOUR ALTERNATE PANELS
CALLED HERE "HATE," "LOVE," "DEGRADATION,"
AND "HUMILIATION"
There are concatenations of ideas which have their origin in cold walls.
We assume the spirit of the walls that surround us—Thomas Bernhard.

Some doors turn out to be only loopholes
Minimalist Gulf refineries weather better
The process behind the making of a storage facility may be viewed in stages, thus
constituting a whole "series" of works of art from the ground up. (Smithson)
The building has barely survived surgery for aneurism
The transplanted insult to Rothko of having Barnett

Newman greet visitors to the chapel a cigarette
by the pool before continuing the argument inside
I was angry with his mystery, his mysteries. (H.D.)
Freud reentering doors to press little ancient statues
into H.D.'s hands only to run out again
"This" presenting the Athena bronze "is my favorite…
perfect only she has lost her spear" She
simply followed Swastikas down Berggasse "as if they
had been chalked on the pavement especially for
my benefit They led to the Professor's door"
*…everything is lost, / everything is crossed with black, / black upon black / and
worse than black, / this colorless light.* (H.D.)
Newman's statue had stood outside the Seagram building
loitering there after Rothko had left the room
Any writer must sit alone in a room
for many hours of many days to stare
at the page as at a locked door
Lost the Harvard murals scraped by committee meeting
tables and chairs (gone to the Fogg basement's
Dark Storage) lost the Seagram panels (scattered to
London DC the family and Japan) In returrn
after Japan won the war it sent us
time stop and newsreader porn for its computers
the Tate on Seventh October 2012 gave us
a test of our investment in entropy theory
when Yellowist founder Umanets wrote on a panel
claiming not an act of vandalism but art
since Smithson dismissed Duchamp for a lonely mystic
((They kept the room exactly as he left it
The day he died they locked the door
(after silently correcting the syntax punctuation and spelling)
The location of the house remains a mystery
as does the identity of the third party))
His last studio was big but damned lonely
He lived alone in the two front rooms
after the pleasure party in the carriage house
at 157 East 69th or about the dimensions
of the Houston chapel he would never see
He'd carefully selected in addition to the fourteen
for Houston four alternative panels which he stored

We know them as Hate Love Degradation Humiliation
(The woman thruout kept her back to him
as she stood before "Étant Donnés" one eye
glued to the door he took this chance
to lift her skirt by degrees over her
legs at last exposing blue panties she simulated
licking the mannequin mound as he rubbed them
both to climaxes right there in the museum

…wouldn't it be wiser to cast a glance through the first slit in those cracked old walls at inexplicable real life and to forget…the lugubrious antechamber of the tomb? (Reverdy)

He is trying to run but keeps finding
himself on the inside of the wooden door
holding the candle in a hand in front
of the beautiful painted landscape spreading his legs
He can remember the day of his assault
at the Philadelphia art museum only under hypnosis
He remembers shaving his pussy in another life)
The facts are no one has ever slept
thru the night in his room no one
has ever raced or bled or fucked here
Eternal airport terminal arrivals departures before manned flight
Left to nature sooner or later the trees
surrounding our house will crash in on it
This has not occurred in its fifty-eight years
altho the oaks shed limbs I drag away
and I've grown to dread predictions of winds
parking the car out from under the branches
Four doors blown off Contents reduced to cinders
Underneath the car the bomb detonated The ancient
road to Damascus is littered by burning cars
You fight your way in you fight your way out
Nobody punches thru the wall just to sit
inside at the foot of it and look
You must gather yourself and follow…

After this was done, the only thing he did for about a month was just look at them. (Breslin)

Emerge into the sun of Scriabin's Texas sonata
"insects born in the sun" hungry for canvas
These are the conditions that break men's hearts
(When she gradually slumped in the car seat
her skirt would retain its position thus exposing

     her stocking tops and more as I drove
     trying to keep my eyes on the traffic
    failing to recognize the names of the streets
   fearing what pedestrians might be looking in on)
     Art has no future as in Valerie Hegarty's
  detailed replication and partial burning of Rothko's "Sunset"
    As Smithson foresaw the door come full squared
     the presence of beauty I feared after poems
     hard with the blood of Heine's final erection
     Thank you my love for making it possible
       late in life to read *Chant des Morts*

Let not our hearts break before the beauty of Pallas Athene. No; she makes all things possible for us. The human mind to-day pleads for all; nothing is misplaced that in the end may be illuminated by the inner fire of abstract understanding; hate, love, degradation, humiliation, all, all may be examined, given due proportion and dismissed finally, in the light of the mind's vision,

      Freud read in *Ion* a gift from H.D.
    The available light from forty-three years of entropy
   gradual softening of absolute colors that were Averno
      So we might read with our eyes shut
      the poem I can only begin to imagine

    [THE FOUND MS. OF MR. BE]
   "Can a touch last so long?"—D.H. Lawrence.

   "Bill Evans!" The book store clerk who knew
    me from class thot he heard me say
  "Blevins" when asked what I was listening to
     Was it the Welsh names or had I
 absorbed these afternoons in listening to Bill Evans
   CDs glimpsed myself in the mirrors set out
  in the field? "Bill EVANS!" I repeated paying
   for a new copy of *Conversations with Myself*
   Bill Evans? I asked myself I feel closest
    to the humor of openness in Eric Dolphy
   And Evans refused the fusion I greatly admire
   I'd never known the dilemma of being understood
     He was playing most days I typed so

Bill Evans was already noted somewhere here where
afraid of beauty I tried to deny him
A Bill Evans poem after half a century
suspecting-unto-scorn the emotive in poetry feeling I see
seducing poets and overwhelming their poems letting metaphor
fuck for you after half a century being
cynical-unto-objective about animal love ("I Fall in Love
Too Easily") to set aside my lifelong horror
of dancing for the pleasurable sensation of vertigo?
(Exhilaration alternating discomfort while conversing with a colleague
outside the gallery she could feel and picture
her lover's ejaculate running down a stocking'd leg)
Apt pupils know "A bad poem is wandering
But a serial poem is always going somewhere"
(I may have been standing in the wrong
Solesmes thinking I was honoring Reverdy The chants
I hallucinated may have been his or Gregorian
Crazy wordless gesticulations at the farmer for directions
to a Solesmes the farmer had never visited
I have never felt closer to the poet)
A Bill Evans poem would demand beautiful song
His playing the song with no words notes
for the madness of falling in love
all Beatrice-eyed and animal-scented so that *nothing is
displaced* (H.D.'s coda) tho Pallas Athene be reduced
(It's Courbet's Origin of the World this time
the frame has a door and the door
has a glory hole available at Joanna's height)
to a relic of beauty in our time
Be unafraid of beauty where you find it
I do not mean lust or the lurid
Fucking is greater than art Art lasts longer!
Beauty equally despises pursuing women and looking at
art or pursuing art and looking at women
The earth has many keys…
Classical art is funereal next comes the pursuit
of beauty first in the chapels then bed
(The empress commands you to take her ass
making you a dead man if you do
or a legendary fuck up if you can't)

Here things get ugly Why should expressionism (Orphee's
second look) be so ugly eventually involving fucking
with space then abstract fucking with the mind?
Call me a rube in Arcadia for seeing
no beauty in Rubens' fat fashion made flesh
(A woman spread open in a pastoral landscape
is something different than peeking thru a peephole
at a woman spread open in a landscape
The barred door renders pornographic her beautiful sex
This same dichotomy put d.a. levy on trial)
...*Beauty is nature's fact.* (Dickinson)
Be unafraid of beauty as you remain fearless
of all ugliness Nothing can be displaced So
we might read with two detached retinas Bill
Evans' song playing *is* the painting I am
seeing eyes closed listening It's Kees I seek
at the piano he plays for a typewriter
This door is opened by a piano key
If in my notebooks the Mark Rothko Intro
appears as "MR" then the law of seriality
declares the new Bill Evans poem is "BE"
Together they make bookends to end my book
opened to where its sense is being made
Given that Lawrence is not a masturbatory aid
you jizz reading the novels of Henry Miller
For this exam write an essay on beauty
in Miller's ugly city versus Lawrence's ideal beauty
Be unafraid to equate kalos and eros
Her headstone "Greek flower; Greek ecstasy" in Bethlehem
It is forbidden to write about certain beauty
Beauty that flourished without sound beyond color
The beauty of a Burne-Jones vamp come alive
Black kief black coffee black stockings black curls
Black bread black lipstick black jazz black listed
Beauty men lined up for with their wives
But if some flame splashes over from my arab hours.../ And burns you...." (Rosemary Tonks)
I'll let one who did know the East
do the talking for the silent film star
Because Theda Bara is *Death Arab* to write
about the beauty of her Ohio Jewess eyes

from Circle of the Raft . . . . rich blevins

Add to end of #1.

vi. ~~ANDANTE~~ AFTER DEBUSSY
   Adagio mortoi

Picnics lapse again -- into sand,
the smooth ocean reclaims our campfire
          in one long shadow. Cronus.
          Watery arms, lapse, into full
          ≥ ← gnomonshadow.
          Lips part,
          legs alike
          released! ~~dropped out~~ fallen
          from the fire-balling
                  night
          to will. ∧Arms of Victory / white column of ~~Cronus~~. or
          ~~of~~ close.

          Whence the Latin figure,
     flagrare :
flame, to burn with "soot-black smoke
from flame." Words collapse, afterall
back into words. Firewater! Mouths
harden a dull shellspeech, ∧whispers
litter a coney-dog shore. Surfaced, ~~poems~~
poems surface
are reclaimed into idea.
     Joyce-again's   o song without words! reversed
               into tunes. *Salvaged* From childhood,
          a memory of glass *A good idea*
          the high shelf of horned things
highly involved surfaces crusty from Continued ~~Exposure~~
to the sun press, press of gray fingers whetted
                                              Notes

boot back from California

— shore. Shipwrecked
poems surface,
to float
outside of unity
Indian
Shipwrecked
within a formlessness
to be reclaimed
into idea.

*to float
wout unity
to be*

*into tunes. A (work of)good idea
Salvaged, from childhood
a memory of glass*

a new vehicle of dance!

(the black rings around her eyes matching lips
offering eyes as the fourth and fifth hole)
risks the penalties of sudden death by terrorists
or the cremation of your body of work
or the leveling of both of your houses
Dame Edith Sitwell lives in the same neighborhood
Old crony "Inside her oriental dressing-gown of dust..."
In front of the blank screen of Rosemary
Tonks' two detached retinas decades into silent retirement
a boy at a piano telling the plot
The cinemas / Where the criminal shadow-literature flickers over our faces....
I want to read about the artist's childhood
at my age I still read biographies first
as if the key to creativity might be
the bookmark left behind by a previous owner
I'd turn directly to the death bed scene
as a young man testing the old artist
After all the poems I have never told
what I wanted to tell that first poem
George James Hopkins' big break with Bara's Cleopatra
Having deleted color sound motion until a few
still frames remain the serial sets about reconstructing
all the lost minutes of Theda Bara's *Cleopatra*
This is how Smithson's last motel room looked
This is how Smithson's last motel room looks
There is no progress *No MS. will be
considered if you've submitted a table of contents
for the serial poem* There is only perpetuity
His plagiarization of "MS. Found in a Bottle"
found in the poet's computer after his death
matches a carbon copy unearthed in a file
Together with a handwritten version in his diary
the three identical texts demonstrate the master's progress
leading to the crown of his *Pym Erasure*
(Poetry sits between two suitors who work together
one touches her nipples the other her thighs
Then they switch and one touches her nipples
the other who was first touches her thighs)
My big attempt at beauty's portrait "Roman[zero]" ruined
when she refused to sit still for it

It was never a question of aesthetics before
now and now it's too late to start
Deep within this unhappiness he stumbles across Stendhal's
"Beauty is never any more than a promise
of happiness" and he knows it was never
a question of the possibility of beauty but
always the fact of his era's great unhappiness
I'm sending this postcard from the unknown peninsula
Calasso's account of Baudelaire's Dream of the Brothel-Museum
following chapters on the painting of beautiful women—
Jupiter arrested by his desire to fuck Thetis
the open invitation extended by Mme de Senonnes
or the derangement of the obsessive Turkish baths—
lacks only the detail of a Tsalalian hieroglyph
The absence of women in *Moby-Dick* and *Pym*
results in the creation of an abstract beauty
an Amerikan whiteness terrifying in its sexless aspect
Ishmael sat three days before his favorite panel
portent of the daytime moon attempting to plumb
frozen pipes with a candle means this winter
will last a boy's entire childhood The Ice-Bound
Stream of Time his favorite panel A rush
of suddenly freed water startled awake his Urania
in her floating bed at long last harpooned
Reger stranded every other day for thirty years
on his peninsula bench extending into "White-bearded Man"
The earth has many keys. / Where melody is not / Is the unknown peninsula. (Emily Dickinson)
For the last track he played the same
line with each hand an ocatave apart Two
voices Bill Evans with Mark Rothko saying so-long
The octave in Petrarch's usage is the opening

His last paintings were doors
Dead at 66 this very year I turn 66
I will do it alone by myself
"He hit a wall he couldn't paint on."

Is Rothko in this room or his absence?
Are we supposed to be thinking about him?
(Blue Matisse is alive in his homesick chapel
arthritis free and cohabitating with his young nun
the saint avoiding the cripple diarist of Vence)

The facts are no one has ever slept
thru the night in this room no one
has ever wagered or bled or fucked here
Eternal airport terminal arrivals departures before manned flight

The fact is she will not be there for you
as she was not present for the beginning

Each panel depicts the first and the last

remembers for us our first sight at birth
and before dying the final face we distinguish

[March 2015; May 2016]

About the Cover: I have come lately, over time, to see the serial poems collected in this volume, many of them reprinted here from ephemera partially buried in the Kent State Special Collections, and my enduring preoccupations with history and place, in terms of "Partially Buried Woodshed," created on site by Robert I. Smithson on my home-state undergraduate campus, and the common fate of that work of art. In January 1970, Smithson directed his sculpture to be built adjacent to the Liquid Crystal Institute building, which became a focus for our May 1970 demonstrations against the Vietnam War and against government-funded projects on university campuses. The May 4 shootings initiate a poem in serial time: the young Smithson was dead by 1973…his widow was forced to engage attorneys in attempts to protect the land art which had been labeled an eyesore by the university…remains of the shed were burned under mysterious circumstances in 1975…there followed decades of *entropy* until, today, it is planted over so only the shed's foundation is visible, if you know where to look. In its present state, "Partially Buried Woodshed" remains a so-called *new monument* to the creation of art beyond official sanctions. It asks us to consider again art's eventual return to its origins and sources among the arable mud of Ohio I played in as a boy. (The name *Duchamp* means "of the ground.") After a decade of attempts, by 1979 I was ready to initiate a serial poetry by arriving at, and departing from, the post-Smithsonian notation "There is nothing here to see / but those who come to see it." (PHOTOGRAPH BY DOUGLAS MOORE. COURTESY OF THE KENT STATE UNIVERSITY LIBRARIES, SPECIAL COLLECTIONS AND ARCHIVES.)

www.ingramcontent.com/pod-product-compliance
Lightning Source LLC
Chambersburg PA
CBHW081341080526
44588CB00016B/2345